The Single Life

# THE
# SINGLE
# LIFE

## Unpatriarchal Manhoods in English Renaissance Literature

**JORDAN WINDHOLZ**

THE UNIVERSITY OF ALABAMA PRESS
Tuscaloosa

The University of Alabama Press
Tuscaloosa, Alabama 35487-0380
uapress.ua.edu

Typeface: Adobe Garamond Pro

Cover image: *Portrait of a Young Man Seated Under a Tree / Portrait of Henry Percy, 9th Earl of Northumberland*, by Nicholas Hilliard, c. 1590–1595; Rijksmuseum, Amsterdam
Cover design: Sandy Turner Jr.

Cataloging-in-Publication data is available from the Library of Congress.
ISBN: 978-0-8173-2242-7 (cloth)
ISBN: 978-0-8173-6213-3 (paper)
E-ISBN: 978-0-8173-9570-4

# Contents

# Acknowledgments

This book has felt, for most of its writing, like an impossibility, and it would have remained so without the generosity, intellect, care, and humor of so many.

Michelle Dowd saw promise in the proposal for this book and saw it through what were then unimaginable storms. Dan Waterman shepherded this book forward through setback after setback, and in his patience and care, seemed to conjure a fire from ashes. I owe the deepest of thanks to the anonymous readers of the manuscript, each of whom provided salient critiques and revision suggestions, all of which improved the work greatly.

Stuart Sherman taught me how to write by example and direct instruction. If there's anything in the prose that shines, it does so by reflecting his gentle light. I am in a long line of those who owe so much to Heather Dubrow. As a scholar, teacher, and mentor, Heather is the picture of both tenacity and generosity. I do not know how she does all that she does. Much of my pedagogy and scholarship is merely an attempt to live up to her example. Mary Bly taught me to read oh-so-many plays and to read them carefully, and Mark Caldwell consistently coaxed my hunches into workable ideas. When I was beginning to think about the shape of this book, Ed Cahill guided the way; he helped me see how to give this book form.

Anna Beskin, Anthony Brano, and Christi Spain-Savage: who would I be without you? You have provided years of friendship, comfort, and commiseration. The pages of this book have so many of your insights. And Anna, especially: your care and outreach in a time of need saved me, in more ways than you can know. Thank you.

The English faculty at Shippensburg University have provided no shortage of inspiration and comradery. I am in awe of the scholarship and creative work my colleagues produce. A primary reason I sought to get this book done was simply to keep pace with them. From my first day on campus, Shari Horner has steered me through the numerous snags of academic life. Her brilliance as a scholar and teacher is matched by her magnanimity and humor as a colleague. Michael Bibby made my decision to come to Shippensburg an easy one; he has been a tireless advocate from the start.

Laurie Cella is indefatigable in her joy and in her commitment to her students. I have become a better teacher through her example, and I thank her for the many (many) office conversations about parenting, teaching, and researching. Neil Connelly has been a friend and mentor, one who has tried to teach me how to keep my head level. One of these days I will start listening. In both how and what he teaches, Tom Crochunis has shown me all the ways literature exceeds the confines of the classroom, and that we should honor its many surprises. Shannon Mortimore-Smith has inspired me in how to design and teach courses well, and how to balance academic life with a family life. Matthew Cella provided necessary and early mentorship when I was just getting my legs under me. Over my years at Ship, Erica Galioto has remained game to discuss the intricacies of pedagogy and literary analysis; she continually teaches me that the research we love can and should be the beating heart of our pedagogy. Sharon Harrow has championed my work day in and day out and believed in this book when I did not. She knows how to bring people together, and I feel lucky that she saw fit to bring me into the fold. Carla Kungl has taught me that the academic life can be a happy one, that there are pleasures among the sometimes-stultifying work, and that it is good to get things done. Rich Cook has consistently shown me what the work is and what it is not, and where and how to set limits that have preserved my sanity. Kim Van Alkemade taught me how to quietly get to writing amid sometimes grueling teaching loads, and her warmth and care carried me through my early years at Ship. Jonathan Dubow provided so much friendship through so many years at Ship. There really are not enough words to encapsulate my gratitude for Nicole Santalucia, whose unrelenting support for her students and colleagues is unrivaled. She has kept me sturdy in the roughest moments. William Harris has read draft after draft of this book, and provided much needed critique and encouragement. Thank you so much, William. You kept me going. Cris Rhodes has also read too many pages of this book, and graciously listened to me talk about it (and many other things). She's a truly brilliant scholar, teacher, and friend.

Many of the ideas in this book came to life in the classroom, and my students have been so integral to their development. I want to say a special thank you to Kaylee Beattie, Chris Carragher, Anne Long, Erica McKinnon, Kyle Gearity, Sarah Davison, Sierra Higgins, Andrew Houpt, Kelsey Kohler, Henry Le, Gina LoPresti, Sarah Markins, Emily Mitchell, Courtney Putnam, Kristina Rhoades, Heather Ritter, Tyler Rock, Rachel Smith, Peggy Trahey, Trent Betham, Ash Chapman, Abigail Cox, Ryley Flanagan, Casey Leming, Veronica Ponti, Nia Primus, Jhonna Slaughter, Adolfo Alvarez,

Kelsey Clevenger, Kaitie McCann, Nate Mull, Nicole Potts, Katie Spengler, Kimberly Braet, Rena Charles, Trevor Dixon, Emily Dziennik, DeeDee Floyd, Taryn Good, Josiah Horst, Bailey Joseph, Pierce Romey, Sydnie Simmons, Paige Armstrong, AJ Barnett, Nell Behta, Hanna Cornell, Piper Kull, Bryce Mentzer, Madison Mummert, Julianna Vaughan, Carleyrose Wagner, Bruce Washington, William Ayars, Kyra Brown, Abigail Stevens, Dean Burghard, Makayla Carr, Emilia Conners, Rose Hannon, Charles Herrick, Lea Holler, Katelyn Mader, Lauren Pool, Jenny Russell, Kyle Saar, Alyssa Sheriff, Faith Sprecher, Ashley Toms, Travis Weaver, Maggie McGuire, Meg Geronimos, Autumn Jones, and Brooke Powell.

Anna D'Orazio, Ashleigh Kennedy, and Isabella Brignola served as research assistants for respective summer public humanities projects. In addition to being incredible students who have helped me piece together my ideas in the classroom, they are marvelous thinkers, writers, and scholars in their own right. I'm excited to see what they do next.

I would not have been able to complete this work without the help of Shippensburg University library faculty. I especially want to thank Melanie Reed and James Sterner.

In addition to all of those at Shippensburg University who have supported me, I owe so much to friends and colleagues far and wide: Stephanie Pietros, Kirk Quinsland, Valerie Billing, Ari Friedlander, Stephen Spiess, Joey Gamble, Holly Dugan, David Sterling Brown, Carol Mejia LaPerle, William Germano, Christine Varnado, and Julie Crawford. I owe a very special debt of gratitude to the Early Modern Trans Studies community, and especially Colby Gordon, Simone Chess, Will Fisher, Hamit Arvas, and Sawyer Kemp. You have informed so much of my research, my teaching, and my thinking. I hope that I was able to do justice to your brilliance, that at least some of it shines through these pages.

In many ways, I could dedicate this book to Mario DiGangi, whom I had the pleasure of meeting in a Folger Shakespeare Library seminar. That seminar seeded many of the ideas for this book, and Mario has never stopped championing me or my work. Long before I knew him, I learned so much from his scholarship. His rare genius for organizing ideas into salient, close, and careful readings of early modern literature remains an inspiration to me. Thank you so much, Mario.

My love of literature began in my undergraduate days. My first English class with Peter Kerry Powers was difficult but awe-inducing. It made me want to be an English major. Thank you, Matthew Roth, Paul Nisly, Crystal Downing, David Dzaka, and Samuel Smith, my first teacher of Shakespeare (and Milton!).

To Lucas Sheaffer, to Michael Flatt, to Rivers Erickson, to PJ Drost: you have been such life-changing friends. I love you all very much.

That I would even seek a life of learning, and that such a life could be possible, is a result of my family and the foundation they have provided. My parents, Tami and Fred, asked nothing more than that I go to college, a dream of theirs that they made a way for me to step into. They championed every step I took thereafter. I am lucky to have such wonderful siblings, Colby and Rachel, who have loved and supported me day in and day out, as have their partners, Alyssa and Tim. Jan, Jo, Don, Kyle, and Nicole are more than any son-in-law or brother-in-law deserves: you have sustained me with your love, intellect, and companionship. I have also been buoyed by the joy and humor of my nieces and nephews: Grayson, Mia, Annabelle, Willow, Eddie, and Theo.

I owe the greatest of debts to Erin Ryan, whose intellect, love, care, and time have made this book a book. You are a special kind of magic. I am so thankful you have chosen and continue to choose to share this life with me. And to Hazel and Bly, thank you for your laughter and love, and for bearing with me all these years. The book is done. What's next?

Even as I acknowledge all that I owe to colleagues near and far, to friends and to family, I also want to make some room to acknowledge the conditions through which this book emerged. The humanities and literary studies are no strangers to a lack of public and institutional support, but these last few years have witnessed an intensified erosion of it. Most of our profession labors under such conditions. Strain and burnout abound; precarity is commonplace. I want to acknowledge this because I want to acknowledge so many of the brilliant scholars whose work has been restrained and restricted, whose labor has been exploited, whose time has been stolen. There are those whose work we will never read but who nonetheless make an impact in their communities, their institutions, and their classrooms. We—our professional organizations, our research cohorts, our consortiums—might do better to create more opportunity and room for those who desire to do the work they love.

Portions of chapter 1 were published as "The Queer Testimonies of Male Chastity in *All's Well That Ends Well*," *Modern Philology* 116, no. 4 (2019), and portions of chapter 2 were published as "Ballads, Journeymen, and Bachelor Community in Shakespeare's London," *English Literary Renaissance* 46, no. 2 (2016).

The Single Life

# Introduction

## The Single Life in English Renaissance Literature and Culture

Shakespeare begins his sonnets by confidently contending, "From fairest creatures, we desire increase," but the speaker cannot sustain his conviction for long. In the face of the recalcitrance of the young man, the sonnet's rhetorical powers of persuasion collapse to uneasy queries.[1] The problem is not a matter of capriciousness or even of his sublime beauty but of the young man's marital status. The speaker cannot make sense of his single life. By sonnet 3, the speaker insists: "die single, and thine image dies with thee" (3.14), but this is also the sonnet where opening assertions twist into insistent interrogations:

> For where is she so fair whose uneared womb
> Disdains the tillage of thy husbandry?
> Or who is he so fond will be the tomb
> Of his self-love, to stop posterity? (ll. 5–8)

Sonnet 4 follows suit in its inquisitive concatenations; of its seven sentences, four are interrogative. As if to salvage themself from foundering in endless, unanswered pleas, the speaker, in the twinned sonnets 5 and 6, turns to seasonal conceits of posterity and decay to reflect on the timeliness of bearing heirs, and then, in sonnet 8, consolidates the seasonal conceits to a much shorter diurnal frame, as if insisting an overdetermined urgency: time is running out. These arguments seem to fail. Sonnet 8 begins again with a question—"Music to hear, why hearst thou music sadly?"—and sonnet 9 likewise opens with a pleading question: "Is it for fear to wet a widow's eye / that thou consum'st thyself in single life?" (9.1).

What does the single life mean? These early sonnets ask the question again and again. Writing on the peculiar epistemological crises that the single life inaugurates, Michael Cobb observes, "singleness is now always figured as a conundrum, and, if all goes according to plan, a conundrum to be solved by coupling off, and as soon as possible."[2] But Shakespeare shows that the single life was a conundrum in early modern England too, and his sonnets thematize the impasse that the single life poses by making of that impasse an occasion for poetic invention. What is notable about the opening sonnets of Shakespeare's sequence is that precisely when the young man's marital status surfaces into textuality, precisely when the attributes of fairness and beauty, of procreation and of aging, of legacy and patrilineality, give way to the condition of marital status, the rhetoric of the sonnets shift from what can be asserted as normative to what must be interrogated as somehow not. Scholars do not normally frame the early sonnets of Shakespeare's sequence as invested in questions about the merits and demerits of the single life, but as the marital status of the young man—or should we say single man?—becomes a subject early in the sequence, the speaker cannot help but render it enigma that will not settle into evident meaning.[3]

Perhaps that is making too much of too little. Most English renaissance sonnet sequences, after all, dramatize the plights of single people, most of whom are single men. But it is Shakespeare's sonnets where the single life emerges—is in fact identified—as incongruent with the projects of courtship, patriarchal marriage, and heteroerotic desire. Other sonnet sequences feature single men, but Shakespeare makes of one a subject of inquiry. That's worth thinking about, or so this book argues. Like Shakespeare's sonnets, it asks a series of questions about the meanings of the single life in English renaissance literature and culture, though its arguments and ends are entirely different than those in Shakespeare's verse. If the sonnets' speaker cannot help but ask *why* the single man of the sonnets remains single, I ask why, throughout much of the period's literature, the single life of men invites a series of interrogations and examinations that early modern patriarchy sought to quell, recuperate, or otherwise subsume in its prescriptive conceptions of sexuality, labor, gentility, emotion, and embodiment. I answer that question in several ways throughout this book, but my central argument is that representations of the single life of men were both integral and inimical to the organization and institutionalization of early modern patriarchy, and that thinking critically about the representations of the single life of men in English renaissance literature and culture can expose patriarchal ideology to new, salient forms of feminist and queer critique that permit us to think more deeply about the limits and capacities of the meanings of manhood running throughout the period's literature.

Given his keen attention to the friable edges of genres and the tropes that knit them together, it is not surprising that Shakespeare would so quickly turn to the single life of the young man in his sonnets, nor that the very mention of the young man's marital status would instigate a dramatic shift in their rhetorical protocols. What is surprising, however, is that scholars of English renaissance literature and culture have not, on the whole, asked many questions about what the single life of men might mean in early modern England. There is, to be sure, good reason for this oversight. In much of the period's literature, single men are married men in due time, cast as universal subjects, so representationally ubiquitous as to be invisible, or so marginal as to be seemingly insignificant. This book, however, recenters the single life in an effort to demonstrate how integral early modern conceptions of single men were to the organization and operations of patriarchal social order. Early modern writers were often quite explicit about the legibility, and at times, viability, of the single life. In *The Haven of Health* (1584), for instance, Thomas Cogan argues, "Saint Mathew in his gospel setteth downe two estates of men in generall, both good and godly; the one married, the other unmaried."[4] While Cogan insists upon its equity with a married life, the single life was not often represented as "good and godly." Instead, in much of early modern literature, the single life pluralizes beyond rigid moral frames or paradigms of cultural normativity.

To account for its variety, I excavate and analyze five types of unmarried men that populate English renaissance literature but whose marital status has not featured heavily in literary studies: chaste youths (chapter 1), journeymen bachelors (chapter 2), true gallants (chapter 3), incel scholars (chapter 4), and unmarried eunuchs (chapter 5). Examining each in relation to respective English renaissance discourses of sexuality, labor, gentility, emotion, and gender, I respectively demonstrate how early modern patriarchal ideology takes shape against these negating and antagonizing forms of what I call unpatriarchal manhoods: types of manhood that resist patriarchal ideals of marriage, family, procreation, patrilineal inheritance, and embodiment. By focusing on the varied representations of unmarried men in English renaissance literature, this book proposes not only that singleness was a significant category of social definition in early modern England but also that figurations of the single life were central to the gendering of men in the period. It further theorizes that more than a means of organizing economic and social relations, the dialectic between marriage and the single life organized a variety of discourses that sought to naturalize patriarchal social order and institutionalize its power structures.[5]

In what follows, I first delve into my typological methodology and explain its relationship to other methods of conceptualizing early modern manhood and masculinity—before I then articulate this book's primary intervention in early modern gender and sexuality studies. After explaining my methodology and intervention, I try to pay some debts: those due to feminist scholars who historicize and critique (early) modern patriarchy, and then, in the subsequent section, the wide range of scholars whose work has already touched upon meanings of the single life in early modern gender studies. Parsing single men from the more localized definition of "the bachelor," I then explain why and how singleness was an operative, and even desirable, form of social definition in the early modern period, which some scholars have described as prior to any such saliency. The saliency of the single life in early modern England, I then go on to show, had both rhetorical and epistemological forms prior to the early modern period that then became redeployed in the renaissance. However, these forms have also come to inform some of the foundational modern theoretical texts of histories of sexuality and gender. Finally, I conclude with brief chapter summaries.

## The Single Life and Unpatriarchal Manhood

Because there is no single kind of single man in English renaissance literature, this book approaches its readings of the single life of men in relation to a series of examinations of how patriarchal institutions and discourses seek to capture and direct manhood to fulfill, for lack of a better term, their ideological operations. In doing so, and as a means of making this book's interventions more or less manageable, I use a typology to localize how thinking about the single life of men offers pathways to analyzing the operations of early modern patriarchal discourses, which, I demonstrate, often mobilize types of single men to naturalize and normalize patriarchy's reification through and as marriage. My use of a typology of single men draws upon recent work in sexuality and gender studies to conceive of how types, as opposed to identities, become deployed or mobilized to organize ideological formations. In his study on how early modern literature represents sexuality through characters constructed by social matrices of familiarization and estrangement, Mario DiGangi argues that "sexual types," whatever the literary pleasures they afford readers or observers, "are also motivated by ideological concerns," and that to address them is also "to address the complex dramatic and ideological functions" that put them into textual circulation. DiGangi notes, however, that while such types often serve ideological ends and operate discursively, they "can also function to expose and critique the ideologies that make them intelligible."[6] In contrast to identities, which may be produced by texts but imply forms of embodiment and subjectivity, types (including stereotypes) might be thought of as discursive, deployed, and imposed effects not so much of behavior or even self-identification but of the operations of identifying—though this does not mean they cannot also be redeployed, appropriated, or garnered by those so "typed," and so come to inform identity categories. Though he does not use the language of typology, Ari Friedlander explains this distinction between identifying and being identified in his study of the "rogue," a literary and social type that figures forth a series of subtypes and categories of roguery. Throughout rogue literature—a category that expands from prose pamphlets to include the works of Shakespeare, Jonson, and Milton—"rogues [comprise] a 'socio-sexual identity'—a durable, reproducible discursive category of personhood," which is less a category of "self-representation" and more a result of "the process by which early modern culture *identified* rogues as objects of knowledge that then become *identificatory* possibilities for early moderns in positions of power over them."[7] Central to this dynamic is a type's recognizability; as DiGangi affirms, types are "recognizable figures of literary imagination and social fantasy."[8] Following the insights of DiGangi and Friedlander, I focus on types of single men, not to historicize or theorize the single life as it concretizes into a form of social identity but to examine how ways of imagining the single life are themselves entangled in the varied, contradictory ideological operations of early modern English patriarchal social order—but not necessarily captured by them. The types of single men that I focus upon in each chapter are recognizable, but the project of this book is also to do the work of such recognition, to make them so.

While I anchor and organize this book around five types of single men, I also argue these types of single men register "unpatriarchal" forms of manhood more broadly. I intentionally use the term "unpatriarchal" to index the negating potentialities that the single life holds in relation to patriarchal ideals of manhood, such as marriage, procreation, patrilineality, and social mastery. As I demonstrate, patriarchal discourses often latch onto and fixate upon the single life of men because of the disruptive capacities and abounding possibilities such a life affords men against the rather prescriptive and restrictive roles of patriarchal manhood. Such capacities were often mobilized to undermine, subvert, or dissolve trenchant patriarchal gender norms. However, in many cases, representations of the single life actively sought to reimagine manhood as a form of power—one that might oppress others—outside those roles of husband, father, and master that patriarchy reifies.

To a certain extent, scholars of early modern manhood have recognized such contingencies. While patriarchy might be understood as the dominant form of social order in early modern England, it was not by any means coterminous with representations or meanings of manhood in the period.

Attending to the plurality of manhood in early modern England, Alexandra Shepard has demonstrated manhood was achieved and practiced in relation to a number of rituals, behaviors, and metrics. Shepard, in particular, has sought not only to understand more fully the gendering of men in the sixteenth and seventeenth centuries but also to rethink historiographies of manhood and patriarchy, especially those that would see "different species rather than different generations" of men at either end of the period.[9] For Shepard, the social forces that gendered men remained remarkably consistent even as access to social positions shifted. Too often, Shepard argues, the pronounced differences between early modern and modern, the Renaissance and the Restoration, are a result of incongruous comparisons between, for example, discourses on the household and the court. In an attempt to acknowledge powerful continuities while at the same time doing justice to multiple and sometimes contradictory figurations of manhood across these centuries, Shepard has proposed four key kinds of manhood operative across the period: *patriarchal manhood*, aligned with marriage and householder status; *subordinate manhood*, associated with male servants, often unmarried, within households; *antipatriarchal manhood*, a form of manhood in direct opposition to patriarchal norms; and *alternative manhood*, forms not so directly antagonistic or tied to patriarchal norms, including those adopted by vagrants or migrants.[10]

Shepard's categories of manhood provide some way to disaggregate patriarchy from the gender formations it produces, but, to a certain extent, Shephard reconstitutes the influential theorization of masculinities by R. W. Connell, who developed, and later, in conjunction with James Messerschmidt, further reformulated the concept of "hegemonic masculinities."[11] Connell defines "hegemonic masculinity" as "not a fixed character type, always and everywhere the same. It is, rather, the masculinity that occupies the hegemonic position in a given pattern of gender relations, a position always contestable."[12] Reformulating this original concept, Connell and Messerschmidt emphasize, "the concept of hegemonic masculinity presumes the subordination of nonhegemonic masculinities"—though it should be noted that not all nonhegemonic masculinities share that presumption.[13] Connell further emphasizes that various iterations of masculinity can have particular relations with a hegemonic form: subordinate, complicit, and marginalized.[14] Constituted relationally to a hegemonic masculinity, a subordinate masculinity is denied legitimacy, a complicit masculinity lacks legitimacy but does not challenge (and even abets) hegemonic masculinity, and a marginalized masculinity may obtain hegemonic status in one aspect of the social order (in terms of class, for example) but is otherwise marginalized (in terms of sexuality, for example). As Ben Griffin has observed, Shepard's categories of early modern manhood both fit within and extend Connell's categories, as Shepard offers up an "antipatriarchal" model that contests and resists the hegemonic form of patriarchal manhood, and yet Connell's formulation of hegemonic, subordinate, complicit, and marginalized, with the addition of a resistive or antihegemonic formation, remain useful for thinking about the relational, contingent, and mediated ways manhood is produced in relation to patriarchy.[15]

My formulation of "unpatriarchal manhood" draws from the work of both Connell and Shepard, but it seeks to resist the categorical impulses of their conceptual framework. Both Connell's formulation of "hegemonic masculinities" and Shepard's more historicized categories offer some ways of thinking about the single life in renaissance literature as outside the culturally dominant form of patriarchal manhood. Similarly, my use of "unpatriarchal manhood" seeks to capture, without limiting, the broad but negating capacities of the single life as it relates to patriarchal ideals of manhood. However, in using the term "unpatriarchal manhoods," I am not so much seeking to categorize as I am aiming to mark an oppositional openness the single life affords men in the period, an openness renaissance literature often itself draws upon both to distance manhood from patriarchal norms and to reaccommodate manhood's relation to power and privilege. The unpatriarchal manhoods of the single life may antagonize patriarchal forms of manhood, but that does not mean they are antipatriarchal in an ideological sense, for they may likewise seek to target and oppress women, children, servants, and other men with as much or greater force. For this reason, this book resists synthesizing the single life into a unity in opposition to patriarchy. Thus I insist the single life is *un*patriarchal as opposed to *anti*patriarchal, and in this way, my use of "unpatriarchal" finds an analytic in the negating energy of its prefix—of attending to what is unformed, what is possibly unknown or unknowable, and what might be undone. It seeks to resist the prescriptive impulse of identifying what the single life constitutively "is" that it might leave a space for what is or what might yet be possible in the single life. As this book hopes to demonstrate, writers of English renaissance literature mine the possibilities of the single life to articulate unpatriarchal forms of manhood that work to negate patriarchal claims to power and privilege, if only to realize power and privilege by other means.

Given that it was defined in large part against the definitive, legally codified, and culturally central married life, the single life signified a potentially boundless space, and early modern literature and culture recognized both the allure and danger of its dilatory capacities. In Sir John Davies's poem "The Bacheler," for example, the titular speaker both acknowledges and revels in the temporal limbo he occupies:

> How many things as yet are deere alike to me,
> The field, the horse, the dog, loue, armes or liberty.
> I haue no wife as yet, whom I may call mine owne,
> I haue no children yet, that by my name are knowne.
> Yet if I married were, I would not wish to thriue,
> If that I could not tame the verist shrew aliue.[16]

The poem is everywhere conditioned by the adverbial "as yet," which playfully negotiates the patriarchal norms of marriage and patrilineality. Outside the bounds of procreative legibility, this bachelor possibly cuckolds other men and has any number of children; while this bachelor revels in a form of sexuality outside of the patriarchal norm, one premised on illicit fornication and bastardy, he also voices a patriarchal, misogynist manhood predicated on disciplining and controlling a woman.[17] Inhabiting a dilatory "as yet," this bachelor recognizes a youthful, subordinate manhood, entertains an antipatriarchal sexuality, and comes to parrot a complicit, patriarchal manhood by the poem's end. The bachelor of Davies's poem evinces the ways the single life does not readily settle into one particular form of manhood, the ways it might bask in how its expatiations forestall the "chronobiopolitics"—to borrow Elizabeth Freeman's phrase—of patriarchal social order even as it may anticipate fitting smoothly within them.[18]

In his adverbial impishness, Davies's bachelor plays to type. He understands the timings and trajectories of becoming a man in early modern England. And manhood in the period was, in so many ways, teleological. While there were a variety of social practices and behaviors that acculturated people to masculinity, and while social rank, vocation, or region might shift, alter, particularize, or prioritize certain modes of behavior, on the whole two primary metrics established differences between men in early modern England: marital status and age. Both supplemented and revised an ideal of manhood drawn from the ancient concept of "the golden mean," but it was marital status that held greater sway, "since married men were accorded higher status than their elders who were still single."[19] Both marriage and age crucially took time. Both, too, could be mutually reinforcing, where marriage could confer maturity upon a man even if he remained relatively young in relation to unmarried, older men.[20] Davies's bachelor knows this and speaks the patriarchal vernacular in a manner that once affirms the pathways of manhood before him and yet imagines alternatives.

In another sense, however, Davies's "bacheler" does not play to type at all because he possesses a social identity ostensibly comprised of his marital status alone: unlike the young man or youth of the sonnets, he is a bachelor, an unmarried man. As a legible type of single man, "bachelors" do not predominate in English renaissance literature and culture in part because the metrics of marital status and age had an asymmetrical impact upon gendered persons in patriarchal social order. Men tend to be represented as young or old and women tend to be represented as maids, wives, or widows in English renaissance literature.[21] This difference between the gendered application of metrics of age and marital status reflects the governing ideology of a patriarchal society. Single men are conceived as young men insofar as they can be imagined as *supplementing* and *not supplanting* a patriarchal teleology. If women are always already conceived in a patriarchal society as property of men, and if marriage is the institution through which women are possessed and maintained as property, then it follows that marital status would inflect their social identities and literary representations. To read the single life in renaissance literature and culture, then, is to locate it within a metric of age because the single life is so often both imagined and validated for men in relation to it. The title page of Joseph Swetnam's *The Araignment of Lewde, Idle, Froward, and vnconstant women: Or the vanitie of them, choose you whether* (1615), for example, exemplifies this common framing; it is advertised as "Pleasant for married men, profitable for young Men, and hurtfull to none." The single life is coextensive with youth, and, in fact, Swetnam naturalizes the single life through metrics of age when he claims "with *Diogenes*, it is too soone for a young man to marry and too late for old men."[22] Shakespeare's sonnets similarly shift from questions of marital status to questions of age and time, of selfhood and privacy, rhetorical maneuvers that universalize, perhaps, the sequence's investments in gender, love, desire, and even racial formations.[23]

As the example of Swetnam suggests, the single life was crucial to the gendering of men in the period, but it manifested not always as the single life but as a youthful life. By insisting upon the *single* life of men (as opposed to "youth," say), this book aims to read against early modern patriarchal modes of gendering men, which inordinately prioritize a patriarchal conception of time that focuses on the durability of marriage and family and singleness as a youthful phase. There's an ideological consequence to this patriarchal formation: a good portion of the misogyny that comes to underwrite the privileges of men is enlivened, as in the case of Swetnam, through endorsements of the single life as a perpetually young or youthful. Such a framing often permits virulent misogyny to be contained within a temporal frame of youth that can always simply be outgrown (the modern common exculpatory phrase goes "boys will be boys" and not "men will be men"). My focus on the single life also resists those forms of social history that are organized around the family, useful as they may be, and follows that work—namely of Judith Bennett and Amy Froide—that has focused on singlewomen.[24] Thus, throughout this book, I am, at times, reading the single life into categories of manhood by which it is readily subsumed because as marital status serves as a category of social definition for women and not men, the social relations for men are expanded beyond the circuit of marriage while the social relations of women are constrained by it. While this trend is changing, early modern English social history and especially social histories of gender, have not read against these early modern patriarchal modes of gendering men, inordinately prioritizing a patriarchal conception of history that focuses on marriage and family. Literary critics have likewise sometimes conflated the social category of manhood with early modern patriarchal beliefs, such that either the single life dissolves into insignificance or it is subsumed by the subjectivity of married men and anxious patriarchs.[25] In his otherwise excellent study on *Shakespeare and Masculinity*, Bruce Smith, for instance, barely touches upon marital status, and when he does, he downplays the significance of the single life in the ideals of saucy jacks and gentlemen, obscures its relation to passages of time and space, or simply forgets its presence in Shakespeare's comedies where single men and women are proleptically cast as "marrying couples."[26] In her study on early modern manhood, Elizabeth Foyster saliently critiques patriarchal ideology but also at moments reinscribes its terms of power. At the very outset of her study, she explains, "men were all too aware that their honour depended on the actions and words of their wives."[27] There are essentially two axes of social definition at work here, but they are not equally applied. In this scheme, the category of "men" exists outside of the marital relation and is not subject to its conditions whereas the category of "women"—the unstated term of the binary—is replaced by "wives." Feminist historians of early modern England have especially done a great deal to think beyond marriage to expose women's roles in literary, social, and cultural production, but scholars have not yet done enough to consider how marital status gendered men, and have too often left men as uninterrogated subjects of the patriarchal institution that benefited so many of them.[28]

While this book seeks to intervene in a body of scholarship on early modern manhood, it primarily thinks about the meanings of manhood in relation to the single life not to supersede or overturn the contributions of the deep and wide body of scholarship on early modern manhood and its literary representations. Through English renaissance literary and cultural texts, the single life not only pops up in strange places; it also proves central to numerous arguments, ideas, and interrogations that gender men. And that should be expected. As Judith Butler has observed on kinship, marriage bears an outsized force upon the social norms that organize gender, such that deviations of gender or sexuality are framed as at once localized to those subjects understood as produced by "dyadic heterosexually based family forms" (for example, the queer child born of straight parents), as well as generalized to all as "perilous to the putative natural and cultural laws said to sustain human intelligibility."[29] Butler writes of early-twenty-first-century American gender politics, and while Butler does not cite Foucault here, such observations echo his more insistent characterization that the early modern period's regulations of sex "were all centered on matrimonial relations: the marital obligation, the ability to fulfill it, the manner in which one complied with it, the requirements and violences that accompanied it, the useless or unwarranted caresses for which it was pretext, its fecundity or the way one went about making it sterile, the moments when one demanded it (dangerous periods of pregnancy or breast-feeding, forbidden times of Lent or abstinence), its frequency or infrequency, and so on. It was this domain that was especially saturated with prescriptions."[30] The locus of scrutiny of much recent scholarship on early modern gender and sexuality has, perhaps, shifted away from the prescriptions of marriage, but as Butler acknowledges, marriage still functions powerfully to order a whole host of sexual and social norms that have tremendous bearing upon sexuality, gender, and kinship relations, what kinds of lives, and whose, are possible and livable—and whose are not. Because of the endurance of the centrality of marriage to patriarchal social order, this book attends to the stakes of marital status in early modern England to put commensurate pressure on those types of single men, who, once recognized, reveal how patriarchal discourses sought to capture and enfold them into patriarchy's real and imagined hierarchies.

## The Single Life and Early Modern Patriarchy

This book's primary contribution to early modern gender and sexuality studies is its focus upon the single life of men where it has or would escape attention, but its arguments rest upon a substantial body of scholarship on manhood, patriarchy, and gender in early modern English literature and culture that has to some extent already recognized the unpatriarchal manhoods that the single life makes possible.[31] While this study examines the representational range and meanings of the single life in English renaissance literature, it does so as a means of analyzing patriarchy as both a sociohistorical phenomenon and an ideological apparatus. Patriarchy feels like an old, if not tired, concept, one that perhaps seems out of fashion for scholarly analysis. When it comes the naturalizations and normalizations of gender and sexuality, we are more apt to talk about heteronormativity, heterosexuality, or cisheteronormativity—as we should. As Merry Wiesner-Hanks has observed, "Patriarchy . . . seems to have lost its edge," but as she goes on to argue, it yet requires further historicization and theorization.[32] Indeed, its gender and sexual norms remain entirely too present; the recent flurry of "trans bans" and the rollback of abortion rights in the United States, for example, confirm its edges remain vital and violent, and because it remains an oppressive and repressive force, one of the goals of this project is to treat patriarchy as a useful subject of critique and analysis, to denaturalize it yet again, and to begin to think about the homosocial, heteronormative, and cisnormative productions of its institutions and structures, as well as what possible alternatives remain extant in an early modern culture that naturalized and normalized a patriarchal social order that continues to ramify into the present.

If patriarchy and patriarchal norms are not new today, neither were they new in early modern England. As Anthony Fletcher once observed, "patriarchy was very old when Queen Elizabeth ascended the English throne."[33] Early modern patriarchy was defined by the material and symbolic links between marriage and family with the economic, social, and political order.[34] The meaning of patriarchy was salient; "patriarch" meant "chiefe father," and the ethos of such a system was one of paternalism.[35] It privileged a procreative manhood predicated on systems of patrilineality. Its central figures were fathers, husbands, and sons. As a social system, "patriarchy" in early modern England can be thought of as "the institutionalised male dominance over women and children in the family and the subordination of women in society in general."[36] The institutionalization of patriarchy in Fletcher's definition is significant because it suggests the formal or structural elements of patriarchy as a hierarchy that organizes both private and public space—through institutions like the university, livery company, the court, or marital household, for example—as well as those laws, bylaws, and norms that govern such institutions. Such institutionalizations of patriarchy, moreover, evince Heidi Hartmann's definition of patriarchy as "a set relations between men, which have a material base, and which, though hierarchical, create or establish interdependence and solidarity among men that enable them to dominate women."[37] Hartmann's definition is perhaps too totalizing, as it collapses the ways particular forms of manhood that do not fit within white, ableist, cisnormative models are excluded from the solidarity and interdependence central to maintaining its hierarchies. Nonetheless, it suggest the ways patriarchy finds form through material and institutional relations, around spaces and places in which a variety of manhoods might be lived or practiced, and which, to a greater or less degree, a host of other people are marginalized and excluded.

The unpatriarchal manhoods of the single life that I analyze in this book are indebted to a feminist methodological commitment to denaturalizing and rehistoricizing patriarchy in the early modern period and in English renaissance literature. Judith Bennett has address the historical problem of what she defines as "patriarchal equilibrium," those ways in which patriarchal institutions and social order recalibrate their hierarchies to maintain the status quo.[38] In attending to the single life, this book focuses on such moments of discursive, structural, and institutional patriarchal calibrations. The unpatriarchal manhoods of the single life that I examine in each chapter of this book are historically discrete insofar as they are produced through and imagined in relation to early modern discourses and institutions that commute across time in ways far more inelastic than the gender identities and relations they themselves might produce. The single lives of journeymen are determined through their specific relation to the early modern institution of the livery company, its hierarchies, and its sociopolitical rituals, but their status also shows the ways patriarchy more generally forges a relation between material precarity and the viability of marriage in economic terms. Alternatively, the single life of the celibate scholar has a specific relationship to discourses of early modern melancholy produced within England's universities, but it also bears unsettling witness to more recent violent, affectively organized forms of manhood like the modern "incel."[39] If, as Bennett argues, patriarchy consolidates itself across time through achieving equilibriums by multiplying across sites and organizing institutional hierarchies, then this book seeks to attend to the representations of such sites and institutions in English renaissance literature to analyze patriarchy where the unpatriarchal manhoods of the single life might antagonize or reconstitute its normative and normalizing social structures.

Because of its commitments to critiquing patriarchal ideologies and institutions through an examination of the single life, this book is a return, in some ways, to earlier concerns in feminist scholarship with the ways patriarchy—as both a form of social order and cultural formation—produces itself and the ways early modern literature variously enables and resists such productions. In *Man's Estate*, Coppélia Kahn at once acknowledges the power early modern patriarchy grants men while analyzing how that power runs through women and the mediating roles of mother and wife that patriarchy requires of them, but Kahn also makes a case that Shakespeare's timelessness hinges upon his perceptions about manhood and patriarchy, which has maintained transhistorical salience.[40] In her psychoanalytic, feminist study of Shakespeare's plays, Janet Adelman exposes the early modern patriarchal family as fraught with psychic trauma and violence because of its necessary investments in the sexuality of women that it cannot fully symbolize or recuperate into sociality. So it is, for instance, that in *Hamlet* the single prince comes to militate against marriage itself as a polluting force.[41] As conflicted as early modern patriarchy appears in such psychoanalytic accounts, later work came to rematerialize the productions and circulations of manhood, understanding it less as exhibiting universal, if historically realized, crises in patriarchal social formations. Instead, Shakespeare's historically emergent universality comes to traffic rather local, oppressive, racist, and patriarchal modes of textual and dramatic production. Examining the ways Shakespeare's theater produces a range of representations through a rather narrow coterie of players and playwrights, Dympna Callaghan has pointed out, for example, that "Shakespeare's plays both demonstrate and complicate the paradox whereby theatrical representation depends on its functioning—even in the moments of self-reflexivity—on the absence of the thing it represents."[42] The plays are so often marked by whom they exclude but represent, namely, white ciswomen and Black men and women. Like these early studies, this book seeks to keep early modern patriarchal culture, Shakespearean and otherwise, in mind in a manner that would acknowledge, rather than negotiate, its histories of violence and exclusion.

## The Single Life and Early Modern Gender Studies

While this book primarily orients its arguments around the question of the single life, it is also heavily indebted to scholarship on manhood that has conceived of its social construction and embodiment as a contingent, procedural, and material process. Manhood was always in a process of being fabricated under early modern patriarchy. Men could and did appropriate, improvise, and otherwise subvert the norms of patriarchal manhood, often in relation to early modern literary plays and playhouses, which afforded both real and imagined spaces to rethink masculinity. Youth culture flourished in such spaces, as Amanda Bailey has demonstrated, and so, "by enabling young men to appropriate the proper use of costly apparel, to reinscribe its traditional value, and to remap its assigned contexts the theatre turned status into style," a style that did not align with elite and status-conferring distinctions.[43] If Bailey shows how sartoriality enables new ways for men to draw upon cultural artifacts to refashion their gender, Will Fisher likewise has demonstrated the degree to which manhood requires its accoutrements, arguing "early modern masculinity was in crucial ways prosthetic."[44] From codpieces to beards, early modern masculinity required supplementations and extensions to reify what patriarchy would imagine as embodied, natural, permanent, and essential. Social rank and social practice, too, insofar as they were integral to constituting manhood in the period, were also sites of improvisation and mutability. In a manner that accounts for how spatial logics and cultural performance can mutually constitute conceptions of manhood, Jennifer Low argues that, despite differing social ranks offering differing conceptions of manhood, "the duel in early modern England became an overdetermined sign of masculine identity that helped to stabilize significantly volatile notions of both rank and gender."[45] Alternatively, focusing on the ways discrete forms of manhood were constructed in and through lower social ranks, Ronda Arab has productively supplemented a gap in the literature on masculinity, which, as she observes, often treats it as a universal quality or attends to elite forms, to consider how renaissance literature represents artisan and lowborn men as possessing manly bodies that challenge aristocratic forms of masculinity that privileged moderation, autonomy, and control.[46] Early modern patriarchy extended considerable effort to stabilize what was fundamentally mutable, and in attending to the single life of men, this book likewise interrogates how the literature of the period negotiates the coaxings and coercions of early modern patriarchal ideals of manhood.

Part of examining such negotiations also depends upon the recent work of early modern transgender studies scholars, who have challenged the transparencies of manhood at the heart of much early modern patriarchal culture and have demonstrated the degree to which transgender histories constitute the histories of gender itself. Examining the plurality of double crossdressing plots in renaissance literature, many of which seemingly abet patriarchal marriages, Simone Chess has revealed the potentials such texts hold for "modeling queer relational gender," and how "these characters offer possible sites for audience and readers to experience . . . some of the experiences and effects of gender swapping."[47] In these texts, the single life serves as a proving ground for such pleasures, and so can provide pathways in which the very heterosexuality that patriarchy produces might be queered beyond a locus of dimorphic cisgenders. Reading histories and representations of the early modern Ottoman court (and English renaissance literary engagements with it), Abdulhamit Arvas draws our attention to eunuchs, who were nearly always required to live a single life, and whose "bodies were re-formed, re-figured, and re-inscribed, and ultimately existed beyond the male-female binary" in early modern literature and culture. Such processes, he goes on to show, created space for queer, gendered embodiment while also entrenching processes of early modern "racecraft."[48] Despite patriarchal prescriptions, gender could be reimagined, refashioned, and rematerialized a number of ways. Through the evidence of a particular—but spectacular—example of how early moderns might resist or redeploy patriarchal ideals of gender, the body, and even species, Holly Dugan examines "a 'bestiary' of premodern tranimals created by a (possibly) trans-identified young student in the Renaissance, . . . a single manuscript, made of vellum and folded concertina-style . . . likely made in the mid-seventeenth century in England, as part of an educational writing task designed to foster, practice, and enforce Puritan religious ideals about what constitutes a moral life"; however, as Dugan succinctly notes: "yet it does not do this." Instead, the manuscript permits all sorts of permutations, at one point even allowing the ostensible original couple of Adam and Eve to become something more than one flesh: "a sequence that flows from Adam-Eve-Siren can create a merman if the top flap (depicting Adam) is moved back into place before the bottom one."[49] Indeed, Colby Gordon shows how just this kind of technogenesis not only inhered in early modern artisan culture more widely but also animates Shakespeare's sonnets in particular: Nature fabricates the sonnet's single youth as master-mistress through the art and artifice of pricking.[50] Given the materials of patriarchal gender norms, individual actors, partners, or persons might reconstitute or transform them into something more experimental, experiential, amenable, and livable.

Even when the single life has not featured explicitly in their studies, other scholars have demonstrated how the single life was very much a lived and imagined possibility made available by English renaissance literature. Scholars working on early modern gender and sexuality have observed that, despite the centrality of marriage to patriarchal social order, numerous literary, religious, political, and economic texts do not always prioritize or valorize its nexus of gender roles or orders of desire. English renaissance literature often functions as a site where the patriarchal norms might be tested or reconfigured. In its ranging investments in biblical accounts of Eden, "early modern culture," Catherine Belsey has argued, "which embraced love as a humanizing force, marriage as the divinely endorsed remedy for desire and the family as the source of civil society, also recognized passion, even in its socially approved form, as all too human, and potentially dangerous and destructive"—and so Shakespeare's romantic comedies, Belsey concludes, revel in the pleasures of courtship by deferring the consummations of it.[51] Like Belsey, other scholars have demonstrated how literary genres can be a powerful organizing force for alternatives to patriarchal manhood and sexuality. Stephen Guy-Bray examines how extensively renaissance pastoral poets, by drawing upon a Virgilian and Theocritan literary tradition, create and sustain "homoerotic space," often against oppressive, insistent patriarchal ideals.[52] Where Catherine Bates has shown how renaissance lyric poetry variously facilitates forms of perverse, abject masculine subjectivity that cannot be recuperated by patriarchy, Per Sivefors has interrogated how the satires of Donne, Hall, Marston, and Guilpin negotiate patriarchal ideals of manhood as they relate to self-control, violence, husbandry, and age.[53] Attending to the ways that the heteronormativity of early modern patriarchy is not historically inevitable or even natural, James Bromley has convincingly shown the range of ways patriarchal marriage does not readily accommodate modes of interiority and relationality, namely access to intimacy, that we might otherwise expect. As Bromley demonstrates, numerous renaissance literary texts provide compelling alternatives, such that, even at the moment companionate marriage was consolidating itself as a cultural norm, "the contraction of the intimate sphere around coupling was hotly contested through . . . representations of alternative possibilities for affective relations."[54] Those relations might even find evidentiary possibility outside the ostensible discourses and genres that might imagine them. Despite the period's patriarchal social order, its discourses on love, especially those written by political writers, contain very little of it. Rather than valorizing marriage, companionship, or courtship, such literature instead meditates on masochism, violence, eroticized submission, promiscuity, and other queer or even antisocial desires.[55] As these scholars, among others, reveal, the single life could enable a range of possible, desirable, and beneficial social, political, erotic, and intimate relations.

While this book draws upon the critical work that has investigated the fissures in early modern patriarchal structures, and likewise acknowledges the fact that English renaissance literature especially provided alternatives to patriarchal ideals of marriage and companionship, it also recognizes that patriarchal structures and incentives nonetheless had a powerful effect in organizing social life and gender norms in the early modern period. Even literary texts that seem to be animated by troubling patriarchal ideals of power could reify them, and the single life they imagine might serve as useful patriarchal fantasies. Looking closely at the material and sexual incentives of marriage for single men, Jennifer Panek has shown, for example, the extent to which widow plays of the period promulgate fantasies of economic and gender mastery for single gallants. Often in these plays, Panek argues, financial precarity could be overcome by sexual mastery, and so "men obtained the reassurance they needed to seize their economic opportunity through the construct of the lusty widow, which provided a kind of compensation against the threat to a second husband's masculine domestic authority."[56] Literature could contest patriarchal ideals, but it could also allow men to rehearse the gender roles central to it. For example, the literature that came out of early modern universities, often overlooked in early modern histories of drama, and which abounded with and were nearly exclusively composed of single men, could abet patriarchal ideals of social, sexual, and gendered authority. As Christopher Marlow argues, university dramas came to gender dramatic performance itself as a "manly act," and, while they could hold a complex and contradictory relation to patriarchal ideals, they also "gave students the opportunity to 'try on' hyperconventional subject positions, such as 'man' and 'father,' that were as yet unavailable to them because of their youth" and so might "'shore up authorized male roles."[57] The single life in each of these cases became a time and space of vested interest for patriarchal social order, and literature could provide a way to access fantasies of privilege and power for single men.

Early modern patriarchy was not just a matter of gender and sexuality, however; it was also deeply invested in racial formations. Literary histories of patriarchy are also those of white supremacy and colonialism. It should come as no surprise, then, that much of the work on early modern gender and manhood has been done by those scholars who have attended to the period's racial formations but have also been too often overlooked as substantively contributing to early modern gender studies. Perhaps no other scholar has done so much integral, if also foundational, work on the intersections between gender and race as Kim F. Hall. In *Things of Darkness*, Hall points out "the threat of interracial desire . . . is a key to the establishment of an ideal of patriarchal authority," and in the context of *The Tempest*, Caliban's enforced singleness indexes and aggregates the threat of rape he comes to embody in relation to Prospero's "obsessive attempts to control his environment and his daughter's sexuality."[58] In reading the circulations and citations of Dido in renaissance texts, Joyce MacDonald likewise shows how "marriage becomes the defining medium through which patrimony is preserved, paternal authority reproduced, racial purity proclaimed," and further insists upon the integral role marriage has within imperial projects to racialize men: "In these tales of empire, this difference between orders of men is constituted within race."[59] More recently, Dennis Austin Britton has shown how early modern Protestant theology came to invest marriage and procreation with the power to create Christian identity—often for women more than men—and the ways early modern English tragicomedies "revise and recuperate the infidel-conversion motif" whereby English Christian men convert women through marriage.[60] In such a context, the single life holds enormous power and consequence for English Christendom. As these scholars, among others, evidence, to analyze early modern patriarchy is to also contend with how its gender and sexual politics are entangled in the legacies and histories of early modern racecraft, colonialism, and imperialism.

## The Single Life in Histories of Bachelorhood

Even as this book variously draws on the insights of these scholars, it also makes a pointed intervention in literary studies scholarship that has focused upon single men only to carve out a space in which the single life holds significant social meaning only sometime after the early modern period. Those few studies devoted to the examination of the single life often circumscribe it to the identity of its modern exemplar, "the bachelor." Circumscribed by this representational terminology, such studies that focus on the single life tend to render it invisible in early modern England but easily discoverable in modern England and early and modern America. In an otherwise compelling argument that considers how subcultures of single men are integral to constructions of manhood in general, Howard Chudacoff argues "the age of the bachelor" was fin de siècle and early-twentieth-century America. According to Chudacoff, as America became increasingly industrialized and young, unmarried men left rural homes for prospective work in cities, a distinct bachelor identity emerged as an effect of this industrial migration and the conservative social policies responding to it. New norms privileging domestic life and heterosocial bonds arose, and as subculture of single men coalesced against these norms, a definable bachelor identity likewise emerged.[61] John Gilbert McCurdy, however, qualifies Chudacoff's dating of the emergence of bachelor identity, situating the rise of bachelor identity far earlier in the American imagination and concurrent with its founding. Thoroughly reading early American "bachelor laws," which obligated single men to specific kinds of civic duties that married men were not obligated to fulfill, including military service and paying higher taxes, McCurdy contends that the increased public scrutiny over unmarried men worked to fashion an engaged citizenry out of them and to shape a concomitant sense of individualism that became engrained into American civic consciousness at large.[62] Though specifically focused on literary representations of bachelor identities, Katherine Snyder similarly argues that bachelor narrators of mid-nineteenth and twentieth-century American fiction, such as Miles Coverdale of Hawthorne's *The Blithesdale Romance* or Nick Carraway of Fitzgerald's *The Great Gatsby*, embody the paradoxical and conflicted norms of bourgeois domesticity and serve as threshold figures that indicate, violate, and remap the boundaries of high and low culture, manhood, and cultural normativity.[63]

There is a pattern to these studies that ascribe an emergent and distinct gender identity to historical epochs which, as Eve Sedgwick has argued, instantiates an epistemological paradigm that extenuates what is thought to be known in the present to resolve what can and cannot be known about the past.[64] No doubt the single life found localized meanings in the genres examined and historical contingencies interrogated by Chudacoff, McCurdy, and Snyder, but it can also be said that the literary forms and social, legal, and cultural phenomena in which single men become legible as such have corollaries in early modern England. If single men are constituted in a socially legible identity through significant migrations from rural homes to urban centers, as Chudacoff argues, then sixteenth- and seventeenth-century London, which saw similar patterns of migration, might likewise find itself roiling with a subculture of single men. An anonymous prose work originally attributed to Thomas Dekker, *The Bachelors Banquet* (1603), attests to such a subculture. It describes its tales of beleaguered householders as "A banquet for bachelors: wherein is prepared sundry dainty dishes to furnish their table, curiously dressed and seriously served in."[65] Insofar as some of its readers are those single men consigned to subordinate positions of service, such a text might equally speak to the juridical distinctions between married and unmarried men that McCurdy finds arising in the early American republic. Or if it is true that the stories of domesticity that single men tell draw and test the thresholds of cultural normativity, as Snyder contends, then we need only look at the at the diabolical visions of Nashe's Pierce Penniless or at Herrick's verses to find single men challenging normative models of gentrified manhood. For example, in "No Spouse but a Sister," Herrick proclaims, "A bachelor I will / Live as I have liv'd still, / And never take a wife / To crucify my life." Herrick imagines access to patriarchal manhood by intensifying and eroticizing the kinship bonds that organize it: "A sister (in the stead / Of wife) about I'll lead; / Which I will keep embrac'd, / And kiss, but yet be chaste."[66] As the spousal relation is refracted through the poem's erotics of incestuous chastity, what is licit and what is illicit blur into a rather queer vision of domestic bliss.

Invested in seeing the single life through the emergence of the bachelor rather than seeing the bachelor as one form of unpatriarchal manhood of the single life, these studies are further narrowed by an over reliance on etymological readings of history.[67] The result is a kind of history that uncovers what it creates. Where Snyder reads the *OED* and concludes "only in the mid-eighteenth century did the current primary meaning [of bachelor] arise: an unmarried man of marriageable age," McCurdy asserts, "the word *bachelor* dates back more than seven hundred years and since then the basic definition has remained the same. First and foremost, a bachelor is an unmarried man."[68] McCurdy is correct on this point—the *OED* lists this meaning originating in the late fourteenth century, citing Chaucer's *Canterbury Tales*—and yet Snyder is right to point out that the identity of a bachelor was more fully imbricated and enmeshed in the early modern period in institutional hierarchies dependent upon mastery and subordination, which she simplifies to an "apprenticeship system."[69] The *OED* indicates several concurrent meanings for "bachelor" in the sixteenth and seventeenth centuries. In addition to a bachelor being defined as "an unmarried man (of marriageable age)," a bachelor could be "a young knight, not old enough, or having too few vassals, to display his own banner," "a junior or inferior member, or 'yeoman,' of a trade-guild, or City Company," or "one who has taken the first or lowest degree at a university, who is not yet a *master* of the Arts."[70] Often, such "bachelors" were also unmarried men, and their social status precluded the possibility of marriage or mandated a single life until the terms of their service were fulfilled. McCurdy draws a broad atomizing effect from the single life's relationship to early modern English institutional hierarchies, claiming "the unmarried were a fragmented group, dispersed throughout society without a collective identity."[71] He does so from a perspective that writes its social history in etymological terms and thus draws a conclusion about the early modern past with only a partial understanding of it.

To be sure, the single life did mean different things in early modern England than it does today. It more readily indicated one's social status, for instance. But it does not follow to presume one's unmarried status constitutes a more unifying element of social identity in the present than it did in the past or that bachelors in early America constituted a unified and undispersed group in terms fundamentally different than those in early modern England. One might make the opposite assertion, in fact. Insofar as marital status was the primary means of gender difference between men, single men could be thought of as a unified group even if dispersed across a more gradated hierarchy of social rank. Take, for example, Thomas Deloney's ballad "Salomon's Wife." It conceives of its audience as single men unified, and not dispersed, across the social hierarchy. "May bachelors of each degree," its speaker warns, "in choosing a beauteous wife / Remember what is joy to see / May lead to woefulness and strife."[72] Lexicons contemporary to the sixteenth and seventeenth centuries likewise suggest that the very term "bachelor" could collectively gather a diverse array of single men into a broad, complex, and uneven social category. In *A World of Words* (1598), Florio translates "Baccalaro" as "a batcheler in any arte, a scholler, a licentiate, a clerke. Also taken for a fond self-conceited fellow."[73] The line between institutional rank and marital status is less than clear, or so blurred as to be beyond distinction: "fellow" might refer to something like a companionable person, but it more likely points to the fellow of a university, that is, one whose life is supported by a fellowship and who was, by statute, a single, celibate man. Florio's other citations of "batcheler" open it up to even more possibilities. He translates "Donzello" as "an appointeer, an officer, a sergeant, an apprentise at the law, a clark. Also a batchelor, a waitingman, an vnmarried man, a page, a squire, a custrell, a waiter, a seruingman"; for "Pizzocolo," he translates, "a lone man, a single man, a batcheler, an vnmarried man" while for "Polcello," he writes, "a yong lad, a batcheler, a virgin boy."[74] In part because of its etymological history and semantic pliability, "bachelor" accreted a range of meanings, prejudices, and expectations and itself came to be enfolded into other social and cultural identities. Single men were in equal measure imagined virgins and bawds, celibates and fornicators, but the most telling aspect of Florio's translations is the association of "bachelor" with vocational role or institutional rank. Consider his translation of "Donzello" where the modern notion of "bachelor" as "an vmarried man" interrupts a chain of service roles: "a waitingman . . . a page, a squire, a custrell, a waiter, a seruingman." On the one hand, the broad application of "bachelor" to various Italian words for types of men indexes etymological shift occurring from the medieval to the early modern era. The word "bachelor" is believed to derive either from old French or Italian; its association with youth, as in Florio's translation of "Polcello," for example, thus resonates with a medieval shift in application, where the French term *bachelier* came to replace the Latin *puer* to denote adolescence.[75] On the other hand, as ABC's long-running reality television shows *The Bachelor* and *The Bachelorette* demonstrate, single men have no problem playing to type, readily lending themselves to puerile representations today.

To reduce the single life in early modern England to the matter of being a "bachelor," therefore, not only narrows the range of its significance in the culture at large but also obscures the possibilities of the single life. If you simply look for "bachelors," you will not find many, even though you will find plenty of maids. There are exceptions, of course, such as the aforementioned anonymous prose work *The Bachelors Banquet* (1603), but on the whole the single life of men does not manifest as legible in the same way the single life of women does (for already-explained reasons). A quick survey of the drama of the period is revealing. While single men are in plenty of the period's plays, they do not appear to be the titular subject of them. In an age where "the maid" abounds as topic of Elizabethan, Jacobean, and Caroline drama—there is *A Greek Maid* (1579), *The Maiden's Holiday* (1586), *The Fair Maid of London* (1598), *The Maydes Metamorphosis* (1600), *The Fair Maid of Bristow* (1603), *The Two Maids of Moreclacke* (1606), *The Maid's Tragedy* (1610), *The Fair Maid of the West, Part 1* (1610) and *Part 2* (1630), *A Chaste Maid in Cheapside* (1613), *Love's Cure; or the Martial Maid* (1619), *The Maid of Honour* (1621), *The Maid in the Mill* (1623), *The Puritan Maid, Modest Wife, and Wanton Widow* (1623), *A Fool and Her Maidenhead Soon Parted* (1624), *The Fair Maid of the Inn* (1625), *A Maidenhead Well Lost* (1625), *The Vow Breaker, or The Fair Maid of Clifton* (1625), *The Maid's Revenge* (1626), *Lovesick Maid or the Honour of Young Ladies* (1629), *The Constant Maid* (1636)—the single man can claim no such cultural cache. The first play forthrightly proclaiming that its subject is a "bachelor"—William Congreve's *The Old Batchelor* (1693)—appears a full three decades into the restoration of the monarchy.

But if much of the literature is not expressly about "bachelors," a good deal of it is written with single life of men in mind. Take Shirley's *The Constant Maid*, the plot of which revolves around the financial and marital crisis facing Hartwell, who calls himself "A Bachelour" within the first line of the play. So-called "widow-plays" market themselves to the plights and fantasies of single men. Sir Thomas Overbury's *A Wife Now the widow of Sir Thomas Overbury* (1614)—one of the most popular character books of the period (eleven editions had been printed by 1622)—is an illuminating example of the problem of identarian representation I have been tracing. With one exception (which I address in chapter 5), the "bachelor" does not appear in early modern character books as a character, and Overbury's text is no exception.[76] And yet the single man seems to be everywhere in Overbury's text as it works to construct a reader that is constitutively unmarried. The volume includes Overbury's titular poem, printed posthumously (Overbury died in 1613), and appended with character descriptions *"written by himselfe and other learned gentlemen his friends."* Overbury's poem seeks to persuade a single man to marry. If its audience is imagined to be a single man that is in no small part due to the poem that precedes it: "Of the Choice of a Wife," the speaker of which is a single man debating the merits and demerits of marriage. Like Touchstone of *As You Like It*, the speaker finds "much virtue in 'if,'" casting the poem in a hypothetical, subjunctive mood: "If I were to chuse a Woman, / As who knowes but I may marry, / I would trust the eye of no man / Nor a tongue that may miscarry."[77] Marriage is not a foregone conclusion here. This is a man who not only privileges his choice but also embraces his cool nonchalance—"As who knowes but I may"—regarding the marriage question. What is striking about this speaker is not that he is a single man but that the single life is conditioned as a discerning and fundamentally asocial, a person skeptical of what the community sees—that "trust[s] the eye of no man,"—as well as what it says—"nor a tongue that may miscarry." Adam Zucker has observed that late-sixteenth- and seventeenth-century England bore witness to various kinds of classificatory texts, of which the character book is emblematic, and that such a text "offered its authors and readers alike an opportunity to imagine themselves as sophisticated observers of London's socioeconomic landscape."[78] In this prefatory poem, the single man is just such a sophisticated observer, and he casts his discerning eye upon both the means and meanings of patriarchal manhood, for he does not imagine achieving his manhood by marrying a well-portioned maid or a rich widow. Rather he personifies a form of unpatriarchal manhood, one predicated on the notion of a choice that would except him from a mandate to marry, and yet would also universalize his discerning, urbane sensibility as an ideal form of manhood and readership. The ubiquity of the single life of men in English renaissance literature should not entail its invisibility. Instead, we are better served thinking twice about it so that we can understand more clearly how the single life in English renaissance literature imagines gender relations that both effected it and were affected by it, and to see those unpatriarchal forms of manhood early modern English patriarchy would rather leave illegible.

## The Single Life and the Double in Early Modern England

If this book resists some of the representational strategies of early modern literature that would absorb the single life into metrics of age or into those social positions where marital status seems less at issue, it also seeks to think with the literature too. It might be true, as Foucault claims, that the early modern period was governed by "the law of marriage" and "the order of desires," but one of the ways such law and order found continual inscription was through a dialectic between "the single life and the double."[79] Early modern writers often conceived of patriarchal manhood by grappling with the meanings of the single life. One of the animating tropes of the period cast the single life in terms of freedom and the married one in terms of obligation. "The difference betwixt, a single life and a double," the refrain often goes, is "the batchelor's pleasure, and the married man's trouble."[80] Notably, it is the difference between the two—and not the single life it-self—that pleasures the bachelor and so troubles the married man. It is as if the speaker recognizes not only a form of double consciousness but also, in that recognition, a desire for individuation.

As playful as it is, that refrain is not innocuous. It neatly encapsulates an "early modern apprehension of marriage as an economy of scarcity," that develops, as Frances Dolan has argued, from three conflicting but mutually-informing early modern marital concepts: "marriage as hierarchy, as fusion, and as contract." These result in an indelible insistence that "there is only room for one full person" within the marriage relation.[81] For the imagined married man in the ballad, the single life constitutes a kind of prelapsarian, premarital utopia when the burdens and responsibilities of marriage did not diminish his personhood, a time he might have been an Adam without an Eve. The single life sticks to the marital one in this case because it enables a fantasy of autonomy upon which marriage seemingly impinges. That single men might take pleasure in the "trouble" of married men, however, like-wise promulgates a fantasy of independence in which the real conscriptions of economic agency, of certain legal privileges, and of elevated social and gender status become occluded by way of an imagined escape from marital obligations. On either side of the dialectic of "the single life and the dou-ble," then, manhood is imagined as essentially a matter of achieving an ide-alized single life in which autonomy and individuality constitute gendered experience. As Dolan concludes, "The notion of marriage as an economy of scarcity facilitates the development of a particular kind of subject, but only one. The other spouse serves as the object to the subject. Thus for one spouse marriage and selfhood are mutually constitutive and for the other marriage and selfhood are radically incompatible."[82] That selfhood, I want to argue, is negotiated through early modern representations of the single life of men—even ideas about the husband and his obligations cannot be extricated from the ways the single life comes to inhere in the "double life" of patriarchal marriage.

In the course of tracing the violent legacies of marriage inaugurated in early modern England, Dolan asks, "what does it mean to *be* married?"[83] I suggest that that question cannot be answered without addressing another: what does it mean to be single? The rise of Protestantism and influence of Erasmian humanism led to cultural venerations of marriage, but they often did so through engaging and reconstituting an entrenched, misogamist (an-timarriage) discourse that asked whether or not a wise man should marry.[84]

Proposed by the Roman rhetorician Quintillian and, through a fragment that appears in Jerome's *Adversus Jovinianum*, the Greek philosopher Theophrastus, that question, for example, figures heavily in sixteenth-century rhetorical and logic texts. Both Thomas Wilson's *The Rule of Reason* (1551) and *The Arte of Rhetorique* (1553) refer to it.[85] In doing so, texts like those of Wilson reinvigorated a tradition dating back at least to Juvenal and extending forward to Chaucer. As Katharina M. Wilson and Elizabeth M. Makowski document, the question was central to classical and medieval misogamist literature. The question traditionally took two forms: whether men in general should marry, or whether particular kinds of men should marry. According to Wilson and Makowski, that topos also had three distinct, but by no means mutually exclusive, traditions: the ascetic, the philosophical, and the general.[86] Drawing from Pauline doctrines of marriage found in the seventh chapter of *1 Corinthians*, the ascetic tradition came to value a celibate, single life as superior to a married one because it required a mortification of the flesh and full commitment to spiritual things. It became the central pillar of the early and medieval church. The philosophical tradition emphasized the financial, mental, and temporal burdens a wife and family brought to a man's life; in this instance, the question was not a matter of spiritual versus worldly concerns so much as it was a question of how best to allocate a man's finite resources. The more general, popular form of misogamous discourse is epitomized in Juvenal's Sixth Satire (whose arguments are repurposed by Truewit in Ben Jonson's *Epicene*). Ironic and often misogynistic, this tradition often emphasizes the "faults" of women and the woes they bring to men.

So often in the early modern period, even those texts ostensibly about marriage cannot help but entail representations of the single life. Take, for example, Edmund Tilney's *The Flower of Friendship* (1568). A relatively popular renaissance humanist text, *The Flower of Friendship*, is, as the title page indicates, "A brief and pleasant discourse of duties in Mariage." Tilney, who would serve as Master of Revels from around 1578 until he died in 1610, wrote the text when he was an unmarried man of thirty-two. He would not marry until fifteen years later, at forty-seven. Valerie Wayne situates Tilney's work as a response to antecedent misogamist texts—including those of Jerome, Theophrastus, Walter Map, and Chaucer—and she aligns it with the humanist works of Erasmus and Vives, whose arguments (and personages) it includes. For Wayne, because Tilney's text synthesizes a range of dominant humanist ideas about marriage, and identifies differing ideologies through its dialogic form, the text might serve as "a kind of fictional record of the available ideologies of marriage" when it was published.[87] It certainly serves as evidence that the positive value of marriage was a position in need of defense; marriage produced, and continued to produce, a discourse, of which Tilney's *The Flower of Friendship* was a significant contribution.

The dialogue begins with the personage of the Spanish humanist, Pedro di Luxan (whose *Coloquios matrimoniales* functions as source text for Tilney's own) insisting, "I will first declare unto you, the vertues of the matrimoniall estate, which (setting virginitie aside, as the purest estate) is both holy and most necessary."[88] While the text is devoted to examining marital roles and the benefits of marital union, it premises its argument by acknowledging the greater value of the single life (so long as it is virginal). In the space of a parenthetical, the single life flashes as an ideal, viable, and desirable alternative to marriage that the text will nonetheless leave unexamined except in the quickly dismissed misogynist and misogamist diatribes of one of the text's interlocutors, Master Gualter.[89] A text like Tilney's *The Flower of Friendship* can, as Valerie Wayne argues, tell us something about the residual, dominant, and emergent ideas about marriage in the period. And yet, inasmuch as Tilney's *The Flower of Friendship* has much to say about marriage, it is also compelling in terms of what it cannot say about the single life, which, acknowledged but not debated, hovers as an impossibility in the text—except, of course, that all of the characters in the text who are discussing "the vertues of the matrimoniall estate" are single, unmarried people.[90] Here, then, is one of the Renaissance's significant document about marriage that features only single people who become preoccupied with marriage as means of negotiating, exploring, and otherwise debating gender and sexual roles. Tilney's text is notable because the merits of marriage are valorized not by married people but by single people. It is as if its ideological aims skate on its surface; it thematizes the ways early modern patriarchy requires the interpellation of the single life as always already invested in and anticipating the married life.

## The Single Life and Histories of Sexuality

Thinking about the single life in English literature and culture can make clear what the literature refuses to represent about it, but it can clarify the role the single life has played in theorizations of gender and sexuality studies more broadly. In *The Epistemology of the Closet*, for example, Eve Sedgwick draws upon Quintillian's distinction between infinite and definite topoi that is so central to premodern and early modern misogamist discourses to analyze "the contradictions . . . internal to all the important twentieth-century understandings of homo/heterosexual definition, both heterosexist and antihomophobic." The first contradiction, Sedgwick explains, is that between the "minoritizing view" and the "universalizing view" of sexuality, that is, whether or not questions of sexuality are primarily a matter of concern for those deemed as a discrete and specific sexual identity or whether or not they are a matter for all sexual identities.[91] Sedgwick's distinction between "minoritizing" and "universalizing" discourses refigures a premodern rhetorical tradition of distinguishing between definite and indefinite topoi, though Sedgwick draws upon it to critique contemporary epistemologies of sexuality. In making a connection between Quintillian and Sedgwick, I want to suggest how the capaciousness of the single life provides a means of thinking forward and thinking backward, or, perhaps, thinking recursively, about the saliencies of patriarchal ideology across time. If Sedgwick was tackling twentieth-century epistemologies of sexuality by using a Quintillian model exemplified by the question of whether or not a single man should marry, she also evinces the ways this earlier epistemology seeded modern epistemologies about sexuality and homophobia, and how the form of a question circulating around single men accommodates new epistemological contents centuries later.

In their organization around definite and indefinite topoi, early modern epistemologies of the single life may ramify into modern epistemologies of sexuality, but at least one instance of unpatriarchal manhood of the single life has also structured the debate around the history of sexuality as such. In *The Epistemology of the Closet*, Sedgwick notably troubles the very divide between the premodern and the modern, and the epistemologies that organize it by challenging the paradigm shifts central to Foucault's *The History of Sexuality, Volume One*. I am not going to restate that debate.[92] Instead, I want to briefly trace how the single life of men intervenes in Foucault's history of sexuality. A good deal of attention has been paid to Foucault's distinction between (premodern) acts and (modern) identities, but far less attention has been paid to the figure—rather than the archive and discourses—upon which he makes that distinction. What heralds the division between the premodern and the modern for Foucault is the life of Don Juan, "the great violator of the rules of marriage." As Foucault asserts, "There were two great systems conceived by the West for governing sex: the law of marriage and the order of desires, and the life of Don Juan overturned them both."[93] Foucault is being playful here. Nonetheless, the figure of Don Juan operates as a kind of rhetorical fulcrum. For Foucault, Don Juan not only embodies the ideal diagnostic subject, an epistemological closet case readymade for psychological and sexological discourse because endlessly open to analysis and analytic revision; he also functions as *the* historical actor in his history of sexuality, one around which modern sexualities and their discourses emerge from the premodern swamp of sex acts. What Foucault refuses to say about the single life of Don Juan structures his genealogy of sexuality. The sexual regimes imagined to fall on either side of that threshold of the consummate single man of Don Juan allow Foucault to define sexuality as that which remains outside of marriage, and the single life of Don Juan shimmers with sexual identities the modern era might diagnose and pathologize. Foucault demurs and speculates, "We shall leave it to psychoanalysts to speculate whether he was homosexual, narcissistic, or impotent."[94]

Impotent, narcissist, homosexual: the single life contains multitudes. It proliferates into any number of possible, unpatriarchal manhoods. Don Juan indexes the histories of sexuality in the proliferation of possibilities he figures forth, but he also introduces into them the synchronically motile, even unhistorical, temporalities literature itself enables. Don Juan has numerous lives and afterlives. Originally published in 1630, Tirso's *El burlador de Sevilla* is set three centuries prior, in the fourteenth century, although the life of Don Juan is perhaps best known in Mozart's eighteenth-century opera and Byron's epic, unfinished early-nineteenth-century poem.[95] When is Don Juan? His stories dilate the synchronic scenes of his single life across thresholds of diachronic histories. Did Don Juan abolish the law of marriage in a premodern, medieval past, a liminal, emergent renaissance, or a modern present?

I turn to Foucault not only to suggest that the single life has been under-historicized and under-theorized in histories of sexuality but also to insist that histories of gender and sexuality must contend with how the unspoken histories of the single life of men function within what Valerie Traub has identified as "certain recurrent metalogics that accord . . . over a vast temporal expanse a sense of consistency and, at times, uncanny familiarity" which yet manifest "as *cycles of salience*—forms of intelligibility"—or in this case, unintelligibility—"whose meanings recur, intermittently and with a difference, across time."[96] Foucault's placement of Don Juan genders that history in a manner that reifies the privileges of single men as essentially transhistorical in a manner that abets, rather than subverts, patriarchal social orders. (Why him, as opposed to Moll Cutpurse, say?) Yet, in denaturalizing marriage, the same history naturalizes the single life as outside of, and thus disruptive to, those cultural systems of law and order. The result is a perpetuation of an Enlightenment conception of the individual that is itself highly gendered and abstracted from the material, racialized conditions that made such a life more or less free. If the single life in English renaissance literature functions as one kind of metalogic that Traub discusses, and I argue it does, the forms of manhood that it makes salient are not so much antecedents in historical genealogies as they are recursive instantiations of the gendering of men in and across time and texts within patriarchal systems that prioritize marriage as a primary social good. Early modern England may be before heterosexuality and prior to modern sexual epistemologies as such, but I contend a more useful metalogic for understanding the gendering and sexuality of men in English renaissance literature is that concerned with the difference between the single life and the married life, for it provides a matrix for reading the gendering of men and the constitution of patriarchy as it is constructed in relation to a variety of discourses and institutions without having to reduce identity to any single formation of gender or sexuality.[97]

Given that the single life of Don Juan generates a crux in Foucault's history of sexuality, it is perhaps not surprising that the single man comes to exemplify those methodologies of queer theory that have both drawn on and critiqued Foucault's genealogical methods. For Eve Kosofsky Sedgwick, it is the figure of the bachelor in the works of William Makepeace Thackeray, George Du Maurier, and Henry James that catalyzes what would be "the inaugurating investigation" of *Epistemology of the Closet*.[98] Here Sedgwick offers up the bachelor as a kind of genealogical antecedent to modern identities classified by sexual orientation, one which "both narrowed the venue, and at the same time startlingly desexualized the question, of male sexual choice."[99] Observing that the figure of the bachelor predominates in late Victorian literature as a character no longer beholden to the association of the single life with a particular life stage—the category of "youth," say—Sedgwick argues the bachelor emblematizes the internalization of homosexual panic by bourgeois masculinity. Such a representation of the single life compounds an epistemological crisis, appearing as simultaneously like other men but fundamentally different from them.[100] Theorizing a queer politics against the symbolic narratives of the Child, In *No Future: Queer Theory and the Death Drive*, Lee Edelman likewise sees the single life as metonym for the queer. Focusing on those narratives of antagonism between the perpetually young and the unmarried old—Tiny Tim and Ebenezer Scrooge, Peter Pan and Captain Hook, Harry Potter and Lord Voldemort—Edelman translates his reading of the Symbolic binary between the Child and the Queer into the local examples of children and old bachelors, and the single life of such villains is quickly subsumed by "the queerness of queer sexualities."[101] Marital status becomes an implicit lynchpin in his polemic—a term I use without condescension—because, for Edelman, the single life queers teleological narrativity insofar as it resists marriage, one of his primary symbols of cultural normativity.

There are good historical reasons scholars like Sedgwick and Edelman situate the single life of men as central to their critiques. Because marriage has been an institution historically denied to same-gender couples, the single life has been the social and legal status for anyone who was not straight. But rather than see this crisis as localized to a historical or cultural development—of one particular to the nineteenth-century novel, for instance—we might situate it within a context of literary production in which marriage itself is at issue or at any point in which the meaning of the single life is at question. Insofar as marriage normalizes one form of sexuality by crucially obfuscating sex acts of the marital couple, as Jonathan Goldberg has argued, the single life will always exist as a kind of epistemological quandary.[102] When marriage is the norm—and in patriarchal regimes, it is *the* norm—we can always ask *why*, as Shakespeare does, the single person is not married. From Austen to James, the nineteenth-century domestic novel seems ripe for such a reading, for teasing its readers with questions of *why* and even offering some answers, but it is by no means the only genre that begs such questions. Take, for instance, the sixteenth-century satirical, epistolary prose text, *The Image of Idleness* (1555).[103] Like so many nineteenth-century novels, it is deeply concerned with the single life, and is even narrated by a single man, Bawdin Bachelor, who at first cannot, then later will not, marry. Popular enough to go through three editions and to influence later writers, *The Image of Idleness* mocks its bachelor on precisely those terms that Sedgwick suggests are emergent two centuries later.[104] Rehearsing a familiar (and ancient) misogynistic logic of the *querelle de femme* while simultaneously acting as inept failure, Bawdin Bachelor is presented as, to use Sedgwick's phrase, "*at the same time* an aspect of a particular, idiosyncratic personality type *and also* an expression of a great Universal."[105] And of course he is: he is a character who rehearses those misogamous question of Theophrastus, Quintillian, Juvenal, and a host of early modern writers. Here the universal language of misogyny is spoken by the egotistical Bawdin, a character any reader, single or married, would feasibly mock. The single life inhabits a structural contradiction in patriarchy that is still salient today: that of the static categorical binary between unmarried and the married as well as a teleological, temporal one in which single people eventually couple off and marry. When the meanings of the single life elevate its identarian possibilities to intervene in or interrupt a martial narrative of supersession, it effectively queers patriarchal normativity by rendering permanent and possible an erstwhile temporary state.

Finally, the turn to the question of marital status helps us understand how patriarchal institutions, and the single lives that either militate against or conform to them, can surface the very epistemologies of sexuality evident in so much of the period's literature. Consider, for example, the single lives of the playwrights of Francis Beaumont and John Fletcher. In his *Brief Lives* (1693), John Aubrey describes the living arrangements of Beaumont and Fletcher in marital terms: "There was a wonderfull consimility of phansey between him and Mr. John Fletcher, which caused that dearnesse of friendship between them. . . . They lived together on the Banke side, not far from the Play-house, both batchelors; lay together—from Sir James Hales, etc.; had one wench in the house between them, which they did so admire; the same cloathes and cloake, &c., betweene them."[106] It is one of the more tantalizing passages in Aubrey's biographical project. Scholars have parsed this passage to comprehend just what, exactly, it means for these playwrights to have "lived together." As a coda to his study on the interweaving discourses of textual and sexual production, Jeffrey Masten turns to this account to clarify his thesis on the homoerotics of dramatic collaboration in the Renaissance. This account is notable, he observes, for its "seeming obliviousness to the public/private distinctions we have come to see as central to a modern discourse of sexuality, the way in which there seems to be nothing to cover, no need for closet space in this shared household."[107]

It's true. Aubrey, after all, makes none of the insinuations or accusations that the period's moralists were inclined to make about exactly the kind of confraternity the public playhouses encouraged and provided. Where Phillip Stubbes frets "every mate sorts to his mate" after seeing a play, Beaumont and Fletcher dwell "in their conclaves," and Aubrey seems not to care whether or not they "play *the Sodomits*, or worse."[108] But the reading here crucially turns upon the social identities Beaumont and Fletcher share— "both batchelors"—and the act that follows: they "lay together." Their single life is organized around the bachelorhood as much as their bachelorhood is informed by their friendship. These are not transparent terms. The scene oscillates between what Alan Bray has traced as the public, sanctioned displays of private homosocial affection and a homoerotic, polyamorous set of relations.[109] There is nothing to cover here because Beaumont and Fletcher are bachelors in a manner akin to the bachelor of Davies's poem. What is represented depends on what cannot be known.

Another reading of Aubrey's account is likewise premised on its transparency. In his own biography on Beaumont, Charles Mills Gayley, like Masten, believes Aubrey "records the obvious," but diverges as to which parts are obvious and for what reasons. He concludes that the information regarding the particulars of their living—that they "lay together," that they "had one wench in the house between them"—is suspect because "so far as inferences are concerned the account is to be taken with at least a morsel of reserve."[110] Believing he's clarifying his point, Gayley notes "popular tradition" conferred the "wench" to Fletcher exclusively, only to recount how Oldwit—an old, married man—of Shadwell's *Bury-Fair* (1689) reminisces about dining with Fletcher and kissing his maid, Joan. But it is not entirely clear what Gayley wants his readers to see in this scene. At first, Gayley suggests Beaumont and Fletcher would not share "a wench . . . between them," but then Oldwit's anecdote implies Fletcher's maid was indeed shared as a sexual object, which would undermine his earlier assertion of Fletcher's monogamous relationship with her. Finally, it seems Gayley, who writes at the beginning of the twentieth century, offers these contradictory readings to displace any inkling that Beaumont and Fletcher might just be lovers, for he concludes, "It is hardly necessary, in any case, to surmise with those who sniff up improprieties that the admirable services of the original 'wench,' whether Joan or another, far exceeded the roasting of pork and the burning of sack for her two 'batchelors.'"[111] Gayley's conclusions—if we can call his deferrals and demurrals conclusions at all—are convoluted, but symptomatically so, for Gayley identifies a "closet space" in this text Masten does not acknowledge in his otherwise careful reading of Aubrey's puns of these playwrights "living near the Play-house; playing house."[112] Even as Gayley's reading shifts the terms of whose desires Beaumont and Fletcher's single life facilitates—they are "her 'batchelors'"—it also demonstrates how the single life's oscillation between being emblematic of an overdetermined homoeroticism or heterosexual chastity abets sexual assault. Represented as having a "common body," Joan, a servant, is kissed, touched, and possibly raped, but the chastity believed to inhere in the shared single lives of Beaumont and Fletcher create a space in which Joan might not be believed, for the facts cannot be known.[113] As "both batchelors," Beaumont and Fletcher benefit from patriarchal norms that afford them a kind of privacy from scrutiny. They are single men living double lives as bachelor spouses, their erotic desire becomes mutually directed, otherwise denied, or rendered unverifiable as a sexual assault intimated but never evidenced. Thus, by attending not only to the meanings of the single life but also to how it arranges the gendering of men, we can see the complex, plural relations unpatriarchal manhoods have within patriarchal systems. The closet spaces of homoerotic desire and polyamory that seem so out in the open also condition the possible exploitation of Joan as a servant in the bachelor household of Beaumont and Fletcher. The single life of men is never so singular.

## CHAPTER DESCRIPTIONS

Because there is no singular meaning to the single life in English renaissance literature and culture, I analyze its possible meanings in a series of contiguous chapters that, while they inform each other, do not map onto a chronological or cohesive developmental narrative of the meanings of the single life in the period's literature. My first chapter resituates the single man in relation to early modern Protestant histories of marriage to show how they organize themselves around the figure of the chaste youth. Drawing on the work of asexual scholars and scholars of asexuality, it shows how such histories construct an early modern notion of "compulsory sexuality." Shifting our attention away from allosexual norms to queer asexuality, the chapter recontextualizes the sexual politics of the single life in Shakespeare's *All's Well That Ends Well* to reread Bertram's proleptic and analeptic riddles of refusing consummation of his marriage with Helena. In doing so, the chapter examines the rhetorical effects of early modern histories of marriage and illuminate forms of the single life that are not alloerotic but imaginable as asexually queer and unpatriarchal.

The second chapter also attends to a Shakespearean marital comedy—*Much Ado About Nothing*—and to his perhaps most famous "bachelor," Benedick, only to recontextualize the institutional and socioeconomic communities Benedick's stated desire to live a single life might come to include. Where chapter 1 examines the theoretical stakes of the single life for early modern marital discourse, chapter 2 attends to the single life as it aggregates around the early modern meanings of bachelorhood as denoting both marital and labor status. Drawing on and developing a growing body of research on early modern English artisans, I read the single life in relation to institutional hierarchies and discourses of labor to provide a new literary history of bachelors that might include Benedick's desire to live as one but that is also not restricted by *Much Ado About Nothing*'s treatment (or the genre of Shakespearean marital comedy's treatment, more broadly) of the term. In an effort to recover literary audiences often overlooked in histories and cultural studies of labor, I tease out the capacity of a type of bachelorhood to demarcate the London journeyman, and further argue that ballads and literature that explicitly address bachelors, including Dekker's *The Shoemaker's Holiday* (1599), Dekker and Middleton's *1 Honest Whore* (1604), as well as those texts that gesture to them, including Shakespeare's *A Midsummer Night's Dream* (ca. 1595) and *Much Ado About Nothing* (ca. 1598), productively mobilize a cultural fantasy that translates the institutional prescriptions that attended journeywork into a bachelor's social and economic freedom.

Expanding chapter 2's focus on the meanings of the single life in early modern London, chapter 3 turns from journeymen to gentlemen, specifically the gallant so central to Jacobean city comedy. Situating the gallant within seventeenth-century consumer culture, critics have characterized the gallant's urbane masculinity in terms of his sartorial performativity and self-referential theatricality. In such studies, the gallant is a product of the market, a consummate consumer. Reading Jonson's *Epicene* (1609) and Middleton and Rowley's *Wit at Several Weapons* (1613) alongside contemporary debates about the nature of gentility, I demonstrate that the constitutive singleness of the gallant enables his mastery over the market, not his subjection to it. Tracing how the gallant uses his wit both to manufacture and to exploit economic exchange, I argue the single life of the gallant underwrites a reassuring conception of social privilege, one newly significant for a gentry that was deeply concerned with London's ability to swallow heirs and mint newly-moneyed merchants. This conception, I ultimately contend, becomes central to the emerging discipline of political economy where the rational action of *homo economicus* comes to personify the values of capitalism as civic values. In Jonson's *Epicene* and Middleton and Rowley's *Wit at Several Weapons*, the gallant anticipates such a figure, for he does not, like so many of his contemporaries, resort to marriage to remedy his financial insolvencies. Instead, he remains single by outwitting others, transforming his wit into wealth, his economic virtuosity into a gentlemanly virtue, and secures a form of unpatriarchal manhood that he realizes through market manipulations.

Chapter 4 retreats from the hubbub of London's streets and enters the solitude of the university to analyze the misogynistic violence produced by and productive for melancholic, single men. Drawing on the feminist analytic philosophy of Kate Manne, I forge an analogy between the modern figure of the murderous "incel" and the early modern university fellow—who was also an involuntary celibate of another kind. Unlike the chaste youth, the bachelor journeyman, and the true gallant, the incel scholar was mandated to live a single life by institutional bylaw, one that did not change until the nineteenth century. He was often also the gallant's foil, a man who could not translate his deep and broad knowledge into economically rewarding rational action. In this chapter, I examine two canonical texts of the period that focus on the abjection of sad and angry scholars—Shakespeare's *Hamlet* (1601) and Burton's *The Anatomy of Melancholy* (1621)—to theorize how their representations of the scholar's single life circulate *melancholer*—a feeling of entitlement, despair, and rage over not having access to patriarchal privileges. Reading early modern accounts of the single life of the scholar in relation to modern incel discourses, I demonstrate how early modern representations of the feelings of the celibate scholar inform the modern ideology of the incel.

My final chapter reconsiders the unpatriarchal manhood of the single life as constitutively cisgender. Placing Shakespeare's *Twelfth Night* and Middleton and Dekker's *The Roaring Girl* in relation to Crooke's *Mikrokosmographia*, this chapter interrogates how early modern patriarchal marriage produces the cisgender couple that it also labors to naturalize. In doing so, it considers how the single life enables forms of gendered embodiment supplemental to, but ultimately displaced from, early modern English gender binaries integral to materializing the cisgender, heterosexual body. For much of *Twelfth Night*, Viola identifies as Cesario, the single eunuch servant of Duke Orsino, and she does not forsake that identity at the play's end; Moll valorizes the single life because they can "lie o'both sides o'th'bed," an assertation that suggests the single life emancipates Moll from the strictures of a mutually constitutive gender binary. But both the euonyms of Cesario and Moll Cutpurse pun on castration, a pun that suggests the ability of these character to transform bodies, theirs or others, in a manner that would align embodiment with identity. Each of these plays, I argue, operationalize the single life of the eunuch to inaugurate processes of gender classification, speculation, and revelation.

As I hope this book makes clear, there is no one way to think about the single life, but that does not mean that we should not think about it. Early modern writers and readers surely did. They wrestled with both the possibilities and impossibilities it might afford them. Through a variety of means of representing the singe life, they imagined alternatives to patriarchy or recalibrated its promises of gendered manhood. While there are far more types of single men than I identify or examine in this book, I hope to show that by attending to a range of meanings of the single life in early modern literature and culture, we might formulate new literary histories of manhood that might disrupt those patriarchy would seek to remember.

# Chapter 1

## The Single Life of the Chaste Youth

### Early Modern Asexuality and the Naturalization of Desire in *All's Well That Ends Well*

There is something unbelievable about a single man who does not want sex—and not just to the modern imagination.[1] It is a commonplace in renaissance literature to find single men characterized by their erotic desires. In *A Chaste Maid in Cheapside* (1613), Sir Walter Whorehound lives up to his name, cuckolding the wittol Allwit (with his permission). In the Petrarchan sonnets of the 1590s, poets pine for their Stellas, their Delias, their Elizabeths, and their Ideas. In his lyrics, Donne anatomizes a flea to elaborate the metaphysics of a threesome and imagines his hands as colonizers roving over his mistress's "full nakedness."[2] In Greene's prose narratives, prodigal gallants spend their wealth on buying wares and wooing women.

Shakespeare's works might be thought of as an exception to this pervading cultural horniness. His single men deny desire as much as they pursue sex. Adonis runs from Venus, and if it is "from fairest creatures we desire increase," the sonnet's young man seemingly does not. Yet even some of Shakespeare's earliest readers found such sexual refusals of young men unbelievable. Tracing the early reception and circulation of the sonnets, Gary Taylor has observed that Sonnet 2 ("When forty winters have besieged thy brow"), which many modern critics read as addressed to the young man, was entitled "To one that would die a maid" as well as "A Lover to his Mistress."[3] According to these textual variants, willful virginity remains far more likely a state for a single woman than a single man.[4]

Early modern literary scholars have likewise found the willful virginity of a young man difficult to imagine, and have read such ostensible refusals of sex as encoding desires that are more or less unspeakable. The sonnets have generated compelling and evocative theorizations of queer pleasure as "sex without issue" even as they could just as well be described as being issued without sex.[5] *Venus and Adonis*, a poem in which a young man is perhaps more adamant about not having sex than any other in Shakespeare's oeuvre, has proven quite generative for theorizations of desire in this regard. Whereas the epyllion insists not only that "love [Adonis] laughed to scorn," but also that, with "leaden appetite," Adonis is "unapt to toy" and "frosty with desire," scholars have read these demurrals as assents to same-gender desire, finding *Venus and Adonis* to be an "explicitly homoerotic text."[6] Adonis's refusal of sex with Venus indicates that he "might desire something else."[7] Even when critics are less emphatic of the poem's homo-eroticism, they nonetheless find desire otherwise abundant in the poem. Madhavi Menon, for example, insists upon a desiring Adonis but, at times, conflates Venus's desires with Adonis's demurring. In one telling moment, Menon aggregates various forms of sexual refusal and pursuit into one categorical example of failed desires; "the Adonis who dies, the Adonis flower that withers, the Venus whose desire remains unconsummated are all markers of failure precisely because they have no remainder—no reminder—to show either for or of themselves." These instances, she writes, indicate "*their* desire has no tangible witness, no material residue," only to conclude, "this is not to say desire is invisible in the poem, or even that it is ineffable; it is to assert that desire in *Venus and Adonis* lacks an object by which either its presence or its success can be measured—desire exists offstage even as it is itself insistently theatrical."[8] Desires—however deferred—effuse.[9] Absence of evidence makes of absence evidence. What is not present must be, nonetheless, pursued.

In this chapter, I attend to what both early modern readers and modern scholars alike have found impossible: the chastity, or, if you will, asexuality, of the renaissance youth. I do so to historicize how renaissance representations of the single life of the chaste youth come to naturalize desire itself and come to structure desire as expressive, purposive, and recuperable by patriarchal marriage. My argument draws upon the work of asexual scholars and scholars of asexuality who have defined compulsory sexuality—that set of assumptions, norms, and practices that insist upon the universality of sexual desire and further interpellate individuals as desiring subjects who should experience desire, should act upon that desire, or possess a sexuality or sexual identity.[10] This chapter argues in part that the history of compulsory sexuality runs through early modern England and the rhetorics swirling around the single life of the chaste youth. Against the figure of the chaste, single man, the early modern period witnessed an intensification of compulsory sexuality and the naturalization of sexual desire in an effort to institutionalize patriarchal marriage as an historical epiphenomenon. In his poetry, Shakespeare draws upon the figure of the chaste youth if only to militate against the viability of a chaste, single life. While both his sonnets and *Venus and Adonis* contain instances of the chaste youth, Shakespeare more fully extrapolates the dimensions of the chaste single life and dramatizes it as a structural problem in his comedy *All's Well That Ends Well*. As this chapter will show, a range of early modern marital discourses framed chastity as a kind of closet space in which the ostensible lack of desire intimated a host of illicit ones. If *All's Well* "underscores the deep incompatibility that separates sexuality from marriage," as Janet Adelman argues, it does so by rendering the chaste, single life, and not the promiscuous one, impossible and perverse.[11] Unlike Adonis, Bertram does not typify the single life of the chaste youth, but the play also ensures that he will not and cannot—even as it often aligns his social and sexual perversities with wider culture figurations of chaste men. Throughout the play, the chaste single life is repeatedly cast and recast as unhistorical, unnatural, unthinkable, and inauthentic by proleptic and analeptic—or forward looking and backward gazing—logics. *All's Well That Ends Well* may stand as one of Shakespeare's enduring problem comedies, but that is because it makes the single life of the chaste youth such a problem for the ends of comedy.

## Rethinking the Single Life of the Chaste Youth in *All's Well That Ends Well*

Insofar as the patriarchal culture of early modern England sanctioned sexual activity within the bounds of marriage, the single life was in theory, if not in practice, a chaste life. But "chastity" is a term fraught with contradictory and compounding meanings in early modern England. Nominally denoting refrain from extramarital sex, chastity could indicate a form of fidelity to God, to a friend, or to a spouse. Imposed by others or espoused by a self, chastity, in the words of Kathryn Schwarz, "is not a straightforward mechanism of hierarchical imposition but a complicated and always potentially contested interplay of constraint and will."[12] In *All's Well*, the more normative meanings of chastity as sexual abstinence are associated with Diana, who, "titled goddess," clearly embodies the virtue.[13] But as a site of epistemological contention, chastity is associated with—if never entirely realized by—Bertram, for it is Bertram who first insists upon his chastity as a stay against sexual consummation with Helen. At the moment when his will is constrained by the King, he contests his marriage by writing two letters— one to his mother, and the other to Helen—in which he adduces a chaste vow designed to undo his marital one. He tells his mother, "I have wedded, not bedded [Helen], and sworn to make the 'not' eternal" (3.2.20–22), his pun tangling his sexual refusal into the marital knot. In his letter to Helen, Bertram explains to his erstwhile wife, "When thou canst get the ring upon my finger, which never shall come off, and show me a child begotten of thy body that I am father to, then call me husband. But in such a 'then,' I write a 'never'" (ll.57–60). Scholars have tended to read this rejection of intramarital consummation as a desire for extramarital sex. That is, in denying what the *Book of Common Prayer* (1549) specifies as "one cause" of the institution of marriage—"the procreacion of children"—Bertram entertains what its second ordinance asserts marriage helps the unmarried avoid, namely, "fornication."[14]

I do not deny this reading; it is there, and it is one the play itself offers up. However, while Bertram's subsequent pursuit of Diana maps this trajectory of desire, this reading of the plot too readily overwrites ends with means, and so overlooks how the play's treatment of chastity queers the marriage plot's march toward socially normative allosexuality.[15] Whatever Bertram eventually does, he first understands that his claim to a chaste, unmarried life—its eternal "not," its "never"—has the power to disrupt the consummative "then" of procreative, marital sex. In other words, in a play whose plot hinges on the realization of reproductive futurism, Bertram's letter echoes, if it does not literalize, what Lee Edelman has claimed is the driving force of queer politics: the refusal of a futurity predicated upon the promise of the symbolic Child.[16] Overwriting his marital vows with a riddling declaration of chastity, Bertram employs just this sort of queering mechanism, a rhetoric that disturbs in such a way to prompt and to frustrate readings that would align sociality with sexual expression, that would direct desire toward a future it reproduces out of the present.[17]

If the very idea of the chaste, single life in *All's Well* seems an absurd proposition, it is not only because the play itself works to construe it as such but also because scholarship on early modern chastity has on the whole contained chastity within early modern discourses of gender and sexual normativity. Chastity can figure as the "pure resistance" of ciswomen to patriarchal sexuality, or, alternatively, it might rescript patriarchal homosociality as the "sovereign amity" of homonormative friendship.[18] Within the structures of patriarchal sexuality, chaste single men do not make sense in any normative way. An allosexuality repressed, disciplined, or displaced does, however, because it might be recuperated, but chastity refuses the very premises of procreative desire. In other words, while allowing for resistive potential of the homonormativity of chastity, insofar as it stands against the heterosociality of marriage, we might also think of the chastity of single men as it circulates in *All's Well* as something closer to the "celibacies" that Benjamin Kahan traces in American modernist literature. What Kahan theorizes as modern celibacy Bertram rehearses in his epistolary riddle. For Kahan, celibacy registers "as sexuality in its own right . . . as synonym for unmarried . . . as a choice, performative, vow . . . as a political self-identification . . . as a resistance to compulsory sexuality . . . as a period in between sexual activity."[19] All might be said to hold in Bertram's case. Having written to Helen and his mother, Bertram tells his compatriot Paroles, "I have writ my letters, casketed my treasure, / Given order for our horses, and tonight, / When I should take possession of the bride / End ere I do begin" (2.5.24–27). This little speech is a cathexis of the chastity's dissident meanings in *All's Well*: it is a riddling of the marital vow, a wish for a perpetual single life, a resistance to compulsory sexuality, and a political evasion "to other regions" (2.3.284). All cite, though they do not ultimately come to be realized as, varieties of a chaste, unpatriarchal manhood.

To conceive of chastity in *All's Well* in early modern English culture more broadly as queer in relation to patriarchal marriage, we must strive "to understand," as Heather Love has proposed, "queerness as an absence of or aversion to sex,"[20] and "to trace," as Ela Przybylo and Danielle Cooper have advocated, "asexuality in unexpected, and perhaps even undesirable locations."[21] Shakespeare's *All's Well That Ends Well* is not exactly an undesirable location for analyzing the single life of the chaste youth, but it is a bit of an unamenable one. Perhaps more than any other of Shakespeare's comedies, it is formally obsessed with the marital teleology of comedy—but this is also why, I contend, the varied and even contradictory meanings of chaste, single life circulate in the play. To trace its various representations and evasion in the play, and to both theorize and historicize them within an early modern context, this chapter situates the meanings of a chaste, single life in relation to by what Patricia Simons refers to as "the neglected realm of semenotics," a neologism she uses to conceptualize an early modern patriarchal sexuality of cismen.[22] According to Simons, early modern semenotic discourse imbued "substantial meaning (or semiotic valence) to three nonpenile factors: semen, testicles and what was considered the concomitant matter of innately masculine 'heat.'"[23] Unlike Freudian and Lacanian semiotics of sexuality that fetishize the erect penis as the symbolic (and disembodied) phallus, the early modern *semenotic* discourse of sexuality understood the testicles as the primary, embodied signifier of desire.[24] If for Freud and Lacan desire is a psychic phenomenon constituting human subjectivity, then in an early modern semenotic sexuality, desire is conceived as a somatically marked expression, an evocative presence resulting in an evacuated absence. As Simons further explains, in this patriarchal discourse "the penis was a means to an end, that purpose being the release and delivery of semen to another body, aided in forceful ejection by innately masculine heat and the pressure of built up *pneuma* or essential spirit"; thus, "as producers or repositories of semen, the testicles were more vital to a man's virility than any other genital part."[25] The significance of the testicles in the early modern semenotic discourse informed and was informed by a contemporary etymology that understood the testes to share an origin with the Latin "testis" or "witness."[26] As seventeenth-century physician Helkiah Crooke observes, "The Stones are called *Testes* because they are witnesses of *viriltie*."[27] Lusty men were believed to have large, round, hairy, hot testicles, while in the words of Ambroise Paré "those on the contrary that have them cold are slow to venery, neither do they beget many children . . . and their testicles are small, soft and flat."[28] Unlike the testes (or ovaries) of ciswomen, the testes of cismen could be tested. Because of the testimonial import of testicles, a man's impotence could nullify a marriage whereas a woman's could not, for her testes (or ovaries) could not bear witness to her fertility as a man's could his virility.[29]

*All's Well That Ends Well* is a play obsessed with bodies—what they desire, what they do not, what ails them, and what might cure them—and it is not subtle about aligning bodily health with social health. But the play's obsession with bodies has also made analyzing the meanings of the chaste, single life in the play difficult. Where critics have attended to the play's bodies, they have more readily focused upon Helen and not Bertram. In a reading that productively explores the homophonic and dilatory plentitudes of the play, Jonathan Gil Harris, for instance, neglects its numerous references to testicles to focus upon Helen's swelling body. Harris is concerned with the "deconception" of the marriage plot, a term he uses to indicate "movement of swelling without clear issue or resolution."[30] Harris orients his reading around the King's scolding of Bertram when Bertram disdains Helen for her low station. Defending Helen, the King explains to Bertram, "it is a dropsied honour" that would privilege titles over deeds (2.3.129). Prompted by the King's diction, Harris cites an early modern gynecological discourse where dropsy and tympanites symptomize gestational phantoms, a strategy that leads Harris to pathologize Helen's pregnancy and to privilege the significance of her swelling body—a swelling that, as Caroline Bicks has argued, is very much in question at the play's end.[31] But this reading overlooks the extent to which early modern diagnoses of dropsy focus on the genitals of men. As Jennifer Evans has shown, watery and windy swellings, whether hydroceles or hernias, served as ready etiologies for male impotence and sterility.[32] With its references to gems, stones, cannonballs, drums, and rings—in short, a variety of variously round or hollow tropes for testicles—*All's Well*, in fact, pays little attention to Helen's belly and instead continually draws attention to Bertram's "balls," which, according to Paroles, "bound" in movement and tumefy with "noise" (2.3.298).[33]

To read for a chaste single life in *All's Well* is to read against the grain of the play, for the play itself works hard to displace and discipline the chaste life into patriarchal marriage. However, to read for the chaste life in the play is also to understand how the play's sexual epistemology depends upon—but also poses a particular challenge to—an early modern patriarchal semenotic discourse that naturalized desire as fundamentally testable and embodied. For if, as the courtier Fabrito explains in George Whetstone's *An Heptameron* (1582), "Mariage is the most honourable euent of Love: and that a Single lyfe, is the greatest testimonie of Chastytie," then Bertram's various refusals and deferrals of sexual consummation with Helen bear witness to a chastity that is and is not what it seems, a chastity that must succumb to a proof of the body that the play cannot ultimately provide.[34] When Bertram writes his epistolary riddles to his mother and Helen, he invokes a form of chastity that testifies to both a virility that will not desire and an impotence that cannot, and he further testifies to a form of early modern asexuality that might challenge the naturalization of desire as such. This kind of chastity does not make sense within in the patriarchal semenotic discourse that Simons documents because it queers its logics that would naturalize desire's somatic etiology. Helen thus sets out to prove Bertram a perjured witness or a cured impotent (or both), but as she does so, the play raises the possibility of chastity as a queer mode of asexuality made purposive by the single life, and in doing so, it cites a form of unpatriarchal manhood that refuses to testify to a procreative social order that would make all well.

## Making Early Modern Marriage History

The history of marriage is a comic plot. It was being written in early modern England, and the chaste, single life of cismen was often at the center of it. *All's Well That Ends Well* gestures to this historiography and its comic, if often ridiculous, sexual epistemology. Early in the play, the Clown Lavatch imagines chastity of single and married men as absurdly natural and naturally absurd in a song that tells "truth the next way" (1.3.58–59):

For I the ballad will repeat,
Which men full true shall find:
Your marriage comes by destiny,
Your cuckoo sings by kind. (ll.60–63)

Identifying himself as a "prophet" (l.59), Lavatch seems to offer the ballad as a cipher to the play's marriage plot. The ballad invites a reading, one Lars Engle explores, that would see Bertram fated to marry Helen in order to cover up his cuckolding by the King.[35] Lavatch traffics in a familiar logic of patriarchal sexual anxiety, but as he explains what he means, he complicates the erotics of cuckoldry in more compelling ways than might first be evident. The song in fact concludes a long riff that he begins when the Countess enjoins, "Tell me thy reason why thou wilt marry" (l.27). Lavatch responds accordingly: "My poor body, madam, requires it: I am driven on by the flesh, and he must needs go that the devil drives" (ll.28–30). In this paradigm, chastity is an impossibility of "the flesh": it is a condition out of which desire incubates, a practice of abstinence evidencing the desire denied. Ironically, however, chastity resurfaces as a desirable state within marriage, where it manifests not as a discipline of procreative desire but as an evacuation of desire outright. Having asserted, "I hope to have friends for my wife's sake," Lavatch explains to the Countess why he invites his cuckolding: "for the knaves come to do that for me which I am aweary of. He that ears my land spares my team, and gives me leave to it in the crop; if I be his cuckold he's my drudge" (ll.39–40, 42–46). Lavatch, in essence, becomes a chaste wittol who benefits from his friend's sexual labor. Fulfilling the letter but not the spirit (as it were) of the law, Lavatch thus offers a parody of Protestant marital doctrine by introducing to it a variation of homonormative friendship, for the marriage Lavatch envisions accomplishes all three mandates of the Protestant justifications of marriage. The husband is able "to auoide fornicacion" while his marriage guarantees "the procreacion of children" within a "mutuall societie"—all so he "might liue chastlie in matrimonie."[36]

Lavatch tells a good joke, but in telling it, he also alludes to a contemporary debate over the meanings of the single life of chaste young men occurring between, as the Clown puts it, "young Chairbonne the puritan and old Poisson the papist" (1.3.52–53). After 1563, when the Council of Trent affirmed the excellence of celibacy in the face of continual Protestant denigrations of it, the lines between Protestant and Catholic marital doctrine were drawn in terms of the distinctions and connections between celibate devotion to God and chaste fidelity to a future or present spouse. The chastity of the single life could either signify a rejection of marital sexuality or a preservation, if also anticipation, of it. This distinction was consequential for the meanings of chastity in Shakespeare's England, and especially for men. Scholars, however, have tended to overlook this significance. In her book *Pure Resistance*, for example, Theodora Jankowski, documents how Protestant marital polemics can be understood as both particular arguments against Roman Catholic discourses on virginity as well as more general historiographic arguments venerating marriage as an original and natural state.[37] But Jankowski wrongly surmises, "the Protestant discourse of chastity is packaged specifically for women," because she excises from her reading of Protestant marital discourse what would be a pivotal text in the Catholic and Protestant debates regarding priestly celibacy and the chastity of single men: Erasmus's *A ryght frutefull Epystle deuysed by the moste excellent clerke Erasmus in laude and prayse of matrimony* (1536), more commonly known as his *Encomium Matrimonii*.[38]

In the *Encomium Matrimonii*, Erasmus tries to persuade a young man to marry, and he does so by making the case that "bachelershyp is a forme of lyunge bothe barren and unnaturall."[39] The *Encomium*'s arguments have been linked to Shakespeare's sonnets. It is not hard to see why: Shakespeare repurposes much of Erasmus's argument against the chaste, single life. Yet the *Encomium*'s resonance with *All's Well* are just as substantive: both are concerned with a recently bereaved noble youth who will not marry and who must be persuaded to do so.[40] The *Encomium*, however, was not just a fruitful source text for Shakespeare's poetic and dramatic works. It proved far more impactful for emerging Protestant polemics valorizing marriage as central to Christian faith, becoming an important source text for their own venerations of marriage. Its arguments against the chaste, single life enjoyed wide circulation after its publication in Latin in 1518. In 1536, Richard Taverner translates it into English and dedicates it to Thomas Cromwell, explaining, "he thought it a thynge full necessarye and expedyent, . . . when he considered the blynd superstition of men and women / which cease nat day by day to professe and vowe perpetuall chastyte before or they suffyciently knowe themselves and thinfirmite of theyr nature."[41] Shortly after Taverner's translation of the *Encomium* appears in England in 1536, Thomas Becon, writing under the pseudonym Theodore Basille, copies near verbatim a passage from the *Encomium*. "For can christen matrimony be any other wyse than a thynge of great excellency and incomparable dignite, seynge it was not ordeyned of Minos of Creta, nor of Licurgus of Lacedemonye, nor yet of Solon of Athenian, but of the moost hygh immortal God him selfe?" he asks.[42] While Protestant marital polemicists do at times inveigh against sodomy, their venerations of marriage take shape against the figure of the single man who seemingly embraces chastity and rejects procreativity. So it is that Becon argues, "Lette others prayse Chastitie so much as they lyste, yet wyl I commend matrimony." His commendation, however, takes the form of historiography:

> Were not the holy Patriarchs marryed men? Did not the Prophettes of God liue in the christen state of holy wedlocke? Dyd not God in the olde lawe both wylle hys prestes to marry, and also appoynt them, what wyues they should haue? Was not Christ borne in maryage? Were not the Apostles of Christ marryed men? Dyd not Christ garnysh maryage with the fyrste of his miracles, whan he wyth his mother and his Disciples were at a wed-dynge in the Citie of Cana Galyle? Was not Philipphe the Euangeliste a maryed man, and had foure doughters excellently learned in holy Scriptures: Were not many other holy men both Byshoppes and prestes: maryed longe after the Apostles tyme, as we read in antentyke hystories?[43]

Such appeals to history proved irresistible for later English venerations of marriage. It was a rhetorical move to which a number of early modern defenders of marriage would return. Whereas Erasmus points out, "Lycurgus made a lawe that they whyche maryed nat wyues, shuld in somer season be dryuen from the enterludes and other fyghtes, and in wynter go about the market place all naked and curse themselues, because they wolde nat obey the lawes," Barbaro Francesco would write over a century later in *Direction for Love and Marriage* (1677), "Lycurgus . . . hath branded them with Ignominy, who continued their Celibacy thirty-seven years; and he prohibited them, who as yet had not attained the Nuptial State to appear at the Wrestling Schools."[44] Erasmus means for history to plot a persuasive fiction; he reprimands the *Encomium*'s chaste, single man, "And without any more a doe, will ye knowe how much our olde Auncesters heretofore estemed Matrimonie?"[45] The chaste, single life, in other words, is constructed in this discourse as an unhistorical, and so unnatural, state for men, but it is also the ballast against which Protestants construct a history of marriage to naturalize desire as expressive and procreative of both humanity and history. Across early modern marital historiography, the chaste, single life manifests as an oppositional alternative to patriarchal, procreative sexuality.

Protestant representations of the chaste, single life was not devoid of anti-Catholic connotations. It readily signified Catholic doctrines on celibacy. Upon its publication, the *Encomium*, for instance, was quickly viewed by Catholics as a thinly veiled attack on a celibate priesthood. The metonymic and synecdochic relation between a universalized chaste, single life and more localized priestly celibacy was inescapable—it was baked into the structure of the *Encomium's* rhetorical project. In his defense of his *Encomium*, Erasmus argues that as a form of "Greek *melete* or Latin *declamation* . . . the situation I treat is not a general one, but one hedged in by circumstances. I depict a noble youth from the best of families, whose entire hope of propagating depends on one thing; for this man I prefer marriage, not for all."[46] Framing it as an example of classical rhetoric rather than a theological treatise, Erasmus insists his *Encomium* rehearses an exemplum on the relation between infinite and definite topoi, a relation notably elucidated by Quintillian.[47] As I noted in the introduction to this book, Quintillian introduces this relation through the question of whether or not it is better in general to marry or whether a wise man in particular should marry. In the *Encomium*, the exemplum becomes recontextualized through a specific theological debate regarding the meanings of the chaste, single life. The most notable repurposing of this Erasmian deployment of Quintillian occurs in Thomas Wilson's *Arte of Rhetorique* (1553), which anthologized the *Encomium* for sixteenth-century English audiences. Wilson, like Quintillian, makes the distinction between infinite and definite topoi in the introduction of the volume. Infinite questions "are propounded, withoute the comprehension of tyme, place, and person, or any such like . . . as thus, whether it be best to marie, or to liue single."[48] Definite questions, on the other hand, "set furthe a matter, with the appoynctment, and namyng of place, time, and persone. As thus. Whether now it be best here in Englande, for a Prieste to Marie, or to liue syngle."[49] Yet because infinite and definite topoi are linked by the logic of synecdoche, Wilson concedes, "that whosoeuer will talke of a particular matter, must remember that within the same also, is comprehended the general."[50] Thus a specific argument for a married priesthood could inhere in a more general argument against a chaste, single life. Unfortunately for Erasmus, the theologians at Louvain, like Wilson, concurred; they understood "that whosoeuer will talke of a particular matter, must remember that within the same also, is comprehended the general," and so found in Erasmus's specific argument against the decision of a noble youth a more general denigration of priestly celibacy. By the time the text was printed in England, Erasmus had been branded a heretic and his writings banned by the Catholic church.[51]

Jonathan Dollimore has argued that the recovery of lost histories of perversion exposes "normative and prescriptive teleologies, and the regimes of essential and absolute truth which those teleologies underwrite."[52] We might reverse that paradigm. Recovering prescriptive teleologies exposes lost histories of perversion. The lost history of the single life of the chaste youth reveals—and denaturalizes—early modern constructions of compulsory sexuality. As the infinite topos of the chaste, single life comes to overwrite the definite topos of Catholic priestly celibacy in Protestant polemics and marital historiography, the idea of the chaste youth comes to be enfolded into the ecclesiastical rhetoric of heresy reserved for celibate priests. But the meanings of chastity also shift. As celibacy as a devotion to God is applied in general to the laity in Protestant marital polemics, chastity transforms into an unnatural denial of a procreative desire the polemics themselves seek to naturalize. The very subject of the *Encomium*, the chaste youth, becomes the spectral presence of the Protestant marital tracts that follow, constituting a kind of inertia against which they establish their histories of marriage and desire. As these texts naturalize marriage, they naturalize not only a desire for procreative sex but also, and more readily, a desire for marriage as history, of a marital history propagated both backward into the past and forward into the future. In Protestant historiographies of marriage, those who oppose such propagation are not primarily men who engage in fornication or sodomy, which can, under their logics, be recuperated by marital union, but chaste youths who seemingly desire nothing at all.

What remains queer, then, in Bertram's "'not' eternal" and his "never" in *All's Well*, which, although not a history of marriage is likewise invested in the comic plot so central to such a history? Queer theorists have argued that the meanings of sex cannot be contained by the meaning of history, and that, as Lee Edelman posits, "heterosexuality succeeds . . . in dissociating itself from the anarchy and ahistoricism of sex by virtue of its socially valorized (re)production of the 'after'. . . of sex through the naturalization of history."[53] In other words, to lay claim over history, heterosexuality must posit itself as a chaste or ultimately sexless relation, a relation in which sex or desire is not about sex or desire but about history and futurity. If this is true, then the history of modern heterosexuality owes a great deal to early modern Protestant histories of marriage, for it is these histories that emplot history not only as marriage but also, and more consequentially, as the "after" of marriage. The singe life of the chaste youth would put an end to such histories.

If we account for the single life of the chaste youth in Protestant histories of marriage, we might also recalibrate how we understand the histories of sexuality in the period, and the various forces that collaborate to produce what Valerie Traub has termed "domestic heterosexuality."[54] Marriage may have become more companionate throughout the period, but insofar as patriarchy prioritizes marriage as product and producer of its history, we might query to what extent marriage functions as something other than heterosexual, or the degree to which the renaissance can be thought of on such terms that precede "the invention of heterosexuality."[55] Protestant histories of marriage situate sexuality within marriage and imagine asexuality outside of it only to flip that dynamic. Posited against a chaste, single life, marriage insulates domestic heterosexuality as merely social reproduction. That is, Protestant marital histories do not treat such domestic sexuality as a sexuality, exactly. Insofar as patriarchal marriage organizes the saliency of the historiography of heterosexuality, heterosexuality evades recognition as sexuality as such. Eve Sedgwick recognized this, observing in *Tendencies*, "Thus, if we are receptive to Foucault's understanding of modern sexuality as the most intensive site of the demand for, and detection or discursive production of, the Truth of individual identity, it seems as though this silent, normative, uninterrogated 'regular' heterosexuality may not function as a sexuality at all."[56] Thus what is at times identified as "not heterosexual" in the premodern past yet looks an awful lot like it in part because of the problem Sedgwick identifies.[57] This is not to say that the institution of marriage and heterosexuality are the same thing; Julie Crawford has productively explored all the ways in which they are not.[58] However, they can amount to the same thing, and we might account for the ways that they are not not the same thing.[59] In *All's Well*, the joke, as Lavatch sees it, is that it is not history but chastity that serves as the "after" of marriage. He, like Sedgwick, recognizes how heterosexuality within marriage does not operate like sexuality at all, in part, because it launders the perversity of the chaste, single life into marriage's virtuous, if hermetic, relation. When Bertram writes his epistolary riddle that overwrites the "then" of sexual consummation with a "never," he literalizes the Clown's joke, but in doing so, he also seems to embrace a chaste, single life that his marriage imagines impossible, one that the *Encomium* and later Protestant tracts understood as a form of "bachelarshyp, which bryngeth mankynd to destruction" because it refuses to supplement a history, that, like comedy, saw marriage as an end that would make all well.[60]

## VIRGIN SOLDIERS AND SIEGING VIRGINS

If the chaste single life can be imagined as a perverse, unnatural rejection of the history of marriage, it also could have more valorous, if potentially, antisocial figurations. In *All's Well*, Bertram's retreat from his marriage is also a pursuit of war. Following the work of G. Wilson Knight, critics of the play have understood Bertram's turn to war and away from Helen as dramatizing a contest between two forms of honor: the masculine honor of martiality and the feminine honor of chastity.[61] But we can also think of this dyadic formulation as one between two competing early modern conceptions of chastity. Insofar as chastity signified either a latent procreative capacity and not blatant impotence, it also signified a capacity for martial prowess. The Elizabethan poem "The praise of Chastitie," for example, normalizes the chaste, single life in terms of its bellicosity; in it, chaste men "compare with men of war" because they contain a vital, testicular heat.[62] In the semenotics of Galenic humoralism, the chaste, single life could house a latent repository of martial strength. Testicular semen fired the heat that forged men into soldiers. Immediately after his betrothal to Helen, Bertram reframes his rejection of sexual consummation with her in exactly these terms; "I'll go to the Tuscan wars, and never bed her," he tells Paroles (2.3.274). Paroles is even more explicit about the semenotic system Bertram negotiates, explaining to him:

> He wears his honour in a box unseen
> That hugs his kicky-wicky here at home,
> Spending his manly marrow in her arms
> Which should sustain the bound and high curvet
> Of Mars' firey steed. To other regions! (2.3.280–84)

Shakespeare draws upon this paradigm elsewhere. As Rebecca Bach has demonstrated, this dichotomy animates the plot of *Henry V*, where "ball" puns proliferate.[63] So it is that Paroles finally affirms Bertram's decision with such a play on words, exclaiming, "Why, these balls bound, there's noise in it" (2.3.298). As Susan Snyder observes, "it is as if war calls up love as its natural antithesis, so that asserting hatred of the latter demonstrates one's adherence to the former"; this dialectic, however, informs a semenotic discourse that posited martial chastity against marital sex, as seminal heat was essential to both.[64]

Before Bertram can charge into the battlefields of Tuscany, however, his turn as chaste soldier has already been proleptically cast as a dishonorable retreat from his marital obligations as procreative husband. In the first act of the play, Helen and Paroles engage in a tête-à-tête about the meanings of virginity that anticipates Bertram's eventual refusal of Helen. Just before Paroles enters the scene, Helen professes in a soliloquy her desire for Bertram:

> 'Twas pretty, though a plague,
> To see him every hour, to sit and draw
> His archèd brows, his hawking eye, his curls

In our heart's table—heart too capable
Of every line and trick of his sweet favour. (1.1.94–98)

As he enters the scene, Paroles asks Helen if she is "meditating on virginity"
(l.112), and although she most certainly is not, she entertains the question.
Mocking Paroles as having "some stain of soldier in you," Helen permits him
to play the part, requesting he "unfold to us some / warlike resistance" so
women might "barricado" their virginity (ll.113, 118–19, 115). Paroles insists such a cause is not only hopeless but foolish: "There's little can be said
in't; 'tis against the rule of nature. To speak on the part of virginity is to accuse your mothers, which is most infallible disobedience. He that hangs himself is a virgin; virginity murders itself, and should be buried in highways out
of all sanctified limit, as a desperate offendress against nature" (ll.137–43).

In denigrating virginal maids, Paroles implicates chaste, single men,
however. This scene has been linked to the Erasmian colloquy, "Proci et
Pullae," a dialogue between a chaste maid and a sieging soldier in no small
part because these are the roles that Paroles and Helen presumably play
even though it is Bertram who eventually acts the chaste soldier and Helen
the sieging maid.[65] Given the ironic tenor of the dialogue between Paroles
and Helen, it seems more an inversion of "Proci et Pullae" than a translation of it. Their musings on virginity more readily cite Erasmus's *Encomium*.
The arguments Paroles levels against virginal maids were often also directed
at chaste, single men.[66] Whereas Paroles says virginity dishonors mothers,
in the *Encomium*, Erasmus asserts that chaste, single men dishonor fathers
when he asks, "What is a more unkynde acte than to denye that to your
yongers, which if ye toke nat of your elders, ye could nat be that myght
denye?"[67] Even Paroles's argument that virginity "murders itself" echoes the
Erasmian argument that a chaste man "shalbe judged a trayterous murdero-
ure of your lygnage."[68] Paroles's contention that "virginity is peevish, proud,
idle, and made of self-love—which is the most inhibited sin in the canon"
(ll.145–47) also reformulates the Erasmian supposition that "what is more
hatefull then the man which (as though he were borne onely to hymself)
lyeth for hymselfe, seketh for hymselfe / spareth for hymself / doth cost to
hymselfe / loueth no person, is loued of no persone."[69] That Paroles par-
rots this Erasmian rhetoric is betrayed at a moment of linguistic slippage.
Halfway through his screed, Paroles switches the gender of his rhetorical
target—"He that hangs himself is a virgin" (l.140)—only to switch it back
again. In short, in order for Paroles to make his argument about the absur-
dity of women remaining virgins, he must draw upon arguments about the
perversity of chaste, single men.

One need not look to Erasmus to see how Paroles's screed against virginity draws its polemical energy from humanists attempting to persuade single men to abandon their chaste lives. Shakespeare is elsewhere fond of such rhetoric. In *Venus and Adonis* (1593), Venus admonishes Adonis for his coldness, saying, "Thou was begot; to get it is thy duty."[70] Paroles may argue that "virginity by being once lost may be ten times found; by being ever kept, it is ever lost" and that "within the year it will make itself two, which is goodly increase, and the principal itself not much the worse" (ll.132–33, 144–45), but in *The Sonnets* (1609) this conceit is used against the young man. In "Sonnet 6," Shakespeare argues that semen, like money, may be productively invested, telling the young man: "That's for thyself to breed another thee, / Or ten times happier be it ten for one. / Ten times thyself where happier than thou art, / If ten of thine ten figured thee."[71] By insisting virginity "dies with feeding his own stomach" (l.145), Paroles creates an argument whose conceit fits within Shakespeare's first sonnet, whose chaste, single man "feed'st light's flame with self-substantial fuel, / Making a famine where abundance lies," and so is a "glutton" who "eats the world's due" (1.6–7, 13, 14). If Paroles rails against virginity like a stereotypical sieging soldier, he is repurposing Shakespearean arguments, which regularly deploy criticisms not of chaste maids but of chaste, single men.[72]

In standing against the naturalization of patriarchal procreativity, the chaste, single man suggests a form of unpatriarchal manhood, one in which the intelligibility of desire itself is at stake. Reading desire back into representations of chaste, single men, scholars have observed that Paroles characterizes virginity as unnatural, but in doing so, they have too readily conflated chastity with sodomy, reading the former as the sign of the latter in a manner that espouses Helen's own reading of it. Thus it is true that Paroles "represents the preservation of virginity as nothing less than a *perversion*," as Nicolas Ray contends, but this perversity does not mean that it is equivalent or reducible to sodomy, the perversity of which constituted not an absence of desire but the wrong kind of sex.[73] This very conflation between absent desire and perverse desire, however, is also one of the play's strategies for denaturalizing the chaste, single life, for Helen herself aligns chastity with sodomy. At the end of her debate with Paroles, Helen returns to the question of military honor. Assenting to Helen's compliment that he was "born under a charitable star," Paroles specifies, "under Mars, I"; Helen wittily responds: "I especially think *under* Mars" (1.1.194–95). Will Stockton has observed that at this moment "Helen translates the fearful and fashionable fop into Mars's catamite, re-inscribing him within the very same sodomitical terrain that Paroles sought to position virginity."[74] He is right. As they signify forms of sexual abstention and perversity, respectively, the terrains of chastity and sodomy come to map the same territory. Their perversities become coconstitutive. While Paroles insists, like Erasmus, that chastity is perverse because it seemly refuses to testify to procreative desire, Helen associates it with sodomy that simply misplaces desire. In aligning chastity with sodomy, however, Helen translates asexuality into allosexuality, and so begins a process of reframing the seemingly inexpressive into the wrongly expressive, a legible desire that might be converted into normativity. For Helen, the chaste soldier always bears false witness, for in preserving testicular heat for war, Helen suggests, the chaste soldier testifies not to martial honor or marital duty but to other desires he will not name.

The ramifications of Helen's recontextualization of the chaste, single life as a sodomitical perversion of martial honor prove consequential in the marriage plot. Bertram, after all, will later align himself to Paroles's astrological benefactor: "Great Mars, I put myself into thy file. / Make me but like my thoughts, and I shall prove / A lover of thy drum, hater of love" (3.3.9–11). To prefer war over sex is, as Helen tells Paroles, to move "so much backward" (1.1.202). To be a chaste soldier is really only ever to desire sodomy, and of course, Bertram, in his courtship of Diana, literalizes that supposition: his hot pursuit of the namesake of chastity in the play is also a pursuit of extra-marital sex, an act that could be enfolded in "that utterly confused category" of sodomy as it could that of fornication.[75] Nonetheless, like Lavatch's joke, the dialogue between Helen and Paroles deploys a rhetoric that acknowledges how queer the single life of the chaste youth might be even as it proleptically renders the chastity of such a life impossible in relation to the marriage plot. When Helen asks Paroles, "How one might do, sir, to lose it [virginity] to her own liking" (ll.152–53), Paroles speaks "like a double meaning prophesier" (4.3.99–100), as Bertram will later call him; he tells Helen, "Marry, ill, to like him that ne'er it likes" (1.1.154–55). Paroles responds with stinging irony, but Helen hears the truth in the jest. Whereas Helen originally seemed resigned to a fate where only her "idolatrous fancy / Must sanctify [Bertram's] relics" (ll.99–100), she now aims to script her own destiny. After her conversation with Paroles, she insists:

Our remedies oft in ourselves do lie
Which we ascribe to heaven. The fated sky
Gives us free scope, only doth backward pull
Our slow designs when we ourselves are dull. (ll.218–21)

With "intents . . . fixed" (l.231), Helen fulfills her desires by aligning them with a comic plot that would restore patriarchal order, and thereby, as Kathryn Schwarz observes, "returns husband, father, and king to the roles from which they have fallen away."[76] But if Helen's relentless pursuit of Bertram comes to expose patriarchy as a fantasy predicated upon women's work, as Schwarz argues, it does so by both invoking and obviating the viability of a chaste, single life as it is evinced in Bertram's retreat to war. For all to be made well in *All's Well*, the virgin soldier must be conquered by a sieging virgin.

## THE QUEER TESTIMONIES OF THE CHASTE SINGLE LIFE

Patriarchal marriage ascribes testimonial weight to a single man's sexual desire. Under patriarchal sexual norms, to desire someone is to desire matrimony itself: this relation comes to naturalize marriage as historical epiphenomenon. To not desire someone is not to desire matrimony, and to not desire matrimony is to desire wrongly—or to not desire at all. *All's Well's* plot gives comic form to this series of relations, first aligning the chaste, single life with a martial honor reconstituted as retreat from matrimony, and secondly associating it with a speculatively diseased body. In *All's Well*, that body is associated with impotency and eunuchry.

As chaste, single man, Bertram must be convinced to become a procreative patriarch in a France in want of them. Patriarchs are either dead, like Bertram's father, or gravely ill, like the King. In an effort to realize her desires, Helen works to restore the play's patriarchal order by curing "the King's disease" (1.1.230). "Notorious" (l.36), the disease, a fistula, pervades the opening scenes of the play. Julia Lupton has read the King's disease as symbolizing the "weary mood of gentle decline" of the French court, "its mounting impotence, its need for new transfusions and infusions of 'life.'"[77] The impotent mood Lupton reads in the King's fistula may be more than figurative. Paroles suggests the King suffers from real impotence. Making a pun on the French word for "father" ("père"), Paroles alludes to it when he condemns "old virginity . . . which is like one of our French withered Pears; it looks ill, it eats drily" (ll.162–64). The play never specifies the location of the King's fistula, but there is no reason to believe that Shakespeare would depart from the plot's source material.[78] In Boccaccio's tale, the disease is a swelling on the breast, a location the King seems to confirm when, responding to the young lords of the court wishing him health, he confesses, "No, no, it cannot be. And yet my heart / Will not confess he owes the malady / That doth my life besiege" (2.1.8–10). The heart may want what the heart wants, but according to early modern semenotics, the heart wants what the testicles want. Early modern physiology cast each as intimately linked organs because both were integral to the sanguification process. Often, the quickest way to a man's heart was not, as it were, through the stomach but through the testicles. So it is that Helkiah Crooke observes, "Finally, in excellency the Testicles are like vnto the heart; for that Cordiall *Epithymatious* applied to the Testicles in great languishments of the of the spirits doe little less auaile, then if they were applied to the heart it selfe."[79] If the King's heart will not confess its malady, another organ may.

Daughter of the "famous" physician "Gérard de Narbonne" (1.1.26, 27), Helen is herself a very good doctor, one conversant in contemporary practices of healing a fistulated King. Her association with her father's craft also allies her with a practice that tested and healed genitalia. As Cathy McClive has demonstrated, surgeons were often called upon to examine the genital function of cismen.[80] Before Helen meets the King, Lafeu suggests that she might cure him with the kind of remedy Crooke describes. As she comes to visit the King, Lafeu tells him,

> I have seen a medicine
> That's able to breathe life into a stone,
> Quicken a rock, and make you dance canary
> With sprightly fire and motion. (2.1.70–73)

Lafeu revels in his bawdy. He further promises that Helen's

> simple touch
> Is powerful to araise King Pépin, nay,
> To give great Charlemagne a pen in 'is hand
> And write to her a love-line. (ll.73–76)

But his revelry need not preclude his diagnostic insights, for Lafeu's bawdy catalogues the King's revivification along a physiological system that prized a literal venality linking genital health to vascular health. Helen's medicine would revivify the King's "stones" or "rocks." Her healing his fistulated heart will grant the King an erection capable of seminal ejaculation.

Whatever the specifics of its application, Helen's cure works. The King reemerges from his sick bed "Lustig," and his healing secures Helen the choice of husband from a "youthful parcel / of noble bachelors," the wards of the King, of which Bertram is one (2.3.43, 53–54). The restoration of one patriarch works to create another. As Helen proceeds to choose a husband, the semenotics of the King's disease and his healing dictate the meanings of sexual desire as it is interpreted by onlookers. In both literal and figurative terms, the King's sexual reinvigoration is mapped onto the wards. Interpellating them through his newfound patriarchal sexuality, the King, now virile, conceives of their sexual agency as an extension of his royal will, assuring Helen that she "hast power to choose, and they none to forsake" (ll.57). These bachelors are legally compelled to marry, but this legal mandate is presented as supplemental to a supposedly natural sexual desire. As the King insists the wards have no legal right to deny Helen, Lafeu reads the courtship in semenotic terms, projecting his sexual desires onto the bachelors. He muses, "I'd give bay Curtal and his furniture / My mouth were no more broken than these boys' / And writ as little beard" (ll.60–63). Equating the wards' sexual vigor with that of a young stallion, Lafeu naturalizes their sexuality through an animal that was castrated for purposes of compliance and believed to hold an aphrodisiacal power to remedy impotency.[81] As Helen moves from bachelor to bachelor, inquiring of their interest and then passing to the next, Lafeu thus wonders, "Do they all deny her?" (l.87).

Lafeu crucially misreads this scene—Helen refuses them and not they Helen—but his misreading is telling. Their denial is an impossibility he cannot fathom, for it would mean they, unlike the King, would be denying the physiological testimony of their testicles, choosing chastity over procreative sexuality. It is an impossibility Shakespeare has explored before. In *Venus and Adonis*, when Adonis attempts to stay the sexual consummation between his courser and the jennet, Shakespeare calls him a "testy master," a pun that evinces Adonis's irritation and perhaps his own mastery over a testicular desire for sex with Venus (l. 319). Like Adonis, Lafeu imagines himself a "testy master" of another sort, sadistically musing, "An they were sons of mine, I'd have them whipped, or I would send them to th' Turk to make eunuchs of" (ll.87–89). Lafeu's wish that these men be made eunuchs cites early modern discourses that analogize chastity to gelding. One such discourse is that of early modern English encounters with the Ottoman empire, where the eunuch figured as "the perfect servant," a discourse that also has significant implications for the gendering of men in the period (which I explore more fully in chapter 5).[82] The other is that of Protestant marital tracts where the eunuch is the only kind of chaste man permitted. As one Protestant writer puts it, eunuchs "ought not to seek after marriage: for by those signes of impotencie God sheweth that he calleth them to live single."[83] This supposition also worked in reverse, as it does in Lafeu's reading, such that "he that never felt the power of this love may be esteemed as some Eunuch, or sot, or else of a super-humane temper."[84] These doctrines are derived from a biblical source: the nineteenth chapter of the Gospel according to Matthew. There, Christ describes three types of chaste men:

those born eunuchs, those made so by others, and those made so by their own hand—the marginalia in the Geneva Bible (1560) indicates "gelded" is translated as "chaste."[85] Protestants tended to ignore the two latter reasons because the Catholic Church used them to support doctrines of priestly celibacy. Instead, they imagined chastity as a bodily abnormality—a visible or invisible deformity of the testicles in particular or the genitals more generally—which had the effect of denaturalizing any form of chastity, including priestly celibacy, as a physical aberration of ideal anatomy. Lafeu's thinking reflects this logic. Because these bachelors seem to deny the testimony of their testicles, Lafeu proposes a violent gelding that would remove the offending organs so that their bodies would comport with a semenotic system of embodied desire where chastity is only sanctioned as genital disability.

In Lafeu's eyes, when Bertram thus denies Helen in the courtship scene, he testifies either truthfully or falsely, bearing witness to his impotence or denying his virility. In the former, he recalls the erstwhile impotent King who "nor wax nor honey can bring home" and so requires Helen's healing touch (1.2.65); in the latter, he offers a kind of queer testimony of chastity that Lafeu wrongly attributes to the other bachelors, who behave like eunuch servants who will not serve their "testy master," the King. Proposing to know which, Lafeu proleptically asserts, "I have known thee already" just before Helen proposes (2.3.102). The aside comes tantalizingly close to construing chastity as a kind of dissident sexuality, which, according to Foucault, "one had to try to detect . . .—as a lesion, a dysfunction, or a symptom—in the depths of the organism, or on the surface of the skin, or among all the signs of behavior" by "contacting bodies, caressing them with its eyes, intensifying areas, electrifying surfaces, dramatizing troubled moments."[86] The courtship scene culminates in casting Bertram's sexual dissidence as political rebellion, translating possible violation against natural law into a violation lèse-majesté. Like the "noble grapes" of Helen's medicine Lafeu earlier hoped his "royal fox," the King, might "eat" (2.1.68, 67), Bertram is "one grape yet" that would sustain the King's sovereign power (2.3.100). Whether or not Bertram has already become a "cuckold" and the King has already served as his "drudge"—as Lavatch earlier prophesies—the sexual exchanges circulating in Helen's courtship of Bertram come to localize around the way his testicles might testify to the will of patriarchal authority. After Bertram initially refuses Helen, the King reprimands him, "It is in us to plant thine honor where / we please to have it grow" (2.3.157–58). As if literalizing a patriarchal, procreative ideology, he is effectively reminding Bertram that he has authority over Bertram's testicles and that their seeds are his to sow.

## THE VELVET KNOWS

As the play turns and returns to the meanings of chastity, it frames the single life as unhistorical, unnatural, and abnormal, proleptically casting Bertram's epistolary riddles as queer testimonies to an impossible desire of not desiring sex. In a play that David Scott Kastan has called "Shakespeare's most insistent exploration of the nature of the comic assertion—indeed of the idea of comedy itself," such an insistence on the necessity of an expressive allosexuality is a formal necessity, for Shakespearean marriage plots are impossible without what Shakespeare's other reluctant bachelor Benedick concludes in *Much Ado About Nothing* (1623): that "the world must be peopled."[87] But as *All's Well* comes to test the limits of comedy, it also comes to test the limits of an early modern semenotic discourse in which the single life should testify to a latent desire for sex, what Erasmus calls a "desire for issue," and not an absence of such a desire.[88] In this scheme, Bertram's refusal of Helen would be recuperated as a chastity that signifies a desire merely deferred, though ultimately captured, by patriarchal marriage. In other words, the marriage plot labors to have Bertram's chastity testify not to the absence of desire but to a desire only mastered and muffled, an act of willful rebellion against a natural order, a rebellion akin to self-castration, a perverse embrace of impotence, or a misplaced procreative desire. This is the reading the play would seek to uphold, but only by a coercive logic that reads the ends of social utility as evidence of an a priori allosexuality.

The history of sexuality is, of course, an epistemological one—a process of interpreting desire as a means of knowing something about somebody. That history takes for granted desire itself as a thing to be read, as expressive and conducive to reading, and so, to certain extent, histories of sexuality have also naturalized desire as such, and so, it must be said, asexuality has not figured significantly in them. Insofar as *All's Well That Ends Well* has proven a productive text for the study of sexuality in English renaissance literature, and insofar as English renaissance literature has something to say about histories of sexuality, Shakespeare's play may remain integral because it dramatizes how the period came to naturalize allosexualities at the expense of asexualities. It is a play where the chaste, single life is made a problem that must be solved, a thing to be rendered impossible so that patriarchal marriage and the allosexuality that it depends upon may be made inevitable.

If for most of the play *All's Well* relegates the chaste, single life as an impossible one through scenes of proleptic recasting of chastity as a misplaced desire to procreate or the symptom of a diseased body, it finally attempts to salvage its marriage plot by analeptically inscribing the chaste, single life as having always been expressive of procreative desire. It does so through the bed trick, where Helen not only answers Bertram's epistolary riddles but also obtains the means by which she might testify to desires he would otherwise deny he has. By the end of the play, the queer testimonies of the chaste, single life are shown to operate through an epistemology of the closet, one in which sexuality is conceived not through a binary of normative and perversive allosexuality but through a semenotic dialectic of seminal preservation or projection, of impotency or potency. Wedded to a teleology of marital history, early modern Protestant discourses insist that chaste men unnaturally preserve a procreative capacity that should be expressed in and as marriage, thus becoming impotent men in function if not in fact. Thus justifications for a socially expressive sexuality, which is to say a procreative, marital sexuality, are often constructed against the impossibility of the chaste, single life, which comes to structure the social legibility of sexuality as such. In Erasmus's *Encomium*, chastity comes either to testify to a man's impotence or to desires that have no social legitimacy. As he explains, "Forthermore nat he onely geldeth hymselfe which lyveth without a wyfe, but he whyche chastly and holyly doth thoffyce of wedlocke. And wold god they were trewly chaste, so many as cloke theyr vyces under the gloryous tytle of chastite and castratyon, whych under the shadow of chastyte doo more fowly rage in fylthy and bestely abhomynation."[89] For Erasmus, the single life of the chaste youth is an act of gelding that is itself substanceless. Chastity can never provide a true testimony, Erasmus insists, for it must only ever cloak, and so license, those unspeakable desires roiling within its shadow. Helen could have been a careful reader of Erasmus, for she seems to understand the epistemology of "the shadow of chastity," which I want to suggest, structures the bed trick in *All's Well*. Helen describe that trick as "wicked meaning in a lawful deed, / And lawful meaning in a wicked act, / Where both not sin, and yet a sinful fact" (3.7.45–47). For both Erasmus and Helen, the meanings of chastity abet the proliferations of sex acts and licit desires, the shadows of chastity intensifying speculations of deeds done in the dark.

The problem of the bed trick in the play is ultimately a problem of knowledge. It has been read as both an "explicitly sexual event" as well as one that "enable[s] marriage less by legitimating sexual union than by magically doing away with it altogether."[90] Understood as the shadow of chastity, the bed trick is neither and both of these things. As "pitchy night" (4.4.24), the bed trick happens in the shadows, but it also thematically functions as the shadow of that other lacuna in the text: the King's healing. In one Helen raises the king from his "sickly bed" (2.3.112), and in the other she translates Bertram's "sick desires" into healthy, procreative sex (4.2.35). But this parallel also imbues the bed trick with the King's disease, a testicular ailment of impotence, and so Helen's healing of Bertram's "sick desires" can be conceived as not merely a rerouting of extramarital sex into marital sex but as a revivification of impotent Bertram's testicles, for we should recall that the only evidence of Bertram's virility is Helen's eventual testimony that she is pregnant by him. Bertram might very well be an impotent man put to use by Helen's healing hands, or he might be chaste man forced into marriage by the King's law, or he might be an erstwhile chaste youth whose desires are sick because they cannot be made to accord with the norms of an early modern allosexuality.

Helen achieves her desired ends through various substitutions, the most obvious of which is her substitution with the maid Diana. When Bertram attempts to woo Diana in act four, scene two, Diana follows a script written by Helen even as Bertram seems to follow one written by Paroles: the wooing scene echoes the virginity debate between Helen and Paroles in the first act. Like Paroles who tells Helen, "that you were made of is mettle to make virgins" (1.1.131–32), Bertram will tell Diana "now you should be as your mother was / When your sweet self was got" (4.2.9–10). Yet in this scene Helen does not merely coach Diana about what to say to Bertram; she essentially mobilizes the whole discursive apparatus that would require a chaste maid and a sieging soldier. Helen knows this dialectic because she tested its rhetorical contours with Paroles at the beginning of the play. Largely following Paroles's original script but for a slight though significant emendation, Helen will demand that the symbols of Bertram's chastity be equally at stake in his courting of Diana. In that original debate, Paroles argues that pregnancy is the only sign of virginity's loss, essentially laying the burden of proof of sexual consummation on cis-women. However, in stipulating that Diana demand Bertram's ring in exchange for her virginity, Helen gains proof of his chastity's loss. With Diana's help, Helen effectively develops a "military policy how virgins might blow up men" (1.1.123–24).

Scholars have long held that Helen's proof of her fulfilment of Bertram's riddle is her pregnant body.[91] Such criticism focuses on the wrong person, thus undermining both the reach of Helen's political and sexual agency and the extent to which Shakespeare problematically constitutes that agency through the containment of the range of meanings of the chaste, single life that circulate around Bertram. Through the bed trick and the final scene at court, Helen routes the proof of her pregnancy away from her body and back onto the men she heals: the King and Bertram. She does this through acquiring their rings. Rings might symbolize all sorts of things in Shakespearean comedy. In many, the ring symbolizes the vulva when given by heroines like Portia and Nerissa as symbols of their sexual honor and promises of sexual consummation. But in *All's Well*, rings do not belong to women but to men, to the King and to Bertram. These circumstances have led scholars to transmute one penetrative logic for another, and so the rings in *All's Well* have, on the whole (so to speak), come to symbolize the anus.[92] But rings are not just hollow. They are also round, and could hold a precious stone. In an early modern semenotic discourse, they would not symbolize a penetrable anus but the projective testicles. When Bertram insists in his letter that Helen must "get the ring upon my finger, which never shall come off, and show me a child begotten of thy body that I am father to" (3.2.57–59), he equates the loss of the ring with a procreative ejaculation, the transfer of his testicular seed to Helen's impressionable womb. The image also reveals a fear of castration, a loss not just of his seed but of the entirety of his testicles. The image of the ring sliding off his finger is resonant with Lafeu's projections of castration over the contract scene, but it also implies the mechanics of procreative sex: a transfer of testicular semen along a phallic channel, which then comes to be possessed by Helen. Trafficking in this semenotic logic, Diana also works to equate Bertram's ring as the symbol of his chastity and its loss. When Bertram at first refuses to give it to Diana because "it is an honour 'longing to our house, / Bequeathèd down from ancestors" (4.2.41–42), Diana sees in Bertram's honor an analogue to her virginity:

> Mine honour's such a ring.
> My chastity's the jewel of our house,
> Bequeathèd down from many ancestors,
> Which were the greatest obloquy I' the world
> In me to lose. (ll.45–49)

Playing with the associations of a "jewel" with testicle, Diana would have Bertram's body testify to his sexual honor in the ways her "ring" is believed to speak for hers. Upon Diana's later presentation of Bertram's ring, the Countess will similarly emphasize its testimonial weight, calling it "that gem, / Conferred by testament to th' sequent issue" (5.3.96–97).[93] Like a functional testicle, Bertram's ring will come to bear witness to a naturalized, patriarchal desire for procreative "issue."

Through the bed trick, Helen thus not only comes to fulfill Bertram's epistolary riddle, but, in doing so, she also secures the very object that Bertram constructs as the sign of his chastity in his letters, suggesting that the "never" of chastity can always be recuperated by the "then" of procreative sex. Emerging from the shadow of that event, Helen presents herself at court as the possessor of two rings: that of the King and of Bertram. It is perhaps too indulgent to say that Helen has these men by their family's jewels, but the play's ending suggests as much. Having healed the King and won Bertram's hand in the bed trick, Helen presents herself as the possessor of both of their rings. Where Bertram's word was before enough to defame Diana as "a common gamester to the camp" (5.3.189), it now holds no weight as testimony, for without his ring, he, much like a castrate, has no right to testify as a witness. Pressed by the King as to how she came to possess the very ring he gave to Helen upon his healing, Diana responds, "the jeweller that owes the ring is sent for / And he shall surety me" (5.3.296–97). Rings in hand, Helen possesses the somatic symbols of the witness, and can thus legally testify not only to Diana's innocence in the face of Bertram's slander but to her own pregnancy. In doing so, Helen not only presents the King and Bertram as her eunuch servants but also bears witness to the role their testes played in effecting her pregnancy, reversing the visible signs of procreation from the swelling belly to testifying testes.

The play does not, however, entirely cede the triumph to Helen. Despite her careful plotting, the single life of the chaste youth casts its shadows across the end of the play, structuring what can be known about desire, or the nonexperience of it, and what cannot. As almost all readers of the play observe, what is proclaimed evident at the end of the play is everywhere conditioned by qualification. However clear the testimonies of the rings are to the rest of the company, Bertram insists upon a clarity that, given Helen's fulfillment of the terms laid out in his riddle, would prove impossible. When he states, "If she, my liege, can make me know this clearly, / I'll love her dearly, ever, ever dearly," he not only revises the original contract but also betrays a suspicion seemingly inviolable to any kind of proof (5.3.315–16). Nor can the King entirely incorporate the marriage of Helen and Bertram into the fantasy of a happy comedic ending: "All yet seems well, and if it end so meet, / The bitter past, more welcome is the sweet," he pronounces (ll.333–34). The perfect rhyme of his final couplet dilates with temporal qualifier—"all yet seems well"—that pushes the boundaries of resolution beyond the scope of the plot.[94] That "yet" recalls the conditionality of the ring exchange, for the rings Helen offers as the proof of her pregnancy testify to the virility of two men. Only Helen knows whether or not—or which of—these men are impotent or virile, cuckold or father, for only she, as physician, has tested their testicles.

As the chaste, single life variously signifies an unhistorical denial of pro-creative sexuality, an unnatural inexpression of desire, a physical, genital disability, or unspeakable sex acts done under its shadow, the marriage plot struggles to localize these possibilities into one determinative and recuper-able meaning. As the riddle at the center of the play's sexual epistemology, the enduring possibility of the chaste, single life inheres in a qualified mar-riage that, through a bed trick, Helen consummated under the shadow of chastity. Thus Helen herself cannot escape it either; she presents herself to Bertram as "but the shadow of a wife . . . / The name and not the thing" (5.3.306–7). As feminist critics have pointed out, this shadow is constituted in no small part by the double standard of sexual honor Helen at once ef-fectively negotiates but from which she cannot entirely emancipate her-self.[95] But if Helen presents as the shadow of wife, Bertram appears likewise as the shadow of a husband, a would be single man coerced into marriage. What remains a problem in this problem comedy is the way in which the marriage plot presents the varied possibilities of Bertram's single life as irrec-oncilable to the otherwise feminist ends of Helen's will.

How to understand, then, the ending of *All's Well*? I would suggest that the play itself dramatizes and suspends that question rather than propos-ing answers to it. When Bertram returns from the Tuscan wars, he appears "with a patch of velvet on's face" (4.5.95–96). Bertram appears so marked just after Helen, Diana, and the Widow confirm the bed trick's success in a previous scene. Like the bed trick, the patch of velvet engenders witnesses that can only testify to the ends and not the means of its effectuation. What lies beneath Bertram's velvet patch, one presumes, is a cut, but its exact na-ture, let alone its cause, resists knowing. It might hide "a scar nobly got, or a noble scar," as Lafeu asserts, and so "is a good liv'ry of honour" (l.100–01), or a "carbonadoed face," as Lavatch argues (l.102). That would be a livery of a different sort. In its opacity, it both testifies to the martial honor of a chaste soldier and to syphilitic sex acts done under chastity's shadow. But it might signify neither of these. The velvet remains merely a surface to be read, one that generates interpretations by the very fact of its occlusions, its testimony queering testimony. As Lavatch observes, "whether there be a scar under't or no, the velvet knows, but 'tis a goodly patch of velvet" (4.5.96–98). Like Bertram's original epistolary testimony to the chaste, single life, the patch of velvet bears witness to a resounding "never," a "'not' eternal," not an affirmation but a recursive negation that can only testify to what it will not say. If as Lavatch and Lafeu speculate, the patch hides a scar, such a wounding lends an ironic edge to Paroles's earlier quip, for so cut, Bertram "married is a man that's marred" (2.4.299). Such a marring need not speak to the antifeminism underwriting Paroles apothegm, for it might just as readily mark the violence a marriage premised on an early modern semenotics of allosexuality does to all sorts of possibilities that inhere in the single life, chaste ones as well as any number that marriage and its histories would render unhistorical, unnatural, abnormal, and unthinkable. We might ask with the play's onlookers what the velvet knows, might yet acknowledge the chaste, single life in histories of sexuality, and the possibilities and impossibilities to which it testifies.

# Chapter 2

## The Single Life of the Journeyman Bachelor

Paronomasia and Communities of Labor Outside
(and Inside) *Much Ado About Nothing*

The desire to live a single life is not one particular to Bertram. Shakespeare's comedies brim with characters seemingly allergic to marriage, but there is perhaps no character in the Shakespearean canon who so forthrightly insists upon the single life than Benedick of *Much Ado About Nothing* (c. 1598). Like Bertram, Benedick also emphatically embraces the single life; early in the comedy, he declares, "I will live a bachelor."[1] These are fated words to utter in a Shakespearean marital comedy. By uttering them, Benedick unwittingly catalyzes his marriage plot. Shakespeare's comedies may begin with bachelors like Benedick, but they end with husbands. Benedick's mistake is one of genre: he does not realize he is in a Shakespearean comedy, even though he does seem to recognize that Shakespearean comedies are no place for a bachelor, for when he says he wants to live the single life, he does not turn to the plots of marital comedy to imagine his bachelorhood. Instead, he looks at a kind of literature that valorizes the single life he longs to live. For Benedick, the single life of the bachelor is best imagined in ballads. He explicitly draws on these "paper bullets of the brain" (2.3.222), as he elsewhere calls them, to dissociate from his present company and to invoke a community of like-minded men for whom his claim would resonate. "Prove that I ever lose more blood with love than I will get again with drinking," he tells Don Pedro, "pick out mine eyes with a ballad-maker's pen and hang me up at the door of a brothel house for the sign of a blind Cupid" (1.1.233–36). His violation of his vow to live a single life would make him an effigy around which other bachelors could fraternize.

Benedick is being witty, but the textual materials of his wit suggest ballads—a form of literature at home both in the imaginative space of plays and in the physical space of playhouses—contest the comedic script in which Benedick finds himself. This chapter follows bachelor Benedick's lead. It tries to imagine bachelorhood with him by relocating what it might mean to "live a bachelor" outside the plots of Shakespearean marital comedy and inside a denser semantic network of ballads and other popular print forms. While the meanings of Benedick's desire "to live a bachelor" may seem self-evident—he wants to live as an unmarried man—this chapter argues that the meanings of bachelorhood are less transparent than they first appear, and that the motility of its meanings across economic, social, and gender hierarchies constitutes a form of unpatriarchal manhood that can be imagined as free from patriarchal social obligations as well as the precarities of wage labor. This fantasy of the single life draws upon the materialization of bachelorhood as a liminal rank within institutional hierarchies, primarily London's livery companies, where it designated communities of laborers, namely journeymen. If Benedick desires "to live a bachelor," he may not only be imagining living as a single man; he may just be imagining living like a journeyman of one of London's many livery companies—among a host of other possible lives. As a journeyman bachelor, Benedick may be seeking a community of likeminded bachelor journeymen with whom he might revel.

To thicken the meanings of Benedick's bachelorhood within Shakespeare's London, and, in turn, to trace the entanglements of gender and labor status, I first turn to the past and present etymologies of the term "bachelor" to show how this word oscillates amid and across semantic registers like a pun. I then turn to the ways early modern lexicographers define the word to think about not only what kinds of men might identify or be identified as bachelors but also what it might mean to live as one. Drawing upon these meanings of the word, I then read it across a range of popular literature written for and to bachelors, especially ballads. Benedick would imagine the single life of the bachelor through the recursive and iterative form of the ballad, a type of literature given to refrains, choruses, and frenetic reduplication as print. If *Much Ado About Nothing*, as scholars have observed, is "both a product of, and a participant in, England's ballad culture," then the bachelor life it is fond of noting has a paratextual life outside it as well.[2] Ballads are particularly useful for thinking about the single life of the journeyman bachelor because, unlike plays, they were a genre suited to a granularity of address. As Natascha Würzbach has argued, "because of its particular mode of communication and distribution the street ballad as a literary form is both suited to, and compelled to adopt, a personalization of its message."[3] Reading ballads and other popular literature addressed to bachelors in relation to Benedick's desire to live the single life, this chapter hopes to think about social ranks and labor statuses encoded in the single life of bachelors, meanings Benedick might have in mind but about which Shakespeare's *Much Ado About Nothing* has next to nothing to say.

## BACHELOR PHILOLOGY

Is there a history of the single life in the etymology of "bachelor"? Is there a history of manhood? Of a kind. In *Queer Philology*, Jeffrey Masten reminds us that etymology is "the history of words (history *in* words)," but as Masten goes on to enjoin, "we need . . . to be more carefully attuned to the ways etymologies, shorn of their associations with 'origin,' persist in a word and its surrounding discourse, as a diachronic record of practice in the midst of language as a synchronic system."[4] Past meanings find present uses; past uses bend to the transumption of present meanings. Masten makes these claims in relation to the word "sweet," a "very old English word," to consider what "lingers" in it, such as those erotic and affective charges between men that it encodes, cites, and circulates.[5] Masten advocates, in part, for attending to the paronomasiac qualities of words, their capacities to pun their histories into affective, erotic, and relational registers extant in early modern texts but not necessarily recorded in past and present lexicons. Observing that "Word-play . . . is to etymology, as synchrony is to diachrony," Derek Attridge similarly troubles the evidentiary force of etymology only to reinscribe its rhetorical power as paronomasia.[6] As a method of reading the pun, etymology records polysemous play both in and across time. A single soldier in a marital comedy who sees ballads as bullets, Benedick is no stranger to the pleasures of puns. He is a bachelor who wants to live like a bachelor. What could that mean?

The word "bachelor" has a history of having a history. Diachronically, synchronically—however you cut it—it shimmers and shakes. Its homonymic features trouble its etymological history. The word "bachelor" is often cast as an etymological problem—or, perhaps more accurately, has served as an example of the problems of etymology itself—for quite some time. Criticizing etymologists before him, the first-century Roman rhetorician Quintilian mocks etymologists by focusing on the meanings of the single life that the word "bachelor" might come to include. "Gavius thought himself a perfect genius," Quintillian mocks, "when he identified caelibes, 'bachelors,' with caelites, 'gods,' on the ground that they are free from a heavy load of care. . . . Modestus is not his inferior in inventive power for he asserts that *caelibes*, that is to say unmarried men, are so called because Saturn cut off the genital organs of Caelus."[7] Quintillian scoffs at how social biases force linguistic affinities. What associates "cælibes" and "cælites" is not so much homonymy, Quintillian argues, but a contemporary belief about what would render such similarities historically meaningful: that castrates cannot or should not marry. Quintillian demonstrates, instead, the ways in which etymology produces social meanings by insisting upon homonymic relations between certain words. The saliency of the liberty (gods) or sterility (castrates) of the bachelor is produced through etymology itself. Such associations may strain logic, but they make for persuasive rhetoric. The meanings of "bachelor" that premodern etymologists forge—and that Quintillian himself mocks—stick around in the early modern period. They recur in the ballads this chapter will later exam and, as chapter 1 notes and chapter 5 will further examine, they ramify throughout Shakespeare's comedies and other popular texts about the single life. As bachelors and beyond, single men are variously represented as gods or eunuchs, among other things.

For semantic theorists, "bachelor" has served as a case study; they have long mulled over its somewhat hermetic, homonymic qualities. Tracing the word's place in twentieth-century semantic theory, H. Joachim Neuhaus explains that the polysemy of the term—it can mean an unmarried man, a young knight, a person with the lowest academic degree, an unmated fur seal during breeding season—has led theorists into ever more convoluted diagrammatic structures of its meanings and their redounding upon each other; early tree diagrams of the word, drawn from and meant to aid lexicographical and dictionary applications, Neuhaus documents, become ever more complicated by later ones that are "a series of overlapping 'circles.'"[8] These latter diagrams effectively trace the complex polysemy of the homonyms of "bachelor," and its variant spellings, even as they serve no practical lexicographic purpose because lexicography tends to prioritize more hierarchical and historical representations of meaning—and so, Neuahus surmises, "conventional dictionary definitions are hardly foundations to build a semantic theory on."[9] In Shakespeare's corpus alone, as Neuhaus explains, "there are twenty-four occurrences of the lemma *bachelor* if the suffixation *bachelorship* is included in the count," and perhaps because Shakespeare so often dramatizes the causes and effects of marriage, the containment of that word's meaning to being unmarried applies in nearly all cases.[10] Despite the rather narrow meanings of the term in relation to marriage, Neuhaus explains, "a simple dictionary definition is probably not enough to describe it adequately."[11] Bachelors may most often be unmarried men in the context of the Shakespearean corpus, but the meanings of each of those terms redound upon one another in a manner that founders, rather than solidifies, its denotation of a type of single man.

If the history in the word "bachelor" runs through but ultimately outside of Shakespeare's *Much Ado About Nothing*, it also encodes the overlapping, and, at times, mutually reinforcing, relation between social status and marital status in early modern England. We can go some way to finding the possibilities imagined in Benedick's bachelor life, discover its textures, complexities, communities, and contradictions, if we notice how it at once registers meanings localized within institutional hierarchies of London as well as those condensed by patriarchal norms of conjugality. In the early modern English lexicon, as in modern ones, the word "bachelor" could denote an unmarried man. *Huloets Dictionary* (1572) defines a "Bachiler" as "one unmarried, or having no wife," but it defines the plural "Bachilers" as "yong men, they that have passed the tender tyme of chyldhoode."[12] Interpellated through a patriarchal telos that collapses age and marriage as markers of manhood, single men in a crowd of peers become youths.[13] While early modern lexicons did attend to the marital meanings of "bachelor," they just as readily defined bachelors not in terms of marital status but in terms of their position within institutional hierarchies, especially those of London's livery companies. For example, in *A Dictionarie of the French and English Tongues* (1611), Randle Cotgrave primarily focuses on these institutional meanings; a "Bachelier" is "a bacheler; a youth of sixteene, or eighteene yeares of age; also he that hath passed Master in a trade, but is not yet swerne of the Companie; also a Batcheler of Art; also a title of gentrie inferior to Banneret, and superior to Escuyer; a young gentleman that aspires vnto Knighthood, and the priviledge of bearing a Banner in a field; also, the Lord of a castle, fort, great house, or Place, that is derived from (but in jurisdiction equal with) and Earledome, Viscountie, or Baronie"; but we also read in another record that "bachelier" denotes, "Bachelery, bachelerlike; of, or belong to, a bacheler."[14] Given their positions within the social hierarchy, all of these bachelors would be, presumably, unmarried. But even as a bachelor realizes their social position within institutional hierarchies, their visibility as a type of single man concatenates in Cotgrave into self-referentiality; the French and English words are orthographically indistinguishable. Bachelors are always bachelorlike. The institutional meanings of "bachelor" that Cotgrave enumerates also populate other early modern lexicons. In his *The Interpreter: or Book Containing the Signification of Words* (1607), John Cowell narrows in on Cotgrave's definition of "he that hath passed Master in a trade, but is not yet swerne of the Companie." Ignoring entirely the word's marital meanings, Cowell defines his bachelor as a journeyman, one out of their apprenticeship, and he focuses intensely upon the institutional meanings of the term. According to Cowell, "those that be called Bachelers of the Companies in *London*, be such of each company, as be springing toward the estate of those that be imployed in Councel, but as yet are inferiors."[15] He further emphasizes the commonality of this body in the great companies: "For every company of the twelve, consisteth of a Master, two Wardens, the Liuerie, which are assistants in matter of Councell, or at the least, such as the Assistants be chosen out of, and the Bachelers, which are yet in expectance of dignititie among them, and have their function onely in attendance vpon the Master and Wardens."[16] Far from obtuse, the institutional meanings of such bachelors that Cowell documents would resonate within a commercial theater that, as Ronda Arab has most recently demonstrated, had historical and material connections with London's livery companies and its affiliated artisans.[17] Benedick, in other words, may have a rather narrow idea of bachelorhood as a matter of remaining unmarried, but the actors and audience members, many of whom would be living as bachelors too, would have a much wider, semantically dense, and experiential sense of these institutional and social meanings.

As early modern lexicons indicate, the difference between a bachelor as an unmarried man and a bachelor as a subordinate in a social hierarchy was a little less than kin and more than kind. In early modern England, the threads tying marital status to age, social status, or vocation were more clearly visible and socially meaningful (though no less knotted) than they are today. While the single life might be a universal status across categories of age, social status, or vocation—anyone might be unmarried for any number of reasons—an individual's place in early modern social order often predominated as the primary meaning of the single life. If, as Keith Wrightson has argued, sixteenth- and seventeenth-century England witnessed a transition away from a medieval notions of three "estates" or "orders" that privileged one's social function to one that came to privilege one's hierarchical status, then it would be expected that the category of "bachelor," so integral to the hierarchies of such estates, would bear the marks of this shift. According to Wrightson, early modern social theorists "abandoned the habit of conceptualizing society in terms of the three estates of medieval social theory and developed an alternative convention of social description derived from their preoccupation with 'degree.'"[18] As institutional lexicons shifted from prescriptive to descriptive in tenor, the meanings of "bachelor" likewise shifted. In the hierarchies of so many early modern institutions—not the least of which, the livery companies and the universities—bachelorhood designated one's rank or degree, and often that degree precluded (by statute or by custom) one from marrying. The degree of bachelor signified a novitiate status; such a bachelor was one who was no longer an apprentice or child, yet he had not yet gained the civic or social rank of master. Usually, but not always, these social circumstances meant he did not have the social standing or capital to make marriage feasible.

Because early modern bachelor journeymen were often bachelors, early modern texts often attended to the paronomasia of the single life. In his *Arte of English Poesie* (1589), George Puttenham writes of paronomasia, "Ye have a figure by which ye play with a couple of words or names much resembling, and because the one seemes to answere th'other by manner of illusion, and doth, as it were nick him, I call him the *Nicknamer*."[19] Bachelor journeymen are nicknamed bachelors, and their meanings could nick each other. Benedick likely knows this, and he also seems to know that ballads might be especially good at surfacing the diachronic accretions of bachelorhood into the synchronies of living a single life. Consider, for instance, Thomas Deloney's ballad, "Salomon's Wife," which I touched upon in the Introduction to this book. It records this distinction between a bachelor's marital status and his institutional rank to pun upon them and to imagine a much wider community of single men:

> May bachelors of each degree
> In choosing a beauteous wife
> Remember what is joy to see
> May lead to woefulness and strife;
> Beauty is not a brave outside
> Beauty within is beauty's pride.[20]

By situating "bachelors" in relation to social hierarchies, Deloney carries over the meaning of the word as indicating a specific rank, but he also privileges the meaning of marital status in the poem. Here, the poem suggests, the shared single life among bachelors binds them into a collective that transcends their particular social rank as bachelors. That this Elizabethan balladeer makes a point to divide the marital meanings of bachelorhood from its other institutional or social meanings also points to the ways that the designation of bachelor could just as easily tangle into a denser knot. In Webster and Dekker's *West-ward Ho* (1607), Birdlime asks a servant, "By your leaue Batcheller: is the gentlewoman your Mistriss stirring?"[21] This servant's status as a bachelor marks him simultaneously as a subordinate and a single man. Birdlime plays with the connotations of bachelorhood later in the play, when she gestures not to a servant but to Honeysuckle, mockingly calling this married man "that honest batchiler" (5.4.226). In this case, Mistress Honeysuckle understands Birdlime to mean "unmarried man," as indicated by her response: "Motherly woman hees my husband and no Batchelers buttons are at this doublet" (5.4.228–29).[22] For Birdlime, the designation of bachelor elaborates a pun on the sexual and social roles men might inhabit; it points to the difference between masters and servants while also raising the question of who services Mistress Honeysuckle (or who is in the best social or sexual position to know if she is stirring from her bed). In this respect, as a constitutive element of a man's social identity, the single life contains a germ of democratizing power, even if that power is more potential than actual. Birdlime suggests bachelors, as single men, might be masters in sexual matters because of the illicit and even private knowledge they may have as bachelor servants. In short, each case demonstrates how marital status could be mobilized to imagine a community of single men in such a manner that supplanted differences of rank even as it registers such a difference.

## Keeping Company with Bachelors

The history of the single life as traced through the "bachelor" is a lexicographical and etymological history, or one, at least, that can be traced, not unproblematically, through lexicography and etymology. Etymology can only take us so far, however, and it ultimately indicates the extent to which the single life of the bachelor is one bound up in early modern institutions where the matter of marital status and social rank impinge upon each other. Perhaps no institution, or rather, network of institutions, impacted the lives of so many early modern Londoners than its livery companies.

Single men predominated in London's livery companies as bachelors. The period of apprenticeship was synonymous with the single life; John Taylor, the water poet, describes apprenticeship as "a vessell that is both singular and single, for none but single persons must boord her; and (to auoyd double dealing) she hath bannished Matrimony out of her quarters for seauen yeares or more."[23] Despite this fact, scholars have tended to characterize livery company culture in terms of age rather than marital status. Since Natalie Zemon Davis described youth groups and their institutional history to explain festive misrule and charivaris in early modern France, several scholars have examined livery company culture in early modern England as an analogue for youth culture.[24] Much of this scholarship has focused on apprentices, their position as adolescents, as well as their confraternity and conviviality.[25] While deepening our understanding of how festive practices within livery company culture consolidated group identity, this scholarship has mostly ignored Davis's own emphasis upon the organizing power of the single life in French charivaris.[26] In emphasizing age and in seeing a parallel (if an inexact one) to the French charivaris Davis historicizes, literary scholars and social historians have thus overlooked the liminal period between apprenticeship and householding that early modern English journeymen occupied, a period in which a man's marital status was a more pronounced concern, and thus more significant for their social definition.[27] Besides simplifying the nuanced interrelations between livery company estates as well as those between masters on the one hand and their social subordinates on the other, this oversight has by and large erased from early modern social and gender histories not only the meanings of the single life and its relationship to labor but also the place of journeymen and their institutional proximity to, and differentiation from, apprentices and householders within London's livery companies.

One significant difference between the single life of apprentices and the single life of journeymen is the social and economic agency granted each under early modern law. An apprentice was legally conceptualized as a child; a journeyman was not. This difference mattered a great deal. After their apprenticeship, most men transitioned into journeywork, laboring for wages, though often still receiving room and board from their employers. Unlike apprentices, journeymen had earned both the freedom of their company and the City. On the whole, they were citizens and they—like Ralph of Dekker's *The Shoemaker's Holiday* (1599)—could theoretically marry. However, most of the journeymen in early modern London were probably unmarried men. While no law barred journeymen from marrying in early modern England—in this, they differed from their continental counterparts—it is unlikely that many did due to the legal restrictions and economic constrictions of their wage labor. A journeyman had to earn enough capital if he wanted to establish his household and indenture apprentices.[28] Thus while the single life of a journeyman was contiguous with that of an apprentice, the journeyman's single life had a markedly different socioeconomic and institutional meaning. If a journeyman were unmarried, even if by choice, his single life signified his social and economic status. It indicated that he had not attained enough capital to marry and establish a household. The journeyman's unmarried status was thus constitutive of his social and economic identity *as a freeman*. If the single life defined the artisan communities of London's livery companies on the whole, as John Taylor suggests, it was journeymen in particular who were readily conceived as a community of bachelors.

Because the journeyman had earned the freedom of his company yet had not obtained householding status, his single life became a clear marker of his social position as a subordinate laborer. His status as such was first codified in 1549 in "An Acte concernyng reteyng of Jo'neymen," which did away with day labor for unmarried journeymen, mandating contracts of at least a quarter of the year.[29] Building upon this early law, *The Statute of Artificers* (1563), which regulated wages, specified contract lengths, and nationalized the terms of indenture, primarily uses marital status to designate and to delineate the requirements of journeywork. Addressing "every person being unmarried, and every *other* person being under thage of thirtie yeres, that after the Feaste of Easter next shall marrye," the Statute specifies that such persons, "shall, duringe the tyme that he or they shall so be unmarryed, or under the saide Age of xxx^tie yeares, uppon request made by anny person using the Arte or mystery, wherin the saide person so required hath beyne exercised as is aforesaide, be reteyned and shall not refuse to serue according to the tenor of this statute."[30] While *The Statute* includes various sorts of workers from country to city, it puts great emphasis on the journeyman, he who has been "brought upp in anny of the saide Artes, craftes, or sciences" or has practiced the trade for three years or more but who is without any claims to estates.[31] Put more simply, the statute addresses journeymen as single men, and it does so to delineate the parameters of living as one. Such men needed to be retained, because they were no longer indentured as apprentices. The journeyman's freedom from apprenticeship paradoxically required his obligatory consent to employment by any master. Between forms of institutional emancipation, economic precarity, and legal conscription, the journeyman's marital status demarcated his social visibility. In *De Republica Anglorum* (1583), Sir Thomas Smith, for example, similarly uses marital status to differentiate types of laborers. After characterizing apprenticeship as a type of covenantal bondage, Smith turns to those "full free men and women" who "be hired by the yeare for wages, and be called servaunts or serving men," and explains, "all servaunts, labourers, and other not maryed, must serve by the yere."[32] For Smith, the single life is the primary metric by which he thinks about a vocational status that is neither fully bonded nor fully free. As he elsewhere observes, "necessitie and want of bondmen hath made men to use free men as bondmen to all servile services."[33] For social theorists like Smith, it was expedient to classify subordinate laborers not by their institutional rank but by their marital status.[34] And the journeymen of London's livery companies were just this kind of laborer: they were freemen of circumscribed economic and social agency because they were also single men.

While *The Statute* and *De Republica Anglorum* use the single life to index the legal restrictions imposed upon journeymen and other servants, livery companies conceived of journeymen not just as single men but as bachelors in particular, a status that was particularly vexed by the relation between service and freedom, especially as they informed early modern England's relationship to bondage, service, and enslavement that Urvashi Chakravarty has recently examined.[35] The distinctions between service and freedom could be both grand and granular within these institutions. In early modern London, the livery company hierarchy could be divided into two distinct bodies: the livery and the yeomanry.[36] Composed of a master, wardens, and court of assistants, the livery was the elite governing body of the company, while the yeomanry was the popular body composed of both journeymen and householders, or those "out of the livery." It contained the majority of the company's members, and thus served as a significant institution through which economic, political, and social identity could be imagined and realized.[37] In the twelve great companies, the members of the yeomanry—both journeymen and householders—were commonly understood as the bachelors of the company. The Merchant Taylors called their yeomanry the Bachelors' Company—in part because of the company's historical roots in medieval fraternities of journeymen—and the Mercers, the Drapers, and it seems the Goldsmiths as well, referred to their yeomanry members as bachelors.[38] Yet despite the inclusion of householders within their ranks, these "bachelors companies" were often associated with unmarried journeymen. Not only did journeymen constitute a sizeable constituency within the livery company as a whole, they also could hold significant sway over the yeomanry.[39] Moreover, it was through the yeomanry that a journeyman's economic and legal agency was most often realized, for it provided the means through which journeymen could influence company ordinances—such as how many apprentices a master could indenture—that had direct bearing on their employment and earning power.[40]

When Benedicks insists he "will live a bachelor," the life he conjures is one conditioned by the homologies between the bachelor as an unmarried man and the bachelor as the journeyman. He surely means he desires to live a single life, but in doing so, he could be imagining keeping company with the journeymen of London's livery companies, for they possessed social visibility as bachelors. It was this order, for instance, that was publicized when a member of the company was elected Lord Mayor. During the Lord Mayor's show, which the yeomanry was responsible for funding and organizing, some members processed as the bachelors of the company. As Tracey Hill observes, these civic shows were "*public* events" that "were still closer to the quotidian lives of early modern Londoners than court or aristocratic cultures."[41] As prominent members of the companies, the bachelors were likewise publicized. They had their own ostentatious barge in the water pageant, and certain bachelors from the yeomanry were selected to process—as per custom, the youngest were first—during the pageant and to attend the feast at Guildhall. Moreover, these bachelors had their own gowns, which were often extravagant.[42] The Goldsmiths' Company made distinctions between these bachelors selected from the "young men of the Company."[43] There were "budge" and "rich," wearing lamb's skin and satin respectively, as well as whifflers (those who maintained the boundary between procession and crowd).[44] To be selected to one of these roles during the lord mayor's election was thus a great honor, though it carried financial costs for each man chosen. According to Steve Rappaport, when Chris Draper of the Ironmongers became mayor in 1566, forty-six men had to pay for their own hoods and gown, and thus "the honour . . . was expensive, for two-thirds of the men paid from 10s. to more than £3 for the privilege of wearing the bachelors' livery."[45] Promotion as a bachelor in these circumstance carried financial ramifications even as it elevated one's social visibility, but it is also true that the bachelor status was by no means monolithic. For instance, the Drapers made distinction within distinction. A small clutch of bachelors, dressed in fine apparel, directed and oversaw a larger group, also richly attired, who provided table service to senior members of the company.[46]

Social historians and literary scholars have generally understood this promotion to pertain to the wealthier members exclusively, but records also suggest that journeymen could serve as bachelors in these events, even if they did not always welcome the promotion.[47] Tracey Hill records that in 1597 the Skinners, depleted of funds from recent building construction, conscripted journeymen to be bachelors of the procession. Seeking to swell the ranks of their bachelors so that the company might exact funds from them, they suggested instituting fines of £5 on freemen who did not speedily enter their apprentices into the freedom of the Company, thus inaugurating them as yeomanry members and journeymen.[48] The pecuniary strain that sometimes accompanied bachelorship might even be seen as reverberating in *Much Ado*. Justifying his decision to live as a bachelor, Benedick wittily claims the life is "the fine . . . for which I may go the finer" (1.1.229). Benedick may be punning upon the undue financial burdens that sometimes attended wearing the bachelor's livery in the Lord Mayor's show.[49] Contemporaries often noted the sartoriality of such bachelors. In his diary, Henry Machyn details the sumptuousness of the bachelors as they processed in the Lord Mayor's pageant "all in leveray, and skar lett hods" and "cremesun damaske hodes" in 1553 and

1562, respectively.[50] Such bachelors could be of the kind Benedick imagines himself to be. In a 1635 engraving of the "Ages of man," the Lord Mayor's pageant serves as analogy for progression of manhood in general. The "youth" is identified as a "whiffler" of that procession (fig. 1).[51]

Figure 1. "Next place of office which I do attaine / is swashing whiffler w[ith] my staff and chaine / In which hot office when I long have been / I swaggering leave to be stayd begin." Edward Calver, "Youth," in *Passion and Discretion in Youth and Age*, London, 1641.

John H. Astington asserts in his examination of these emblems that "it [the whiffler] is quite unrelated to any *permanent* social role outside the festival."[52] But this is only partially true; Astington misses the larger picture of manhood these emblems paint. Because manhood in the early modern period was not a permanent state, and rather one moved into and out of as one aged, the emblem of the whiffler to represent a young, unmarried man indeed represents a single life that was far more intractable, and even desirable, for journeymen. Whifflers maintained, even as they inhabited, the borders of the processionals of the Lord Mayor's show. They in particular typify those contingencies of livery that, as Chakravarty observes, "constitutes a limit case for the slippages between consenting service on the one hand and bondage on the other"; as journeymen, they marked an institutional threshold as well as a gendered one.[53] Such journeymen likely would never attain the livery, however much they might hope for it. In rejecting marriage for the single life, Benedick too espouses a social role that is marginal but also perhaps desirable, for like the whiffler journeyman, he insists on a form of unpatriarchal manhood that would license sartorial display and forms of affiliation marginal to patriarchal householding status.

If the single life of the journeyman was often conceived as the single life of a bachelor, then "to live a bachelor" in early modern London, as Benedick desires, was to live within communities realized and imagined through institutional affiliation and conditioned by marital status. These meanings collided in one social designation of bachelor, but not always in transparent ways. At least one historian, Henry Wheately, a contemporary of W. C. Hazlitt, seems to let the semantic interrelations between marital and livery company status get the better of him. Reading livery company records, Wheately wrongly surmises, "all the livery companies possessed a class of young unmarried members called 'The Bachelors.'"[54] While Wheatley is probably incorrect—he seems to conflate the word's marital meanings with a designation of the yeomanry, which included both married and unmarried men—his error is understandable. It seems some of the livery companies made little distinction between kinds of bachelors in their companies. Wheatley cites a reference to a residence in Sir Walter Prideaux's history of the Goldsmiths.[55] That record reveals that there was indeed a visible and sanctioned community of unmarried journeymen in the Goldsmith's company who lived as bachelors in a manner that conflated institutional and marital status. The residence was colloquially called, as Wheatley also confirms, "Bachelor's Alley" or "Bachelor's Courte." It was located on Gutter Lane (a street that met Maiden Lane at its north end), just southeast of Goldsmith's Hall. First cited in a 1595 record, the residence seems to have existed well before this, and it remained an established and managed property well into the seventeenth century. Perhaps similarly reading the "invisible ink that mapped, controlled, and demonized" urban spaces that Mary Bly finds overwriting "various liberties in London," the company clerk recording the 1595 entry postulates, "Bachelor's Alley appears to have derived its name from, and to have been appropriated to the residence of, that portion of the Company denominated 'The Bachelors'—a body of members which was common to all the Livery Companies."[56]

Perhaps Benedick imagines living on "Bachelor's Alley." In any case, we might understand it as a particularly salient example of those early modern London locales Amanda Bailey and Roze Hentschell suggest "communicated gendered messages—whether by means of overt exclusion or tacit inclusion" and that "created the conditions for certain uses and misuses, alliances and identifications, as well as new forms of mobility and constraints that had far-reaching consequences for the articulation and comprehension of gender."[57] When the lease for Bachelor's Alley was extended on December 12, 1655, the company authorities again conflated the journeyman's institutional rank as a bachelor with his marital status as one. Under the presupposition that only "death, marriage, or otherwise" exempted a resident from his lease, the ordinance further stipulated that "every person admitted tennant bee a batchelor, and a freeman of the Company of Goldsmithes, and of sober life and good conversacion, and conformeable to the good governement of the Company."[58] Here was a community of journeymen living as bachelors in two mutually reinforcing senses: they were unmarried journeymen, or bachelors, of the yeomanry, that is, the bachelors' company of the Goldsmiths.[59]

The records of the Goldsmiths suggest how London's livery companies sanctioned the single life of the journeyman because it was instrumental to the patriarchal hierarchies of those institutions. Conceived as a threshold of freedom and obligation, the journeyman's single life marked a boundary space into which apprentices graduated but over which the livery maintained its powers of promotion and governance. As the meanings of bachelorhood bled outward from the institution, the single life of the bachelor journeyman could signify a far more subversive and antisocial form of unpatriarchal manhood. While livery companies sanctioned the gathering of their bachelors in residences like Bachelors Court, congregations of unmarried journeymen could just as easily herald a breakdown of patriarchal order. Writing toward the middle of the seventeenth century, on December 29, 1662, Henry Newcome registers a concern over the social round that derives from the confraternity of bachelors common to and sanctioned by livery company culture. "I hear ys day of ye confederacy of ye yong men to ye feasts & meetinge," he states, only to add that these gatherings are a "sad omen to ye towne."[60] In his study of early modern youth culture, Paul Griffiths sees Newcome's entry as "evidence that young people (especially young men) did organize feasts and drinkings which imparted a sense of age-differentials."[61] But he may misread the dynamic of Newcome's documentation precisely because he overlooks the role livery companies played in endorsing such confraternity and conviviality. Newcome tells us these are "quarterly feasts" attended by young men who "are out of their time & unmarried."[62] These young men are likely journeymen who have completed their apprenticeship ("out of their time") and yet remain single men. If such young journeymen did organize these feasts, they did so in relation to a livery company that sanctioned them. According to the early modern chronicler William Harrison, quarter day feasts—of which the yeomanry could hold its own—were known for their ostentatious displays, being "nothing inferior to the nobility."[63] Moreover, they were deeply invested in the local economies of the town, as much of the food was drawn from "great store in the markets adjoining, beside souse, brawne, bacon, fruit, pies of fruit, foules of sundry sorts, cheese, butter, egs, etc."[64] Suffused with the spirit of charivaris, the feasts over which Newcome frets lubricate livery company hierarchies and concretize the various ranks within them.

Newcome's diary entry reveals the ways institutional culture could conflict with the larger culture, the way one patriarchal system might undermine another as each operated through different institutions, social practices, and social distinctions. For Newcome, these young men seem temporally dislocated; they remain between the two social hierarchies—one of labor and one of marriage—that were meant to complement each other. Reveling in their bachelorhood, these journeymen are, in a literal sense, out of order, for they seem to have embraced a single life naturalized by the vocational status they have attained. What is institutionally normative—plenty of journeymen could not and did not marry—ramifies outward as a social problem. Through Newcome's eyes, these feasts, in their power to solidify fraternal bonds, could also broadly undermine patriarchal rule because they valorize the single life. "A linking of young Men into good fellowship before they are entered into the world and they must all be brothers & so cannot meet in the streets but must go together to drink, & so the Men that should bear sway of the Town the next Generation shall be debauched," Newcome breathlessly worries.[65] The homosocial order of the livery company is, for Newcome, the constitutive element that genders the bachelor journeymen as unpatriarchal and perhaps even sodomitical, if he finds in these journeymen the social and confraternal practices that constitute the city-destroying "familiar vices" of sodomy that Mario DiGangi has examined in early modern representations of fellowship between men.[66]

The homosociality central to these institutions and their bachelor companies is not merely a matter of what is "between men"; it marks the ways that which comes "between" can produce "men" of differing degrees, marital statuses, and even orders of desire. When Eve Sedgwick first theorized homosocial desire, she understood it as a structural and contiguous formation that implicated a range of social and sexual roles and identities, all bound up "in an intimate and shifting relation to class."[67] Using Shakespeare's sonnets to theorize the triangulated, rivalrous relations between men in relation to women, Sedgwick observes how these relations draw upon spatial and temporal tropes. Sexuality, for Sedgwick, instantiates a diachronic relation, sociality, a synchronic one.[68] What Newcome sees as devolution of manhood into debauchery depends, crucially, on its spatial containment within interior, private space: they "cannot meet in the streets." The hermeticism of the meeting prompts a temporal problem and the imagined decay of the next generation. As homosocial practices of the livery company retreat into privatized space, the specter of sexuality surfaces, and they come to evince a homoerotic fellowship that would end procreative, patriarchal order. Newcome's fretting demonstrate how a specific socioeconomic status animates a particular patriarchal concern. When Newcome reads the feast as signifying licentiousness and applies that reading to this otherwise sanctioned social act, the danger of liberty becomes more pronounced because that liberty operates within an otherwise normative social structure. "They must all be brothers," Newcome asserts, as if their fellowship is enforced—and, to an extent, it is. A gathering of bachelor journeymen meant to shore up an institutional order of obligation, service, and mastery paradoxically comes to undermine patriarchal manhood because that gathering heralds bachelor status *apart from* householders over and above a bachelor status *subordinate to* them. For Newcome, it is precisely the conflicted relation between one form of bachelorhood and another that so troubles him. He is concerned that these bachelor journeymen are becoming journeymen bachelors, men so accustomed to the single life that they will come to prefer it over a married one.

## JOURNEYMEN BACHELORS AND LITERATURES OF THE SINGLE LIFE

London was full of journeymen, whose identification as bachelors became institutionalized through livery company hierarchies, labor contracts, and cultural practices, and the plural, and even contradictory, meanings of their bachelorhood suggest the ways gender can be realized through institutions and their hierarchies. If Benedick wants to "live a bachelor," he might look to an early modern London to imagine such a community, but he might also look back into Shakespeare's plays. Prior to *Much Ado's* performance, Shakespeare had already envisioned such a community, though he does not call them bachelors. In *A Midsummer Night's Dream* (ca. 1590–1596), he dramatizes a fraternity of laborers for comic effect: the artisans—the weaver Nick Bottom, the carpenter Peter Quince, the bellows mender Francis Flute, the tailor Robin Starveling, the tinker Tom Snout, and the joiner Snug—are a coterie of bachelor journeymen, though they are not called such (the only use of the term "bachelor" in the play occurs when Hermia suggests that Lysander's sleeping apart from her "becomes a virtuous bachelor and a maid"). The motley nature of these laborers is not necessarily a dramatic device, and might in fact be representative of the realities of journeywork. While livery companies were incorporated as trade organizations, not all of their members practiced the titular trade of the company. As Ian Archer points out, by the seventeenth century, journeymen clothworkers and blacksmiths might find themselves within the same livery company, and thus their fraternity would have to draw on social matrices beyond those internal to the companies.[69] Nor is their theatrical endeavor entirely parodic even if it is highly comical. Playing companies had connections with livery companies, and actors were often apprenticed through companies themselves. Medieval guilds, of course, produced seasonal theater, including Midsummer shows and mystery plays. Early modern players were inheritors of this tradition as well as the legal ordinances that helped shape it. In order for players to bind apprentices, they had to be a member of one of London's livery companies. Members of Shakespeare's playing companies—the Lord Chamberlain's Men, and later, the King's Men—were also members of livery companies. John Heminges, actor and one of the compilers of the 1623 folio, was a freeman of the Grocer's Company. As a freeman, Heminges could bind apprentices, and as David Kathman has demonstrated, Heminges actively used his livery company membership to bind apprentices for the playing company. (While one had to be a member of a company to bind apprentices, apprentices so bound did not, in fact, have to learn the trade of the company through which they served their contracts.)[70] These young players would play the roles of women just as Flute does in the mechanicals' production of *Pyramus and Thisbe*.

In *A Midsummer Night's Dream*, the material connection between livery company and playing company are explicit. When the artisans gather, Peter Quince asks, "Is all our company here?"[71] Given that this group of men is also a collection of laborers, the term "company" thickens their relation beyond that of playing: here is a bachelor company as a playing company. The language used by these men also registers their company affiliations even as it fine tunes the joke. They continually refer to each other as "masters," a designation denoting their freedom of their company, however much they fail to master their stagecraft. Upon hearing the name of the play, Bottom tells his compatriots, "Masters, spread yourselves" (1.2.15), that they might receive their roles from Quince, and when Quince distributes these roles, he repeats the title: "But, masters, here are your parts" (ll.91–92). Bottom and Quince repeat these terms when they rehearse the play as well.

What is notable about Bottom and Quince's use of "master" is its difference from its uses in the rest of the play. Bottom and Quince (and later Snug) use it to refer to their equals, the other members of their company. When it appears elsewhere in the play, it signifies hierarchical relations. Early in the comedy, Theseus uses the term to explain to Hermia the consequences of her renunciation of Demetrius. She must subordinate herself either to the law, the penalty of which is death, or to chastity. If Hermia chooses the latter, Theseus expounds, she joins those "Thrice blessed . . . that master so their blood / To undergo such maiden pilgrimage" (1.1.74–75). To be a master in this context is to control one's desires. Later in the play, Puck uses the term to refer to Oberon; mistaking Lysander for Demetrius in the Athenian wood, Puck soliloquizes, "This is he, my master said, / Despised the Athenian maid" (2.2.71–72). For those associated with the elite—fairy or human—mastery is never a term to denote equity of rank. That the artisans use this term to refer to one another then not only suggests the egalitarian nature of their fraternity but also that, as laborers, they are also masters or freeman—that they are, in fact, unmarried journeymen as opposed to apprentices.

Shakespeare's artisans are a rather remarkable representation of journeymen in an egalitarian community of bachelors. While they hope to be "made men" through their playing for Duke Theseus (4.2.18), and thus amelioriate their economic precarity, they are not represented as indentured workers to a household. Rather, they are believed to hold relative independence; "Have you sent to Bottom's house?" Peter Quince asks Starveling (ll.1–2), a question that, if nothing else, suggests Bottom rents or even owns a residence.[72] Otherwise ensconced in the world of mythological Athens, these journeymen seem insulated from the practicalities of early modern labor. It is a stark contrast from other early modern representations of journeymen. Most early modern drama represents journeymen in strict relation to their status as subordinate workers of a household. Their position as single men, while represented, does not as readily supplement the marriage plots of city comedy. For example, in both *The Shoemaker's Holiday* (1599) and *1 Honest Whore* (1604), Thomas Dekker represents journeymen overseeing apprentices and extending or actualizing the authority of their masters. Despite often being associated with apprentices, *The Shoemaker's Holiday* focuses heavily on journeymen and their work. It not only depicts Eyre's London shop as a business maintained by a fraternity of journeymen—here, the foreman Hodge, Firk, Ralph, and eventually Lacy disguised as the German shoemaker Hans—but also accentuates the singleness of both Hodge and the "fine firking journeyman" Firk by contrasting their merry lives to the hardships that befall the newly married, but conscripted, journeyman Ralph Damport.[73] As his name insinuates, Firk—with a homophonic pun on "fuck"—embodies the vigorous, loyal journeyman whose status as a single wage-laborer indicates a raucous sexual energy not usually associated with married householders.[74] Though not as explicitly, the sexual proclivities of journeymen are similarly mobilized in *1 Honest Whore*, which Dekker wrote with Thomas Middleton. Donning the livery gown of his master Candido at the wishes of Viola, Candido's wife, the journeyman George attempts to make his infamously patient master "horne mad."[75] George's status as a bachelor is never explicitly commented upon because it never needs to be; Viola treats the two as coterminous when she hopes to exploit a presupposition that his status as a single journeyman provides him the proximity and means to act upon a desire to replace his master as Viola's lover and business partner.

Libidinous journeymen are not confined to city comedy, however. Even in the pages of conduct literature, a genre that presumably addresses single men of all kinds, journeymen are sometimes represented as a significant if not primary audience. For Alexandar Niccholes, author of *A Discourse of Marriage and Wiving* (1615) bachelors are journeymen. The title of the prefatory poem to the marriage treatise specifies its audience as "the Youth and Batchelary of England, hote blouds at high Revels."[76] While the title makes plain that the treatise's intended audience is "a body of unmarried men," the poem's text is more specific about what kinds of men constitute this body.[77] These are not just any unmarried men; Niccholes imagines incipient journeymen. They are laborers at a vocational threshold first and foremost, unmarried men second. Niccholes writes:

Therefore to you, whose weary bonds yet keepe,
Severing the Armes wherein you long to sleepe;
That have before-hand, many a tedious howre,

Wisht that approaching minute in your powre,
Which when arriv'd, most slowly brought to passe,
Cancels but Parchment to inroule in Brasse;
What not so short a terme of years shalle end.[78]

These opening lines recapitulate the ideal trajectory of the young craftsman. He moves from one type of institutional restraint, apprenticeship, to another, marriage. Niccholes emphasizes the young laborer's timebound body. The terms of his service are full of "many a tedious howre," which makes him attentive to the "approaching minute." But even as the poem gestures toward approaching freedom, it also undermines that freedom by transferring the terms of service to marriage: that minute "cancels but parchment to inroule in Brasse." The single man transfers his contract of service for another, far more permanent one. Indeed, the terms of service now appear stricter. Unlike his timebound contract, no "short a terme of years shalle end" the marriage. Like those unmarried men in *The Statute of Artificers*, the audience that Niccholes addresses is composed of a set of bachelors whose single life is mutually constituted by vocation and marital status.

Niccholes has a reason for making the transition to marriage a matter of tedious timekeeping. He believes these single men are still in need of instruction: "lest your to forward hast should stray / Here is beforehand chalked out a way" he states.[79] The lines intimate a larger patriarchal concern over the transitional moment between apprenticeship and householding, childhood and adulthood.[80] Focusing on how marriage made public a man's credit network, Jennifer Panek has argued that this concern is a sustained topos of early modern prodigal husband plays. Because "the gendered nature of early modern English credit relations meant that a man's sexual, economic, domestic, kinship, and friendship ties became, upon marriage, both disconcertingly intertwined and a matter of public interest," Panek contends, prodigal husband plays often depict the anxieties of newly married men thrust into public view.[81] However, Niccholes poem suggests that this multitude of relations was of public interest at the threshold before marriage as much as it was at the moment after it. For Niccholes, the very institutional constraints meant to bridle premarital excess come to provide opportunities for young men to practice living as single men and not as husbands:

But you whose lustes this limit shall not tye,
For more inlargement of variety,
That will not any your owne proper call,

The better interressed to commerse with all.
As when your Lord and Lady downe are laid,
Behind the dore to woe the Chamber-maid:
Or amongst neighbors, where you lead your lives,
To be the more familiar with their wives,
Or any place where ere you do espye,
A pretty morsell pleasing to your eye,
To seize it more suspectlesse, being knowne
Then hee that hath at home a wife of's owne.
Well take that blessing, but withal this curse,
To walke on weake legges with an empty purse.[82]

The printed marginalia next to this passage indicates that Niccholes differentiates these single men from the ones he spoke to previously; this final section of the poem is addressed "To those that forebeare marriage for more liberty of sin." Like those journeymen with the freedom of their company, these single men possess a "liberty" of lingering in between estates to practice a form of manhood more antagonistic than complementary to patriarchal householding. Like *Much Ado*'s Boracchio, whose staged encounter with the chambermaid Margaret is used by Don John to indict Hero as unfaithful, such single men use their subordinate position to license their "variety."[83] At Borachio's moment of deception in *Much Ado*, Shakespeare imagines a similar "batchlery" as Niccholes does. When Borachio confesses to Conrad, he identifies his likeness to those "hot-bloods between fourteen and five-and-thirty" (3.3.128), imagining a community of men who, like Niccholes's more specific youths, use their status as "knowne" servants to access and to proposition any number of women within the household.[84] In *Much Ado*, it is precisely this public knowledge about such bachelors—and the women they woo—that Claudio and Don Pedro draw upon to falsely accuse Hero.

While the tropes Niccholes uses to sexualize these bachelors are common enough—these journeymen are "bettered interressed to commerse" and they are left with an "empty purse"—their proximity to "batchelary" here renders legible the material conditions of their gender construction. The bachelor's sexuality proceed from his economic status; the amassing of wages is integral to having enough capital to establish a household. That "empty purse" is both his treasury and his testicles; he is spent. But perhaps more significant is the way the final lines of this prefatory poem gesture to the problems of men too readily embracing a social or gender role enabled by a single life. As a denomination of a community, "batchlery" uneasily aggregates a group of social subordinates who are also practicing libertines. Such men could be youthful laborers of restrained passions or, just as easily, of unbridled lasciviousness. As late apprentices coming out of an institutionally mandated single life, such men might just be imagining the benefits of a journeyman's bachelorhood.

Niccholes presumes a "batchelary" whose private indiscretions are built into their economic status, and like Niccholes, early modern balladeers also accounted for the economic realities of journeywork when they represented bachelors. Broadside ballads demonstrate that general appeals to an audience of bachelors often encoded institutional paradigms in order to imagine what it meant to "live a bachelor" in Shakespeare's London.[85] Despite the fact that ballads were consumed across all ranks of early modern society, they were associated with lower order laborers. When Bottom—the most recognizable journeyman bachelor in Shakespeare's canon—awakens from his dream as an ass, he struggles to articulate his experience. "Methought I was—there is no man can tell what," he mutters in disbelief; "Methought I was—and methought I had—but man is a patched fool if he will offer to say what methought I had" (4.1.206–9). Yet Bottom has a solution to his problem of discernment, one that promises extended rehearsals of interpretation. He tells himself (and the audience), "I will get Peter Quince to write a ballad of this dream: it shall be called 'Bottom's Dream,' because it hath no bottom; and I will sing it in the latter end of a play, before the Duke." (ll.212–16). Not only is Shakespeare aligning ballads as products for and of London's laboring ranks, but he is also advertising the sale of such a ballad in the playhouse, one perhaps sung by the company of players once Robin Goodfellow—that other servant bachelor of the play—implores, "Give me your hands, if we be friends, / And Robin shall restore amends" (5.1.423–24). Might Bottom sing his ballad thereafter in a performance the play cannot record? Both Bottom and Benedick understand ballads as complementary with playmaking and playwatching even as they recognize they "have no bottom," that their circulation is not so easily contained inside set times or places.

Bachelors do appear in early modern ballads, and often, the bachelors in these ballads recontextualize the meanings of their bachelorhood as liberating, single life. Read within and against the context of livery company institutional hierarchies and their social round, these texts not only "shew the Complexion of the times," as early modern jurist John Selden said of such literature, but they also do significant ideological work, capitalizing upon the material constraints familiar to journeymen to shift available discourses about manhood, principally fiscal and misogynistic ones.[86] In so doing, they reinterpret the social limitations resonant with a journeyman's vocational station and marital status, and in turn they imagine a community of bachelors that is not composed solely of such laborers. In other words, these ballads enlarge London's bachelor community in a manner that blurs distinctions between ranks and orders separating journeymen from gentlemen, the laborer from the lawyer. It is this kind of expansive, plural, if also entirely fantastical, bachelor community within which Benedick imagines himself living.

One ballad that epitomizes this expansive reconstitution of the bachelor is "The Batchelors Feast," and it seems like one Benedick—whom Beatrice mocks as "a very valiant trencherman" with "an excellent stomach" (1.1.48–49)—might have in mind when he imagines living a bachelor. Organized around a bibliophagic trope, the title puns on the formal and informal conviviality institutionalized in bachelor companies. The bachelor's feast variously constitutes his conduct, the misogamist representation of husbands and family, as well as the ballad itself that bachelors buy and read to imagine their community. In the ballad, the feast signifies the bachelor's social and economic freedom born from group affiliation. As the song reconstitutes the bonds of service into an imagined autonomy, its bachelor brags,

> No Cradle have wee to rocke,
> nor Children that doe cry,
> No land-Lords rent to pay,
> no Nurses to supply:
> No Wife to scould and brawle,
> now wee still keep good company
> With them that take delight,
> to live at liberty.[87]

That "liberty" can point to the journeyman's civic relationship to the company and the city as well as a general sense of possibility. The ballad translates this liberty to civic rights as a liberty from marital restraints. With "No land-Lords rent to pay"—because he likely lives under the roof of a householder—this bachelor enjoys the benefits of shelter without the responsibility of paying for it. As the ballad continues, this liberty is actualized by public performance and communal living:

> We Batchelors can flaunt,
> in Country and in Towne,
> And in good company,
> may merely spend a crowne.[88]

As the ballad portrays the conviviality that sustains these single men, it translates individual identity through fraternity. Although the original speaker of this ballad, a husband, "heard *a Batchelor* / within an Harbour sing," (emphasis added), this overheard bachelor reconstitutes his solitariness as a communal condition; the voice overheard is a decidedly plural "we." Indeed, that collective identity has already been intimated in the ballad's title: "The Batchelor's Feast" can also be read as "The Batchelors' Feast," or the more active "The Batchelors Feast." This ballad also suggests that this collectivity has positive economic benefit. The bachelors' "good company" turns camaraderie into cash savings, and that company itself can be read in institutional terms. The economic restraints imposed upon journeymen as a class of workers is here translated as fostering a frugality born of membership within a company of bachelors.

According to "The Batchelors Feast," to "live a bachelor" is to live a communal life. It is also to live as a consumer. In this respect, such English broadside ballads promote a bachelorhood that accords with those social identities that Merry Wiesner argues the early modern German journeymen fashioned for themselves. As Wiesner observes, Germanic journeymen rejected the patriarchal ideals of domestic authority, and instead favored an identity predicated on an homosocial community in which "transience, prodigality, physical bravery, and comradeliness made one a true man."[89] The English broadside ballads reflect a similar bachelor ethic. The primary object of consumption in the ballad (besides its rhetoric) is apparel, and in this regard the ballad has much in common with other ballads about bachelors. In "The Lamentation of a new married man," for instance, a bachelor is what he wears. A husband grieves,

> You Batchelors that brave it
> So gallant in the street,
> With Muske and with Rose-water,
> Smelling all so sweet:
> With Shooes of Spanish leather,
> So featly to your feete,
> Behold me a married yong man.[90]

Notable here is the social power the young husband attributes to the bachelors, and notable too is their plurality. He does not speak to one man but many whose collective sartorial choices enable and naturalizes their unpatriarchal manhood. The bachelors "brave it" insofar as their fashion challenges normative displays of masculine restraint, and the leather is "featly," a word that denotatively suggests propriety—"fitly, properly," but also, in its ho-mophony with "feete," naturalizes the bachelor's sartorial accouterment.[91] The clothes make the man, but these single men make of the clothes a style, they fit so well. This performance exemplifies how, as Amanda Bailey argues, "a certain group of men used clothes to make something out of what had been made of them" even as their braving tropes the pageant processions of the Lord Mayor Shows that made bachelors visible in London as sartorially marked members of their respective companies.[92]

Bachelors are not reducible to journeymen in every such ballad, of course. Imagined communities of bachelors are expansive and not homogeneous. In "The Lamentation," for instance, the economic divide between bachelor and householder similarly becomes a way to reinterpret individual liberty, but it is everywhere inflected with the social scene of London's West End. The husband bemoans how he must attend to his wife, providing fare and fashion to her, fetching "Cheries, / And dainty Kather'n Peares" as well as "a new Gowne" with "a dainty fine Rebato."[93] It is not clear that this husband is a householder, though his wife's response to his complaint tell us she "hath won [him] credit," that social currency Craig Muldrew argues mediated economic and social relations for many early modern men, householders especially.[94] The bachelors, on the other hand, are notable because they seem to embody the husband's past economic freedom, when he "knew no cause of strife" because he "lived single."[95] According to the husband, these men are not entirely integrated into credit networks like he must be. The divide between bachelor and husband is the difference between cash and credit here; one has a payment on hand and the other can only promise to pay. In this ballad, marital status is tied to different modes of economic behavior. What the bachelor consumes and how he consumes it signify not just culturally but economically. By squarely positioning the bachelor within a market where one might buy or borrow, this ballad revises the terms through which the bachelor engages the husband and householder. Bachelorhood comes to signify economic agency and not subordinated standing because the single life is a life imagined free of credit obligations. Here, the bachelor, not husband, has purchasing power.

In many of these ballads, bachelors buy like the wives that husbands bemoan. As the "Collegiates" of Jonson's *Epicene* (1609) emblematize, early modern sexist stereotypes caricatured women and wives as consumers par excellence. There is thus an implicit paradox in these ballads. On the one hand, they depend upon a broadly held misogyny that equated a wife's sexuality with a voracious appetite, yet on the other hand, these ballads depict the bachelor as a man receptive to the very consumer practices relegated to new wives. To effectively translate such consumption into a masculine and not feminine behavior, these ballads displace and redirect misogyny toward husbands.[96] In the ballad "The Batchelor's Delight," puns transmute scrotal containment into uterine incontinence: the husband's pockets "bleed" and his purses are "always weeping." The husband becomes, to repurpose Gail Kern Paster's terminology, the leaky vessel "known by [his] loss of corporeal being—loss of content, form, and integral identity."[97] Because his wife consumes, the husband menstruates; while the bachelor buys, the husband bleeds. In such ballads, manhood has less to do with the quantity of financial resources than it does with one's control over them. Even if they in reality have little money, bachelors delight in buying because they never fret over what a wife has bought.

## MUCH ADO ABOUT BACHELORS

One can only postulate that Shakespeare had ballads like these in mind when he wrote *Much Ado*. I bring them into conversation with the comedy not to suggest that the play is about journeymen in some fundamental sense. It is clearly not. Rather, I want to suggest that Shakespeare appropriates the culture practices of such bachelor communities even as he excises their direct representation from the aristocratic world of Messina. Throughout *Much Ado*, the single life is imagined as predicated on communal affiliation structured by consumer practices. However much Beatrice mocks Benedick for his bachelorhood early in the comedy, she nonetheless entertains the emancipatory power such a life might entail. Like Benedick, she does so by imagining the single life as a communal, fraternal one. After her uncle Leonato, Hero's father, chides her for remaining unmarried, she claims her own place within a community of bachelors; she tells Leonato that upon her death St. Peter will direct her to "where the bachelors sit, and there live we as merry as the day is long" (2.1.42). Beatrice makes this assertion after Leonato insists, "you may light upon a husband that hath no beard" (lll.31). Observing "he that hath a beard is more than a youth, and he that hath no beard is less than a man," Beatrice argues for her single life because "he that is more than a youth is not for me; and he that is less than a man, I am not for him" (ll.34–39). The quip riffs on Diogenes's adage that marriage comes too early for young men and too late for old men that Joseph Swetnam turns to misogynistic ends in his *Arraignment*. Beatrice, however, goes on to allude to another maxim, concluding "Therefore I will even take sixpence in earnest of the bearherd and lead his apes in hell" (l.40). Forfeiting her apes to Satan, she then ascends to heaven, which she imagines not as a Maiden Lane but a Bachelor's Court.

The various jokes about feasting and fashioning that animate much of the comedy in *Much Ado About Nothing* can be understood as gesturing to the wider cultural associations of the single life of the bachelor with confraternity, feasting, and conspicuous consumption. For example, aligning Benedick's fraternal choices with his sartorial ones, Beatrice quips, "He hath every month a new sworn brother" because "he wears his faith but as the fashion of his hat: it ever changes with the next block" (1.1.67–68, 70–73). Beatrice's criticism emphasizes how closely the sartoriality of men signified their bachelorhood, and thus it is not surprising that Benedick, the comedy's self-proclaimed bachelor, uses sartorial tropes to negotiate the bonds between his fellow unmarried men, Don Pedro and Claudio. After Don Pedro and Claudio observe how a married Benedick would provide fodder for the cuckold jokes of bachelors, Benedick gains the rhetorical upper hand by likening their wit to a shoddy garment, chastising them: "Nay, mock not, mock not. The body of your discourse is sometimes guarded with fragments, and the guards are but slightly basted on neither. Ere you flout old ends any further, examine your conscience" (1.1.266–69). Bendick's point is that he is the better bachelor because his words flaunt an original style. But his tropes also evidence his communal affiliations. As Thomas Becon emphasizes in his preface to Heinrich Bullinger's *The golden boke of Christen Matrimonye* (1543), unmarried men, who "spend in wanton and ryottous companye" are known by "theyr vayne jagged and garded apparell."[98] As in ballads, there is an economy at work behind these sartorial decisions; Becon situates this argument regarding the bachelor's apparel in a wider conversation about those who object to marriage because of its financial responsibilities; he worries about financially precarious bachelors remaining bachelors.[99] Decrying the false accusations of Don Pedro and Claudio, Antonio, Beatrice's father, likewise focuses on sartorial display to cast the manhood of Don Pedro and Claudio as regression from adulthood. He calls both of them, "Scambling, outfacing, fashion-monging boys, / That lie, and cog, and flout, deprave and slander, / Go anticly and show outward hideousness" (5.1.94–96). These braving bachelors flaunt something like a toxic masculinity.

Alongside sartorial tropes, Shakespeare uses bibliophagic tropes to demarcate bachelor communities in *Much Ado*. These tropes echo those found in ballads on two counts: they evince the convivial practices associated with bachelors, and they also emphasize how a particular misogamistic discourse binds bachelor communities and facilitates the imagining of them. Bachelors are what they eat. In *Much Ado*, these bibliophagic tropes occur at significant conversion moments in the comedy's marriage plots when bachelors rescind their oaths to live a single life. When Claudio betrays his bachelor companion Benedick by falling in love with Hero, Benedick not only wonders if he will see "a bachelor of threescore again" (1.1.188), he also imagines Claudio's newfound love language as a veritable feast of words.[100] Benedick marvels that while once Claudio "was wont to speak plain and to the purpose, like an honest man and a soldier," he has now, "turned orthography" (2.3.18–21). Claudio's speech becomes Benedick's food; his "words are a very fantastical banquet—just so many strange dishes" (2.3.18–21). The trope resonates not only with the ballad "The Batchelor's Feast," but also that of a popular prose work, *The Bachelor's Banquet* (1603). Originally attributed to Thomas Dekker, but now generally attributed to unknown author, it is a translation of a fifteenth-century French original, *Les Quinze Joies de Mariage* (late fourteenth–early fifteenth century), and it went through five to six reprints throughout the seventeenth century.[101] *The Bachelor's Banquet*, the title page indicates, is "A banquet for bachelors: wherein is prepared sundry dainty dishes to furnish their table, curiously dressed and seriously served in."[102] Those dishes are, in fact, tales about the humors of wives, "their quickness of wits and unsearchable deceits," and many of the tales, like the first one about "The humor of a young wife new married," illustrate the plight of householders, a subject in which unmarried journeymen would relish. Such revisions evidence the degree to which there existed a collection of men that imagined themselves as fashionable, feasting bachelors even if they were in reality a householders' subordinate journeymen. In a manner consonant with the imagined audiences of the ballad "The Batchelors Feast" and the prose work *The Bachelor's Banquet*, Benedick insults Claudio to mark Claudio's betrayal of an imagined bachelor community and to indicate his own place within it.

*Much Ado* also deploys bibliophagic tropes to represent Benedick's conversion, and Claudio's reversion, as a matter of appetite. After overhearing Don Pedro, Claudio, and Leonato speak about Beatrice's infatuation with him, Benedick conceives of his conversion as a change of appetite as well as a sign of maturation, concluding, "A man loves the meat in his youth that he cannot endure in his age" (2.3.229–31), a commonplace assertion found in contemporary recipe and medical books.[103] Later in the play, Benedick and Beatrice revise earlier tropes of feasting and fashioning, marking a transition from one form of manhood to another. When Benedick swears his devotion to Beatrice, she wonders, "Will you not eat your word?" Benedick responds, "With no sauce that can be devised to it" (4.1.277–78). Not only will he not wear his loyalty like he does his hat, but he will also no longer eat the bachelor's dish. The very texts, like ballads, that sustained the bachelor life he imagined living, no longer nourish him.

Whereas Benedick's change of appetite marks his conversion from the single life, Claudio's turning to the table confirms his newfound devotion to it. Rejecting Hero at the altar, Claudio acts the bachelor more forthrightly than Benedick did, and the drama marks his conversion by his turning to the feast. When Benedick challenges Claudio to a duel to defend Hero, both Claudio and Don Pedro see this challenge as an opportunity to feed their wits. They render Benedick's confrontation as an invitation to a banquet, thus posing one form of manhood against another.[104] Witness Claudio's transmutation of Benedick's challenge into a more digestible dish:

> *Benedick*: You have killed a sweet lady, and her death shall fall heavy on you. Let me hear from you.
>
> *Claudio*: Well, I will meet you, so I may have good cheer.
>
> *Don Pedro*: What, a feast, a feast?
>
> *Claudio*: I' faith, I thank him, he hath bid me to a calf's head and a capon, the which if I do not carve most curiously, say my knife's naught. Shall I not find a woodcock too? (5.1.146–54)

Punning upon the homophony between "meet" and "meat," Don Pedro quickly renders Benedick's challenge into a bachelor's feast. Unable to acknowledge the legitimacy of Benedick's proposal, Claudio then encodes the honorific duel into symbols he can utilize. Fencing turns into feasting, and Benedick's duel becomes a dish "to carve most curiously." In Claudio's eyes, Benedick is both a foolish, if young, cuckold ("calf's head") and a castrated man ("capon"). In a move that inverts Benedick's own transaction of wit for the blade, Claudio now can only imagine mockery as the sign of his potency; if he cannot adequately make Benedick food for his thought, then his "knife's naught."

By the end of *Much Ado*, Benedick renounces his desire to live as a bachelor among bachelors. Instead of reading ballads, he writes love poems; his practice of a new lyric discourse reflects his transition from one kind of bachelor to another. But not all the comedy's bachelors are so easily recuperated by the play's generic prescriptions. At the comedy's final scene, Don Pedro, still unmarried, lingers at the margins. The great author of Benedick's marriage plot remains the play's most conspicuous bachelor. Benedick even chides him, "Get thee a wife, get thee a wife!" (5.4.120), a bit of dramatic irony given that earlier in the comedy Don Pedro proposed to Beatrice, who refused him (2.1.300–303). Appearing "sad" (5.4.120), Don Pedro resembles his melancholic, fugitive, bastard—and single—brother, Don John.

While the comedy converts most of its bachelors into husbands, it cannot do so for all of them. Rather than providing, as Jean Howard contends, "Benedick and Beatrice understandings of self and other that serve his own ends," the marriages that Don Pedro orchestrates only accentuate the ends he cannot achieve for himself.[105] Even his authority is qualified by his bachelorhood. The betrothed Benedick, not Don Pedro, gets the final words of the comedy. The final lines of the play are his: "Strike up, pipers!" (5.4.126). The bachelor's feast becomes a wedding party. Amidst that music, Don Pedro remains a single man without a bachelor community. Perhaps like the real journeymen watching the play, and some of the actors performing it, he will imagine a meaning for his single life that finds substance outside of the comedy, by other communities, in other locales, and in other texts.

# Chapter 3

## The Single Life of the True Gallant

Economic Men and Entrepreneurial Action in
*Epicene* and *Wit at Severall Weapons*

Single men might resist patriarchal ideals of manhood by testifying to a chastity not easily interpretable or amenable to procreative ideals,
or they might reimagine their bachelorhood through confraternity and consumerism. But the single life might also rescript patriarchal privileges while
rejecting obligations to householding and patrilineality. Single men could
be imagined as revising the tenets of patriarchy without themselves taking
up the call to be patriarchs. Francis Bacon makes just this sort of case. Revising and expanding his *Essayes* of 1597, Bacon published a new edition
in 1612. Among the new essays, Bacon includes, "Of Marriage and Single
Life." It opens with an affirmation of the social and economic merits of living as a single man. "Hee that hath wife and children, hath giuen hostages
to fortune," Bacon begins, "For they are impediments to great enterprises,
either of vertue or mischief. Certainly the best works, and of greatest merit
for the publike, haue proceeded from the vnmarried, or childlesse men,
which haue sought eternity in memory, and not in posterity; and which
both in affection and means, haue married and endowed the publike."[1]
Unlike Shakespeare's visions of memorialization that run through the early
sonnets to the single man, desired increase here is not a matter of posterity
but of prosperity. One's legacy depends not on a tender heir but instead on
a public that will bear one's memory.

Even if the tenets of Bacon's veneration of the single life—that a wife and
children are impediments to a man's ambition—suffused early modern English culture, his conclusion that the single life was more socially beneficial
than marriage was relatively novel. Marriage remained a central institution

for obtaining manhood, in no small part because it served as a primary institution through which a man exercised social mastery as husband and father.[2] Bacon's essay offers up a type of manhood that is at once unpatriarchal but still privileged. Rejecting domestic relations for the public good, his single man of "great enterprises" translates one early modern meaning of economy, that is, "household management," for another, namely, the relations of human society as a whole, even as it anticipates a much later, and modern, definitions of economy as a matter of markets, commerce, and exchange.[3] Somewhere between the late medieval "entreprenour" ("a person who undertakes a venture or enterprise") and the modern "entrepreneur" ("a person who owns and manages a business, bearing the financial risks of the enterprise"), Bacon's single man stands above and apart from the society he endows, emerging as an individual whose private activity subsidizes the public good.[4]

Bacon's vision of the single life is unpatriarchal primarily because it challenges the political economies of primogeniture and patrilineage central to early modern England's patriarchal culture, especially as they organized the transference of capital and property among the socially elite. But that does not mean it is not an enticing one, and enticing to both early modern and modern audiences alike. This chapter considers how Bacon's vision of the single life underwrites a form of unpatriarchal manhood in Jacobean city comedies contemporaneous with its publication and how two of those comedies—Jonson's *Epicene* (1609) and Middleton and Rowley's *Wit at Severall Weapons* (ca 1613)—valorize the single life as socially restorative and economically efficacious. While these plays bear the marks of traditional city comedies, they also diverge from them in a significant way: both of their plots revolve around a gallant in pursuit of his inheritance who refuses marriage as a remedy to his financial plight. In most city comedies, the marriage plot either provides a gallant an estate in the form of a woman's dowry or widow's assets, or it functions as a kind of amelioration of social divisions that also proves the desert of the young man who seeks his patrimony from a reluctant, elitist elder. That is not what happens in these plays, however. *Epicene*'s Dauphine Eugenie and *Wit at Severall Weapons*'s Wittypate win their inheritance by proving they are wittier than their elders, not morally superior than them, and in doing so, they also demonstrate their autonomy from them (or anybody) by remaining single and not resorting to patriarchal marriage to secure their financial futures. Their plots do not make them husbands; instead, they reveal them to be entrepreneurs. In dramatizing the witty hijinks of their single gallants, Jonson's *Epicene* and Middleton and Rowley's *Wit at Severall Weapons* do something more than lay bare the economics of patriarchal patrilineal inheritance. They also champion a form of unpatriarchal manhood resistant to normative patriarchy but entranced by—and ensconced within—its privileges. The gallants of these comedies epitomize Bacon's ideal of the individual man, who, unencumbered by marriage and family life, might fully endow the public through his entrepreneurial spirit. They at once shore up patriarchal order while exempting themselves from the prerogatives of patrilineality.

The plays themselves are quite explicit about their vision of economic men. The patriarch of Middleton and Rowley's *Wit at Severall Weapons*, Sir Perfidious Oldcraft, baldly states this entrepreneurial ethos at the opening of the play; "Give me a man that lives by his wits," he propounds, "And never left a groat, there's the true gallant" (ll.63–64). And so begins the plot: to demonstrate he is worthy of the wealth that primogeniture promises, Wittypate must first prove that, like his father, he does not require it because he knows "how to match and make my market" (l.54).[5] If this ethos were not so central to an early modern city comedy, we might call it modern, or rather, we might call it modern because its alignment of wit with market optimization has been so central to modern fantasies of neoclassical and neoliberal capitalism. Aligning the single life of gallants with a faculty for entrepreneurial ingenuity, Jonson's *Epicene* and Middleton and Rowley's *Wit at Severall Weapons* champion a type of manhood that would become central to modern political economy: the rational, self-interested, market actor *homo economicus*. These plays perform the kind of economic thought that Bradley Ryner argues circulates through much of the drama of this period, but they also propound a vision of economic agency that would prove foundational for later neoclassical models.[6] Though often critiqued, the theoretical *homo economicus* has proven an intractable avatar for a variety of capitalist fantasies.[7] This figure of "economic man" emerged in economic discourse in the late nineteenth century, in critiques of John Stuart Mill's theory of political economy. In his "ethology" of *homo economicus*, Joseph Persky documents how early critics of Mill, like John Kells Ingram and John Neville Keynes, lambasted his supposed treatment of "imaginary men," and "an 'economic man,' whose activities are determined solely by the desire for wealth."[8] While these early critiques of *homo economicus* framed the desire for wealth as a kind of vice, later political economists transmuted it into a virtue. An eminently useful type, *homo economicus* came to be characterized through five central qualities: "individualism," "optimizing behavior," "full rationality," "universality," and "exogenous preferences."[9] The animating desire for wealth might be said to characterize much of Jacobean city comedy, but with plots evacuated of their marriage plot, and with their protagonists acquisitive desires valorized rather than deprecated, both *Epicene* and *Wit at Severall Weapons* elevate a durable ideal that economies organize themselves to benefit the single life of the true gallant and insist that the true gallant best organizes and optimizes markets to benefit the social order writ large. In these city comedies, the single life of the true gallant evinces the ways capitalist political imaginaries insist not only that the individual is the ideal, authentic economic actor but also that an economic actor is the ideal, authentic individual. They offer up a fantasy where market values enumerate social values.

While this chapter argues that the antecedent to the neoclassical ideal of *homo economicus* can be traced through the single life of the true gallant, it also contextualizes the utility of the gallant's single life within an early modern patriarchal economy of primogeniture and patrilineage, one in which questions of gentility were debated, negotiated, and refashioned. In what follows, I first situate the concerns over inheritance and desert that fundamentally drive the plots of these plays in a larger social context around the meanings of gentility among the landed gentry. I then demonstrate how the characterization of Dauphine Eugenie as a single gallant is central to his economic agency and how the property of his wit determines and secures his eventual wealth. Following this analysis of *Epicene*, I turn to Middleton and Rowley's *Wit at Severall Weapons*, the plot of which similarly instrumentalizes an exchange between wit and wealth but which also more explicitly elevates the aptitude of its central protagonist, Wittypate, as an entrepreneurial figure who facilitates the preservation of the gentry. Subordinating its marriage plot, the play dramatizes a shift away from the ideal of patrilineage to a market-measured form of merit typified by its true gallant.

## GENTILITY AND PATRILINEALITY IN UNGENTLE GENTLE LONDON

*Epicene* and *Wit at Severall Weapons* dramatize a very specific problem for a very specific type of person. Dauphine and Wittypate are gentlemen and heirs, a knight and a knight's son, respectively, who are threatened with the loss of their patrimony. Their loss of their means to wealth would leave them members of the gentry in title alone. As these plays engage with the question of where the value of social status might inhere—in wealth or in heritage—both plays can be understood as engaging a larger social concern over the migration of England's gentry into the country's urban center, a concern King James himself voiced in a series of proclamations urging the gentry to return to their country estates.[10] These concerns are also circulated in most seventeenth-century English city comedies where gallants and gulls intermix with artisans and merchants. Inasmuch as Dauphine and

Wittypate resemble the gallants of other city comedies, their plots (and the ways they come to engineer them) offer up an entirely different vision of economic agency, one that comes to affirm the benefit of patrilineal inheritance while also sidestepping the marital mechanisms that secure generational wealth in a patriarchal system. These gallants maintain their gentility not only by securing wealth but also by demonstrating they do not require patriarchal marriage and patrilineal systems—though the money is nice—to secure their economic futures.

The gentry symbolized the primary aspirational category for new wealth, and, accordingly, it was the social order around which political and economic subjectivity was theorized most heavily. As new, wealthy merchants moved into its ranks and longstanding families faced financial hardships, the gentry became the site over contestations over the meanings of gentility in the period.[11] It was beguilingly simple to be accounted a member of the gentry: you just needed "gentility." Yet by the seventeenth century, gentility itself had become a much-contested concept. Historically, gentility required lineage. Lineage, however, was not just a matter of blood, for the intelligibility of noble blood relied upon proof of land tenure over time. As Felicity Heal and Clive Holmes observe, this "conjunction of blood and tenure . . . defines and legitimises individual status."[12] Yet gentility also (or perhaps more rightly always) required wealth, and specifically "the acquisition and retention of landed wealth."[13] In this respect, wealth was the necessary, though not sufficient, condition of gentility. For those in the country, the historical territory of the gentleman, wealth could be taken for granted as a signifier of gentility insofar as it most readily materialized as lineage, the maintenance of land by blood relations over time. The risk of wealth's loss was thus often framed in terms of generational disturbances. A gentle family might become insolvent by not producing a male heir, or if it did produce a male heir, there was always the chance that son would squander his inheritance. But so long as wealth coincided with lineage, gentility might be theorized in terms of the latter instead of the former.

As London grew in population and local and global trade expanded, there were not only new opportunities for the gentry to increase and diversify their holdings and wealth; the means to wealth became available to more and different kinds of people, giving merchants and the middling sorts the means to purchase the traditional signs of gentility. These concerns were also intimately entangled within and conducive to early modern formations of race.[14] Kim F. Hall has demonstrated how increased global commerce in the Jacobean period was everywhere informed by a sense of "commercial interaction inevitably fostering social and sexual contact," and plays and masques focusing on whiteness, Blackness, and mixed marriages mobilize such concerns even as they reify an alignment of Englishness with whiteness.[15] The economic shift beginning in the Elizabethan era and continuing into the Jacobean period that Hall examines would lead Sir Thomas Smith in *De Republica Anglorum* to cite the primacy of wealth, and not land, in constituting the gentleman: "and to be shorte, who can live idly and without manuall labour, and will beare the port, charge and countenaunce of a gentleman, he shall be called master, for that is the title which men give to esquires and other gentlemen, and shall be taken for a gentleman."[16] But that did not mean that landholding was insignificant. While those in the gentry most likely remained the largest buyers of land, the newly wealthy professional ranks, merchants, and artisans were buying country estates, in part because estate ownership remained synonymous with gentility, permitting its resident to live a life of leisure while also providing opportunities to ingratiate into the county community through intermarriage.[17]

Writing in *De Republica Anglorum*, Smith was both observing this changing composition of the gentry as much as he was ratifying it. His eye on the commonwealth as a whole, he saw few ill effects for the nation so long as the gentry remained stable as a social order. The maintenance of the group took precedence over the attributes of any individual composing it. Smith was also a realist, recognizing the degree to which titles may be bought. The heralds of the college of arms were long believed to "give . . . for money, armes newly made and invented."[18] Under Stuart rule, titles themselves would only be further distributed; in desperate need of funds, the Crown sold them to the highest bidder with secondary interest in a family's ancestry.[19] But Smith's cold realism was not fully accepted even if the changes he cited were widely recognized. We only need look at Ben Jonson's earliest city comedy, *Every Man Out of His Humor* (1599), to see Smith's definition satirized. Sogliardo, a wealthy yeoman, comes to the city that he might be reputed gentle. Like Smith, he understands gentility as both acquisitive and performative. Speaking to his companion Carlo Buffone, Sogliardo proclaims, "I have land and money, my friends left me well, and I will be a gentleman whatsoever it cost me," and Carlo confirms the salience of this claim, calling it, "A most gentleman-like resolution."[20] The scene contains both a concession to the changing face of gentility that Smith recognizes while also annotating a resistance to it. Sogliardo and Carlo Buffone are fools, and by the end of the play, Jonson exposes them as pretenders. Though he may have land and wealth, Sogliardo bears the marks of labor. Malicente displays Sogliardo's hands at court, which are calloused from "holding the plough" (5.2.115). However monied and leisured he may become, this yeoman, it is intimated, cannot attain gentry status because the marks of his body betray his low birth.[21]

In *Every Man Out of His Humour*, Jonson premises his satire of aspirational wealth on the material effect London had on the intelligibility of gentility. Jonson knew that because gentility was historically tied to the acquisition and maintenance of land, London's urban spaces would radically alter the meanings of gentility, for the meanings of gentility were susceptible to geographical contingencies. As Jonson's contemporary John Selden wryly observes, place conditions the legibility of the gentleman's gentility: "What a Gentleman is, 'tis hard with us to define; in other Countries known by his Priviledges; in *Westminster-Hall* he is one that is reputed one; in the Court of Honour, he that hath Arms."[22] Selden here highlights what Michelle Dowd has defined as the "sociospatial" dimensions of lineage in the period, which, though it required temporal narratives for its legitimation, often required rhetorics of space for its social intelligibility.[23] Where one finds the gentleman determines those qualities deemed constitutive of his gentility. In *Every Man Out*, Sogliardo hopes to manipulate the geographical contingency of gentility; in the country his labor is evident, but in the city he might purchase gloves to hide his callouses. Unfortunately for Sogliardo, what works in Paul's Walk does not work at Court.

If Sogliardo goes to London to become a gentleman, he does so because London was quickly becoming the place where gentlemen were both made and unmade. When the play was first performed, landed gentlemen had already been spending more time away from their estates and in the city, with their visits largely seasonal and in accordance with the law terms.[24] The gentry's increased presence in the city further cultivated interest in its domestic and imported goods, and new trends in urban architecture even influenced the style of manorial houses in the counties.[25] The volatilities of London's economy, however, could also be felt more acutely the closer the gentry resided to London. The early modern complaint that the viability of the dynasty of a landed family was inversely correlated to their proximity to London seems to have been correct. There was indeed greater turnover of land in those counties closer to the capital.[26] For some, London's growth had real consequences for the early modern landed gentleman. In *Wit at Severall Weapons*, Middleton and Rowley typecast this fact of London's economy; two of the characters are called Sir and Lady Ruinous Gentry, characters whose wealth London has swallowed up. For all the opportunity London both symbolized and actualized for the gentry, it was nonetheless perceived as a threat to those born gentle.

This turnover among the ranks of the gentry came to intensify a long-standing question of what, exactly, constituted gentility. Even for those contemporaries who, like Smith, allowed for social mobility into the gentry, London's vast and varied communities of laborers—much like the yeoman Sogliardo—were imagined as an invasive threat to this social order. A concern about just this sort of impingement, mostly imagined, of artisans upon the gentry animates the rhetoric of the period's literature on gentility even as early as the mid-sixteenth century. In *The Institucion of a gentleman* (1555), for example, Humfrey Braham explains that the gentry have decayed because of aspirational artisans, "wherby such corruption of maners hath taken place, that almost the name of gentry is quenched, and handycraftemen haue obtayned the tytle of honour, though (in dede) of them selues they can chalenge no greater worthynes then the spade brought unto their late fathers."[27] Titles, Braham observes, can lie; gentility cannot fundamentally inhere in name alone. Braham thus sets out to define what constitutes gentility in the face of social change, so he creates a taxonomy that might parse it, defining the "gentle gentle," "ungentle gentle," and the "gentle ungentle."[28] The mobility of gentility across grammatical kind, from adjective to noun and back again, reflects the mutability of gentility as it was realized in early modern English society, as that which modifies, like Sogliardo's glove, and that which inheres, like his calloused hand. The "gentle gentle" bind virtue to lineage; as Braham explains, the "sorte of gentrye called Gentle Gentle be al those gentlemen which haue folowed the steppes and done the noble dedes of their fathers: who for theyr vertue as the firste obtayned the name of nobilitie, and nowe their posteritie in doyng lyke dede be lykewise called noble men."[29] The "gentle ungentle" are those men who degrade their noble blood by vicious deeds. Against such men, Braham introduces, as if to censure, the "ungentle gentle." Such a man is he who, "taking his beginninge of a poore kyndered, by his vertue, wyt, pollicie, industry knowledge in lawes, valliency in armes, or such like honest meanes becometh a welbeloued and high estemed manne, preferred then to great office, put in great charge and credit, euensomuch as he becommeth a post or stay in the communewelth, and so growing rich, doth thereby auance and set up the rest of his poore line or kindred."[30] Braham would understand both Morose of *Epicene* and Sir Perfidicous of *Wit as Severall Weapons* as "ungentle gentle" figures. For Braham, the "ungentle gentle" is not himself a gentleman; rather, he secures gentility for future generations. As Braham observes, "the children of such one commonly called gentlemen, of which sorte of gentlemen we haue nowe in Inglande very many, whereby it should appeare that vertue florisheth among us."[31]

Braham explains the "ungentle gentle" are commonly called "upstarts." Shakespeare would eventually count himself, and even be disparaged as, one such gentleman. Yet there were those who would disagree with this assessment, and take a far harder line on the maintenance of gentility against those deemed outsiders. Responding in part to Smith's *De Republica Anglorum*, John Ferne disdains such upstarts in his *The Blazon of Gentrie* (1586). Ferne directs his invective against "all mechanical artisans, and churles broode."[32] Ferne's conservative assessment is reactionary. Inasmuch as Ferne insists upon a hard line between the gentry and the artisanal ranks, he implicitly acknowledges the complexity and contingency of patrilineage. The second half of *The Blazon* aims to reconstruct the "vncertaine lynes or genealogies of *Lacies*, sometimes Earles of *Lyncolne*."[33] While Ferne insists upon a gentry impregnable from lower orders, his *The Blazon of Gentry* is also a testament, like so many other genealogical treatises, to "the contingencies that both troubled and helped define English inheritance practices, particularly in the late sixteenth and early seventeenth centuries when the system of patrilineage was especially fluid and subject to alteration."[34] In attempting to account for such contingencies, Ferne argues that gentility is a matter of heritability, and as such, marriage, properly managed, both secures and protects it.

Early modern city comedies often engage the dichotomies and dynamics of Braham's early tract and Ferne's later one, mapping and dramatizing the shifting nature of gentility across and between social orders. While their marriage plots circulate around questions of love and desire, they also often raise the question of social status explicitly, such that concerns over status drive the marriage plots of these comedies. Dekker's *The Shoemaker's Holiday* (1599), for example, begins with Sir Hugh Lacy and Sir Roger Oatley discussing the discrepancy of social ranks that the marriage of Rowland and Rose would amelioriate or exacerabte, and ends with the play ultimately affirming their union. The plot both confirms and confronts the hard divide between gentle and ungentle status that Ferne presents in his *The Blazon of Gentrie*; Lacy's pursuit of Rose is one Ferne views as anathema to gentility. Distinguishing between the difference between liberty and service as it pertains to the "noble" and the "base," and promulgating an early modern form of eugenics, Ferne argues if a nobleman were to marry his son "vnto the daughter of any of the foresaid persons . . . be they yeomen, marchants, burgesses, or bondmen, & although the woman be formed of a most excellent proportion of body, her yeeres tender, her beauty fresh, her portion rich, and her heritage very ample, yet for all this, heere is a disparagment, and it is the vnequall coupling in yoke of the cleane Oxe, and the vncleane Asse."[35] Ferne sounds like Lacy's father, and if Dekker is responding to

Ferne—Rowland Lacy bears the namesake of the family of Ferne's genealogy, and similarly, Lacy is also a gentleman of Lincoln—his response is not entirely dismissive of Ferne's central argument. His ending entertains fantasies of upward mobility while simultaneously insulating the gentry from the intrusion of upstart "blood." Honoring the request by the patriarchs Lacy and Oatley to annul the marriage, the king does so only to remarry them and knight them.

In both *The Shoemaker's Holiday* and *The Blazon of Gentry*, marriage function as the social institution through which those in the gentry maintain or corrupt their gentility. While it is true that for the gentry, "marriage . . . was essentially an arrangement to ensure the succession to property, and in return for the settlement of the husband's family estate upon the children which it was hoped would be born," for both Dekker and Ferne marriage comes to ratify the inherent gentleness of those who derive from, or seek to rise into, the upper ranks of the social order.[36] Later city comedies, however, become more explicit about the ways marriage could secure the wealth and property of a dissolute heir and ultimately reinstate both the wealth and gentility squandered in the city. John Fletcher's *Wit Without Money* (1614), for example, dramatizes a rather typical Jacobean concern over a young gentleman forsaking his estate for the commercial pleasures of London. Vallentine, a gentleman heir and the play's protagonist, squanders his patrimony, dismissing both marriage and his obligations to the patrilineal economy of the gentry. The degradation and neglect of his estate is a primary concern among the characters of the play. Lance, one of his yeoman, worries,

> must wee turne Tennants now,
> After we have lived under the race of Gentry,
> And maintaind good yeomantry, to some of the City,
> To a great shoulder of Mutton, and a Custard,
> And have our state turned into Cabbidge Gardens,
> Must it be so?[37]

Vallentine's prodigality violates, in Lance's estimation, a social contract between those of the upper and lower ranks, and even risks a dissolution of social rank that evinces a loss of racialized superiority because of its proximity to the "race of Gentry."[38] Lance goes on to reprimand Vallentine:

> You ought to maintaine us, wee have maintained
> You, and when you slept provided for you;

Who bought the silke you weare? I think our labours;
Reckon, youle find it so: who found your horses
Perpetuall pots of ale, maintain'd your Tavernes,
And who extold you in the halfe crowne boxes,
Where you might sit and muster all the beauties? (B2v)

Vallentine explicitly rejects these appeals and embraces a single life of homosocial fraternity like that examined in the previous chapter. Yet the vehe-
mence by which Vallentine embraces his single life largely comes to signify
the viciousness of his lifestyle. His brother, Francisco, assures us that despite
Vallentine's behavior demonstrating the contrary, Vallentine is "Fraughted
as deepe with noble and brave parts, / The issues of a noble and manly spirits / As any he alive" (1.2.60–62).

The rest of the play will dramatize the righting of the social order
through a marriage plot that will remedy Vallentine's material losses and
validate his brother's assurances about his inherent virtue. Vallentine's salva-
tion will come through marriage to Lady Hartwell, a wealthy widow. In this
case, the marriage plot not only secures for Vallentine new wealth, it also, as
Jennifer Panek argues, secures his manhood. As Panek explains, "the meaning of being a 'man,'" defined at the beginning of the play in terms of wit,
knowledge, reciprocal male friendships and a bachelor's freedom, shifts until it is based entirely on sexual virility."[39] By the end of the play, Vallentine
claims Hartwell's wealth to reconstitute his squandered gentility, and the
complaints of Lance are rectified as her wealth enables the recuperation of
his lands.[40] Through his marriage to a wealthy widow, the prodigal gallant
returns to the ranks of the landed gentry as patriarch.

While *Epicene* and *Wit at Severall Weapons* similarly focus upon gallants
faced with insolvency, marriage does not serve the same function in their
plots. In fact, it does not even occur to the gallants of these plays that they
should marry, and in *Epicene*, marriage is not a benefit but a penalty Morose would use to "thrust" Dauphine "out of [his] blood like a stranger"
(2.5.103). The gentility of Dauphine and Wittypate is not secured or
proven by their becoming patriarchs against the wishes of their elders or
by demonstrating their manhood by mastering a lusty widow. They instead
prove themselves worthy of their patrimony by simply being smarter than
everyone around them. Though both *Epicene* and *Wit at Severall Weapons*, like many other city comedies, depict a vibrant and bustling mercantile London, their central plots are fundamentally about this economy of
patrilineal inheritance and the ever-present concern over the disruption of
generational wealth.[41] The central tension of their plots positions a young

heir against an old patriarch modeled after the senex of Roman new comedy. Both Morose of *Epicene* and Sir Perfidious Oldcraft of *Wit at Severall Weapons* at once embody a traditional patriarchal order defined by patrilineal inheritance and a new mercantile gentry for whom wealth is less a matter of inheritance than it is an effect of savvy investments or financial schemes that can play out in a variety of local and global markets. Both plays thus fundamentally affirm the value of patrilineality while they also realign the mechanisms by which inheritance is secured. No longer is kinship or "blood" the guarantor of gentility. What is instead demonstrative of it is another faculty, one no less inherent, what the plays call "wit."

## ECONOMIC MAN IN *EPICENE*

*Epicene* is a play about the single life of gallant in want of wealth, who, faced with the prospect of disinheritance, must maneuver around and through the legal and economic vagaries of a patrilineal economy. Unlike other city comedies that often portray the depletion of a gallant's funds through his unmitigated consumerism, *Epicene* instead foregrounds the customs of primogeniture and inheritance as impediments to the gallant's free enterprise. But if, as John Dryden recognized in the late seventeenth century, "The action of the play is entirely one, the aim or end of which the settling Morose's estate on Dauphine," the play achieves these ends through a series of scenes that establish the reciprocal relationship between wit and wealth that negotiate the early modern debate about the meanings of gentility for an increasingly urban gentry.[42] As the play moves to its conclusion, Dauphine's wit functions as the means by which wealth might always be secured, and in this way, it comes to resignify his gentility: his having wit evidences his intrinsic value, his being worthy of both his title and inheritance.

By situating Dauphine's wit in relation to the wealth that he desires, *Epicene* recontextualizes wit as something more than the discursive practices of the cultured or the practical jokes of those in the know directed against those who have no clue, even though nearly every instance of what the play calls "wit" are examples of these things. Literary scholars have tended to overlook this dimension of wit in *Epicene*, focusing instead on its discursiveness, those verbal pyrotechnics that evidence a gentleman's urbanity. Yet in the Jacobean era, wit could and did mean rational thought; in his assessment of wit in Shakespeare's *Much Ado About Nothing*, Carl Dennis defines wit as "prudential reason and practical evaluation of sensory evidence."[43] But wit of this nature also manifested as what and how one wrote or spoke. As William G. Crane noted some time ago, wit in Elizabethan and Jacobean England was often associated with literary skill, an *ingenium* or "mental acumen," a kind of affinity for verbal arts.[44] More recent work on wit has focused not on denotative meanings but its social effects, with scholars paying attention to its ability to mark a man's taste. Being witty was one way a gentleman might distinguish himself in Jacobean London, and recent scholarship on wit has done much to trace how wit abets Jacobean urban sociability. Scholars have thus come to distinguish between two kinds of wit: one primarily social and the other primarily antisocial. Martin Butler identifies these as "wit as a social value ('accomplishment' or 'breeding')," which he aligns with Fletcher's plays, and "the 'wit' of Middleton's heroes which represents the capacity to swindle."[45] In a useful survey of Jacobean wit, Leo Salingar traces such representations of wit from the prose works of Lyly to its appearance on the Jacobean stage in the plays of Jonson, Middleton, and Fletcher. Salingar sees Jonson's wit in relation to "sociability" and argues Middleton's wit exhibits "practical cunning, a counter-cunning, and the harshly ironic enjoyment of a jest."[46] Where wit indicates sociality, it marks the elevation of status, and where it indicatives economic activity, it signifies the debasement of exchange as form of swindling.

These distinctions are perhaps too tidy. *Epicene* dramatizes both of these kinds of wit, but it also obscures the relation between the status effects and material rewards of being witty. As Ari Friedlander has observed, *Epicene* fits within a literary tradition invested in the material rewards of wittiness; it alludes to its own legacies in cony-catching literature and the forms of wit practiced as a con game. As Friedlander points out, the play has both topical and thematic connections to cony-catching literature, connections flagged by the homophonic pun of the title, which in the Greek spelling Jonson preferred (*Epicoene*), "could be pronounced eh-pi-koi-eh-nee, or perhaps Epi-cony."[47] Wit thus also signifies the economics of the con game in *Epicene*, but the play also works to exchange what might be understood as cozenage into the social refinement of gentility. As Adam Zucker argues, wit can displace material relations as much as it can fix them in place; he observes that the wit of *Epicene*'s gallants performs a kind of sleight of hand by which social mastery disguises the gallants' involvements in the economic fervency of London's West End.[48] The plots Dauphine fashions to negotiate the patrilineal economy, in other words, come to construct, and ultimately signify, his social status and authenticity of his gentility. He becomes worthy of his patrimony by manufacturing a scenario that secures for him the wealth he believes he deserves, and crucially, his plot requires that he remain unmarried.

Throughout the play, Dauphine proves himself witty, but the ultimate proof of his wit is the acquisition of patrilineal wealth. Unlike Truewit, for example, Dauphine does not desire wit for its own sake; wit is a means to a material end. The primacy of Dauphine's desire for wealth establishes him as a near pure economic agent in Jonson's play, but it also prefigures later ideas of economic agency. This dialectic between wit and wealth, between forms of knowledge and its relation to acquisitive desire, which characterizes Dauphine, renders him a prototypical figure of later, neoclassical economic theory. In his essay, "On the Definition of Political Economy; and on the Method of Investigation Proper to It" (1836), John Stuart Mill proposes the basic tenets of the rational, market-oriented actor that would become central to neoclassical economics. Mill first sets out to define the discipline of political economy as a science. After proposing, modifying, and analyzing a series of definitions (and their limitations), Mill proposes that political economy is the "science which traces the laws of such of the phenomena of society as arise from the combined operations of mankind for the production of wealth, in so far as those phenomena are not modified by the pursuit of any other object."[49] It is from this definition that Mill insists that political economy is "an *abstract* science" drawn "from assumptions, not from facts."[50] His definition of "man," he thus concedes, is also an abstraction more akin to geometry's definition of the line, as "'that which has length but not breadth.' Just in the same manner," Mill argues, "does Political Economy presuppose an arbitrary definition of man, as a being who invariably does that by which he may obtain the greatest amount of necessaries, conveniences, and luxuries, with the smallest quantity of labour and physical self-denial with which they can be obtained in the existing state of knowledge."[51] Insofar as Mill's economic man has a psychological imperative, it is a "desire for wealth," and the extent to which that desire for wealth is fulfilled depends upon Mill's economic man's "existing state of knowledge."[52]

Throughout *Epicene*, such an "existing state of knowledge" is at stake in nearly every scene; the terrain of it enables and impedes the characters' ambitions to attain wealth and status. Fully beholden to the patrilineal economy of the gentry, Morose fixates on the significance of lineage and title as markers and bearers of wealth and status. That is his existing state of knowledge. His plot to undo his nephew, Dauphine, who Morose emphasizes is "next of blood," depends upon the strict maintenance of the patrilineal economy (1.2.17). In this economy, marriage establishes the pathways of wealth's transfer over time and space. Morose knows this. Dauphine knows this too, but he also knows, as the play will come to reveal, how disrupting marital pathways will not only maintain his single life but also organize another economy determined not by marriage but by an individual's wit, namely his own. Because Morose cannot recognize that the patrilineal economy might be upended by his witty single nephew, he fails to recognize how he could be outwitted and instead fixates on stables signifiers of the patrilineal economy of the gentry, specifically, titles.

Shortly after Morose secures his marriage to Epicene, thereby coming one step closer to disinheriting his nephew, he reveals what motivates his plan. "How I shall be revenged on mine insolent kinsman and his plots to fright me from marrying!" Morose rants: "This night I will get an heir and thrust him out of my blood like a stranger. He would be knighted, forsooth, and thought by that means to reign over me, his title must do it: no kinsman, I will now make you bring me the tenth lord's and sixteenth lady's letter, kinsman, and it shall do you no good, kinsman" (2.5.101–8). In this diatribe, Morose reveals himself to be obsessed with status. He is angry that Dauphine is a knight, and so outranks him in the social orders of the gentry. He thus desires to devalue that title by stripping it of the wealth necessary to maintain it. By the end of 1604, James had tripled the number of knights in England to 1,161. To be a knight in 1609, Dauphine would not only have had to pay at least £60 in fees (though probably more) to the heralds and other officials at the ceremony, but he also would have been expected to have an income of £40 a year. But by the time *Epicene* was performed, knightages were being circulated "like stocks and shares, into general currency among London financial speculators."[53] Aware of the commodification of knighthood, Morose seeks to render Dauphine's title as an object of exchange, rendering it a thing apart from the man: "your knighthood itself" (l.108). Repeatedly referring to Dauphine's degree as "it knighthood," Morose objectifies the title and looks to reify into a commodity. He also entertains a fantasy of gentility's decay that begins with knighthood's connection to the markets that underwrite its social value: "it shall be sued for its fees to execution, and not be redeemed; it shall cheat at the twelvepenny ordinary, it knighthood, for its diet all the term time, and tell tales for it in the vacation, to the hostess; or it knighthood shall do worse, take sanctuary in Coleharbour, and fast" (2.5.109–14). The final invocation of Coleharbour is a spectacular image that emphasizes how closely gentility required external materializations, often in estates. Coleharbour was an urban mansion located in Upper Thames Street, which was torn down by the Earl of Shrewsbury in 1598 so that tenements might be built; it was a notorious sanctuary for debtors.[54] The allusion does more than express Morose's desire to make Dauphine insolvent. In recalling an Earl's demolitions of an estate for rent-earning tenements, it cites a concern over a gentility that is no more than exploitative of the public. For most, including John Stowe, who records the destruction, the crumbling of the estate would actualize a crumbling of virtue. But for Morose, the image of Coleharbour crumbling serves as an apt metaphor for the decay he hopes to bring to Dauphine's title. Morose, in fact, cannot stop with this fantasy of debt; "it shall not have money to discharge one tavern-reckoning, to invite the old creditor to forbear it knighthood, or the new that should be, to trust it knighthood," Morose gleefully imagines, only to add, "It shall be the tenth name in the bond, to take up commodity of pipkins and stone jugs, and the part thereof shall not furnish it knighthood forth for the attempting of a baker's widow, a brown baker's widow" (2.5.114–25). Morose hopes to quite literally discredit Dauphine. He looks to tarnish that title so that it lacks power in the various credit markets that structured London's economy. In this diatribe, Morose imagines a loss so great that Dauphine will not have recourse to even the most risky of activities a gentleman might worthily engage: colonial "adventuring," a vocation usually reserved for the youngest of the gentry's sons. Morose prophesies, "It shall not have hope to repair itself by Constantinople, Ireland or Virginia" (ll.130–31). The loss of credit will result, Morose hopes, in a full descent down the London social hierarchy. Being rejected by "all gamesome citizens' wives," "it knighthood shall be to make Dol Tearsheet or Kate Common a lady, and so it knighthood might eat" (ll.126, 132–33). Thus, by marrying, Morose hopes to force his single nephew back into a patrilineal economy, but one where marriage becomes the last resort for his ruined kinsman.

While Morose may know a great deal about the patrilineal economy of London, he is not, unfortunately, very witty. Dauphine knows of Morose's plot. It is not novel. It would be the natural outcome of his marrying and having an heir. As Michelle Dowd observes, "Morose seems to be a model of traditional patrilineal tactics: throughout the play, he actively seeks marriage and a biological heir. From this perspective, Morose is a poster child for ideologically conservative patrilineal strategies, an advocate of direct descent against the claim of a more distant relative."[55] Like Vallentine of *Wit Without Money*, Dauphine might marry to save himself, but such a marriage would prove Morose correct and Dauphine more of an upstart than a worthy heir. That Dauphine maintains his single life thus suggests that he possesses a form of socioeconomic mastery anathema to the patrilineal economy that Morose hopes to exploit. Remaining single, and yet reaping the rewards of patrilineality, Dauphine proves himself a master of that economy, neither subject to it nor a subject within it.

Dauphine also ensures his knighthood signifies his gentility and not its commodification, as Morose so desires. He does so through series of social performances that accord to him a value perceived to be lacking in others who hold the title. In a series of exchanges with Sir Amorous La Foole and Sir John Daw, Dauphine distances the meanings of his knighthood as derivative of mere wealth or mere learning. Measuring himself against two other knights, Dauphine suggests his knighthood's value inheres in his innate gentility and not in the cost incurred by an exchange, and it is his wit that demonstrates his gentility perfect, his lineage authentic, and his learning substantial. When Dauphine and Clerimont encounter Sir Amorous La Foole, Clerimont asserts, "I'll make him tell us his pedigree now, and what meat he has to dinner, and who are his guests, and the whole course of his fortunes, with a breath" (1.3.52–55). Ridiculing La Foole's overeager displays of the accouterments of traditional gentility, including ancestry, hospitality, and wealth, Clerimont seeks to expose La Foole as a pretentious pretender. La Foole does not disappoint. In a speech that is meant to mock the fabrication of ancient armigerous gentility, La Foole explains that rather than come from the county of Essex, as Dauphine wryly suggests, he hails from "the La Fooles of London" (1.4.35). Unwittingly implicating himself by invoking the correlation of true and false lineage with country and city, respectively, La Foole then proceeds to explain, "They all come out of our house, the La Fooles o' the north, the La Fooles of the west, the La Fooles of the east and south—we are as ancient a family as any is in Europe—but I myself am descended lineally from the French La Fooles" (1.4.37–41). Rather than carefully chart a patrilineal line, La Foole seemingly includes all of London and some of Europe too. The bloat of his ancestry materializes in the gaudiness of his coat of arms; it is "yellow, or or, checkered azure and gules, and some three or four colours more" (ll.137). Despite his pretending to ancient gentility (La Foole does note "antiquity is not respected now"), he primarily emphasizes his wealth. Tying his knightage to those cheapened by Essex during his failed campaign in Ireland in 1599—he created fifty-nine in six months—La Foole documents his largess and its uses, explaining, "I went down to my tenants in the country and surveyed my lands, let new leases, took their money, spent it in the eye o' the land here, upon ladies—and now I can take up at my pleasure" (ll.64–67).

Throughout this verbal exchange, Dauphine and Clerimont display their wit less through what they say than through how they manage what is said and what might be thought, mapping and remapping the scene's existing state of knowledge, and demarcating those who are in the know and those who are not. La Foole's very name advertises his ignorance to the audience. Yet despite his self-identification as a fool, his status as a wealthy knight does not seem all that preposterous. He earned his knighthood in military service, and he has land, the rents of which permit him to live a leisured life in London. Many gentleman of the time aspired to such a life. Truewit praises such a leisured lifestyle at the beginning of the play, and Dauphine clearly covets the leisured life that La Foole lives. Rather than establish some essential difference between Dauphine and La Foole, Jonson constructs an exchange between Dauphine's wit and La Foole's wealth, bringing the two into a reciprocal relationship. At this moment, Dauphine negotiates the disparity between La Foole's wealth and his own by making that difference dialectical. Dauphine's wit targets La Foole's wealth and what that wealth provides. Disparities of wealth are here translated into disparities of wit in inverse proportion. Dauphine's lack of funds comes to imply his abundance of wit, and La Foole's abundance of wealth, his lack of wit.

Dauphine's mockery of La Foole as a man merely made of and by money finds its analogue in Sir John Daw, a knight of too many words. Through his exchange with La Foole, Dauphine differentiates wit from wealth, essentially establishing them as mutually exclusive of one another. Possessed wealth precludes wit, but wit so possessed can always acquire wealth. A similar process of differentiation occurs when Dauphine first encounters Daw. If La Foole parodically embodies the wealth presumed necessary for landed gentry, Sir Jack Daw parodically embodies the learning deemed necessary for gentlemen groomed for civil service. Jonson mocks these strains of gentility in other plays, especially when they are totalized and divorced from one another. La Foole anticipates Sir Epicure Mammon of *The Alchemist* (1610), and Daw echoes the pretender Sir Politic Would-Be of *Volpone* (1606). When Dauphine encounters Daw, he and Clerimont labor to make a distinction not between wit and wealth but between wit and learning. Just as it manifests in the scene with La Foole, the wit of Dauphine and Truewit is evinced through negation; it has little shape of its own outside that given to it by the extent of Daw's own ignorance. Dauphine, for example, asks Daw "whom do you account for authors, Sir John Daw?" (2.3.76–77). The instigation can only be considered wit insofar as it forthrightly exposes Daw's ignorance. Daw responds not with authors but with titles of books. Mocking such ignorance is not really substantive. But it does do important work because it differentiates one kind of knowledge from another and it further shows how Dauphine's knowledge of such texts is not merely citational; it is functional. His knowledge of a classical canon is a knowledge to be leveraged, useful not for its information but for its social purposes, for its ability to create difference on the grounds of what one knows and what others do not. Perhaps more importantly, this scene makes a distinction between knowledge one seems to inherently possess and knowledge one might try to buy. Daw buys books, and insofar as many early seventeenth-century books were advertised in terms of title and contents over and above authorship, he is not wrong to cite titles. But this kind of knowledge also marks Daw as a subject in a particular market economy, as a consumer of and not producer or interpreter of texts. His economic activity cannot generate wit; it can only cost him wealth.

Sir John Daw is proven witless because does not understand how to use his learning to shape a reality, only to participate in a current market as a consumer. When Dauphine first describes Daw to Clerimont, he notes how Daw fails to align learning with right action. In his attempt to woo Epicene, for instance, Dauphine observes, "Daw does nothing but court her, and the wrong way. He would lie with her, and praises her modesty; desires that he would talk and be free, and commends her silence in verses, which he reads and swears are the best that ever man made. Then rails at his fortunes, stamps, and mutinies why he is not made a councillor and called to affairs of state" (1.3.14–21). Daw not only demonstrates himself ignorant of the contents of books; he does not even know how to use what he does know. Conflating the difference between the title of a book and the title of a gentleman, Truewit implies Daw's relationship to gentility reflects his relationship to the print market, cursing, "A pox on him, a fellow that pretends only to learning, buys titles, and nothing else of books in him" (1.3.75–77). Like Sir Amorous La Foole who owns *Greene's Groatsworth of Wit*, Daw confuses the power to buy a book with the necessity to understand it and develop one's knowledge effectively, and Truewit aligns such acquisitiveness of literary works with the cheapening of armigerous title. In much the same way that they buy books they do not read, La Foole and Daw, Truewit implies, have bought their knighthoods like upstarts. Against these rubes, Dauphine does not actually demonstrate the inherent worth of his title so much as he distances it, through negative example, from his presumed social inferiors. In doing so, he suggests the value of "it knighthood" does not inhere in wealth, lineage, or learning. It inheres, instead, in something far more amorphous but more deeply inherent: wit.

## WIT KNIGHTHOOD

Like Dauphine, Truewit, as his name suggests, knows how to wield wit in a way that would shape an existing state of knowledge. After he learns of Morose's plan to disinherit Dauphine, Truewit barges into Morose's home and attempts to dissuade him from marrying by repurposing Juvenal's sixth satire, a single man's screed if there ever was one (2.2.17–42). Unlike Daw, who mistakes the titles of books for the names of authors in his poor courtship of

London ladies, Truewit nowhere notes his borrowing. Like an actor, he personifies Juvenal. However, as Adam Zucker observes, Truewit's wit inheres less in his ability to readily recall Juvenalian satire than it does in his ability to write the classical onto the contemporary.[56] In vitiating marriage, he remaps London through a single man's eyes. The Thames becomes a river "wherein you may drown so handsomely," and "London Bridge at a low fall with a fine leap, to hurry you down the stream"; notable cathedrals become not spiritual houses of heavenly realms but expeditious edifices, offering access to the afterlife: "such a delicate steeple i' the town as Bow, to vault from; or a braver height as Paul's" (2.2.20–24). We might say Truewit's Juvenalian improvisation conditions the play's audience for an end that they do not yet know. John Dryden famously praised *Epicene* for these kinds of proleptical moments. He admires how, throughout *Epicene*, Jonson, "when he has any character or humour wherein he would show a coup de maître, or his highest skill, he recommends it to your observation by a pleasant description of it before the person first appears." This formal maneuver, Dryden suggests, "prepares you to receive them favourably, and when they are there, even from their first appearance you are so far acquainted with them, that nothing of their humour is lost to you."[57] Through Truewit's eyes, London transforms into a city that tempts a man to kill himself rather than marry, a land in which only single men would remain and thrive.

But if Truewit's Juvenalian screed reimagines London as a city of single men, it also reveals the degree to which he operates within the same patrilineal economy that Morose looks to exploit. Truewit's single men are not economic men; they are merely misogynistic ones, and Truewit himself, despite his grasp and application of literary allusion, remains locked into the same patrilineal economy that Dauphine plots to evade and Morose hopes to exploit. Believing, as he later tells Dauphine, "I have forbid the banns . . . I have been with thy virtuous uncle and have broke the match" (2.4.5–6), Truewit aligns his literary ingenuity with a material outcome: Dauphine's inheritance. It is no wonder then that Morose sees through Truewit's charade. Fed up with Truewit's Juvenalian rehearsal, Morose asks, "Good sir! Have I ever cozened any friends of yours of their land? bought their possessions? taken forfeit of their mortgage? begged a reversion from 'em? bastarded their issue? What have I done that may deserve this?" (2.2.43–46). Drawing upon the various economic, legal, and sexual means by which a gentleman might disenfranchise another in the patrilineal economy of the gentry, Morose clearly sees Truewit's speech as a kind of economic discourse. This scene presents a familiar exchange between a single man and soon-to-be-married one, a witty gallant who has a wealth of words and would-be husband hoarding patrimonial wealth, but both operate within the suppositions of a patrilineal economy.

Because they share an existing state of knowledge about the same economy, Morose has no problem seeing through Truewit. Only when the nightmare scenario Truewit paints is realized, when the silent Epicene becomes "a manifest woman," who "can talk" and, as Epicene herself asserts, "govern" (3.4.40, 46, 52), does Morose default to seeking the aid of his nephew Dauphine. Having proven that his gentility inheres in his wit by differentiating it from both La Foole's wealth and Daw's learning, Dauphine mobilizes his wit to secure what he has desired all along: Morose's estate, which would substantiate his title with wealth and property. Dauphine's revelation at the end of the play that Epicene is a boy in disguise realizes Morose's wildest dream, whereby a marriage would force a member of the gentry down the social hierarchy and into a marriage with a sex worker. Morose is now, instead, a victim of his own fantasy. Here, the single gallant Dauphine coaxes Morose into confessing his impotence, effectively casting him as a eunuch, and thus ensuring he will live a single life until he dies.[58] Dauphine navigates the patrilineal economy of Morose not by becoming a patriarch in his own right but by embracing a form of economic agency embodied by and necessitated by his single life while simultaneously ensuring his uncle remains single, and so without recourse to a patrilineal economy that Morose knows too well.

If Dauhpine's single life enables an unpatriarchal form of manhood, it is one decidedly privileged and predicated on mastery. That mastery is not so much a mastery over others as it is a mastery of existing states of knowledge, one shown to be much wider than others had previously perceived it to be. As Truewit states, "Well, Dauphine, you have lurched your friends of the better half of the garland, by concealing this part of the plot! But much good do it thee, thou deserv'st it, lad" (5.4.220–22). Thus, though, as Marjorie Swann argues, Dauphine's theatrical trick at the end of the play, "elides the hereditary transmission of wealth with a form of commercialized, all-male theatrical practice," it also reifies his status as an economic man who is very much an authority because he is a kind of author of his own life.[59] Unlike Truewit or Clerimont, Dauphine is not so much an actor playing a role as he is an entrepreneur organizing and negotiating a series of market relations. While at first appearing as a character within a city comedy, he proves himself the comedy's central plotter. Unlike the rest of the company, he is not beholden to the dramatic conventions of the genre, where marriage secures and signifies the reordering and righting of the socioeconomic relations of the dramatic world.

*Epicene* suggests that Dauphine deserves the wealth he wins because he proves he does not need wealth to prove his desert: he can, in the words of a popular saying contemporary to the period, "live by his wits." Such a fantasy would be appealing to the young gentlemen that Michael Shapiro imagines frequenting the Whitefriars theatre, those "members of the upper classes who felt their social status to be precarious: either old-line aristocrats struggling to maintain their standing; or gentry, *nouveaux riches*, and young inns-of-court men striving for higher status."[60] Though Dauphine does seemingly "live by his wits," this aphorism nowhere appears in *Epicene*. Jonson does, however, use it in a later play, one that is similarly interested in cozening gullible gentlemen of their wealth: *The Alchemist* (1612). Seeking Subtle's tutelage, the young gull Kastril asks Face if the alchemical doctor can "teach / living by the wits too?"[61] Face assures him he can, explaining, that young gentlemen who frequent ordinaries "live by their wits . . . that have vented / Six times your fortunes" (3.4.52–53). These men are "gallants yet" because they never succumb to their debt, and rather use their insolvency to enact further performances of their wit (l.55). Face rehearses the social fantasy *Epicene* dramatizes, where a gentleman's innate wit produces and procures wealth against even the greatest of odds. Kastril—a young gentleman whose annuity of "fifteen hundred, a year" is equal to Dauphine's own (l.15)—believes in this fantasy.

The single life of Dauphine, and its continued maintenance, is thus not incidental to the economics of the play or merely a social circumstance reflective of a bustling, commercial West End. Given how deeply the plot hinges upon the patrilineal economy of inheritance where marriage is both the means of establishing or disrupting the passage of patrimonial wealth, the single life valuates not only who deserves wealth but the terms through which that wealth finds value. In *Epicene*, the accidents of kinship organize the pathways of patrimony, but they do not ultimately direct the flow of money from one generation to the next. A single man's wit does that. Dauphine can rest in the fact that his wit earned him the patrimony the patrilineal economy says he deserves but does not guarantee. He gets the wealth he desires all while demonstrating he does not need the traditions and mechanisms of patrilineality to get it. He has all he needs already because he has his wit, and the inherited wealth he wins by it merely ratifies his inherent value as the truest of gallants.

## The Single Life of the True Gallant in *Wit at Severall Weapons*

Like Jonson's *Epicene*, *Wit at Severall Weapons* is a city comedy that concentrates on the social and economic problems confronting the gentry in the early seventeenth century. Most of its characters are members of the gentry. Sir Perfidious Oldcraft is an old knight; Wittypate is his son. Sir Gregory Fop, like Sir Amorous La Foole, is a foolish, landed gentleman, and Cunningame, Fop's companion, is a gentleman with much more cunning (as his name suggests) than his master. There is a poor scholar, Priscian, as well as a foolish one, Credulous, Sir Perfidious's nephew. And then there are Sir and Lady Ruinous Gentry. The play is not subtle about its vision of the social order. Bradley Ryner has argued that in another Middleton and Rowley play, *The Changeling*, audiences must negotiate allegorical and mimetic representations of individuals that correspond to questions about their agency in relation to economic systems.[62] *Wit at Severall Weapons* can be understood to negotiate these tensions through its characterizations as well. Its characters are at once mimetic representations of individuals who are understood as economic types. The dynamics between these characters are at once those between city and country, new money and old, but the energy that animates the plot are expressly urban: the city has the power to ruin as well as raise the gentry, if only a witty economic actor would seize the opportunities before them.

*Wit at Severall Weapons* has two plots. The main plot focuses on Wittypate and his attempts to secure his patrimony from his withholding father, Sir Perfidious Oldcraft. The second plot is a marriage plot, a standard of city comedy, but here it further highlights the various economic and social circumscriptions that attended gentry marriages. In the second plot, a younger son, the gentleman Cunningame, outwits his master Sir Gregory Fop to win the hand of Sir Perfidious's Niece (she has no other name in the play). After seemingly failing at winning the hand of Sir Perfidious's Niece, Cunningame asks, "Why should I aim my thoughts at better fortunes / Than younger brothers have?" (3.1.127–28). A younger son, Cunningame both questions why he should hope for better luck or more wealth, and while he does win the marriage game in the end, it is also clear that this is the only kind of game he is permitted to play. Because he is an heir, Wittypate need not resort to marriage to win his wealth. When their respective plots overlap, the social differences between Cunningame and Wittypate are understood in relation to marriage and the single life. As Cunningame tells Wittypate, "Friend, we'll share / The sheaves of gold; only the love-acre / Shall be peculiar" (5.1.9–11). Cunningame's fiscal future is tied to his marriage to the Niece; Wittypate's is clearly not. The divide between their two plots is also marked in the divide between "cunning" and "wit" in the play. The former manifests as the knowledge to navigate within socioeconomic constrictions and to optimize them. The latter manifests much as it does in

*Epicene*: it is a form of managing, constructing, and creating socioeconomic situations that come to benefit oneself. Wit, but not cunning, is managerial and entrepreneurial. This distinction between the two is made clear in the end, for it is Wittypate, not Cunningame, who will finally secure the marriage of Cunningame and the Niece. While both Cunningame and Wittypate prove their desert by bilking Sir Perfidious of his money—a dowry and a patrimony, respectively—the marital status that attends the culmination of each gentleman's plot confirms their respective places in the ranks of the gentry. In this comedy, the single man Wittypate proves the truth of his gentility because he does not need to resort to a marriage like the younger son, Cunningame.

While *Epicene* also represents the single gallant's wit as the faculty enabling his economic action, *Wit at Severall Weapons* more clearly represents wit as the faculty "to match and make" a market (1.1.54). Explaining the reasoning for his testing of Wittypate, Sir Perfidious says to his son: "If I can see thee thrive by thy wits while I live, I shall have the more courage to trust thee with my lands when I die; if not, the next best wit I can hear of carries 'em; for since in my time and knowledge so many rich children of the City conclude in beggary, I'd rather make a wise stranger my executor than a foolish son my heir, and to have my lands called after my wit, thou after my name, and that's my nature" (1.1.74–81). Unlike Morose, Sir Perfidious looks to disrupt the patrilineal economy by modifying its terms of inheritance. Kinship does not determine wealth in his vision; wealth determines kinship. To a certain extent, Sir Perfidious lays bare what, exactly, the patrilineal economy was designed to preserve: the value of land as an asset. Who owns that land is less important than that it reflects a history of ownership. Like Sir Thomas Smith, Sir Peridious thus seems to embrace the turnover of land among the gentry that is elsewhere bemoaned. So long as his land would be maintained by someone witty enough to possess, manage, and maintain it, Sir Perfidious has no problem with the transfer of an ancestral estate to someone other than his kin. His true heir are wits like him.

Sir Perfidious further insists wit comes by experience in the world; inherited wealth, on the other hand, insulates one from the realities of it. He justifies denying Wittypate his patrimony because he believes Wittypate must learn through experience:

Much like the art of swimming; he that will attain to't
Must fall plump, and duck himself at first,
And that will make him hardy and adventurous,

And not stand putting in one foot, and shiver,
And then draw t'other alike, like a quake-buttock;
Well he may make a paddler i' the world,
From hand to mouth, but never a brave swimmer,
Borne up by th' chin, as I bore up myself
With strong industry that never failed me;
For he that lies borne up with patrimonies
Looks like a long great ass that swims with bladders:
Come but one prick of adverse fortune to him
He sinks, because he never tried to swim,
When wit plays with the billows that chocked him. (ll.16–29)

Sir Perfidous's vision that his son "adventure" "with strong industry" elevates the practices of merchants and colonial expropriation. The nautical conceit of sink or swim that Sir Perfidious uses here gestures to the very kind of investments in colonial and imperial trade in which members of the gentry increasingly engaged.[63] "Wit" in this economy is what founders heirs "borne up with patrimonies" and aided by the "bladders" of inherited wealth. It is a force anathema to such wealth; it is that which "plays with the billows" instead that which relies upon them.

Throughout *Wit at Severall Weapons*, Wittypate offers another vision of wit, one not dependent on "adventuring" in colonial exploitation and expropriation but on urban cony-catching. As he manufactures situations in which his father might be parted with his money, Wittypate salvages a traditional model of primogeniture where fortunes are inherited, essentially tricking his father into the patrilineal economy that he otherwise rejects. Rather than survey the various licit and illicit markets in London as his father would have him do, Wittypate, like Dauphine, takes to cony-catching, particularly sharking or plain fraud (and not cross-biting like Dauphine). However, Wittypate's cony-catching is not readily analogous to criminal activity. As Anupam Basu has argued, cony-catching pamphlets are often animated by the questions of industry and leisure, the very themes that Sir Perfidious notes in his monologue of adventuring. Though the vagrancy of rogues is often ascribed to their idleness and sloth in many of the period's moralizing tracts, Basu notes that in cony-catching pamphlets, "The cony-catcher is often depicted as hard working, while the cony is represented not as an innocent but as a complicit victim of his own corruption" so that "the pamphlets collapse the opposition between these positions until it becomes impossible to hold on to any notion of stable identity or morality as the foundation for a social hierarchy."[64] Sir Perfidious in fact relishes this lack of stable social identity, especially as it applies to the gentry, because he profits from this social chaos so long as he can make sense of it; he even admits that he relishes indenturing gentle orphans "to feltmakers, / To make 'em lose and work away their gentry" (1.1.68–69). But for Wittypate, the dissolution of a traditional social hierarchy risks his patrimony. He resorts to sharking not to dissolve social identity but to reinforce it. His deceitful acts become moral because, though fraudulent, they expose the fraudulence of Sir Perfidious's own gentility. Thus, in *Wit at Severall Weapons*, cony-catching becomes a means of asserting that "mastery of marketplace skills and contingencies" that Karen Bix suggests the cony-catching pamphlets "endorse" as "the egalitarian notion that economic talents are randomly dispersed" or that "they more subversively suggest that the *superior* endowments of cony-catchers somehow level the playing field."[65] Wittypate answers his father's deceitful and exploitative market practices with a kind of deceit that would force his father to act more gently with his son and with others.

Wittypate's gentle status, however, qualifies any notion that the cony-catcher's skills are randomly dispersed among the populace. He is not a rogue pretending to be gentle so that he might defraud other gentlemen. Rather, he is a gentleman prompted into roguery by his father, and thus he merely uses cony-catching as a means of performing a gentility that is already presumed inherent. In both *Epicene* and *Wit at Severall Weapons*, cony-catching occurs not across but within social ranks, between members of the gentry. For example, at the first sharking episode of the play, Wittypate capitalizes upon the roles that his compatriots—Sir Ruinous Gentry and Priscian—normally play, a destitute captain and a poor scholar respectively. In the con, they are all members of the gentry pretending to be more or less what they actually are: members of the gentry. In this scene, Wittypate exploits this relationship of members of the gentry acting like members of the gentry, albeit ruined ones, and thus, like Dauphine, Wittypate also exploits the divide between the known and the unknown. As Sir Gregory and Sir Perfidious come upon Wittypate and his party, Priscian regurgitates scripted Latin. The performance appeals to Sir Perfidious because it gives him an opportunity to showcase his own learning. It allows him to act like a gentleman as well, especially for Sir Gregory, the gentleman he hopes will marry his niece. When Priscian gets to the end of his script and begins repeating himself, Sir Ruinous steps in as a poor captain. It is at this moment that Wittypate, disguised in a false beard, interrupts the exchange between his sharking companions, Sir Gregory, and Sir Perfidious. The interruption does not change the deception, however. Rather it intensifies its effect and enhances its monetary reward. Wittypate explains, "I am a poor gentleman, that have little but my wits to live on" (1.2.242–43). The statement interrupts a financial exchange; Sir Perfidious is about to give Priscian and Sir Ruinous "a groat" to alleviate their poverty. This is stingy charity. Seeing their miserliness, Wittypate tells them, "I begin a better example than so," and hands them a whole bag of money, which is actually his share of their previous sharking venture; "There's a pair of angels to guide you to your lodgings, a poor gentleman's good will" (ll.248–50). Shamed, Sir Perfidious and Sir Gregory each give "a piece that if he were divided would make a pair of angels" (ll.257–58). Directly correlating his wit with his wealth, Sir Perfidious interprets his loss of coin as "a little abatement of my wit" (ll.262).

This scene emphasizes the material relation between wit and wealth, a relation best managed by the single gallant. Wit here functions as a kind of capital that is either invested or depleted. It, like wealth, is fungible. Wittypate spends his coins that more coins may be gained. This investment is met with return, but it is his wit that fabricates a situation in which such an investment will pay off. Because he is unknowingly participating in an exchange of his son's creation, Sir Perfidious loses wealth, which he equates with a loss of wit. But it is also important to realize how Wittypate uses specific knowledge for economic gain. Both Sir Perfidious and Sir Gregory are knights, and both are gentlemen. The whole scene is, in fact, gentlemen performing as gentlemen for the benefit of other gentlemen, and as such, the difference between the generosity of Wittypate and that of Sir Perfidious and Sir Gregory is a social norm that Wittypate can manipulate. By seemingly giving up all of his wealth, Wittypate disassociates wealth from gentility to instead emphasize gentility's relationship to generosity. He capitalizes upon the notion that true gentility inheres in the gentleman's virtue, not his coins. In doing so, by his wits alone, Wittypate pilfers coins from gentlemen pressured to act virtuously.

Even as Wittypate defrauds his father, the scene frames his defrauding as a form of payment of patrimony due. In this way, Wittypate does not merely use his wit to acquire wealth. Rather, he uses his wit to reorient the social order in a manner that would acknowledge his claims to patrimony and restore the patrilineal economy that is otherwise in shambles. As Wittypate explains, "For there's the ambition of my wit: to live upon his professed wit, that has turned me out to live by my wits" (ll.308–10). As Wittypate continues, wit more clearly is an analogue for wealth. Alluding to the parable of talents found in the Gospel according to Matthew, Wittypate soliloquizes, "father, you shall know that I put my portion to use, that you have given me to live by; / And, to confirm yourself in me re-nate, / I hope you'll find my wit's legitimate" (ll.315–19). Unlike his father, Wittypate envisions not a change in the gentleman's relationship to urban markets but a return to practices of primogeniture. Sir Perfidious, it should be remembered, ventured from home and to the city, where he participated in a whole host of illicit practices to make his way. Wittypate, on the other hand, aims only to obtain what he views as his by patrilineal right, and he thus reimagines the patriarchal order such that women are not so much subordinate as they are entirely inconsequential. Wittypate redacts the role wives and mothers play in mediating inheritance. Sir Perfidious has already denied the patrimony by blood, and has instead asserted wealth might be passed between two men with commensurate wits. Wittypate repurposes this conceit and turns it into a parthenogenic fantasy in which fathers be-get sons without women. It is single men all the way down, a generational exchange of wealth reconfigured as exchange between market actors. He would have his father "renate" or reborn in him. He quite literally hopes to show his father that he is like-minded, that he deserves the estate Sir Per-fidious withholds not because he possesses his father's name but because his father's love of wit inheres in and as his son.

Wittypate is not only in control of the social and economic milieu of London in *Wit at Severall Weapons*; he is also in control of the very narrative of the foolish prodigal that his father would impose upon him. Wittypate's allusion to the biblical parable of the talents comes to militate against the popular parable of the prodigal son so often circulated as a warning to heirs in the period. Unlike Vallentine of Fletcher's *Wit Without Money*, Wittypate is no prodigal. He does not need a rich widow to save him because he is his own savior (it is hard not to hear the Christological resonance in his desire to have his father's wit incarnate in his person). In *Wit at Severall Weapons*, it is the single gallant who will save the gentry from its economic sins. Wittypate in fact aligns his singleness with economic autonomy at the beginning of the first sharking scene. He disdains that he might only collect "but this fourth, this lay illiterate share" that puts him "beside his wits" (1.2.2, 1). Wittypate must collect a fourth, and not a third, because Sir Ruinous and Priscian have predetermined that any money gained be di-vided not only among the three of them but that Sir Ruinous's wife, Lady Ruinous, be given a share, regardless of whether or not she participated in the fraud. Wittypate, however, rejects such communal obligation, asking, "And what precedent's this for me?" and further disparages the techniques of Sir Ruinous and Priscian, "that never got anything but by accidence and uncertainty" (l.15, 16–17). He returns his share, and continues to excoriate

Priscian with puns on Latin grammar, mocking Priscian's weak handling of the language. These dissociative practices not only enable Wittypate to become the orchestrator of the fraud of his father that follows; they also distinguish him as an individual apart from the rank of the gentry. The abundance of his wit is demonstrated, predicated, and maintained by his willingness to continually throw money away, his willingness to defer small monetary rewards so that larger ones might be gained.

Wittypate has all the success in the world, but he does not fully imbricate himself in London's markets. He has only one cony to catch: his father. Sir Perfidious, on the other hand, demonstrates a deep knowledge of London's various markets, especially its credit markets. Despite Sir Perfidious's ignorance of his son's scheme, he is nonetheless fully attuned to London's credit networks. He knows their power to shift and move wealth from one member of the gentry to another. Like Old Gorinius of *Greene's Groatsworth of Wit*, Sir Perfidious is also near death—as he put it, "I'm grown old now, / And e'en arrived at my last cheat" (ll.93–94)—and so makes way for his funeral and aims to "discharge all my legacies, 'tis so wealthy, / And never trouble any interest money" (1.1.96–97). That is, he seeks to settle his debts and looks to collect on debts owed. Craig Muldrew has pointed out that credit, rather than coin, was the primary means of market exchange in the sixteenth and seventeenth centuries. Muldrew explains that in early modern period, "Money in England had primacy not because it was the means of exchange, but because its value was used as a measure in the pricing of all things."[66] Thus, though Sir Perfidious is wealthy, he is not merely a hoarder of coin. Rather, his wealth is also reflective of his imbrication and negotiation of London's credit networks and markets, for he is both a borrower and a lender.

Recognizing the power of London's credit networks to both empower and ruin the gentry, Sir Perfidious seeks to manipulate them to his favor. In this respect, *Wit at Severall Weapons* divides the meanings of wealth and wit in a manner that associates them with coin and credit. Wealthy men put too much faith in coin as a means of exchange; witty men understand how to use credit to gain coins, though perhaps more rightly, capital, as a measure of market value. Like Dauphine, the wits of London know how to use coin as a metric of wealth and not as the means of exchange, which can be done through credit. Sir Perfidious demonstrates his own wit when it comes to negotiating the relationship between credit and coin; it manifests in his attempted negotiation of his niece's marriage. He first indicates that marriages between the gentry can be deeply affected by London's credit markets. For the gentry, daughters were debt because of their dowries, but such marriages could also exploit the social debt understood to bond gentlemen to each other. Sir Perfidious explains that "for fear some poor earl steal her ('t has been threatened) / To redeem mortgaged land," he has negotiated a husband for his niece that would not too heavily risk his capital. To mitigate this debt Sir Perfidious has "sought out a match for her; / Fop of Fop Hall (I take it, / The ancient'st Fop in England), with whom I'm privately / Compounded for the third part of her portion" (ll.102–5). In what seems like an allusion to Jonson's play, Sir Gregory Fop is very much like Sir Amorous La Foole: a knight who puts great worth in his land and spends his money frivolously. In this case, Sir Perfidious negotiates that he will only pay a third of his niece's dowry.

If *Wit at Severall Weapons* frames its various plots as produced by and productive of London's various credit markets, it, unlike *Epicene*, more baldly establishes a material relation between wealth and wit. If wit is understood as a gallant's mental acumen or *ingenium*—and certainly Middleton and Rowley mean to associate it with the mind in the person of Wittypate—it is also everywhere a material phenomenon, and so dependent upon the movement of wealth from one gentry member to another for its signification. The conclusion of the play emphasizes wit's ability to move wealth, but here it recuperates rather than dissolves the gentry. The ending of the play sees Sir Perfidious bilked of his cash and his various plots ruined by his son. Through a clever handfasting ceremony, in which Sir Gregory consents to marriage without seeing whom he marries, Cunningame tricks Sir Gregory into marrying Mirabell, the niece of the Niece's Guardianess. Wittypate contrives a masque in which all parties are disguised so that Cunningame can run away with the Niece, and then he coaxes his father into paying for the music of the ceremonies (the musicians—actually Priscian, Sir Ruinous and Lady Ruinous—charge an exorbitant fee). This is less wit than "plain robbery," as Sir Perfidious notes (5.2.131). Yet despite such robbery, the ending makes all well. Once the plots are revealed, Sir Perfidious is all too eager to reward his son. His generosity overflows; "Wealth love me as I love wit!" he proclaims to the company. Wit does indeed recuperate wealth, and it raises the ruined. Cunningame tells Sir Ruinous, "your gentry and your name shall both be raised as high as my fortunes can reach 'em" (ll.338–40), a sentiment Wittypate confirms because he will also supply the funds that would make Cunningame's promise a reality. Like Dauphine in *Epicene*, Wittypate's circumstances end where they should have begun in a patrilineal economy. He receives his patrimony. And while all the other characters attain new heights—Mirabell becomes a Lady by marrying Sir Gregory, Cunningame gains a fortune by marrying the Niece, and Sir and Lady Ruinous Gentry are bestowed wealth commensurate with their titles—Wittypate ascends to his original status: an heir. He attains what was already his to possess. His lack of social mobility is further realized through his status as a single man; those who climb the social ladder either do so through fortuitous marriages, or are already married. For someone like Cunningame, marriage becomes a pathway into the securities of the ranks of the gentry; but marriage cannot maintain wealth. One needs wit to do that. It is Wittypate, the single man, who remains free to effect and create the circumstances whereby other members of the gentry might rise. He marries them off, but he does not marry. Though part and parcel of the gentry, he nonetheless appears distanced from it, and his single life reflects his economic exceptionalism, for he neither needs a wife nor wealth to be proven a true gallant. Having demonstrated his wit innate, and thus inherently inexhaustible so long as he lives, Wittypate also and more importantly has demonstrated his wit fungible. He does not need wealth because he has an endless supply of wit that can always obtain more wealth .

If in *Epicene* and *Wit at Severall Weapons* the single man restores the patrilineal economy of the gentry, he does so in a manner that valorizes his wit as an inherent virtue that overwrites titles and wealth as signs of his gentility. His single life signifies his mastery over, and his position outside, of patrilineality. If he inherits anything, he inherits it because he deserves it, having outwitted those who would withhold such financial deserts. It is a powerful fantasy, and one that is not so easily disentangled from the signs of gentility it otherwise supplants: those that remain or become wealthy or titled garner what they deserve because of their wit. These plays ultimately rationalize the logic of the patrilineal economy through a fantasy of market activity. The heirs Dauphine and Wittypate deserve their wealth, these plays suggest, because they earned it through their rational action. In the end, the rich, single gallants at the center of these plays believe their own fictions: that they earned the wealth they worked so hard to inherit. Their financial security is a result of their individual action, their hard work, and their innate sense of how to manage the markets before them. If that is a fiction of the single life represented in these early modern plays, it is also one still eminently appealing to, and enabling of, a variety of capitalist fantasies today, especially those in which wealth comes to signify the just deserts of savvy entrepreneurs rather than the expected effects of generational privilege.

# Chapter 4

## The Single Life of the Incel Scholar

Feelings of Entitlement in *Hamlet* and *The Anatomy of Melancholy*

Although the single life of the true gallant promulgated fantasies of entrepreneurial action and unfettered economic agency, not all such representations of the single life centered on the volitional potentials of unpatriarchal manhood. The single life could be downright sad and lonely. It could be the very picture of melancholy, as it is in the late-fifteenth-century woodcut from the *Deutsch Kalender* (fig. 2).

Figure 2. Anonymous, Melancholy, *Deutsche Kalender*, 1498.

In the other emblems of the *Deutsche Kalender*, each of which represent
the other three humoral passions of the sanguine, the choleric, and the
phlegmatic, men's emotions are made legible in relation to women. Reading the representations of women in the woodcuts of the *Deutsche Kalender*, Gail Kern Paster has observed that "what the woodcuts represent most
clearly is the correlation among heat, gender, and conceptions of agency,"
such that the women merely "provide a neutral social background for the
men's temperamental self-display."[1] These emblems are indeed about men,
as Paster notes, but I suggest the women here are not quite neutral back-
grounds. The choleric man beats a woman with a rod, and she raises her
arms in defense or defiance; the sanguine man forcefully embraces a woman
who, arms draped at her sides, signifies her lack of consent to his presumptive act; the phlegmatic man serenades or sings with a woman, who seems
to equally join in on the music. Even as these woodcuts negotiate the relations between gender, agency, and temperament, they also evince the
ways that men's emotions are not just something they themselves feel; they
are also, and perhaps primarily, behavior that women experience. In these
woodcuts, the very social legibility of men's emotions occurs at the moment
they are visited upon women.

The woodcut of melancholy shares something with its cohort. Like the
others, the represented emotion correlates to a metonymic object. The choleric man's rod materializes his affective relation to the woman as one of
intimate partner violence; the phlegmatic man's lute harmonizes with the
woman's harp; and the sanguine man's arms overtake the woman's torso.
The melancholy pair have their objects too, but the metonymic relation
they hold elaborates a more emblematic relation not to their affective state
but to their marital one. A maid and her distaff; a bachelor and his book:
these two are sad, the emblem suggests, because they are single.

Later emblems of melancholy provide a more forthright vocational depiction of melancholy; head buried in a book, melancholy is a scholar. In
*Minerva Britanna* (1612), the woodcut of melancholy (fig. 3) perches above
a verse, where readers learn that "*Melancholly*," with his mouth bound and
book on his lap,

musing in his fits

Pale visag'd, of complexion cold and drie,
All solitarie, at his studie sits
within a wood, devoid of companie:
Save Madge the Owle, and melancholy Pusse,
Light-loathing Creatures, hatefull, ominous.[2]

With his foot upon the block "plodding *Constance* affordes," "*Melancholly*" is busied with the iterative and endless work of the scholar's vocation. Peacham's emblem reinforces the early modern association of melancholy with study, which, as Bridget Gellert Lyons has noted, braids together two traditions: a genial one that ran through Aristotle, and which associated melancholy with Saturnine genius, and a pathological one that ran through Galen, which looped the inclination to study into its stuporing effects.[3]

Figure 3. Henry Peacham, "Melancholly," in *Minerva Britanna*, London, 1612.

Both of these emblems of melancholy suggest that in viewing a man we are really seeing an emotion. This chapter seeks to invert that paradigm by excavating a type of single man out of his constitutive feelings. To do so, it reconsiders the etiology of early modern melancholy and its emblematization of the single life of the scholar as it ranges across Shakespeare's *Hamlet* and Burton's *Anatomy of Melancholy*. Each of these texts represent the single life of the scholar to different ends, but they also, I show, similarly construct a type of unpatriarchal manhood affectively engendered through an insistent feeling of entitlement. The philosopher Kate Manne has argued that entitlement—"the widespread perception that privileged man is owed something"—is widely universalized within patriarchal systems among men, and that, crucially, any man, however themselves disenfranchised, might nonetheless feel themselves deserving of patriarchal privileges.[4] One of her primary case studies is the modern figure of the "incel."[5] The incel violently erupted into modern consciousness with what has been called the "Isla Villa Killings." On the evening of May 23, 2014, Elliot Rodger killed four men and two women, and wounded fourteen others. After killing his roommates, he targeted women at the University of California, Santa Barbara, and its surrounding community. His murder spree was preceded by a self-aggrandizing video that he posted on YouTube and an extensive manifesto detailing his ideology. He ended his rampage by killing himself before he could be taken into custody. In the days after the murders, the public learned that Rodger self-identified with, and was radicalized by, a group of men who call themselves "incels," short for "involuntary celibates," and Rodger has since become as a kind of perverse "saint" among them, with his image circulating on their multitudinous chatboards and wikis in a variety of memes and videos. Other mass murderers emerged after Rodger: Scott Paul Beierle, Chris Harper-Mercer, and Alek Minassian. When, four years after the Isla Villa killings, on April 23, 2018, Alek Minassian killed ten in Toronto with a van, he praised Rodger and cited him as an inspiration.[6] As self-identified incels, Rodger, Beierle, Harper-Mercer, and Minassian highlight the virulent, violent ways single men weaponize their loneliness and self-loathing as a misogyny that women in particular (but not exclusively) experience.[7] In this chapter, I want to suggest that Manne's analysis of the modern incel registers a "structure of feeling" that ramifies within early modern patriarchy.[8] If, as Manne contends, "incels are but a vivid symptom of a much broader and deeper cultural phenomenon" of entitlement within patriarchal systems, then the toxic masculinity of the modern incel might have, if not an etiology, then a symptomatic relation to the early modern melancholic scholar.[9]

Dislodging early modern melancholy from its synchronic relations to contemporary discourses of genial disposition or humoral pathology, and throwing it into diachronic relation to the incel's affectively organized violence, I argue, abets both a historicization of melancholy as an early modern affective phenomenon and a retheorization of its reciprocity with modern and early modern misogyny.[10] As it presents as a symptom of the scholar's single life, melancholy registers a kind of "ugly feeling," what Sianne Ngai theorizes as an interpretation of obstructed agency. As Ngai explains, such emotions are "unusually knotted or condensed 'interpretations of predicaments'—that is, signs that not only render visible different registers of problem (formal, ideological, sociohistorical) but conjoin these problems in a distinctive manner."[11] Melancholy, especially as it is emblematized, circulated, and represented in relation to the single life of the early modern scholar, interprets a problem that is really not a problem: that of perceived privileges denied. Melancholic scholars have, in other words, no good reason to be melancholy, or they do, but only within the terms of patriarchy. In this respect, they hold something in common with the modern incel. Devoid of a discursive tradition of geniality or a humoralism, modern incels hyperbolize their ugly feelings until they erupt in violence against women. Such incels interpret their predicament as an "involuntary celibacy" because, as Manne points out: "they believe they are entitled to, and have been deprived of, sex with 'hot' young women, who are dubbed 'Staceys.' . . . But an incel will typically want sex and love not only, and perhaps not even primarily, for their own sake. His rhetoric betrays a desire to have these goods for *instrumental* reasons: as a currency to buy status in masculine hierarchies, relative to the 'Chads.' These are supposed 'alpha males,' whose masculine prowess contrasts with the incel's (again, supposedly) lowly status."[12] Unsatisfied with their perceived social status, modern incels read patriarchal norms accurately but too rigidly. They make of themselves a social type because they schematize the social order in a typological way: other men are typical Chads, women are typical Staceys, and so they imagine themselves typical incels.

Early modern scholars could similarly conceive of their melancholy as an interpretation of predicaments of obstructed agency. Within the early modern universities, the scholar was required to live a single, celibate life. Up until the nineteenth century, university students were required by statute to be celibate, single men. They (and others) could likewise conceive of themselves as involuntary celibates. This statutory requirement often framed questions about their sexual agency in the period. In his sixteenth-century medical tract, *The Haven of Health* (1584), Thomas Cogan, for example, explains the broad human need for "Venus" only to then turn to a salient example: "howe live students at this day in Universities that be of anie societie, who may not marrie while they have interest in their Colledge?"[13] As Cogan's question suggests, the viability of the single life of the scholar was predicated upon his relationship to his university. The single life of the scholar makes him melancholic, but his melancholy is an effect of his mandated single life. In his examination of emotion in the Tudor Court, Bradley Irish advocates for an analysis of emotions that does not primarily historicize emotions as objects of study and would instead historicize early modern discourses about emotion to "inform our understanding of how they, and the texts they construct, participate in the Renaissance social world."[14] If an analysis of the modern incel provides some way to theorize

131

how feelings of entitlement index feelings of abjection and antifeminist beliefs, as Manne demonstrates, an analysis of the single life of the early modern scholar provides one avenue to historicize how feelings of melancholy betray feelings of entitlement, especially as they percolate within texts about the early modern university.

By theorizing the melancholic scholar's affective relation to the modern incel, and historicizing his single life within the university, this chapter contends that he can be understood as a type of early modern incel. If we return to the woodcuts, we might see how the incel scholar surfaces through the emblematizing of his melancholy. There is something a bit darker than the humor of black bile impressed in these images. The final couplet of Peacham's verse draws attention to the hand of *Melancholly*, where "A sealed purse he beares, to shew no vice," but that sign of innocence wavers in the next line, which asserts, "So proper is to him, as *Avarice*." In a single gesture, the emblem conflates two conditions of the scholar's single life: his poverty and his celibacy, both of which encode a desire exceeding their state. The "sealed purse" signifies a frugality born of the scholar's poverty only to transmogrify it as an inordinate desire for wealth; read as a scrotal sack, the "sealed purse" signifies the scholar's celibacy as a form of advertised castration that nonetheless evinces his inordinate carnality. There's something false here; something within which passes the scholar's "shew," that leeches outward, only finding articulation in those "light-loathing Creatures, hatefull, ominous." The *Deutshe Kalender* may present its melancholic man as a downcast scholar whose face remains illegible, but if it shares a semiotics with its cohort, where men's emotions register against women who oppose or share them, then here the maid looking away suggests a cause of the man's feeling as much as it registers his feminization as a celibate scholar. Like an incel, this emblematic scholar understands his celibacy and melancholy as an effect of a woman's rejection of him. They may be his emotions, this emblem suggests, but they are caused by a woman's spurning.

Such early modern emblems do not depict melancholy, then, but some other feeling with a sharper edge: the *melancholer*, say, of a fuming incel scholar who might wield his book like a rod. Having spent endless hours observing and documenting incel webpages, forums, and other online spaces, the journalist Talia Lavin argues, "the current that underlies all incel discourse [is] a potent mix of despair and rage."[15] Incels use the trope of the "redpill" to mark their inauguration into an antifeminist worldview that perceives the world, as Laura Bates explains, as a "'gynocracy,' a clever system designed to keep men (the true victims of oppression) in their subordinate place without them even noticing."[16] Incels supplement the antifeminism of the redpill by a further repathologization of their despair at this so-called reality, an act which they call taking the "blackpill," a resignation that "their inherent flaws doom them to a life of utter failure and celibacy that no attempt at self-improvement could possibly alleviate."[17] While Renaissance discourses on melancholy did not widely circulate the trope of pilling—except, as we shall see, in one crucial moment in Burton's *Anatomy of Melancholy*—it nonetheless readily forged a similar connection between melancholy and antisocial behavior that the modern incel so evocatively evinces; as Lawrence Babb documented some time ago, the melancholic was often represented as "the 'malcontent' type."[18] But rather than simply overlay one modern type onto an early modern one, this chapter instead attends to those representations that transmute entitlement as melancholy, melancholy as anger, and blend both into a mélange of *melancholer*. The single life of incel scholars represented in Shakespeare's *Hamlet* and Burton's *Anatomy of Melancholy* are at once very modern and decidedly early modern. They evoke all of the entitlement and misogyny of the modern incel, but their "involuntary celibacy" cites a material relation to their status within the early modern university. In reading the modern incel into these literary representations of the incel scholar, I seek to recontextualize the etiological, institutional, and affective networks that produce such a type (or perhaps more accurately, a prototype). Ultimately, the single life of the early modern incel scholar facilitates a form of unpatriarchal manhood, but that unpatriarchal manhood, through its melancholer, entrenches a misogyny that reinforces and reifies a patriarchal social order that ostensibly has no room for such incels, but does make great use of their violence.

In what follows, I first situate Hamlet's status as a scholar in relation to the meanings of the single life within the early modern university and then consider how recent, lay readings of Hamlet as a prototypical incel reengage a critical tradition that has debated the modernity of Shakespeare's tragic hero in relation to his seeming inwardness, a debate that, I suggest, locates his modernity in the wrong place. Following this reading of *Hamlet*, I read selections of Burton's *Anatomy of Melancholy* alongside Rodger's manifesto, "My Twisted World," to illuminate how each draw on similar rhetorical strategies to position their "celibacy" as "involuntary" and therefore their access to sex as a patriarchal privilege to which they are entitled. I finally conclude by further pressing the relation between Burton and Rodger to show how Burton's representation of the love melancholic casts them— and himself—as an incel, one who frames the amelioration of melancholy through an insistence on misogyny as a form of "pilling." As this chapter shows, both early and late to histories of patriarchy, the single life of the incel scholar enables a form of unpatriarchal manhood that, while it militates against patriarchal hierarchies, fully supports its ideological commitments, and thus manifests as a type of manhood distinctly endemic to patriarchal social order itself.

## The Single Life of the Incel Scholar

Throughout *Hamlet*, Shakespeare represents Hamlet, the Prince of Denmark, not primarily as the heir apparent but as a student of Wittenberg whose life experiences almost entirely derive from that social position, revisions of the source text that Suzanne Stein identifies as Shakespeare's "most salient innovations to the variants of the *Hamlet* story available to him in the late sixteenth century."[19] As a thirty-year-old man, Hamlet is very much a scholar who has insulated himself in, and has been insulated by, the university. Hamlet's position as both a single man and a university student attaches him to a material and an institutional form of unpatriarchal manhood that, while sometimes observed, is rarely surfaced in his associations with melancholy. In the scene in which Hamlet asserts to Gertude and Claudius that "I have that within which passes show," for example, his status as a student is brought to the fore.[20] Claudius tells Hamlet, "For your intent / In going back to school in Wittenberg, / It is most retrograde to our desire," and Gertrude pleads with him, "Go not to Wittenberg" (1.2.113-14, 119). The university is mentioned twice more in this scene—when Hamlet asks of Horatio's presence in the court—and then no more in the play. It is in this scene that Hamlet identifies Horatio as "my fellow student," the only time "student" is mentioned in the play (l.176). These explicit references to Hamlet and Horatio's relationship to the university may appear tangential to the play's plot, but, as Elizabeth Hanson has argued, "*Hamlet* goes to considerable lengths to establish that Prince Hamlet is a student at Wittenberg; his friendship with Horatio is both a sign and an effect of that status."[21] Moreover, as Eric De Barros has argued, from the outset, the play positions him as "one of the first, first-generation students," and in addition to the play representing Hamlet as a literal student, it also evinces his racialized education through which Hamlet learns to selectively forget violent pasts to imagine a self that is free from historical contingency and entitled to present white privileges.[22] Elsinore may be the setting of the dramatic action, but Wittenberg informs much of *Hamlet*'s—and Hamlet's—social world.

One way to understand Hamlet's status as both a student of Wittenberg and the Prince of Denmark is through the development of an early modern conception of the lay intellectual. Tracing the changing meanings of celibacy and the single life as it came to be institutionalized in the universities, John Guillory has argued that the seventeenth century witnessed the emergence of the lay intellectual and natural philosopher as a new social type, and "that early modern philosophy . . . reaches back past humanism to recapture and transform celibacy into a new practice of philosophical bachelorhood."[23] Reading the utopian vision of academic fellowship cast in Bacon's *New Atlantis* (1627), Guillory argues that the social type of the philosopher begins to emerge in the early modern period out of the institutional sanctioning of celibacy within early modern universities. He observes that numerous philosophers, including Descartes, Hobbes, Locke, Hume, Spinoza, Newton, and Hooke, among others, were single men, and suggests that the single life of the philosopher—he uses Nietzsche as the spokesperson of this notion—functions as "the converse predicament of celibacy: it is the *freedom not to marry* rather than the *prohibition of marriage*."[24] This vision of celibacy as freedom and not prohibition did obtain in the period; it recalls a Platonic vision of philosophical celibacy articulated in the *Symposium*, and it circulates, as I show in chapter 2, through a number of ballads and other kinds of popular print. In Plato's vision, either an individual is drawn to physical love, immortalizing oneself through procreative sex and childrearing, or one is drawn to philosophy and craftsmanship, creating legacy not by sexual activity but by intellectual (or artistic) activity.[25] This model of the procreative philosopher informs Bacon's relatively novel seventeenth-century essay, "Of Marriage and Single Life," referenced in the previous chapter. In so loving his mistress Wisdom, the philosopher has no need for real mistresses, let alone the cares of marriage.[26]

Even as Guillory's argument allows us to see how the single life of the scholar came to be privileged within the discipline of natural philosophy, his social history of the philosopher is, like Bacon's *New Atlantis*, a bit utopian. If indeed the seventeenth century witnessed a reclamation of celibacy that became transformed into a new ideal philosophical bachelorhood, it did so against a competing notion of the single life of the scholar as one who, while having a freedom from marriage, was nonetheless restrained by institutional statutes from marrying. Historians of the early modern university have observed that it is an institution particularly inflected with concerns over social rank and status.[27] Like so many other patriarchal institutions of the period, the university was an institution where the line between the married and the single life, between participation in a patriarchal procreative order and an exclusion from that order, organized its internal hierarchies. The freedom not to marry was not so easily separated from its prohibition. The celibacy that emblematized the single life of the scholar was designed to both recognize and reinforce his exception from patrilineal, patriarchal manhood. Those statutes of St. Mary Magdalene College, Cambridge, when founded in 1542, assert that fellows could not be heirs to property, nor could they have claims to wealth; instead, preferences were to be given "to those who are 'docti et pauperes' and intending to devote themselves to theological study."[28] When William Harrison bemoans the influx of wealthy students into the Elizabethan universities, he frets over the granting of fellowships to those of means, in part, because patrilineal heirs were encroaching upon the statutory protections instituted for those who did not benefit from generational wealth. Arguing that the colleges "were erected by their founders at the first only for poor men's sons, whose parents were not able to bring them up unto learning," he goes on to note, "but now they have the least benefit of them, by reason the rich do so encroach upon them."[29] Erasmus, among other humanists, had argued for the literacy and education of the nobility, but for Harrison, the granting of rich men's sons fellowships undermined the primary reason university fellowships were established. Such wealthy sons could not only afford their education, they could afford to establish households. He concludes, "And so far hath this inconvenience spread itself that it is in my time an hard matter for a poor man's child to come by a fellowship (though he be never so good a scholar and worthy of that room)."[30] A form of charity, fellowship was meant to ensure that promising young men from the lower ranks of the social order might find means to study and enter ecclesiastical orders, but it also permitted wealthy young men like Hamlet pathways to the university. Disentitled poor men might find their pathways to the university taken, or imagined to be taken, by the already entitled.

While the introduction of new statutes, the acquisitions of lands and buildings, and the influx of commoners and courtiers to the university system altered the dynamics of the university across the sixteenth and seventeenth centuries, marital status came to increasingly signify one's entitlements within the university itself. Universities became more hierarchical, and a more pronounced fault line grew between the masters on the one hand, and the fellows, from which a Master was originally elected, and later appointed, on the other. Masters were granted privileges subordinates were not, and increasingly marital status reflected one's institutional status. Throughout the sixteenth century, the coronation of a new monarch occasioned new visitations to the universities and new, or sometimes the reinstitution of old, statutes. Though Edward and Mary both revised university statutes, it was the Elizabethan statutes of the 1570s that perhaps had the greatest effect on university fellows and the heads. Shortly after, the governing power of the colleges shifted from regent masters to the heads of the colleges, from a more diffuse form of government in which power flowed from the bottom (or near bottom) up to one where it was established from above. Because masters were not required to remain celibate by statute (the exception being Caius College, the statutes of which required a celibate master), they often took up the opportunity to wed. Elizabeth herself preferred celibacy within the universities, but her statute of 1561 insisting upon the celibacy of university members was revised in 1570 to include only the fellows, with the caveat that the maintenance of family could not occur within the precincts of the colleges. Masters or heads thus moved their lodging further afield from those of the fellows, the geographic distance reflecting a greater hierarchical one.[31] As Victor Morgan argues, the shift toward more authoritarian government within the university "is characteristic of Elizabethan attempts to ensure the greater answerability of subordinate units of government through a more precise allocation of authority."[32] A real and perceived divide between masters and fellows ensued, for as the university was continually analogized to a domestic household and its hierarchies aligned with this patriarchal structure, fellows and scholars were deemed servants, and so "were not enfranchised members of the political nation."[33] When Hamlet tells Horatio, "For what advancement may I hope from thee / That no revenue hast but thy good spirits / to feed and clothe thee? Why should the poor be flattered?" he makes direct reference to Horatio's position within the university hierarchy as a "fellow" student (3.2.53–55).

The single life of the scholar thus signified both his entitlement to university resources and his restriction from other patriarchal privileges as they were realized through marriage. Early modern scholars and university fellows often made much of this fact. It is relatively commonplace, for example, to see the fellows of universities negotiate their access to patriarchal manhood by reinterpreting university statutory restrictions as a special form of exclusive access. In the preface to his *Dyets Dry Dinner* (1599), a catalogue of food and table talk, Henry Buttes makes a qualification regarding his subject matter. While he asserts, "I bid all in general," to partake of his gustatory taxonomy, he in fact prohibits a great many: "I forbid no man but him onely that hath married a wife & cannot come."[34] The phrase reconstitutes the "Parable of the Banquet" found in the fourteenth chapter of the Gospel according to Luke. In the parable, a man holds a great banquet, and invites numerous people; one man cannot accept the invitation because he has just married. Buttes reconfigures a guest's rejection as the host's prohibition. As "Maister of Artes, and *Fellowe* of C.C.C. in C." or

Corpus Christi College in Cambridge, Buttes suggests that the textual feast he has prepared is meant for the single men of England, a marital status that reflects his own institutional standing as a celibate university fellow. The joke likewise inverts the logic of privilege most salient in the university hierarchy, but it has less to do with a philosophical freedom than the homosocial one that was also at work in the ballads examined in chapter 2. In fact, Buttes alludes to the confraternity that marked university fellowship. Medieval statutes encouraged masters, fellows, and servants to dine together to promote a communal ethos within the university. Throughout the sixteenth and seventeenth centuries, this trend was reversed. The master was often expressly dissuaded to eat with the fellows except for specific holidays or celebrations; at St. John's in Cambridge, for example, masters by custom did not dine with the fellows.[35] Thus, Buttes's prohibition is not anomalous or even reflective of personal preferences. In *The Anatomy of Melancholy*, Robert Burton, himself a lifelong "student" of Christ Church, Oxford ("student" being that institution's term for "fellow"), similarly recirculates the phrase from the Gospel according to Luke. Propounding the hardships and social obligations that attended marriage, Burton argues, "In sober sadness, marriage is a bondage, a thraldom, a yoke, an hindrance to all good enterprises ('he hath married a wife and cannot come'), stop to all preferment, a rock on which many are saved, many impinge, and are cast away."[36] Aphorism becomes an ameliorating axiom; to the contrary of Burton's assertion, marriage coincided with preferment in the university system, and as the statutes dividing married masters from single fellows, they enabled masters to have greater interaction with civil and court life while ensconcing the fellow further within the university community. For the scholar interested in social promotion and integration into the world outside of the university, like Marlowe's Faustus, his single life signified his status within an institutional hierarchy even if scholars themselves, at times, reimagined it as a freedom to transcend such institutional prescriptions.

## TYPICAL MAN: HAMLET AND HIS PROBLEMS

As a student of Wittenberg, Hamlet could be counted as one familiar with the single life of the scholar, but in the wake of the Isla Villa murders, lay readers and audience members have been quick to see the sulky prince as a prototype of the modern incel. Prompted by Alek Minassian's vehicular killing spree in Toronto, and four years after the Isla Villa killings, the scholar Erin Spampinato, in a 2018 article for the *Guardian*, combs through a literary tradition that runs from Hamlet to *The Great Gatsby's* Nick Carraway featuring socially isolated and sexually frustrated single men as the protagonists of their stories.[37] The headline for David Cote's review of Robert Icke's 2022 production of *Hamlet* claims that production "misguidedly embraces the Prince's incel-nature," while Cote merely notes that "the resonance comes across as incidental, Hamlet as incel edgelord only vaguely implied."[38] Harford echoes an observation that emerges again and again; writing for the *Daily Beast*, James Poulous, days after Rodger's homicides, turns to "*Hamlet*, another story about a hyperprivileged young man whose fury, fear, and confusion around sex and manliness sent him into a postmodern spiral of self-obsession and carnage."[39] Far from inventing the modern subject in creating Hamlet, Shakespeare may have invented the incel.[40]

These lay readings of Hamlet insist that he is all too modern. In doing so, they iterate what has been an intractable question about the play. When scholars tend to think of the question of Hamlet's modernity, they often turn to the problem of his interiority or inwardness.[41] What makes Hamlet modern in this interpretive tradition is not what Hamlet does (or does not do) but who he is. That problem has had a variety of articulations, but beginning with T. S. Eliot, the questions of Hamlet's modernity could be said to inhere in the mystery of his feelings. For Eliot, the play broadly and the character in particular fails to relay to audiences Hamlet's "feeling of a son towards a guilty mother" as an "objective correlative"; as Eliot explains, "*Hamlet*, like the sonnets, is full of some stuff that the writer could not drag to light, contemplate, or manipulate into art. And when we search for this feeling, we find it, as in the sonnets, very difficult to localize."[42] However insufferable he may be, Hamlet at once feels too much but says too little. Tracing twentieth-century articulations of this "Hamlet mystery" from Eliot to John Dover Wilson and through to Francis Barker, Drew Daniel shows how each situates the intractability of Hamlet's interiority as an impasse of psychology, illusive dramatic representation, or a subjectivity too early for its time.[43] From each of their agnostic readings of *Hamlet*, Daniel seeks to recuperate the modernity of Hamlet by reinscribing it through another affective register: the problem of Hamlet's feelings are themselves emblematic of early modern evocations of melancholy. As Daniel explains, "Hamlet makes us his accomplices, joining us together into a socially extended assemblage as he stages a melancholy which we not only witness but cocreate," and he does this through the technical device of the aside.[44] If Hamlet is modern, this argument goes, he is so because he melancholizes with us by first inviting us to melancholize with him.

We might envision Hamlet's modernity differently, however, and in a manner that would understand his melancholy or feelings as beside the point. When recent lay readings of Hamlet find him an avatar of the incel, they do not preoccupy themselves with his psychology or affective state, not exactly, but instead think about his relationship to his social world. In this respect, these lay readings recall a mode of interpretation theorized by cultural materialists, one far less concerned with subjectivity as such. If Hamlet might be translated into an incel, it is because he seems to "typify" one. In his analysis of art's relationship to culture, Raymond Williams, citing Lukács, explains, "Art, by figurative means, typifies 'the elements and tendencies of reality that recur according to regular laws, although changing with the changing circumstances'; as Williams goes on to elaborate, "in general terms the sense of 'typicality' . . . is that based on recognition of a constitutive and constituting process of social and historical reality, which is then specifically expressed in some particular 'type.'"[45] Types, in this formulation, do not congeal into a transhistorical social identity so much as they express a "dynamic process," a relation between individuals, institutions, material realities, and historical contingencies.[46] Out of this idea of the type developed notions of "correspondences" and "homologies," which served as a means, in part, of analyzing diachronic recursions of social processes that could be said to possess formal qualities, such that, as Williams concludes, those things which correspond, or that which is homologous, function as "examples of real social relationships, in their variable practice, which have common forms of origins."[47] If Hamlet shares something with the modern incel, the correspondences between them do not inhere in what each one feels, then, but in how they feel it, through those relations between themselves and the ideological formations, "those tendencies of reality," that make sense of their feelings.

Hamlet feels melancholic, but others experience his melancholy as violent misogyny. There is nothing particularly new in this observation. It is no secret that Hamlet is a misogynist. Attending to the structuring relationship between mourning and misogyny in the play, Steven Mullaney, for example, reads *Hamlet* (and *The Revenger's Tragedy*) as invested in mourning processes, at times proleptic, for the aging Queen Elizabeth and contends that, for men, "mourning is sometimes difficult to dissociate from misogyny."[48] Hamlet, in Mullaney's reading, mimics his father's misogyny toward Gertrude's sexual vitality by translating a mourning for his mother's future death into a present disgust at her sex life. As Mullaney observes, Hamlet may insist upon the intensity of his grief, as "that within which passes show," but he interprets the illegibility of that inward feeling as a highly legible vitriol: "Frailty, thy name is woman" (1.2.146).[49] We should be careful about corralling Hamlet's misogyny into an ameliorating relation to his grief or melancholy, however. Rather, as Kate Manne has argued, misogyny functions not so much as something men feel but a social effect women experience: "what matters is *not* deep down," as Manne explains, "but right there on the surface."[50] Hamlet's melancholy may be "that within which passes show," as an emotion abstracted into depth and endlessly, publicly rehearsed, but his misogyny is everywhere on the surface of the text; Hamlet cannot help but speak it and effect it.[51] Rather than defining misogyny in relation to men's feelings, which Manne terms the "naïve conception of misogyny," she insists we should define misogyny as "the hostile forces that (a) will tend to be faced by a (wider or narrower) class of girls and women because they are girls and women in that (more or less fully specified) social position; and (b) serve to police and enforce patriarchal order." In Manne's account, misogyny is not psychological so much as it is political, and while it ostensibly targets all women, its effects redound upon women who violate (in actuality, perception, or representation) patriarchal norms; as Manne goes on to summarize: "misogyny primarily targets women because they are women in a *man's world* (i.e., a historically patriarchal one, among other things), rather than because they are women in a *man's mind*, where the man is a misogynist."[52] To Hamlet and his ghostly father, Gertrude behaves like neither a mother nor a wife, appropriate roles under patriarchy. Instead, she exceeds these roles, and behaves like something far grosser and less contained by patriarchal gender norms: a queen, a woman, a person.

Manne's conception of misogyny does some work to reorient us to Hamlet's supposed inwardness and melancholia as inaugurating his modernity. What makes Hamlet modern is not the inwardness of his melancholy but the outwardness of his misogyny. Let us set aside Hamlet and his feelings, then. His psychology is beside the point. What makes Hamlet modern like an incel is his relationship to patriarchal entitlement. Arguing that Hamlet belongs closer to an early modern past than a modern present, Margreta de Grazia has argued that Hamlet's entitlement can best be understood as a matter of a patrimony desired and denied.[53] According to de Grazia, "that within that passes show" might best be understood not as melancholy or grief but as an unspeakable, because politically untenable, claim to a throne that he believes should be his.[54] Recontextualizing Hamlet's entitlement in relation to patrilineality casts the modern Hamlet decidedly into the early modern past. If Hamlet seems modern, it is because modernity mistranslates his political motives and desires into a subjectivity anticipating its present instantiations.

Hamlet may have more material relation to his entitlement, but he feels entitled all the same. Nonetheless, the play does not only represent Hamlet as a prince entitled to a throne his uncle usurps. He arrives to Elsinore as a celibate scholar from Wittenberg, and throughout the play, he very much continues to behave like one. *Hamlet* represents Hamlet as occupying two worlds, one which demands a form of patriarchal manhood conditioned by militarism, conquest, and patrilineal futurity, and the other which requires an unpatriarchal manhood devoted to study, melancholy, and the single life. This dialectic between the patriarchal manhood of a prince and the unpatriarchal manhood of the celibate scholar of Wittenberg everywhere marks the play and Hamlet's character. It is near structural. In remembering his father, Hamlet rages against the theft of a patriarchal birthright while performing his status as a celibate scholar even as he knows—and everyone else knows—that he could be heir-apparent. In her reading of the *amicitia* that informs Hamlet's relationship with his "fellow student" Horatio (1.2.176), Elizabeth Hanson observes the ways the early modern university's culture of social distinction between highborn and lowborn grates upon the social world of Elsinore in a manner that renders Hamlet's status as student superfluous to the tragic plot but nonetheless endemic to the play's dramatic action; as Hanson notes, "When 'Wittenberg' is paired with 'Elsinore' or 'Denmark,' it reminds us that these spaces cannot be occupied at the same time: for Hamlet, Horatio and (in Q1) Rosencrantz and Guildenstern, to be *in* Elsinore is to be *from* Wittenberg."[55] As Hanson goes on to show, Hamlet may desire a return to Wittenberg, but Horatio cannot let him forget that they are not exactly fellow university fellows, as his every address positions him as Hamlet's subordinate and insists upon Hamlet's "noble heart," even at the moment of death, where Hamlet is memorialized not as a fellow student but as a "sweet prince" (5.2.343).[56] Fellow student and sweet prince, neither and both, Hamlet belongs to two worlds that offer idealized visions of manhood that remain fundamentally incompatible.

Those lay readings that identify Hamlet as a prototypical incel do not situate Hamlet's crisis of manhood in historical terms; they perceive it as a structural relation. If his melancholy interprets a problem of obstructed agency, as Ngai theorizes, then we can understand the structural impediment that Hamlet faces in relation to these two incompatible forms of manhood, each of which militate against the other. Hamlet the modern incel arises from a crisis of entitlement born of Hamlet's status as an early modern incel. A celibate scholar who desires to be (but cannot fully achieve being) an heir no matter how violently he seeks to reorient his world, Hamlet is typical in his misogyny. And so typical in his misogyny, Hamlet is an all too typical incel, obsessed with the condition of his manhood as a matter of entitlement. As Drew Daniel observes of the play's ending, "the stakes of establishing and verifying masculinity, and of locating Hamlet in relation to available modes of masculinity, become acutely present at the moment of his death."[57] But perhaps they are not *so* present. As Daniel goes on to note, Hamlet not only dissuades Horatio from committing suicide, but, in countering Horatio's suicidal fantasy of abolishing national identity through an act of Roman stoicism, he also recuperates his manhood as an abstract ideal; where "Horatio has asserted his Roman-ness over his Danish-ness, Hamlet responds by asserting first and foremost his masculinity as a primary quality which precedes, and trumps, national identification as such."[58] What vestiges of that masculinity remain? Hamlet the scholar's melancholy provides affective cover for Hamlet the prince's entitlement, but both forms of manhood traffic in a misogyny the women of Hamlet's world experience as violence. If Hamlet's own "crisis" of masculinity negotiates two very distinctly early modern, institutional forms of manhood, then Hamlet is an early modern incel more than he is a modern one. But so too then are Rodger and his ilk, for they, likewise haunted by patriarchal ghosts, perceive themselves entitled to patriarchal privileges, to women's bodies and their services, and imagine themselves so canonized, if not as sweet princes, then as "supreme gentlem[e]n."[59]

## ROBERT BURTON AND THE ANATOMY OF AN INCEL

If *Hamlet* dramatizes the tragedy of an early modern incel who feels entitled to his birthright under patriarchy, Robert Burton's *Anatomy of Melancholy* lays bare the relation between melancholic feeling and vengeful reaction. An early modern scholar, Burton seems to have known something of Hamlet's character; according to Burton, melancholics are "most part covetous, muttering, repining, discontent, and still complaining, grudging, peevish, *injuriarum tenaces*, prone to revenge, soon troubled, and most violent in all their imaginations, not affable in speech, or apt to vulgar compliment, but surly, dull, sad, austere."[60] In this catalogue, Burton groks how the melancholic's depths of feeling animate his violent reprisals. Understood in relation to Burton's diagnostics, Hamlet plays to type. Yet Burton's diagnosis reaches from the early modern past to describe the disposition of the modern incel as well. The mass murderer incel Elliot Rodger imagines his "tragic life" as "a dark story of sadness, anger, and hatred."[61]

Situating Burton's *Anatomy of Melancholy* between Hamlet and Rodger, I suggest, exposes how representations of early modern atrabiliousness index an incel ideology that is structural to patriarchal social order but also subject to historicization. In his manifesto, "My Twisted World," Rodger, like Burton, insists upon an etiology that forges a dialectic between personal feelings and violent actions and fantasies. He continually conceives of his misogyny as an effect of his melancholy. In that manifesto, he purports to tell the story of his life, which amounts to a chronology of grievances against women (and some men) who do not appropriately recognize his social and sexual value. It is not a complex text, and it rehearses what it asserts from the beginning: how he was "forced to endure an existence of loneliness and insignificance, all because females of the human species were incapable of seeing the value in [him]."[62] He cries a lot throughout the text, and often in concert with a desire to inflict violence or humiliation upon others. In one scene, for example, Rodger recounts, "I passed by a girl I thought was pretty and said 'Hi' as we neared each other. She kept walking and didn't even have the grace to respond to me. *How dare she! That foul bitch.* I felt so humiliated that I went to one of the school bathrooms, locked myself in a toilet stall, and cried for an hour."[63] The episode is emblematic. If one vector of feeling in the manifesto turns inward, pulling toward abjection, loneliness, and sadness, the other looks outward, directing violence and anger to a larger social world. Like Hamlet, "that within which passes show," surfaces into a misogyny everywhere directed outward toward women. Melancholer abounds.

Burton was himself something of an incel. His *Anatomy of Melancholy* is, among other things, the treatise of an early modern celibate scholar. Produced by a celibate fellow who often reflects upon his own status as a single man in a university, *The Anatomy of Melancholy* not only assembles the etiologies and effects of early modern melancholy but also comes to hold a metonymic relation to Burton and the university in which he produced his defining work. Experienced as form that shuttles between and collapses differences of finite generalities and nearly infinite particulars of melancholy, *The Anatomy* reveals itself to readers as "a total unity of unreliability," or it comes to instantiate a "melancholic structure" that describes an exhaustive, effusive world of melancholy through a highly discursive, interiorized (if evasive) speaker.[64] It can be understood as an early modern cure for melancholy insofar as it offers up the experience of reading as ameliorative, or it functions as a political document, offering a subversive critique of the utopianism of the early modern church and state.[65] Exhaustive (and often exhausting), it offers numerous angles of interpretation. The one I offer here displaces a reading of melancholy qua melancholy, and instead interrogates how Burton represents himself as an early modern incel negotiating his feelings of entitlement to patriarchal privileges that, as he perceives it, the university denies him. To do this, I trace Burton's rhetorical strategies in *The Anatomy of Melancholy* alongside those of Elliot Rodger in his incel manifesto, "My Twisted World." Manifestos are polemical, and so rhetorical, projects, and while not a manifesto, Burton's *Anatomy* is likewise invested in various registers of persuasion and logics of totalization. As Susan Wells observes, "while the *Anatomy* is not a book of rhetorical theory, it is certainly a deeply rhetorical text."[66] Hyperglossic, citational, and ruminative, *The Anatomy of Melancholy* shares something of a formal ethos with modern incel internet forums and their seemingly endless discursivity, but Burton's big book also uses similar rhetorical patterns and logical structures as the modern incel discourse. Analyzing incel websites and internet forums, social scientists have identified three recurring rhetorical practices of incels: *discursive distancing, strategic borrowing,* and *fortifying boundaries.*[67] *Discursive distancing* is a practice whereby such men insist on distance from patriarchal power without actually abdicating that power; *strategic borrowing* is a practice of claiming or aligning oneself with a marginalized group as a means of appropriating victim status; and *fortifying boundaries* is a strategy of wielding the language of patriarchal power against those perceived as outsiders. In addition to these central rhetorical practices, incels often engage in hostile sexism and suicidality.[68] Because *The Anatomy of Melancholy* is such a vast and varied text, one which Burton also amended and revised over a number of years, it exceeds the narrow ideology and myopia of modern incel websites, and yet, its ruminations on melancholia are seeded throughout with similar rhetorical protocols, especially when Burton explores the relation between the single life and his statutory celibacy.

Robert Burton was a "student"—a term synonymous with fellow—of Christ Church, Oxford. As such, according to bylaw, he could not marry without forfeiting his privileges and patronage. Burton makes much of his circumstances. His single life surfaces into the text almost from the outset. As Burton teases his own biography, he divulges only those parts of his life that condition his status in the university. He confesses: "Yet thus much I will say of my selfe, & that I hope without all suspiton of pride, or self-conceipt, I have liv'd a silent, sedentary, solitary, private life, *mihi & musis,* in the University as long almost as *Xenocrates* in *Athens, ad senectam ferè,* to learne wisdome as he did, penned up most part in my study."[69] Divulgements of his single life as a celibate scholar often curdle into recriminations elsewhere in the *Anatomy,* however. When Burton turns again to his single life in the university, he often makes it clear that the university impedes his access to patriarchal privilege.

Burton speaks of his melancholy through the *Anatomy,* but it is in his "Digression of the Misery of Schollers" where he meditates at length on his own institutional status in relation to patriarchal manhood. Throughout this section, he engages in a practice of *discursive distancing,* whereby he reinscribes his access to the patriarchal institution of the early modern university as an impediment from patriarchal privileges writ large. He begins by quickly citing those commonplace causes of the scholar's melancholy: how they live and what they do. As Burton explains, the practice of scholarship conduces "this malady": scholars "live a sedentary, solitary life, *sibi & musis,* free from bodily exercise, and those ordinary disports other men use."[70] This type of life is required of the second reason for a scholar's melancholy: "contemplation," an action that produces pathological symptoms of ill health, "all such diseases as come by overmuch sitting."[71] Burton gives these causes little credence, however, and soon turns to the material relations that condition the scholar's single life as impoverished and precarious. Spending too much time on learning, "many poore schollers have lost their wits, or become dizards, neglecting all worldly affaires, and their own healthe, wealth, *esse* and *benè esse,* to gain knowledge [,] for which, after all their paines in the worlds esteeme they are accompted ridiculous and silly fooles, Idiots, Asses, and (as oft they are) rejected, contemned, derided, doting, and mad. . . . Or if they keep their wits, yet they are esteemed scrubbes and fooles by reason of their carriage."[72] If the world perceives the scholar in such humiliating terms, Burton affirms the scholar more or less deserves it: "Because they cannot ride an horse, which every Clowne can doe; salute and court a Gentlewoman, carve at table, cringe and make congies, which every common swasher can doe, *hos populus ridet &c.* they are laughed to scorne, and accompted silly fooles by our Gallants. Yea many times, such is their misery, they deserve it: a meere Scholler, a meere Asse."[73] The comparison Burton makes between what "Gallants" seemingly know and what scholars have failed to learn is an odd one. He implies that scholars have not learned such social practices because they have not been taught; they do not know how to talk to women because they have been prevented from learning how to do so, or worse, scholars are, in some essential sense, incapable of doing what "every Clowne can doe" and what "every common swasher can doe." If such men, as clowns and swashers, are intellectually below Burton, the scholar, then how much more humiliating for him, who cannot rise to their economic or social status.

What makes the scholar so melancholic, then, is the degree to which his learning does not prepare him to perform socially like other men. This rhetoric of *discursive distancing* is common in Rodger's manifesto as well; the incel bemoans, "I always felt like a loser compared to them, and I hate them for it, though I still wanted their approval. I wanted to be one of them."[74] In *The Anatomy,* the scholar relates to the gallant as the incel does to the "Chad." But Burton goes beyond the interpersonal observation to systematize the scholar's social disadvantages. As he imagines an alternative world that "would have good Schollers to be highly rewarded, and had in some extraordinary respect above other men, *to have greater priviledges then the rest, that adventure themselves and abbreviate their lives for the publike good*," he does so to insist that the patriarchal social order privileges the wrong kinds of men: "But our patrons of learning are so farre now adaies, from respecting the *Muses*, and giving that honour to Schollers, or reward which they deserve, & are allowed by those indulgent priviledges of many noble Princes."[75] The problem, Burton goes on to argue, is one of desert: "after all their paines in the *Universities*, cost and charge, expenses, irksome hours, laborious tasks, wearisome daies, dangers, hazards (barred *interim* from all pleasures which other men have, mewed up like hawkes all their lives) if they chance to wade through them, they shall in the end be rejected, contemned, & which is their greatest misery, driven to their shifts, exposed to want, poverty and beggary."[76] Positioned as an aside, the parenthetical interrupts the litany of the scholar's toil to underwrite the premises of his feelings of entitlement. Burton believes scholars like himself deserve more material rewards because they, "mewed up like hawkes," have lived lives of involuntary celibacy. They have foregone, the logic goes, their entitlement to sex with women to live lives of learning, but the public fails to acknowledge and reward them for their personal sacrifice.

What an incel. As he meditates further on the misery of scholars, Burton continually reinscribes his celibacy as an involuntary, institutional imposition upon his agency. Even as he provides a rather brilliant digression on the ways the value of learning becomes a mere matter of utility in relation to a nascent capitalist political economy—wryly observing, "he that can tell his mony hath Arithmeticke enough: He is a true Geometrician, can measure out a good fortune to himselfe; a perfect Astrologer, that can cast the rise and fall of others, and marke their Errant motions to his own use"—Burton maps these material relations to reconstitute his celibacy as both cause and effect of his disenfranchisement by the prevailing patriarchal social order.[77] Likening scholars to the goddess Psyche, Burton extrapolates, "many mortall men came to see faire *Psyche* the glory of her age, they did admire her, commend, desire her for her divine beauty, and gaze upon her; but as on a picture; none would marry her, *quòd indotata*, faire *Psyche* had no money."[78] As Burton analogizes the scholar's poverty with Psyche's own, the scholar's celibacy not only becomes an effect of the material conditions of his labor, but it also comes to effect a gendered relation to those material conditions. While the comparison circulates a homoerotic fantasy in which the scholar can imagine themselves Psyche, and so desired by "many mortall men," it also repositions the scholar in a passive role. "A picture," the scholar may be admired, commended, desired, and gazed upon, but he possesses no power to act or marry. Burton here laments that scholars are melancholic not only because they do not possess capital to wed, but also because, despite their beauty, no one will sleep with them, so, he concludes, "Wee that are University men, like so many hide-bound Calves in a Pasture, tarry out our time, wither away as a flower ungathered in a garden, and are never used."[79]

Like a virgin, Burton simply wants to be touched for the very first time. Such a desire, however, bespeaks his conception of his celibacy as a condition over which he has no control: no one will pluck his flower, which tarries and withers (the incel Rodger uses a similar trope; he "withered in agony").[80] Framing his sexual agency as a matter of what others will not do for or to him, Burton engages in that incel habit of *strategic borrowing*, appropriating the victim status of single women and maids. When, in fact, he turns to the "Symptoms of Maides, Nunnes, and Widowes Melancholy," he cannot help but see in them his own position as a celibate scholar. Burton begins the section much like he did that on the misery of scholars; he documents the supposed humoral, behavioral, and dietary causes of melancholy for such women, and then he makes a distinction between laborers and gentlewomen, the latter of whom—"noble virgins, nice gentlewomen, such as are solitary and idle, live at ease, lead a life out of action and imployment"—"for the most part are misaffected, and prone to the disease."[81] Burton insists that women are expressly victims of melancholy. While he asserts, "I doe not so much pitty them that may otherwise be eased," he does pity others, "those alone that out of a strong temperament, innate constitution, are violently carried away with this torrent of inward humours, and though very modest of themselves, sober, religious, virtuous, and well given, (as many so distressed maids are), yet cannot make resistance; these grievances will appear, this malady take place, and now manifestly shew itself, and may not otherwise be helped."[82] This long meditation on those overtaken with melancholy catalyzes vertigo in Burton; "But where am I?" he asks; "Into what subject have I rushed? What have I to doe with Nunnes, Maids, Virgins, Widowes?"

But Burton does know where he is. He tells the reader in the next lines: "I am a bacheler my selfe, and lead a Monasticke life in a College, *næ ego sane ineptus qui hæc dixerim.*" Constituting his single life as that of a celibate, if monastic, bachelor, Burton self-deprecates, calling himself a fool in his scholarly Latin. From such deprecation, he deprecates himself further. In a move that parallels his earlier analogizing of scholars to Psyche, Burton casts himself as Athena: "I confesse 'tis an *indecorum*, and as *Pallas* a Virgin blushed, when *Jupiter* by chance spake of Love matters in her presence, and turn'd away her face; *me reprimam*, though my subject require it, I will say no more."[83] Conceiving himself as a blushing virgin, Burton suggests his sympathy with melancholic maids is a matter of shared feeling: he does not simply feel for them; he feels with them. So positioning himself on the side of maids, who here cannot speak for themselves, Burton performs a similar silencing only to rescind it in the next line: "And yet I must and will say something more, adde a worde or two *in gratiam Virginum & Viduarum*, in favour of all such distressed parties, in commiseration of their present estate."[84]

Because he is not a maid but a scholar with a book, he will yet speak. However, he does not do so on the behalf of maids alone but on behalf of "all distressed parties," a group which might include him. Strategically borrowing the victim status he has already assigned to virgins and maids, Burton distances himself from patriarchal power to rail at length against those social forces that enforce his celibacy:

> I needs inveigh against them that are in fault, more than manifest causes, and as bitterly tax those tryannizing pseudo-politicians' superstitious orders, rash vows, hard-hearted parents, guardians, unnatural friends, allies, (call them how you will), those careless and stupid overseers, that, out of worldly respects, covetousness, supine negligence, their own private ends, (because, meanwhile, it is well for him), can so severely reject, stubbornly neglect, and impiously contemn, without all remorse and pity, the tears, sighs, groans, and grievous miseries, of such poor Soules committed to their charge. How odious and abominable are those superstitious and rash vowes of Popish Monasteries, so to binde and enforce men and women to vowe virginity, to lead a single life against the lawes of nature, opposite to religion, and humanity, so to starve, to offer violence, to suppose the vigor of youth, by rigorous statutes, severe lawes, vaine perswasions, to debarred them of that, to which by their innate temperature they are so furiously inclined, urgently carried, & sometimes precipitated, even irresistibly led, to the prejudice of their souls health, and good estate of body and minde. . . . Stupid polititians; hæccine fieri flagitia? ought these things so to be carried? better marry then burne, saith the Apostle, but they are otherwise perswaded. They will by all meanes quench their neighbours house if it bee on fire, but that fire of lust which breakes out into such lamentable flames, they will not take notise of, their owne bowels often times, flesh and blood shall so rage and burne, and they will not see it.[85]

As grief over the particular circumstances of maids becomes grievance over all afflicted parties, Burton's invective recalls his earlier description of the misery of scholars, but it also proleptically incorporates the incel logic of Rodger's manifesto. With Rodger, we might imagine Burton decrying, "Not only did I have to waste my entire youth suffering in loneliness and unfulfilled desire, but I had to live with the knowledge that other boys my age were able to have all of the experiences I craved for. It is absolutely unfair and unjust."[86] While Burton encodes such "involuntary celibacy" as a matter of religious doctrine, he applies the veneer a bit too thinly. Having already asserted that he leads "a Monasticke life in a College," Burton cannot fully distance the university statutes from the "odious and abominable . . . superstituous and rashe vowes of Popish Monasteries," which "binde and enforce men and women to vowe virginity, to lead a single life against the lawes of nature." As despair turns to rage and the fires of unrequited lust stoke his choler, Burton's anatomy of the melancholy of maids, nuns, and widows transforms into pure polemic about the involuntary nature of his celibacy. Positioned where the social and symptomatic touch, the single life, for Burton, is a cause of melancholy because it is an effect of patriarchal oppression. Framed within an examination of single life of women, Burton's anatomy of his single life diagnoses not the afflictions of a susceptible body. Instead, it unfolds those social and material relations that prevent him from fully participating in the patriarchal social order. He bemoans his enforced celibacy because, in the end, it makes him too much like the maids with whom he can never have sex.

## FROM GUILDED PILLES TO RED PILLS IN BURTON'S *ANATOMY OF MELANCHOLY*

Later in *The Anatomy*, women who will not sexually service men become a pressing concern for Burton. He begins his third partition by focusing on love melancholy, and it is here a fuller correspondence with incel discourses emerges. The section opens with Burton acknowledging possible critics: "There will not bee wanting, I presume, one or other that will much discommend some part of this Treatise of Love Melancholy, and object . . . *that it is too light for a Divine, too Comicall a subject* to speake of Love Symptomes, too phantasticall, & fit alone for a wanton Poet, a feeling young love-sicke gallant, an effeminate Courtier, or some such idle person."[87] Justifying his choice to focus on love melancholy because "Love is a species of melancholy," Burton then turns to a metaphor to cast this portion of this treatise as a kind of cure: "and these my writings I hope, shall take like guilded pilles, which are so composed as well to tempt the appetite, and deceave the pallat, as to helpe and medicinally worke upon the whole body, my lines shall not onely recreate, but rectifie the mind."[88] Historicizing

Burton's trope, Mary Ann Lund explains that he cites the practice of sugarcoating bitter medicine but argues that Burton goes beyond merely repurposing convention to instead proposing that "reading will 'medicinally worke' on the reader in an equivalent manner" as physical medicine.[89] Burton draws on a long tradition of presenting reading as a healing practice, as Lund goes on to show, but what is notable about Burton's use of the trope is that he envisions not only that reading his text will function as a cure but also that the cure might take the form of an epistemological reorientation; he insists "my lines shall not onely recreate, but rectifie the mind." The love melancholic, who ostensibly sees things unclearly, might read, and in reading, be transformed to see the world anew.

In its purported power to recreate and rectify the mind, Burton's guilded pill preempts the incel's "redpill," the trope incels use to signal their inauguration into an antifeminist ideology by having been awakened to "the 'true nature' of feminism as oppressive to men."[90] Like Burton's guilded pill, the incel's red pill is discursive: what they read (they imagine) rectifies their minds and recreates them. For the incel, the pill metaphor explicitly marks the epistemological shift that reveals to them who they are in relation to the world they live in: they often use the phrase "being redpilled" or "taking the redpill." But Burton's "guilded pill" does not just share a formal consonance with the incel's redpill. It contains the same kind of misogynistic medicine. The love melancholic, in other words, might begin Burton's text with one idea of himself, but by the end, Burton will suggest, such men, having taken his guilded pill, are better off as incels like him.

If in the first partition Burton engages in strategic borrowing to cast the single life of the celibate scholar to claim the victim status of virginal maids, in his meditation on love melancholy, he fortifies the boundaries of patriarchy by "inveigh[ing] against them that are at fault," who, it turns out, are women. Given its etiology, early modern love melancholy limns the ideology of the modern incel, which as Rodger articulates it, blames "all women for rejecting me and starving me of love and sex."[91] Because incels naturalize patriarchal social order and its gender hierarchies, they are also quick to naturalize other social hierarchies, especially racist ones. Incels have little sympathy for women, but they do have sympathy for white supremacy. Burton does too. Guilding his pills, Burton targets maids and single women as the causes of melancholy in men, and here Burton, the incel scholar, sounds a lot like Rodger, the modern incel, especially as both steep their melancholy in white supremacist, racist imaginaries.[92] In his manifesto, Elliot Rodger frames his hatred of women in relation to his hatred of Black men. Recounting his early college experience of learning about the sexual activity of his peers, Rodger wields anti-Black racism to cast his entitlement as something like Hamlet's own: a matter of royalty. He wonders:

> How could an inferior, ugly black boy be able to get a white girl and not me? I am beautiful, and I am half white myself. I am descended from British aristocracy. *He* is descended from slaves. I deserve it more. I tried not to believe his foul words, but they were already said, and it was hard to erase from my mind. If this is actually true, if this ugly black filth was able to have sex with a blonde white girl at the age of thirteen while I've had to suffer virginity all my life, then this just proves how ridiculous the female gender is. They would give themselves to this filthy scum, but they reject ME! The injustice! . . . Females truly have something mentally wrong with them. Their minds are flawed, and at this point in my life I was beginning to see it.[93]

While his racism rehearses stock tropes of anti-Black animus, Rodger also cites a kind of genealogy for his white supremacist thought; he insists on his "descent" from "British Aristocracy." That fantasy indexes both the racial and class dimension that whiteness concatenates for Rodger, but it also corresponds to early modern racial epistemologies. Burton will likewise draw upon them. While the contents of Burton's meditations on the lovelorn melancholic differ, Burton marshals a commensurate anti-Black racism. With just a bit of rubbing, Burton's guilded pill shows itself to contain the incel's red medicine. He sounds a lot like Rodger, for example, when he explains that the cause of melancholy is white women who desire anyone but white men:

> a black man is a pearl in a fair woman's eye, and is as acceptable as lame *Vulcan* was to *Venus*; for he being a sweaty fuliginous blacke smyth, was dearly beloved of her, when faire *Apollo*, nimble *Mercury* were rejected, and the rest of the sweet-fac'd Gods forsaken. Many women (as *Petronius* observes) *sordibus calent* (As many men are more moved with kitchin wenches, and a poore market maid, then all these illustrious Court and City Dames) will sooner dote upon a slave, a servant, a Durt-dawber, a *Brontes*, a Cooke, a Player, if they see his naked legges or armes, *thorosaque brachia*, &c., like that huntsman *Meleager* in *Philostratus*, though he be in all in ragges, obscene and durty, besmeared like a ruddleman, a gypsy, or a chimny-sweeper, than upon a Noble Gallant.[94]

Like Rodger, Burton ameliorates the lovelorn melancholic's lack of access to women by arguing women do not recognize the desert of white men when they see it. For Burton, fair women do not perceive fairly the value of white men. Instead, they render Black men white even as they commodify them; fair women see such men as "pearls."[95] Both Rodger and Burton further dehumanize Black men in similar terms by aligning them with dirt and social subordination. Against the fair, clean incel, Rodger and Burton view a Black man desired by a white woman as "obscene and dirty," "filth," "foul," "a slave, a servant, a dirt dauber." The scopophilic capacity of a fair woman to transform Black men into commodities conditions the rhetoric of Burton and Rodger in what they continually "observe" and "see" about the world, essentially effecting their "pilling" as a form of perception. While both deploy a range of similarly racist tropes, they engage in what Patricia Akhimie has identified as "marking," an early modern (and here, modern) practice of social distinction whereby "the language of 'marking'—observing, interpreting, remarking, labeling—succeeds in branding, permanently marking its objects."[96] As Akhimie explains, race-making and racist thought in the early modern period extends from conduct discourses in which processes of observation and judgment determine reputation. As somatic signs come to signify cultural and social difference, scrutiny might mark such bodies, such that "Blackness as a mark symbolizes that immutable status in which no behavior, good or bad, can alter one's reputation."[97] Positioning themselves as scholar and aristocrat, both Burton and Rodger construct a white supremacy by "marking" Black men as well as the white women who see and desire them. Having swallowed their pills like good incels, Burton and Rodger purport to see the world as it really is.

If the cause of melancholy is rooted in women who refuse to desire the right kinds of men, as Burton and Rodger insist, then misogyny—especially if it can obliterate the object of desire—should cure it.[98] Burton advises that the lovelorn should combat generalizing from one particular case—the beauty of a woman—and instead focus upon a host of other particulars that might refute the love melancholic's conclusions about the woman upon which he has fixated. He must scrutinize her body. As Burton recommends, the love melancholic should: "compare her to another standing by"; "put her in another's clothes," including the raiment of beggars, and behold "her in a frosty morning, in cold weather, in some passion or perturbation of mind."[99] He should examine her mouth, how she smiles, her teeth, by candle and in the morning; he should "carefully consider what comes forth of mouth and nostrils and other bodily conduits," and, moreover, he should "see her undrest, see her, if it be possible, out of her attires."[100] The cure for desire, Burton finally concludes, is hate: "for burning lust is but a flash, a gunpowder passion, and hatred followes in the highest degree, dislike, and contempt."[101]

In this section on the cures for the lovelorn melancholic, Burton rehearses misogamist and misogynist tropes to present the single, celibate man as a man self-mastered, one who can discipline his body and its passions by representing women as undisciplined and tortured. A consummate scholar, Burton deeply knows and widely cites a misogynistic discourse, and like an incel who has taken the "redpill," Burton rehearses a range of misogynistic and misogamist rhetoric—only partially quoted here—to "cure" love melancholy through the practice of "oppressive othering" common to incel forums.[102] The cure itself is likewise meant to compound and intensify the lovelorn's misogyny to ameliorate his melancholy. If Burton insists "I have not writ a tenth of that which might bee urged out of [such women haters]," it is because he does not need to write much more. The lovelorn who takes Burton's guilded pill might, like an incel scholar, do that work for him.[103] Given the present vitriol that circulates on the internet, in chat rooms, message boards, across the whole of the "manosphere," Burton proves prescient when his samples are situated in relation to a continually unfolding discourse of sad and angry incels.[104]

By the end of the subsection on cures for love melancholics, Burton attempts to ameliorate his antifeminist bile by excusing his misogyny as a kind of joke: "If any man take exception at my words, let him alter the name, read him for her, and 'tis all one in effect."[105] Any man, Burton imagines, but not any woman. His appeal leads to a description of the protean nature of his own rhetoric. Burton explains: "My words are like *Passus* picture in *Lucian* of whom, when a good-fellow had bespoke an horse to bee painted with his heeles upward, tumbling on his back, he made him passant, now when the fellow came for his piece, he was very angry, and said, it was quite opposite to his mind; but *Passus* instantly turned the Picture upside downe, shewed him the horse at that site which he requested, and so gave him satisfaction."[106] The image of the picture that can be turned, or the turning picture, is a trope that Christopher Tilmouth sees as structural to Burton's whole project. Here, as Burton provides a picture of melancholy, it turns into misogyny, and back again.[107] Melancholy conduces rage, rage melancholy, until they blur into melancholer.

Guilded pill and red pill: Burton's rhetoric turns and returns to misogyny as a cure for what ails sexless men. Recirculating an early modern incel aphorism, Burton concludes, "A woman a man may eschew, but not a wife: wedding is undoing, (some say), marrying, marring, wooing woing."[108] Fortifying the boundaries between married masters and celibate scholars,

Burton ends his meditation on love melancholy by retreating back into his single, celibate life, both desiring women and denigrating them. But the effect of his misogyny here is not really a matter of his feelings. As he concludes that love melancholics should find solace in the single life of a celibate scholar, Burton also comes to reify the early modern university as a homosocial institution dominated by men and exclusive of women. Melancholy may be felt by the love melancholic and the incel scholar alike, but the misogyny offered as a cure polices the boundaries of the university, which prevents women from entering it, both materially and discursively. Read against his earlier meditation on the misery of scholars and the melancholy of women, Burton's treatment of love melancholy also reframes the dialectic between scholar and the maid: if the celibate scholar is by statutory fiat like a maid tyrannized by institutional keepers, he can, alternatively, imagine himself as one who (unlike the lovelorn melancholic) remains free from the tyranny of women who are kept from universities in the first place. In the final partition of *The Anatomy of Melancholy*, the incel scholar ascends: the lovelorn melancholic might yet transform into a celibate scholar—he simply needs to read the right books, to take the right kind of medicine—and safely ensconced in his university, a celibate scholar like Burton can stew in the burbling, black bile of the incel's melancholer.

# Chapter 5

## The Single Life of the Unmarried Eunuch

### Elaborations of Gendered Embodiment in *Mikrokosmographia*, *Twelfth Night*, and *The Roaring Girl*

In the seventeenth-century character book *Characterismi: or Lenton's Leisures* (1636), readers might come across the description of "A Bachelour" who plays very much to type. "A Bachelour," they are told,

> Is one that carries a great burthen about him, Concupiscence; to which hee is either given over, or in perpetuall combate betwixt the flesh and the spirit; He is never quiet in his mind, for he is continually choosing, and commonly as soone dislikes his owne choyce: a great point of folly in him, to bee provok't to any thing either by opinion or purblind Passion. He is one whose honesty cannot shelter him from suspition, and imputation of his next neighbour, by reason of his supposed vigour. Hee dreames away his best time, and sowes his seed in other mens gardens, (which they reape and are no gainers by it) whilest he hath scarce any left to sowe in his owne. Hee thinkes himselfe happy in that hee hath none to care for but himselfe, whilest he cares not at all for his Nobler selfe, his Soule, and dyes without a Vine to his houseside, or an Olive plant to his Table; so that posterity shall not behold any of his Progeny. Hee courts each handsome object, his veines being full of *Venus*, and his heart of *Cupids* darts, which in short time so sting him, that happily ere long, he salutes *Hymen*, and proves an honest man: for the obtaining whereof in his former estate he was farre out of his way, except made an Eunuch, and consequently been hated by the softer Sex for ever after.[1]

Lenton's characterization traffics in familiar early modern tropes about marriage and the single life. Constituted by his overdetermined sexual desires, this bachelor is all too socially legible. As he moves through his world, his "great burthen" is at once his "Concupiscence" as well as its "imputation," that "supposed vigour" that invites the "suspition" of "his next neighbor." This little sketch traces the contours of the compulsory sexuality explored in chapter 1, though here "the bachelor" appears less a chaste youth and more an early modern fuckboy, one whose only hope is a marriage that might recuperate a wildly inordinate lust into procreative desire. Marriage, in this character sketch, emerges as a kind of membrane, one through which the terms of normative gender and sexuality are tested and controlled; passing through the bower, the bachelor either "proves" an "honest man" or is "made an Eunuch." That earlier suspicion of the bachelor's burdensome lust becomes reconstituted as just that: merely suspicion. Rendered husband or eunuch, the bachelor becomes a person neighbors might know, or, one whom in so knowing, "the softer sex" might loathe "for ever after."

Despite the sketch's insistences on proofs and truths, questions remain. What conditions the candor of the "honest man"? If the "honest man" is honest, then is the "Eunuch" dishonest? If the "softer Sex" comes to hate the "Eunuch" "for ever after," how did they feel about the eunuch before, when they were "a bachelor"? Who or what processes make the eunuch so? What does it mean to be made an eunuch? Insofar as the gender and sexual relations circulating in Lenton's description are "intelligible," they become so because, as Judith Butler has argued, they "in some sense institute and maintain relations of coherence and continuity among sex, gender, sexual practice, and desire."[2] Butler, of course, has taken up the problem of gender performativity and materializations of gender across a body of work, but quite early in *Gender Trouble*, they ask a question this chapter will in part answer: "Is there a history of how the duality of sex was established, a genealogy that might expose the binary option as a variable construction?"[3] Lenton's text evidences one such history of a variable construction of gender, one in which the dichotomy between the single life and the married life organizes a set of relations that seemingly speak the truth about gendered embodiment in terms of who might be a bachelor, eunuch, or husband.

Lenton's character description is full of variables. In situating a "Bachelour," an "Honest Man," the "Softer Sex," and a "Eunuch" each among the other, Lenton's characterization suggests the ways that, within the early modern period, "the duality of sex" was not a duality but a shifting set of relations that operationalized the distinction between the married and the single life to naturalize and normalize particular modes of gendered embodiment through processes of speculation, revelation, and obviation. This chapter argues that the single life of the eunuch was integral to materializing forms of gendered embodiment conducive to patriarchal marriage. Attending to chaste youths, bachelor journeymen, true gallants, and incel scholars, previous chapters have explored how representations of the single life facilitate the imagining of unpatriarchal manhoods in relation to early modern institutions and patriarchal ideologies that organize sexuality, labor, gentility, and feeling. In those previous chapters, manhood remained a rather stable category of analysis so that the register of the "unpatriarchal" might be interrogated from the particular analytics of each chapter. By attending to the single life of the eunuch, this chapter seeks to shift this book's register and to attenuate its organizing premises. It holds fast to the ways the single life promotes "unpatriachal" relations to open what that term modifies: manhood, especially as it might be imagined as an embodied state.

That the bachelor of Lenton's characterology "is made an Eunuch" reveals the ideological operations of early modern patriarchy that this chapter seeks to read and recover. Through its passive formation, it suggests all the ways gender is imputed, manufactured, rendered, fabricated, and ultimately imposed on subjects by abstracted authority. Gendered bodies are made so, and they are often made so in the language of sex. In *Sex Is As Sex Does: Governing Transgender Identity*, Paisley Currah argues that classifications of sex might be better understood not so much in relation to what they "are" but in terms of what they "do." Shifting analytical energy away from the dialectic of gender/sex and toward that of state/sex, he examines how institutions, agencies, and other authorities operationalize sex in contradictory ways to conclude that "sex is not a thing, a property, or a trait, but the outcome of decisions backed by legal authority. And its meaning changes."[4] Currah examines the granular operations of state agencies and jurisdictions in the territories of the United States in the mid-twentieth to twenty-first centuries. What sex is often changes depending on institutional vagaries, but, as Currah shows, whatever sex is or is imputed to be—and it can be "a thing, a property, or a trait" if a state actor treats it as such—depends upon its function as "a technology of governance," such that "the classifications . . . are the effects of decisions, not simple and transparent descriptions of something already there."[5] If, as Foucault argues, the early modern period was governed by "the law of marriage," patriarchal marriage might be understood as operating as one such technology that classified sex as a genital property of the body such that a body could be speculated upon, examined, tested, and imagined as possessing an imputed sex. As exemplified by the excerpt from Lenton, central to this process were representations of the single life of the eunuch, who early modern discourses represented as given over in particular to the revelations of sex.

In examining the central role of the figure of the eunuch to the construction of the patriarchal marital couple, I seek to further historicize and theorize early modern materializations of gendered embodiment. Primarily through the influence of Freud, acts of castration and fear of the gelded body have deeply informed twentieth-century European theorizations of the heterosexual subject even as such theorizations have dematerialized such a body as a relation of the unconscious to the self. Scholars have done much to historicize Freud's theory of the castration complex and its connection to early modern representational antecedents.[6] Examining the single life of the eunuch goes some way to demonstrate how the abstracted heterosexual subject is an effect of the naturalization of patriarchal marriage in Freud's twentieth century, but attending to the eunuch also localizes the materialization of sex in the early modern period. In their own theorizations of the heterosexual matrix and the materiality of sex, Butler has crucially observed "if the materiality of sex is demarcated in discourse, then this demarcation will produce a domain of excluded and delegitimated 'sex.'"[7] In the early modern period, the "eunuch" demarcated this domain of exclusion, and the primary territory of that domain, as already at work in Lenton's sketch, was often that of marriage.

My argument in this chapter attends to early modern representations of the eunuch to contribute to a body of scholarship that recognizes histories of castrated people and their representation as central to histories of gender, sexuality, race, disability, and normativity.[8] Katherine Crawford has argued, for instance, that "castrates were (often deliberately) physically and socially disabled castrated men who were effectively transgendered medically and culturally"; this act upon a body, Crawford goes on to assert, "put castrates at odds with normal and normate social and cultural values, and . . . served as an epistemological point of origin for pejorative notions of deviant sexual identity."[9] In this chapter, I draw upon Crawford's historical arguments but deploy them to different ends. Crawford seeks to trace the history of those who were castrated in relation to "the medicalization involved in the intentional disabling of boys and men in terms of the institutional structures that justified and encouraged castration."[10] In this chapter, I analyze the ways early modern English texts operationalize the figure of the eunuch—a figure who, crucially, may or may not be castrated—to materialize forms of gendered embodiment constructed as conducive to particular forms of life, namely the married or the single life. There were indeed early modern eunuchs, but the figure of the eunuch and the systems of representation, interrogation, and materialization that might construe any person legible as such were deeply imbricated in the institutionalization of

159

patriarchal marriage as a technology of governance. Early moderns could and did imagine castration in terms of gender transition, that is, as "a change of the sex as it were, which by eunuchism makes the body which was virile and masculine to be effeminate, done by the ancients by Gelding."[11] For the purposes of this chapter, however, I am less interested in documenting modes of early modern transition or tracing genealogies of subjects than I am in interrogating those processes by which sex classifies bodies, by which bodies are materialized as sexed, and by which sexed bodies materialize as able bodies. To pay close attention to how early modern English discourses operationalize the eunuch is thus to engage in what Marquis Bey advocates of a Black trans feminism: "an agential and intentional undoing of regulative gender norms and, further, the creative deconstructing of ontological racial and gender assault; a kind of gendered deconstruction, an unraveling that unstitches governant means of subjectivation."[12]

To do that work, to try to do that work, this chapter first examines the single life of the eunuch within early modern marital and anatomical discourses to trace how such discourses labor to classify subjects by sex through and against constructions of the figure of the eunuch. Specifically, it surveys early modern marital discourses and closely reads Helkiah Crooke's *Mikrokosmographia* (1615) to elaborate the ways early modern patriarchy reproduces the gender and racial categories it then seeks to materialize and naturalize through patriarchal marriage. Having established the integral role that the figure of the eunuch plays in naturalizing (what amounts to) the cisnormative marital couple, I turn to Shakespeare's *Twelfth Night* to reconsider how that play similarly mobilizes the figure of the eunuch to organize its epistemologies of race and gender. I then consider the ways Middleton and Dekker align Moll and Laxton with the figure of the eunuch in *The Roaring Girl* to effectuate the gender relations of its marriage plot. These two plays have stood at the center of much feminist and queer scholarship on the early modern period, and if I do not entirely urge the decanonization of them, I hope to show that they operationalize sex classifications to reify cisnormativity even as they leave some room to imagine forms of gendered embodiment subversive to early modern patriarchy. Though to different ends, each of these plays mobilize the single life of the unmarried eunuch to naturalize the marital couple, the transparencies of which depend upon rendering visible the figure of the eunuch—indeed, constructing the single life of the eunuch as one given over to operations of scrutiny and visibility—so that the structuring opacities of cisnormativity might readily translate into the privacies conducive to the marriage relation itself.

## UNMARRIED EUNUCHS AND PATRIARCHAL MARRIAGE

When Lenton insists in his character description that the "bachelor" might be "made an Eunuch" or prove "an honest man," he pushes the single man through the threshold of marriage as means of revealing the truth of a person. "The honest man" is truthful because he becomes, we are to understand, a husband and so demonstrates his willing role in procreative futurity. Both the "bachelor" and the "Eunuch," on the other hand, are figures of perceived opacity, and each are likewise given over to scrutiny: the bachelor's "honesty cannot shelter him from suspition, and imputation of his next neighbour," and the eunuch has "consequently been hated by the softer Sex for ever after." Lenton means for readers to understand "softer Sex" as "women," an interpellation of gendered embodiment that renders a body as essentially a matter of matter, of porousness. That comparative of quality ("softer") supplements the comparatives of gender roles throughout: from bachelor, to man, to eunuch, to the implied women or wives, we might imagine soft and softest genders, as well as hard, harder, and hardest ones. The sexed body here has always ever interrogated other bodies for their sex; the adverbial "consequently" that follow from the characterization of the eunuch imposes a causality that naturalizes the revelation of the sexed body as a matter of affinity and animus, of what has always "been" and will be "for ever after." In Lenton's description, the figure of the eunuch makes the matter of sex matter.

I return again to Lenton's character sketch because it so transparently foregrounds how the figure of the eunuch supplemented early modern naturalizations of gendered embodiment. That Lenton supposes a bachelor may either become an honest man or a eunuch—instead of, say, remaining a bachelor—is in keeping with early modern normalizations of patriarchal marriage and the single life. As I briefly touched upon in chapter 1, patriarchal marriage was one means by which a body became subject to public scrutiny. Canon law stipulated marriages could be dissolved in early modern England through proof of various forms of impotence, which relied upon "remarkable hands-on methods ordered by courts to establish their claims."[13] In his readings on marriage litigations in early modern Spain, Edward Behrend-Martínez demonstrates the degree to which "the basic question of anatomy" were central to these cases in wider European contexts.[14] The bodies of husbands were especially given over to this kind of inspection; it was often wives who brought such cases to the court.[15] Even when not the subject of court proceedings, the infertility and genital health of men pervaded the medical literature of the period. As Jennifer Evans has demonstrated, often medical treatises of the period elevated the likelihood of the infertility, impotence, and sterility of men over and beyond the pro-creative maladies of women.[16]

Given the legal impositions and classifications of sex upon the marital couple, it is not surprising that early modern marital discourses likewise turn to questions of gendered embodiment to align patriarchal manhood with the cisgender body. In his tract, *Of Domesticall Duties* (1622), for instance, William Gouge turns to the question "Of those who may seeke to be maried," and eunuchs serve as case studies in those "Who are to be accounted *able*." For Gouge, there are two exceptions: immaturity (or "ripe-nesse of yeares") and "impotence." Gouge defines impotence broadly in re-lation to a specific biblical passage, the nineteenth chapter of the Gospel according to Matthew, often cited in the early modern period. As Gouge explains, "They are to be accounted *impotent*, and in that respect vnable to performe the essential duties of mariage, who (to vse the Scripture phrase) *were borne Eunuchs from their mothers wombe:* or by accidental occasion are so made: as they who are defective, or closed in their secret parts: or taken with an incurable palsie: or possessed with frigidity, or any other such like impediment."[17] Through his turn to the figure of the eunuch, Gouge not only conceives of the single life as one populated by such persons but also stipulates that patriarchal marriage requires the procreative potential, if not capacities, of husbands.

In Gouge's text, marriage enables and disables bodies, but eunuchs are not simply gelded persons.[18] Here, eunuchry may characterize equally any person whose body, for whatever reason, is not deemed capable of procre-ative sexuality. Much like Lenton, Gouge does not invoke the figure of the eunuch to define eunuchry but instead cites the eunuch to map the borders of the marriage relation and the bodies that define it and are defined by it. Gouge, for example, is not primarily concerned with procreativity, ex-actly. Instead, marriage raises the question of impotency to inaugurate a set of procedures by which bodies might be given over to anatomical inspec-tion. Such is evident in his treatment of barrenness, which Gouge frames as impotency's acceptable corollary. Whereas, Gouges observes, they sin "who conceale their impotencie and ioyne themselues in marriage," those who are barren commit no such sin. As Gouge explains, "there is a great difference betwixt impotencie and barrennesse," for "Impotencie may by outward sen-sible signs be knowne and discerned, barrenness cannot: it is not discerned but by want of child-bearing. . . . Impotent persons cannot yeeld due be-nevolence: but such as are barren may . . . Impotencie incurable: but bar-renness is not simply so."[19] What distinguishes impotency from barrenness is less a matter of function than apprehension. Their difference takes shape through an epistemology that constitutes gendered normativity in terms of what can be examined, seen, and known by others or oneself, of what can be concealed by a eunuch or revealed by an honest man. At the same time, what constitutes the object of examination must not be transparent to society; it must be a site given to the quality of revelation. Eunuchs are central to this question because, while they are technically barren and not impotent—and thus, according to Gouge's own logic but not his dicta, able to marry—they provide Gouge a means of understanding gendered embodiment as expressive of the social purposes of patriarchal marriage. To apply Currah's insights, sex is as sex does here, and what sex does is reveal who can and cannot marry.

Other early modern marital discourses similarly parse the ways marriage genders bodies, as, well, bodies that matter. When Robert Crofts writes of "nuptial love," he argues, "But all of us have bodies as well as soules, wee are composed of humanity as well as divinity, and he that never felt the power of this love may be esteemed as some Eunuch, or sot, or else of a superhumane temper," and so naturalizes the marriage relation to insist upon a universal, ensouled humanity against those who "may be esteemed as some Eunuch," a figure that not only lacks desire but also is implicitly perceived to lack parts of the "body" that "composed of humanity and divinity."[20] In his discussion of "the praise and commendation of a good Wife, or the dispraise, discommendation, yea and detestation of a bad," Thomas Gataker cites the eunuch to naturalize womanhood with the category of wife, such that a "bad wife" can be thought of as a "wife no wife" in a manner similar to the eunuch as "Man No Man."[21] Aligned with the category of manhood but deprived of particular attributes that would otherwise materialize them as such, the eunuch functions in such marital discourses to demarcate categories of gender from which they themselves are excluded.

Such early modern operationalizations of the figure of the eunuch bear uncanny witness to later rearticulations of patriarchal marriage as a technology of gender. In the beginning of the eighteenth century in *Eunuchism Display'd* (1718), Robert Samber, translating and expanding a text by Charles Ancillon, turns to the figure of the eunuch to reveal the ostensible truth of gender as an embodied fact. As the title page indicates, the polemic was "*Occasion'd by a young Lady falling in Love with Nicolini, who sung in the Opera at the Hay-Market, and to whom she had like to have been Married.*" Like Gouge's *Of Domesticall Duties*, the text brings the eunuch into social visibility as a means of defining and policing marriage, and also like Gouge, it insists eunuchs might conceal themselves from possible partners. If the text is explicit about its polemical targets, it is so because it reinforces the relation not between sex classification and gender role so much as it does the relation between sex classification and governance. As Paisley Currah observes, "Rules for sex classification become explicit when it becomes necessary to account for the anomalies of transsexuality, intersexuality, and gender deviance."[22] Faced with the case of a woman desiring to marry Nicolò Grimaldi (Nicolini), a mezzo-soprano, Samber argues that marriage both classifies sex and is only made for those so classified. He is obsessed with the "vanity" of eunuchs, and, in providing a history of eunuchry, defines the category rather broadly, as those who "neither Men nor Women, but were called a third Sort of Men."[23] Following the codification of eunuchs as unfit for marriage drawn from the Gospel according to Matthew and recirculated in Protestant marital texts, Samber states, "An Eunuch then is a Person which has not the Faculty or Power of Generation, either through Weakness or Coldness of Nature, or who is any wise deprived of the Parts proper to Generation."[24] As the polemic argues for the strict protocols of patriarchal marriage, it rewrites gender relations as sexual relations and sexual relations as gender relations. Like Protestant marital discourses, "sex" is a matter of having or not having the "faculty" or "power" to procreate. To make this case, however, Samber turns to marriage, rendering it a technology of governance over bodies and their gendered meanings. Turning to legal definitions of marriage, he explains, "Marriage then according to the general Definition which the Lawyers give, is, *A Consent of Man and Woman, to pass their Lives together in a perpetual Union, which is inseparable, only by the Death of either Party*."[25] While it may seem Samber is concerned with categories of gender, he first pursues the legal question of "consent." He does not want gendered individuals—in particular, women—to consent to marriage on their own terms. The social purposes and erotic possibilities of marriage, namely, those of intimacy and partnership, remain a problem for Samber, and so he explicitly reduces marriage to a procreative relation, one requiring biological reproduction that abets social reproduction: "God then instituted Marriage only for Generation, and that by that means we might live in our Posterity, and in some Sort make ourselves living after Death."[26] By returning to the insistence that marriage institutes a procreative sexuality, Samber concludes, "According to these Maxims, how can Marriage be supported to agree with the State and Condition of a Eunuch? And does it not hence evidently appear, that Eunuchism and Marriage are two Things incompatible and essentially opposite?"[27] The eunuch, according to Samber, should thus be relegated to a single life, so much so that the imagined condition of the eunuch's life, "eunuchism," stands in its stead. The effect is a recapitulation of marriage as a means of naturalizing a relation between two people who are not eunuchs. Unlike eunuchs, such people, Samber argues, were made for marriage.

This proves to be a sticky bit of illogic. It is not so far from us today.[28] If early moderns worried eunuchs might replace men, modern transphobes worry eunuchs will replace women. Germaine Greer famously predicated her politics of feminist liberation upon the insistence that the nuclear middle class family made women eunuchs, a trope that at once naturalizes gender as a matter of procreative capacity even as it argues against the reduction of gender roles to those of reproduction—while all at the same time implying that eunuchs are themselves anathema to the marriage relation. More perniciously, Janice Raymond explicitly has built her transphobic arguments through conflating transwomen with eunuchs, which not only demonstrates the problems of conflating the experiences of early modern eunuchs with those of transwomen but also suggests how cisgender bodies becomes naturalized through the figure of the eunuch in relation to marriage and the single life. Raymond, for instance, spends considerable time insisting transgender individuals primarily long to marry and to essentially replace cisgender women in the patriarchal order, and in this case, their marginalization depends upon the presumption that they should be relegated to a single life.[29] Raymond's transphobia does double work: it targets patriarchal concerns over the sanctity of marriage as well as TERF (trans-exclusionary radical feminist) preoccupations with policing and totalizing any and all space as cisgender space.

## ELABORATING SEXED BODIES IN EARLY MODERN ANATOMIES

If early modern marital tracts, like Gouge's *Of Domesticall Duties*, resort to questions of anatomy to justify patriarchal marriage itself as a means of inspecting bodies for particular parts, early modern anatomies similarly anchor their own inspections of the body in relation to patriarchal marriage's protocols of sex classification. In his *Mikrokosmographia* (1615), Helkiah Crooke insists upon dimorphic gender by resorting not to anatomy but gender roles of patriarchal marriage. He explains, "It behoued therefore that man should be hotter, because his body was made to endure labour and trauell, as also that his minde should bee stout and inuincible to vndergo dangers, the onely hearing whereof will driue woman as wee say out of her little wits."[30] As for women, Crooke stipulates, "The woman was ordained to receiue and conceiue the seede of the man, to beare and nourish the Infant, to gouerne and moderate the house at home, to delight and refresh her husband foreswunke with labour and well-nigh exhausted and spent with care and trauell; and therefore her body is soft, smooth and delicate, made especially for pleasure, so that whosoeuer vseth them for other doth almost abuse them."[31] In an early modern anatomy text, we find the naturalization of marriage, just as in an early modern marital texts, we often find a preoccupations with anatomy.

Crooke's turn to marriage comes at the end of a long examination of genital parts and an argument for their centrality to the human body. And the eunuch plays a central role in his argument. Throughout *Mikrokosmographia*, Crooke presents the body as a matrix of inquiry and interpretation. The book's subtitle identifies it as "A description of the Body of Man. Together With the Controversies Thereto Belonging." Those descriptions and controversies carry with them their histories, and Crooke advertises that fact: the text is itself reconstituted as "collected and translated out of all the Best Authors of Anatomy." If "the norm of sex takes hold to the extent that it is 'cited' as such a norm," and "derives its power through the citation that it compels," then Crooke's anatomy is a rich text to interrogate the gender norms that regulate bodies in early modern England because it so forthrightly literalizes and thematizes its citationality, in fact renders citationality as integral to the discourse of early modern anatomy.[32]

Through a series of citational descriptions, Crooke proceeds to elaborate the body and its parts. I use *elaborate* intentionally. It is the right word. However late, nascent, developed; however proleptical to genealogies of modern anatomy; however ancient, regressive, premodern: Crooke's argument annotates and becomes annotated; it cites and is cited. Functioning diachronically, its "intelligibility rests on its status as a repetition."[33] It elaborates a citational field, one that enfolds the discourse of anatomy, but also comes to include marital discourses. But *elaborate* is the right word, too, because it signifies the last stage of early modern processes of materializing bodies. The final stage in a series of somatic preparations and concoctions, elaboration knits parts to wholes, flourishes fluid seed into flesh; it makes matter matter.

Crooke elaborates his arguments about the body through a literary trope, synecdoche, the relation of part to whole, which, he explains, animates the logic of his treatise on anatomy: the "subject of both kinds of Anatomy as well historicall as Scientificall is a Part," and while anatomists "doth not handle a whole body," they nonetheless approach it through its parts, which Crooke finally defines, following Galen, as "*to be whatsoeuer doeth integrate or accomplish the whole.*"[34] Crooke draws on the logic of synecdoche to develop a kind of poetics of elaboration, which might otherwise be imagined as synecdoche with a telos. When he explains why the "parts of generation" are so significant in relation to what he calls other "Principal Parts"—that is, the brain, liver, and the heart—he rhapsodizes on the fundamental relationship between part and whole: "The parts of Generation belonging to men . . . are verie many, but all conspiring vnto one end, which is to exhibite something out of themselues which may haue the nature of a Principle; by which, and out of which a newe man may be generated. The Principle exhibited is seed, which because it containeth in it selfe the forme and Idea of all the parts (for it falleth from them all) . . . stoode in neede of manifold preparation, coction and elaboration, and therefore the structure of the parts fit for so great and curious a worke is no doubt very exquisite."[35] Crooke's description prizes the labor required to generate bodies out of their "verie many parts" as well as the discursive practices that might make bodies mean something as wholes. Out of bodies, other, new bodies, and all of them "in neede of manifold preparation, coction, and elaboration."

Bodies elaborate themselves out of their parts, and for the most part, Crooke has little trouble anatomizing each and every part he describes. Except for one: he is not sure how to classify testicles. He knows his problem is not a new one. Having done his reading, he knows that both Hippocrates and Galen were also perplexed by them. In seeking to resolve what he saw as their particular peculiarity—their seeming nonessentiality—Crooke does not so much make a novel argument as he elaborates their significance anew for his early modern readers. Turning to the body's "Principal Parts"—those organs defined as integral to life and to the body's systems that sustain life— Crooke agrees with his predecessors that the heart, liver, and brain should be classified as principal parts. Following the lead of earlier anatomists, Crooke elaborates a claim made by Galen as well as medieval anatomists, like Master Nicholas; he explains that the heart, brain, and liver are principal parts not only because of the ways that they are enmeshed within and central to larger systems—veins rise from the liver, sinews or nerves unspool from the brain, and arteries extend from the heart—but also because of the roles they play in the etiology and cure of particular diseases.[36] These systems likewise circulate different faculties—animal, vital, and natural—that remain distinct; as Crooke queries, "how can we imagine reasonably, that three distinct & different faculties, yea oftentimes quite contrary, Reason, Anger, and Concupiscence should reside altogether, as if they were sworne friends in one Organ?"[37] Different systems organized by distinct faculties bring a physiological balance to the body that is by its nature subject to flux, and these systems are governed by their respective, distinct parts. Thus Crooke will concur with Galen that a principal part is that "*which alloweth or affoordeth to the whole either some faculty, or at least some matter.*"[38]

Testicles, however, do not fit this criteria. Crooke knows this and says so:

for while "they are of absolute necessity for the conservation of the kinde, and production of increase . . . the Testicles indeede do not make allowance to the whole body of any matter, or faculty, or spirit, but only of a quality, together with a subtile and thin breath or aire, from which the flesh hath a ranke taste of the seede, and the bodye a strength or farther ability in the performance of his actions"[39] Testicles, in other words, play a part in other systems; they do not organize one. Crooke recognizes that the inconsistency in his definition of principal parts requires an answer, and so in Book Four, "of the naturall parts belonging to Generation, as well in Men as in Women," the first controversy Crooke addresses is "Whether the Testicles be principall parts or no."[40] It is here that Crooke elaborates his argument that like the brain, liver, and heart, anatomists should classify testicles as principal parts of the body.

Another problem quickly emerges. Unlike other principal parts, testicles are disposable. Crooke observes that when you remove a brain or a liver or a heart, the body becomes a corpse, but bodies do not become corpses when you remove testicles. Instead, you have a body without testicles. Crooke calls those with such bodies "eunuchs," and Crooke deliberately turns to eunuchs to shift the terms of synecdoche, and to elaborate again, but to different ends, the relation of part to whole. For Crooke, testicles should be classified as principal parts of the body because those without them transform: "their temperament, substance, habit and dispositions are all altered."[41] Crooke argues further: "We see also that in gelt men called Eunuches, there is a change of the whole habite and proper substance of the body, for they become fatter and smooth without haires; the flower also of their bloode decayeth and their vessels or veines loose their bredth and capacity, and all vigour of lust and desire of ioylity is extinguished; beside the flesh of such creatures looseth the former tast and smell; for whereas before it breathed out a certaine vnsauory and rammish sowrenesse, after they are gelt it becommeth sweete and pleasant to the taste."[42] Marking the threshold between types of manhood, the eunuch also limns the line between human, animal, and fleshly matter. In his insistence on the creaturely characteristics of the eunuch, Crooke promulgates an early modern conception of *"animality,"* what Mel Y. Chen defines as "not a matter of non-humanity or of creatures considered non-human . . . so much as a quality of animalness, one equally attributable to humans as well as non-human animals."[43] Because Crooke is drawing on sources that observed castrated animals, and then applying them to gelt men, the eunuch melts into "the flesh of such creatures" and loses "a rammish sowrenesse...after they are gelt." Crooke's turn to "flesh" transverses the threshold between human and animal, which, gelt and cultivated for consumption, "becommeth sweete and pleasant to the taste." Crooke's classifications of sex bespeak the classification of the human species in a manner that anticipates those dehumanizing examinations of "chattel persons" that C. Riley Snorton has shown reproduces a colonial, white supremacist ideology. Like those histories Snorton interrogates, Crooke's description of the eunuch likewise "raises a number of questions, including how race constructs biology, and whether sex is possible without flesh."[44] As gelt men become eunuchs who become flesh, the body through which classifications of sex arise becomes another species entirely.

Turning to the eunuch, Crooke sows a eugenicist logic, demarcating what kinds of bodies can and should participate in projects of human viability. Echoing Galen once again, Crooke thus argues that testicles should be principal parts because while testicles are not essential to the maintenance of any individual's life, they are essential to the propagation of life in general. We still have parts and wholes, but they are not body parts and the body; they are *bodies as parts* in a larger social and temporal order. Where before the anatomical part of the organ bore a relation to the whole of a bodily system—brain to the life of the body, for instance—now an individual body (to be defined as with or without testicles) will bear a relation to a whole human species and its propagation through time. As Crooke bluntly asserts, "the Testicles, because they are the chiefe Organes or instruments of procreation & by procreation mankind is preserued, are therefore to be accounted principall parts."[45] Never mind that people without brains cannot propagate either, for here Crooke extends the logic of synecdoche to elevate testicles above even all other principal parts, further insisting, "and haply so much are they more excellent than the heart, by how much the species or whole kinde is more noble then one *indiuiduum* or particular of the kinde."[46] Eunuchs may not be corpses, but, according to Crooke's reasoning, they are necrotic to patriarchal social order.

Crooke's introduction of the eunuch into his description of testicles has profound implications for how he classifies sex and materializes gendered embodiment, but scholars have more or less overlooked the figure of the eunuch in early modern anatomies, instead overemphasizing the role that Galenic humoralism has had in the process of materializing gendered bodies in the period. This has meant that the early modern past has sometimes been imagined as an as yet open space where gender had not yet materialized into modern biopolitical categories that too often lead to death or bare life, where everyone is possibly trans but there are certainly no trans people. While it is true, as Jess R. Pfeffer argues, Crooke's *Mikrokosmographia* can provide "a way of thinking about materiality as distinct from a de facto male-female binary," I would contend that Crooke also shores up that very binary by his sustained meditations upon the body of the eunuch and the classification of testicles as principal parts.[47] Throughout much of his text, Crooke draws on Galen and maintains what Patricia Simons has described as an "'unequal two-seed theory,' a scale of hierarchical value between male and female bodies based on the core elements of semen, testicles, and heat."[48] Crooke valorizes such a thermal basis of sex classification, but one dependent on body parts, when he argues, citing Galen, "the power and vertue of the Testicles is very great & incredible, not onely to make the body fruitfull, but also in the alteration of the temperament, the habit, the proper substance of the body, yea & of the maners themselues. In these doth *Galen* place, beside that in the heart, another hearth as it were of the inbred heate, and these are the houshould Goddes which does blesse and warme the whole bodye."[49] Even here synecdoche enlivens Crooke's imagination. It permits him to transpose linguistic morphology for an anatomical one: inside the "hearth" of the testicles dwells a "heart," which houses an original "heat." How quickly the body of man, in form and function, becomes a testicle. The body, in this view, is a temple, and the testicles are its gods. The proof of these ascriptions is not, for Crooke, in the relative thermal differences between kinds of bodies, or that hotter or colder bodies might traverse a gender binary or realize distinct forms of embodiment. To establish that testicles are a fire that forges fleshy matter into those he might classify as men, Crooke deploys eunuchs as a negative example; "Hence it is, that the Egyptians in their Hieroglyphickes doe paint *Typhon* gelt," Crooke explains, "signifying thereby his power and soueraignty to be abolished and decayed."[50]

Although the norm of patriarchal marriage provides Crooke a model for dimorphic sex, he does not arrive at sexual dimorphism through that relation alone. Like Lenton and Gouge, he turns to the figure of the eunuch to construct sexual morphology as dyadic. While early modern marital tracts would concede that one might be born or made a eunuch, Crooke's text often insists the eunuch is a body that is nearly always made so through gelding. By focusing in particular on the gelding of the eunuch, Crooke further institutes dimorphism by gendering the "testes" of men in relation to the "testes" of women. The testicles of men, in short, become gendered parts in this paradigm; unlike the testicles of women, which will be defined later as ovaries, the testicles of men can be cut off and removed relatively easily. Thus, for Crooke, when constructed in relation to the figure of eunuchs, manhood does not reside so much in comportment or temperament or behavior but in a particular body part, which is to say that manhood becomes a matter of anatomy. His answer to the controversy of testicles extends the logic of synecdoche with which his book begins. "For we confesse," Crooke admits to his readers, "Wherefore they [testicles] are principall parts in respect of mankind, not in respect of this or that particular man. For the propagation of mankind is onely accomplished by procreation: procreation is not without seede, seed is only concocted and perfected by the Testicles, to which the spermaticke vessels doe serue as well for preparation as for condution and leading of the seede."[51] These fleshy organs, presumed to hold a symbolic relation to patriarchal order and a material relation to the body, instead possess for Crooke a material relation to patriarchal order and a symbolic relation to the individual body. The gendered embodiment of the individual manifests through the part it is presumed and prescribed to play in a larger social and sexual matrix that requires testicles for its propagation. In *Mikrokosmographia*, Crooke grants testicles more precise and agential forms of embodiment than the individuals who do or do not possess them. When it comes to the matter of testicles, we have bodies in service to their parts rather than parts in service of their bodies. Women, too, find themselves disposed of testicles and redefined by other organs. So it is that Crooke comes to conclude, "The partes of the Female are the wombe and the rest which by a general name are called matrices; the parts of a man are the virile member and the Testicles. And so much shall be sufficient to haue been added concerning the difference of the Sexes."[52] And just like that, the problem of testicles is resolved for Crooke. Bodies serve their parts, and here, an early modern natalism complements the testicularity of men.[53]

If Crooke situates the eunuch as internal to his arguments about the classifications of sex, he does so by insisting that the eunuch is external to early modern England itself. In his many citations, he makes clear that the eunuch does not originate within the borders of Britain. Kim F. Hall has argued that England's increasing global economic reach in the sixteenth century led writers to deploy racialized tropes to construct gender relations, and as Abdulhamit Arvas has demonstrated, as the eunuch organized such relations in the Ottoman court, early modern travel writers made much of the distinction between white and Black eunuchs to reify their own Englishness.[54] Crooke does much of the same; his eunuchs are very much not English. He explains that "*Auenzoar* the Arabian, where he saith, Eunuchs haue a shrill and piping voice, euill manners, and worse dispositions, neyther shall you lightly finde one of them of a good inclination, or not broken witted," and he cites the *Cryopaedia* to reconstitute its conclusions about eunuchs in terms he finds more amenable to their denigration: "Albeit in the seauenth Booke of the *Institution of Cyrus* it is recorded, that this

171

kind of men is quiet, diligent, and especially faithfull: but we may answere that they are quiet because they are dull and blockish; diligent because they are seruile and base-minded; faithfull because they haue so much distrust of themselues."[55] Crooke's text demonstrates the degree to which his project relies upon the eunuch in similar ways to those travel narratives both Hall and Arvas cite in their respective archives, for Crooke, too, invokes the eunuch to construct normative manhood as fundamentally testicular and nonnormative manhood as gelt and foreign.

Crooke was not the first nor would he be the last to invoke the figure of the eunuch to elaborate the inherent testicularity of manhood. Earlier in the sixteenth century, in his *The Byrth of Mankynde, otherwyse named the Womans Booke* (1545), Thomas Raynold had similarly argued: "But truely comparing one man to another, such as be geldyd and want the genitories be moch febler, weeke, and effeminate then other: in voyce woman lycke, in gesture and condition nyse, in saftnesse of skyn, and plumpnesse of the bodye fatter and rounder; in strenght and force unpotent nothing manly ne bold. The which imbecyllite in them may well be named imperfection: for imperfection is when that any properte, instrument, or qualite, which communely, by nature is in all other or the moore part of the kynde: comparying it to other of the same kinde, and not of any other kynde."[56] While Raynolds compares eunuchs to women, he does so to counter an Aristotelian argument that women were imperfect men. On the contrary, Raynolds argues, women are not imperfect; eunuchs are. If Raynolds attempts to sidestep charges of sexism, he nonetheless traffics in an early modern form of transmisogyny, what Julia Serano defines as the cathexis of two complementary forms of sexism, "traditional" and "oppositional." If traditional sexism naturalizes the supremacy of men over women, "oppositional sexism," Serrano states, "is the belief that female and male are rigid, mutually exclusive categories, each possessing a unique and nonoverlapping set of attributes, aptitudes, abilities, and desires."[57] As early modern anatomical discourses document, however, such oppositional sexism requires transmisogyny for its salience. In the early modern period, it is not so much a matter of there being a fluid gender binary so much as it is a matter of there being no gender binary without the figure of the eunuch, who transverses that binary—"in voyce womanlycke . . . nothing manly ne bold"—but exists outside of it. In this respect, the rhetorical protocols through which the eunuch is made legible and against which the eunuch is denaturalized and dehumanized share something with a modern transphobic discourse that insists upon gender as the expressive truth of genital morphology.

Other early modern anatomists will likewise elaborate Crooke's arguments and similarly cite the figure of the eunuch to do so. Where anatomists classify sex in terms of genital parts, eunuchs, not women, appear as exemplary case studies. Paré claims, "The action of the testicles is to generate seed, to corroborate all parts of the body, and by a certaine manly irradiation to breed or encrease a true masculine courage. This you may know by Eunuches or such as are Gelt, who are of a womanish nature, and are oftentimes more tender and weake than women."[58]

As testicles "corrobate all parts of the body," they essentially come to index that body's very wholeness as a body. In *A Directory for Midwives* (1651), Nicholas Culpepper insists testicles "ad heat, strength, and courage to the Body, and that appears, because Eunuchs are neither so strong, hot, nor valiant as other Men."[59] Thomas Bartholin similarly asserts, "Also the *Stones* seems to give strength and courage to Mens bodies, as may be seen in gelded persons, who are changed well-near into Women, in their Habit of Body, Temperament, Manner, &c.," though he concedes a contradiction: "But Eunuchs also are lustful, for they are great Lovers of Women: And Eunuchs are often transported with anger and other Passions of the Mind, but they receive not never the more the Habit of Men."[60] As early modern anatomists elaborate sex as a means of classifying bodies in terms of their gendered parts, they operationalize the figure of the eunuch to give the body itself over to protocols of inspection. In this way, they rehearse a modern gender essentialist logic, whereby "the trans subject" as Gayle Salamon has argued, discursively functions as "necessarily proximate but inassimilable, able to enact and secure gender as a binary system only to the extent that sie is exiled from it."[61] To think about cismen and ciswomen, to make them thinkable as such, early modern anatomists did not really think about cismen and ciswomen. They thought about eunuchs.

## MISTAKING EUNUCHS IN *TWELFTH NIGHT*

If the eunuch played an integral role in the shaping of early modern epistemologies of gendered embodiment, we should anticipate that eunuchs would likewise play more than a marginal role in early modern drama. And they do. They are everywhere. In his cultural history on castration, Gary Taylor records that "The noun *eunuch(s)* appears at least 240 times in at least seventy-eight different English plays written between 1580 and the closing of the theaters in 1642; early modern synonyms for the verb *castrate* appear more than 150 times in the plays of those decades."[62] Shakespeare is not far from his contemporaries. While it is true that apart from Cesario of *Twelfth Night* and Mardian of *Antony and Cleopatra*, Shakespeare does not stage eunuchs, that does not mean that eunuchs and gelding more broadly do not play a central role in the gender relations of several of his plays. Eunuchs are explicitly referenced in *Love's Labor's Lost*, *A Midsummer Night's Dream*, *All's Well That Ends Well*, *Coriolanus*, *Cymbeline*, *Henry VI, Part 2*, and *Titus Andronicus*. We might add to these explicit references to eunuchs references to, or musings upon, gelding in *The Merchant of Venice*, *Two Noble Kinsmen*, *Measure for Measure*, *Pericles*, *Richard II*, and *The Winter's Tale*.

In *Twelfth Night*, however, Shakespeare introduces the figure of the eunuch as a central component of the comedic plot to reinforce patriarchal marriage as a technology of gender assignment. Despite the fact that the eunuch plays a central role in the comedy, scholarship on and performances of the play often overwrite Cesario's eunuchry, either explicitly amending it to boyhood or otherwise qualifying its representational force. As Stephen Orgel has observed, the eunuchry of Cesario "has received very little editorial attention."[63] While *Twelfth Night* has remained an enduring text for early modern gender criticism, Cesario's eunuchry has slipped out of most of the scholarship on the play. Calling it "the comedy's most conspicuous 'forgotten' project," Keir Elam, editor of the Arden edition, points to the editorial tradition of reading Cesario's eunuchry as an authorial oversight, an indication of "Shakespeare's change of plan."[64] When critics do attend to Cesario's eunuchry, the gelded body dematerializes, serving as a sign of gender performativity, functioning as a trace of lost textual sources, or acting as a metatheatrical wink at the relationship between staging practice and dramatic representation. In his attentive and sustained reading of eunuchry in the play, one which does much to contextualize the play's musings on castration, John Astington insists upon Malvolio's humiliation as a "displaced gelding," that "his binding is a symbolic sign of his impotence, of his having been made a festival eunuch."[65] Where is the eunuch but always elsewhere?

In *Twelfth Night*, it would seem then, there are no eunuchs, just bachelors, husbands, wives, and maids. That is even what some of the characters of the play insist. At the conclusion of the play, the Countess Olivia has wed the single man Sebastian believing him to be the eunuch Cesario. Inverting Lenton's idealized schema, Olivia pursues a eunuch for a husband and instead ends up with a bachelor. Seeking to assure Olivia of her marital choice, Sebastian explains,

> So comes it, lady, you have been mistook;
> But nature to her bias drew in that.
> You would have been contracted to a maid,
> Nor are you therein, by my life, deceived.
> You are betrothed both to a maid and man.[66]

The questions that circulate in the play around gendered embodiment not only become resolved in Sebastian's person, who is now a made man, for he is to marry a Countess, but also diffused through marriage, in which context Olivia's betrothal to a maid now signifies Sebastian's eligibility as a bachelor and not Viola's gender. As the eunuch Cesario, Viola is meant to be rejected by Olivia, and, revealed as a maid, Viola herself becomes eligible for marriage.

This passage has stood at the center of much of the foundational gender criticism of *Twelfth Night*. Stephen Greenblatt, for example, finds in it the frictions of fiction, and Stephen Orgel, in a rather elegant reading, sees an iteration of the master-mistress of Shakespeare's sonnet 20.[67] For Thomas Laqueur, this passage epitomizes the early modern commitment to the one-sex model. Serving as the epigraph for his fourth chapter on "Representing Sex," the passage, according to Laqueur, glides through its miraculous transformations because "nothing specifically and fundamentally corporeal peculiar to each sex" grounds those tranformations: "Having a penis does not make the man just as, to quote Feste, 'cucullus non facit monachum' (the cowl does not make the monk)."[68] In drawing this conclusion, Laqueur insists upon an analogy, one evoked in the scene itself, that would equate anatomy (a penis) with sartoriality (the cowl).

But Laqueur is wrong—especially if we recall how integral the figure of the eunuch Cesario is to the accidents of Sebastian's marriage. Sebastian was not mistaken for Viola but for the eunuch Cesario (and Viola was likewise mistaken for them). We might interrogate how the simultaneous invocation and dematerialization of the eunuch Cesario enables a fantasy of gender dimorphism central to Laqueur's one-sex model and much of the scholarship on the play that valorizes its genderqueer elements more or less contained by the cisgender body. In a trenchant critique of gender criticism on this play (and many others in the early modern dramatic canon), Sawyer Kemp has argued that early modern gender and literary history has conflated sartoriality, gendered embodiment, and transgender experience. As Kemp observes, early modern literary gender criticism has yet to fully reckon with the degree to which the staging of gender has presumed a cisgender stage, and thus, "because we persist in reading androgyny or genderqueerness in the performance of a cis actor, we participate directly in constructing the image of androgyny and genderqueerness *from the performance of a cisgender body*."[69] The result, as Kemp notes, is the dematerialization of the transgender body into fictions of its performance by cisgender actors. Kemp aptly concludes, "Dependence on the cis body for these readings then produces a fictional 'trans' body continually defined by the same cisgender norms—a performative fiction of androgyny and genderqueerness that is uninterested in the varied branches of androgyny that medical and social transition have actualized."[70] In much the same way, *Twelfth Night* represents the eunuch as only a ciswoman in disguise; the trans body, in other words, is only ever conceived as a cis body performing genderqueerness.

Kemp provides a way for reading this scene and the various ways presumptions about bodies facilitate this play's radical gender transformations as well as the miraculous marriages that follow from them. Ezra Horbury has similarly interrogated the certainties grounding early modern scholarship on gendered embodiment, reassessing the "cross-dressed page" to argue, "it is not that there is *no* body beneath, but that the somatic body exists only in fantasy."[71] As Kemp and Horbury show, when scholars cite Sebastian's speech, they are often complicit in an epistemology of gender that follows from his vested interests in marrying a Countess. But it is a mistake to take Sebastian at his word. Instead, we should linger a bit on how he imagines Olivia to "have been mistook" and what she is mistaken about. Is her mistake that she took a ciswoman as a eunuch or as a cisman? If so, is she also mistaken in taking a cisman as a eunuch? On what grounds are these actually mistakes? How is it that we know that Sebastian is not a eunuch, that Orsino, that Malvolio, that Valentine, that any number of characters are or are not? Despite the insistences of the likes of Gouge, Crooke, and Lenton, Orsino attests that Cesario and Sebastian are identical, the eunuch and the husband indistinguishable, such that in each, all see "one face, one voice, one habit and two persons: / a natural perspective, that is and is not" (5.1.211–12). If the eunuchry of Cesario has received little attention, then the possible eunuchry of Sebastian, whom Viola models her Cesario after, has received even less. As "both a maid and man," Sebastian can likewise be understood as appropriating the eunuchry of Cesario, even ironically deploying the transmisogyny that denigrated eunuchs as "like" women. Knowing his sister has been disguised like him, Sebastian could be affirming that Olivia now has the real eunuch—"a maid and man"—and so what she has desired all along. Alternatively, Sebastian could be insisting we, like Olivia, should forget such likenesses, such naturalness, and instead privilege the dissimulation of a sister in disguise over and above the simulation of husband as eunuch, eunuch as husband, and the various ways these dissimulations and simulations organize bodies into formations that might result in married couples. Have we been mistook?

The tendency for the eunuch Cesario to slip into and out of view reveals as much as it occludes how readers might perceive representations of gendered embodiment and processes of racialization in the play. I contend that the occlusions and transparencies of gendered embodiment in this play—the various ways it asks us to take and mistake eunuchs for men and men for eunuchs—are inextricably bound to its drive toward the patriarchal marriages and the whitewashing of the marital couple. If we suspend, for a moment, cisnormative presuppositions about bodies and their meaning in this play, attending to the figure of the eunuch might facilitate what Jo Henderson-Merrygold has called "a hermeneutics of cispicison," one in which epistemological and ontological pressure is brought to bear not upon bodies perceived not to conform to patriarchal order but on those presumed to conform to it.[72] *Twelfth Night* seems at least nominally invested in such a hermeneutics given the degree to which the figure of the eunuch organizes the various ways characters are taken and mistaken for cisgender men and women.

## RACIALIZING EUNUCHS AND WHITEWASHING MARRIAGE IN *TWELFTH NIGHT*

When Viola first washes up on the shores of Illyria, everyone is single and most are sad. From the outset of *Twelfth Night*, the single life is bound up with themes of death, loss, and mourning. The play opens with Orsino hoping that his "appetite may sicken and so die"; the music he longs to hear has, to his ear, "a dying fall" (1.1.3–4). Like a stereotypical, melancholic Petrarchan lover, Orsino conceives of his single life as one of frustrated desire. Everyone, moreover, knows he's a bachelor. Viola tells the Captain that Orsino, about whom he spoke, "was a bachelor then," and the Captain informs her, "And so is now, or was very late" (1.2.27). What we know about Orsino at the beginning of the play is what we will know of him throughout the play: he is lovelorn and looking to marry. There is not much to make in that fact. On the one hand, Orsino's status as a bachelor overdetermines the comic plot in much the same way that Benedick's insistence that he will live a bachelor overdetermines the comic plot of *Much Ado About Nothing*. Marriage is on the horizon. On the other hand, unlike Benedick's bachelorhood, Orsino's ongoing status as a bachelor does not suggest liberatory potential or freedom of movement: here it indicates statis and enervation. In *Twelfth Night*, the single life is not conducive to homosocial conviviality. Instead, it resembles a death sentence.

Viola, however, sees in this land populated by single people much possibility. Upon noting the Duke's bachelor status, and upon learning that Olivia will take no suits to her household, Viola comes up with a plan, telling the Captain with whom she is shipwrecked: "Conceal me what I am, and be my aid / For such disguise as haply shall become / The form of my intent. I'll serve this duke. / Thou shalt present me as an eunuch to him" (1.2.50–53). Scholars have speculated why Viola chooses such a disguise, but there are reasons for it if we consider the play's setting as well as those mutually reinforcing relations between the eunuch, bachelor, and husband with which this chapter began. Viola's first question is one about locale; she asks the captain where they are, and learns, "This is Illyria" (1.1.1). As Patricia Parker has thoroughly documented, Illyria, and those regions associated with it, appeared in a number of romances before, during, and after the publication of *Twelfth Night*, a number of which "underscore its proximity to Saracen or Turk."[73] These associations are not incidental. As Parker goes on to insist, "perhaps the most important in relation to *Twelfth Night*—with its references to a 'eunuch' and 'mute,' to the 'Sophy,' and to the transformed Malvolio as a 'renegado'—is the extent of contemporary writing on the relation of Illyria to the Turk."[74] Tracing "the contours of Illyria as a cultural and symbolic geography," Ambereen Dadabhoy has likewise argued that "Ottoman imperial praxis, particularly the same-sex organization of Ottoman societies, influence the spatial arrangements of *Twelfth Night*"; Illyria was literal ground that the Ottomans occupied, as Dadabhoy demonstrates, but Shakespeare also appropriates the Ottoman imperial domestic sites, in particular the harem and its concomitant eunuchs, to represent the respective households of Orsino and Olivia in the "staged Mediterranean" world of the play.[75] As we saw in chapter 1, Shakespeare aligns eunuchs with "the Turk" in *All's Well* as well, and Helkiah Crooke similarly associates eunuchs with Persian, Egyptian, and Ottoman empires, an association that was typical in the period. As Abdulhamit Arvas explains, "In England, with the increased importance of Anglo-Ottoman encounters in the 1580s as a result of England's participation in Mediterranean trade, the figure of the eunuch emerged as an integral, orientalist component of travelogues and stage plays, and as a means of signaling Ottoman otherness," and as he further argues, *Twelfth Night* is not an exception to this pattern, as "Shakespeare's pairing of the eunuch and mute in *Twelfth Night* is mirrored by other contemporaneous accounts that consistently surround the eunuch with other exoticized figures like mutes, dwarves, and hermaphordites."[76] Viola seems to know a eunuch would be a common person in Illyria as well as a welcome servant in Duke Orsino's court. Learning of Orsino's legal authority and his singleness, Viola states that, "haply shall become / The form of my intent" (1.2.51-52), where that "form" finds its habit in the eunuch Cesario, whose name becomes an euonym of their ostensibly self-constituting cut, or gelding.

Much as in Crooke, the introduction of the eunuch to materialize forms of gendered embodiment also inaugurates processes of racialization. While the disguise at once reinforces the trope that eunuchs are proximate to or like women, it also encodes forms of racialized, gender embodiment not so easily parsed. To ascend to a place of favor *as the eunuch Cesario* in Orsino's court could be understood as means of racializing Viola as white, especially given the ways hierarchies of whiteness and Blackness structured early modern Ottoman eunuchry.[77] Asking to be presented "as a eunuch *to* [Orsino]," Viola is also asking to be presented in the role of a eunuch, a subordinate to a superior. The introduction of eunuchry in the context of Illyria also can imply the ways in which the play's other references to Blackness suggest the eunuchry of other characters, like Malvolio, who are likewise associated with cuts and gelding. Such associations further redound upon early modern dramaturgy. As Dympna Callaghan has argued, the impersonation of women on the English stage relied upon representations of the gelded body, such that "the production of an aesthetic of representation that depicts sexual difference defined as the presence or lack of male genitalia" comes to be the telos of early modern dramaturgical practice, a presentation, I would emphasize, that likewise reinforced the naturalization of gender dimorphism that cast the figure of the eunuch as the constituting limit of the cisgender binary.[78] As Callaghan points out, early modern plays did not represent men and women so much as men and eunuchs. In this scheme, Viola's disguise as Cesario renders dramatic mimesis as representational of dramaturgical practice, and in doing so, raises the question of the racializing stage properties that might be involved in being presented "as a eunuch" as a performance that can be readily, visually apprehended on such identitarian terms.[79]

Viola's stated intent is to have the bachelor Duke Orsino mistake Viola as the eunuch Cesario, who will also then come to be mistaken for her presumed drowned brother, Sebastian, who just so happens to look exactly like the eunuch Cesario. Perhaps this would be an easy mistake to make in an Illyria already populated by eunuchs and bachelors who are more alike than they are different. When Cesario appears on stage, they enter a court populated with single people, and the play will come to explicitly align singleness with eunuchry in its later citations, especially in the forged letter of the nineteenth chapter of the Gospel according to Matthew. Orsino's court is one of bachelors, but it might very well also be a court of eunuchs.[80] I want to emphasize *how much we do not know* about the representations of gendered embodiment at this moment in the play, which only come into clearer focus as and when characters are coupled off and married. The elision between the eunuch and the man occurs at the very moment Cesario enters the drama. The stage direction for Viola's first appearance tells readers, "*Enter Valentine, and Viola in mans attire.*" As editors have noted, there is a bit of prolepsis at work here: Viola is likely dressed in clothes that will be identical to Sebastian's when he first appears on stage. The play does not present Viola passing as a man but Viola disguised as a eunuch in man's attire. But it also should not be overlooked that Viola does not enter alone. Valentine accompanies Viola. Given the accidentals of punctuation, that modifier might apply to both Valentine and Viola: both enter "in man's attire." When Valentine first speaks and affirms Cesario's standing in Orsino's court, the effect is of one gentleman speaking to another. Or to put it another way, we have an actor playing Valentine speaking to another actor playing Cesario. We see two single gentlemen, or two eunuchs, or a eunuch and a cisgender servant, of Orsino's court. What's the difference between Valentine and the eunuch Cesario, and why would we presume Valentine is not also, like Cesario, a eunuch of Orsino's court? Or do we presume Valentine's gender because of the legibility of Cesario's eunuchry, or of Viola as Cesario?

Sebastian will, of course, be mistaken for the eunuch Cesario at the end of the play. This mistake of person has led scholars, following Sebastian, to insist upon a mistake in gender, such that some scholars analeptically construe the gendered embodiment of Cesario in relation to that of the presumptively cisgender Sebastian, rather than the other way around. Everyone in Illyria seemingly accepts Cesario to be a eunuch, and they readily mistake Sebastian for Cesario. Orsino, for instance, takes Cesario for the eunuch they present themselves as. When Cesario resists Orsino's charge for them to serve as an envoy to Olivia, Orsino affirms Cesario, stating:

> Dear lad, believe it,
> For they shall yet belie thy happy years
> That say thou art a man. Diana's lip
> Is not more smooth and rubious. Thy small pipe
> Is as the maiden's organ, shrill and sound,
> And all is semblative a woman's part.
> I know thy constellation is right apt
> For this affair. (1.4.29–36)

A variety of scholars have read this passage to similar ends, seeing in it the fluidity and expansiveness of gendered embodiment. But it is worth noting that the comparisons and similitudes Orsino invokes are commonplace in early modern descriptions of eunuchs. As we saw in Crooke and other early modern anatomical treatises, the eunuch, categorically understood as a "Man No Man," was consistently likened to a woman, indeed, as "womanish."[81] By claiming that "*all* is semblative a woman's part," Orsino totalizes Cesario's identity in these terms, and further hints at Cesario's presumptive castration. Lacking testicles, Orsino implies, Cesario's "part" is more like that of a woman than a man, a statement of the patriarchal order that is consistent with representations of eunuchs in early modern English discourses.

Cesario's status as a eunuch in Orsino's court also explains why Orsino is so willing to send Cesario to Olivia to woo her on his behalf. It would make sense that given Olivia's cloistering, Orsino would presume that a eunuch like Cesario might gain entrance, for it was the eunuch who had access to the inner chambers of royal women in the Ottoman empire, and eunuchs were widely understood, as Kathryn Ringrose has demonstrated, as "perfect servants because they were uniquely qualified extensions of the imperial person—they partook of and guarded his numen and they carried with them the divine legitimation and the special powers of the emperor wherever they went in his service."[82] Moreover, beginning with Terence's *Eunuchus*, it was a common dramatic trope to grant a eunuch—or someone disguised as one—access to a maid. Orsino entrusts Cesario precisely because of the presumption that a eunuch is an extension of his person but not one that would be an object of desire to Olivia.

But Olivia sees Cesario differently than Orsino would either hope or expect. Olivia first asks Malvolio "what kind o'man" Cesario might be (1.5.146). The question seems to puzzle Malvolio, who retorts, "Why, of mankind" (1.5.147), an answer that does not satisfy Olivia, nor does Malvolio's response to her question, "What manner of man?" (1.5.148). When Olivia asks, "Of what personage and years is he," Malvolio gives the following response: "Not yet old enough for a man, nor young enough for a boy, as a squash is before 'tis a peascod, or a codling when 'tis almost an apple. 'Tis with him in standing water between boy and man. He is very well favoured, and he speaks very shrewishly. One would think his mother's milk were scarce out of him" (1.5.152–57). Of this passage, Jeffrey Masten observes, "Malvolio's semiotic riffs on her terms only further complicate any attempt firmly to distinguish or categorize Cesario."[83] We can read this passage, as many scholars have, as privileging the inherent indeterminacy of Cesario's gender. To do so, however, is often to map, as Kemp has argued, gender transitivity upon the unmarked cisgender body. As we have already seen, eunuchs were distinguished and categorized in terms of such indeterminacy—of their being *like* a man or a woman without ever being identified as either. The passage does, however, privilege the genital pun of "cod," and even as Malvolio privileges images of thresholds—of being in between states—he also insists upon the permanence of such a stage. We are not at the shores of Illyria, where the tides roll in and out. Cesario is like "standing water" (l.155). As Masten goes on to point out, "In a pool not subject to tides or flow, [Cesario] is *categorically*, not *temporally*, between boy and man."[84] However much Malvolio riffs here, the depiction that he gives of Cesario continually fixates and puns upon genital parts that might speak to the gender of Cesario's whole person.

Malvolio may mean to disparage Cesario, but Olivia likes what she hears. Let us presume Olivia knows something of Illyria—the same something Viola knows and which guided her choice of disguise. Let us also presume that Malvolio's description that situates Cesario as somewhere between "boy and man" tells Olivia all she wants to know: that Cesario is likely a eunuch, and that Olivia desires a eunuch such as Cesario. Only after Malvolio's answer does Olivia assert: "Let him approach" (1.5.158). The field of Olivia's desire—if we might call it that at this moment—radiates into possibilities not so easily encompassed by patriarchal marriage. Olivia may desire Cesario because they are a eunuch, unable to procreate, but still able to enjoy sex and to be a perfect servant of a partner. Or she might also desire the eunuch Cesario because they are a servant without any real power. Her desire for Cesario might be coextensive with a desire to exploit them. In either case, however, Olivia rejects the notion that any desire should lead to procreative sex and marriage. Cesario may insist, "Lady, you are the cruell'st she alive / If you would leave these graces to the grave / And leave the world no copy" (1.5.233–35), but Olivia will have none of it: "O sir, I will not be so hard-hearted. I will give out diverse schedules of my beauty. It shall be inventoried, and every particle and utensil labelled to my will, as, item, two lips, indifferent red; item, two grey eyes, with lids to them; item, one neck, one chin, and so forth" (1.5.236–40). Her rejection of Orsino and embrace of Cesario maps onto a rejection of patrilineal, procreative expectations of patriarchal marriage. Because this is a Shakespearean comedy, however, Olivia's desire for the eunuch Cesario sets in motion the marriage plot of the play as well as the darker comic subplot of Malvolio's humiliation. When Olivia is revealed, quite literally, as a desiring and desirable subject, it is the figure of the eunuch that comes to structure the circuit of desire that surrounds her. Orsino desires Olivia, and sends the eunuch Cesario as his emissary; Olivia then comes to desire Cesario, and just as she does, her servant Malvolio desires her.

Malvolio is invited to act upon his desire for Olivia through a letter. Much has been made of that scene. His humiliation depends upon the presumption that it is absurd that a servant like Malvolio would be desired by Olivia. But, of course, the play has already demonstrated that such a fantasy is plausible. Malvolio even seems to recognize this: just before he discovers Maria's forged letter, he is already entertaining the possibility of Olivia's affections, musing to himself: "Maria once told me she did affect me, and I have heard herself come thus near, that should she fancy it should be one of my complexion" (2.5.21–24).[85] That complexion has largely been whitewashed, in no small part because Malvolio has been traditionally associated with English Puritanism instead of Ottoman eunuchs. But Malvolio's meditation on the desirability of his complexion surfaces the stakes of his racialization as a matter of desirability. He may have the pale skin of a white eunuch or the dark skin of a Black one, though the latter is more likely. Maria has just told her compatriots that "He has been yonder i'the sun practicing behaviour to his own shadow this half-hour" (2.5.14–15). Much like the Prince of Morocco in *The Merchant of Venice*, who describes his "complexion" as "the shadowed livery of the burnished sun," Malvolio's racialization as a "dark" other is likewise projected into the shadow with which he converses below an apposite sun, which in early modern English racial imaginaries often aligned racialized darkness—and concomitant fears of miscegenation—with sunburn.[86]

Malvolio's racialization extends, however, into the contexts of his gendering as it pertains to his social status and his proximity to Olivia as her servant. As numerous early modern scholars of race have argued, racialization is never merely a matter of somatics; it involves fluctuating and variable modes of materializing social difference. When Sir Toby fantasizes that "we will fool him black and blue" (2.5.9), he can be thought of as engaging in fantasies of racialization entangled with status distinctions. In this case, as Patricia Akhimie has demonstrated, "subservience is visible as a stigmatized mark on the body, a 'bruise' that indicates both a moral and social inferiority."[87] Shortly after, Maria conceives of their gulling of Malvolio as a form of religious conversion realized by gelding: "he is turned heathen, a very renegado," and such racialized differences, encoded as they are through religious conversion, come to be quite literally mapped upon Malvolio: "He does smile his face," Maria tells Toby and Fabian, "into more lines than is in the new map with the augmentation of the Indies" (3.2.74–76). The scene ends with a redoubling of the stigmatization and marking of the body; Maria can "hardly forbear hurling things at him," and sadistically imagines, "I know my lady will strike him" (ll.76–78). These stigmatizations of Malvolio build upon Fabian's earlier ascription of him as a "turkey-cock" that "jets" (2.5.28, 29). As Su Fang Ng has observed, the turkey cock was "the

African bird imported through Turkish dominions," and while "jet" mostly immediately describes Malvolio's ostentatious strut, its denotations of Blackness are difficult to overlook.[88] To recognize or see Malvolio as racialized in these terms raises a host of questions and consequences about his humiliation, his binding, and his imprisonment, but it would also be to read such actions as imbricated within processes of materializing both racial difference and gendered embodiment in relation to the play's preoccupations in representing Ottoman eunuchs.

If we take Malvolio seriously at this moment, if we recognize that he has himself grounds to believe in the possibility of Olivia's affections for him, then we also ultimately find ourselves out of step with the play's marriage plot—but not so out of step, for Olivia assumes she marries the eunuch when she marries Sebastian. When Malvolio reads, "Some are born great, some achieve greatness and some have greatness thrust upon them" (2.5.141–43), we may be inclined, as John Astington has suggested, to revel in the irony of Malvolio's incapacity to recognize the allusion to the nineteenth chapter of the Gospel according to Matthew. But it may just be that Maria's forgery here is meant to reinforce an extant fantasy. The forgery at work is not just a forgery of Olivia's hand. It is also, as Maria freely admits, a forgery of Malvolio's person. "I will drop in his way some obscure epistle of love," Maria plots, "wherein by the colour of his beard, the shape of his leg, the manner of his gait, the expressure of his eye, forehead and complexion he shall find himself most feelingly personated" (2.3.150–54). In reading that epistle, and the lines that allude to a biblical passage on gelding, Malvolio may in fact see what he is meant to see: himself. And why wouldn't he? *Twelfth Night* consistently aligns Malvolio and his body with the figure of the eunuch. When, with Sir Toby, Fabian, and Maria overhearing him, Malvolio fantasizes of "having come from a day-bed where I have left Olivia sleeping," he relishes an imagined newfound position of authority in which he commands "Seven of my people, with an obedient start, make out for [Sir Toby]"; in the interim, Malvolio muses on his leisurely waiting: "I frown the while and perchance wind up my watch, or play with my [*touching his chain*]—some rich jewel" (2.5.45–46, 55–58). In its allusive capacities of wealth and testicularity, that "some rich jewel" Malvolio contemplates fondling gestures to a desire for both of those objects he is perceived to lack, but it is especially in the evasion, in the pause, in the fondling of the phallic chain, in which the bawdy pun on genitalia comes to overwrite its supplementation by the priceless stone. A similar impulse to transpose his social role from servant to husband informs his other readings of the letter. The "cut" he reads in "her very c's, her u's and her t's" not only suggests his fantasies about Olivia's body but an affirmation of his own embodiment. Projections though they may be, Malvolio's interpretations confirm the possibility of what he has already witnessed with his own eyes: Olivia may desire a eunuch. However we interpret these lines—that this is "a displaced gelding" or a citation of an actual one—the play, following Maria's logic, would have us laugh at this possibility.[89] Why would Olivia desire a eunuch, one who converses with his shadow in the sun's hard light? Only a fool would make such a mistake.

And, of course, in making that mistake, Malvolio confirms he is just such a fool. But in a play full of such mistakings, his humiliation does more than merely provide cruel jokes their punchlines (and punching bags). It further emplots not only who is desirable in the play but also who is marriageable. Compared to Cesario, Malvolio makes the mistake of acting as a desiring subject rather than a desirable object. He no longer embodies "the perfect servant" to Olivia. If we read both Cesario and Malvolio as court eunuchs, however, their respective fates in Illyria also limn the racialization of the eunuch that Arvas has traced in the early modern Ottoman court and English travel narratives: we can read the desire for Cesario and the disgust at Malvolio as encoding the ways the racialization of white and Black eunuchs in the Ottoman court established hierarchies of beauty and racializations of space and interiority. In the Ottoman harem, Black eunuchs were assigned to interior spaces, those designated for wives and women. Malvolio's proximity to Olivia is everywhere marked in the play. She first enters with him in scene 5, and she veils herself to hear Orsino's suit. As Arvas observes, "after the Ottomans' unique emphasis on separating white and black eunuchs—and assigning black eunuchs to interior feminine spaces—blackness and eunuchism started to be collapsed into one another."[90] Early modern English accounts record this distinction, and often reified this racialization in their own description of eunuchs. Michel Baudier's account of the Ottoman seraglio, translated by Edward Grimeston, for instance, documents: "We haue said elsewhere that the womens *Serrail* hath no other Guard but blacke Eunuches, which are sent young to the Court by the *Basha's* of *Caire*, to be bred vp to that place. The *Sultans Serrail* receiues none but white, the which are chosen in their infancie, out of that pleasing troupe of children well borne, which are taken for Tribute from the Christians."[91] *Twelfth Night* precedes this account, but in its various citations of eunuchs, and interpellations of social status and somatic markers, it evinces, if it does not entirely textualize, an Illyria organized by similarly gendered and racialized forms of service.[92] Cesario, associated with fairness and gentleness, serves Orsino; Malvolio, aligned with darkness and harshness, serves Olivia and is eventually ostracized from the play's social world and marital economy.

If Malvolio makes the mistake of believing himself too much like the eunuch Cesario, he is not alone in making it. Cesario is often mistaken for somebody else in the play. It seems even at times Orsino cannot keep things straight. Desiring a tune he heard the night before, Orsino, states:

> Now good Cesario, but that piece of song,
> That old and antic song we heard last night:
> Methought it did relieve my passion much,
> More than light airs and recollected terms
> Of these most brisk and giddy-paced times.
> Come, but one verse. (2.4.2–7)

Before Cesario can speak or sing, however, Curio steps in to correct Orsino: "He is not here, so please your lordship, that should sing it" (2.4.8–9). Orsino discoverers it was "Feste the jester," not Cesario, who sang the tune the Duke recalls. This is a small moment in the play, and not much is made of it. Cesario is not confused with Feste again, but for a moment, Orsino makes a mistake, confusing the voice of Olivia's jester with the mellifluous voice of his court eunuch.

The play resolves its marriage plots by likewise mistaking eunuchs for bachelors. If Sebastian understands Olivia's mistake as that of confusing two cisgender bodies, that of a bachelor and that of a maid, he does so by overwriting the series of such mistakings throughout the play, a series of mistakings of which he figures as the last: that of taking bachelors for eunuchs or eunuchs for bachelors. In this framing, the eunuch Cesario dissolves from the scene so that Sebastian and Viola might emerge as marriage material, as wife and husband to a Duke and Countess, respectively. The eunuch, it turns out, was never really there: there were just cisgender, marital bodies all along, or so the play's marriage plot would insist, and so might we, if we reduce the play's representations of gender to the operations of that plot. Or maybe Olivia does get what she desires. Viola's choice of disguise was no accident. Presenting as the eunuch Cesario, she took on the likeness of Sebastian, her twin. Given the way so many of the plots of Shakespearean comedy resolve, it is tempting to conceive of patriarchal marriage as their natural end, but in this version, Olivia reimagines what a comedic ending might be. She makes a husband not of a bachelor but of a eunuch.

## Remaining Unmarried in *The Roaring Girl*

*Twelfth Night* associates eunuchs with the single life, and it takes a form of cispicious reading to reformulate the transparencies and opacities of gendered embodiment that otherwise organize the play. However, even as it labors to dispel the figure of the eunuch, it also intimates how there really is no difference between the eunuch and bachelor and the husband: one can easily replace Cesario with Sebastian. You can make of a body what you will.

Neither Cesario nor Sebastian, however, embrace that life in *Twelfth Night*. Despite the long remainder of single people—Feste, Curio, Valentine, Malvolio, Sir Andrew, Fabian, an unnamed servant, a Priest, Antonio, and the Captain—there are very few, if any, who valorize it or explore its potential. But that is not the case in *The Roaring Girl*, which contains one of the renaissance's most salient affirmations of the unmarried state. In that play, Moll Cutpurse adamantly refuses marriage and embraces the single life, asserting to that play's Sebastian: "I have no humour to marry. I love to lie o' both sides o'th' bed myself; and again, o' th'other side, a wife, you know, ought to be obedient, but I fear me I am too headstrong to obey, therefore I'll ne'er go about it. I love you so well, sir, for your good will, I'd be loath you should repent your bargain after, and therefore we'll ne'er come together at first. I have the head now of myself, and am man enough for a woman; marriage is but a chopping and changing, where a maiden loses one head, and has a worse i'the' place."[93] If Cesario and Malvolio are relegated to a single life for the sake of Sebastian's and Viola's respective marriages, Moll rejects marriage because of the freedom the single life affords and the range of gender expressions such a life permits.

Much has been made of Moll in literary criticism of *The Roaring Girl*, and much of what has been made has concerned their gendered embodiment. As Heather Herschfeld has argued, the play's insistence on Moll as an object of inquiry has meant that *The Roaring Girl* not only invites ontological queries over the nature of gender, but also dramatizes a series of epistemological problems about what gendered individuals know and what can be known about gender.[94] Reconsidering just such ontological and epistemological contours of the play, Marjorie Rubright closely reads the play's lexicon to catalog its "transgender capacity," a capacity created through its variety of "semantic opacities that refuse to render the body an ontological site of decipherability, and object of certain knowledge."[95] Rubright goes on to argue that transgender capacities of *The Roaring Girl* depend upon "the opacities of the soma-semantics of gender: the ways in which, at the semantic level, the play refuses to produce classificatory clarifications regarding gender (particularly Moll | Jack's self-expression)."[96] Christine Varnado likewise attends to the way the play represents Moll's gendered embodiment, though to different ends. Analyzing how, in *The Roaring Girl*, "two lovers need, commission, and use an ambiguously gendered third party to negotiate the social, affective, and sexual demands of their prohibited love match," Varnado argues, "that being made instrumental can be regarded as a queer mode of relation, one that can expand our thinking about early modern sexuality and its representations in literature."[97] Varnado goes on to demonstrate the various ways instrumentality, objectification, and agency need not be mutually exclusive of one another, and essentially recenters Moll within the marriage plot by showing how that plot's circuit of hetero-erotic relations run through and are organized by Moll.

As these scholars (and numerous others) demonstrate, *The Roaring Girl* remains a rich text for thinking about gender and desire in the early modern period. Without denying the potentialities of understanding Moll as both object and subject of knowledge, or one who possess the capacity of transgender embodiment, I want to consider how the play's construction of Moll's gendered embodiment underwrites insistent speculations upon their person that reify transgender embodiment itself as that which must be attended by intense speculation and obsession by a cisnormative patriarchal social order. Refusals to produce classificatory systems of gender may be liberatory in some contexts, but not all. Moll may just want to be left alone. While there are "opacities of the soma-semantics of gender" throughout *The Roaring Girl*, those opacities often take the form of plurality: an overproduction of meaning that often, though not always, localizes upon the body of Moll, and, significantly, Laxton. But there are other opacities of gender in the play. The ostensible cisgender bodies of Sebastian, Mary Fitzallard, the patriarchs, the other gallants, and citizens also organize around "opacities of the soma-semantics of gender" insofar that no one speaks much of the gendered bodies in relation to social presentation or genital morphology. The transgender capacities of these characters are simply not recognized by the play. As Simone Chess has argued, "though we can never locate a 'real' gender for the historical Frith or the fictional Cutpurse, attending to Frith/Cutpurse's performance of queer gender makes visible the construction of cisgender and normative gender performances around her, both in the play and in the audiences, just as her queer act of opting out of marriage reveals the artificiality, production, and maintenance of heterosexuality."[98] Chess notes that the play invites a kind of reading of Moll's gender that creates the potential to see the naturalization of patriarchal order. However, I also want to insist that the impossibility of locating Moll's "real" gender is a problem the play invites specifically to naturalize the cisgender body central to patriarchal marriage, and it does so through and a continual alignment of Moll with the figure of the eunuch. As already demonstrated, the figure of the eunuch was cast as fundamentally outside normative gendered embodiment, and so also anathema to marriage. By positioning the eunuch outside the patriarchal gender order, other bodies could be granted the privileges of being inside it, as man and woman, husband and wife. If the transgender capacities of *The Roaring Girl* tend to localize around "Moll | Jack," then to what degree do such capacities depend upon the alignments, from appellative to metonymic, of Moll with the figure of the eunuch? Following the arguments of both Chess and Varnado, I argue that *The Roaring Girl*, much like anatomical and marital discourses of the period, instrumentalizes Moll as a eunuch figure to materialize Sebastian and Mary as a cisgender couple who, in their union, naturalize patriarchal marriage as relation between men and women who might be imagined as "one flesh." The play, in short, represents patriarchal marriage as a technology of governance invested in classifying sex as a property of the body, and Dekker and Middleton operationalize Moll as an instrument in its marriage plot to effect its classificatory speculations.

In their *The Roaring Girl*, Middleton and Dekker characterize Moll as a eunuch to speculate upon Moll's body as a sexed body. The euonym "Cutpurse," much like that of "Cesario," inscribes gelding as constitutive of identity—Moll is one whose scrotal "purse," like that of a eunuch, has been "Cut." The title page of the 1611 quarto capitalizes upon the very spectacle of Moll as a possible eunuch, and further situates what makes them spectacular as a matter of too much signification and not enough. A viewer sees in the woodcut *The Roaring Girle, OR Moll Cut-Purse*, and the caption that runs on the left margin, states, "My case is alter'd, I must work for my living."[99] All the speculations and interpretations that arise around who Moll is and what they might do circulate around the puns on their genitalia: an altered case and a cut purse. Moll, the title page suggests, is a eunuch, but it also implicitly argues that the proof of gender, of Moll even being a "roaring girl," depends upon a localization and a focalization upon genitalia, the "alter'd case." As Christopher Clary has argued, the title page of the quarto renders Moll "a figure who demands exploration. Her body is a site of confusion and multiplication, and its depiction on the Quarto title page invites a reading practice that must contend with these shifting lines of signification."[100] Even in her affirmation of the single life, Moll puns on a humoral difference: having "no humour" to marry, Moll conflates the lack of testicular heat of the eunuch with a personal disposition. If, as Varnado observes, "the play repeatedly raises, without resolving, the question of Moll's genital anatomy," such scrutiny participates within and supplements an early modern project of materializing gendered embodiment in relation to the figure of the eunuch.[101]

189

Such a reading practice of intense speculation over the body extends to the quarto's epistle "*To Comic Play-readers: Venery and Laughter*."[102] The epistle, as many readers of the play recognize, aligns dramatic style with sartorial display, and so it insists, "Now in the time of spruceness, our plays follow the niceness of our garments: single plots, quaint conceits, lecherous jests, dressed up in hanging sleeves."[103] Middleton extends this analogy to consider the implications of interpretation, of the text and of the bodies represented by that text; "and for venery," he writes, "you shall find enough for sixpence, but well couched an you mark it. For Venus, being a woman, passes through the play in doublet and breeches; a brave disguise and a safe one, if the statute untie not her codpiece point!"[104] In these few lines, Middleton invites a speculation over the body that amounts to an assault, a non-consensual violation. Moll is at once abstracted as a woman through the goddess Venus, and thus objectified as a figure of venery, and also materialized through the promise of exposed genitals: what the "codpiece point" neatly occludes but tantalizingly might reveal if untied. The reader, moreover, is invited to look for Venus as Moll (and Moll as Venus) and to continually read for the matter and meaning of Moll's genitals, all of which are "well couched an you mark it." Moreover, the prologue reduplicates this reading practice by forcing an analogy between the spectator's "look" and the reader's "book." It begins, "A play expected long makes the audience look / For wonders—that each scene should be a book / Composed to all perfection" (Pro.1–2). The play invites speculation and then reifies it by characterizing Moll as a body to be read and interpreted from the outset in terms of a classification of genital morphology.

Is Moll *really* a eunuch? That's the question the play asks again and again, implicitly and explicitly, in a manner that overdetermines Moll's gendered embodiment, and the other questions about the "truth" of gender (is Moll *really* a woman; is Moll *really* a man?) become structured by questions intensified upon the body of the eunuch. That question, however, does not require an answer: the play asks it but does not answer it, so that the gendered embodiment of other characters is essentially an answered question that has never been asked. Setting aside the question of how Moll identifies (*who* cares?), however, there are at least two effects to this overdetermination of Moll's gendered embodiment. One is the signifying of a "transgender capacity" coordinated through the figure of the eunuch that could, but does not have to, supplement the play's transphobic fascinations. Constructed as a eunuch, Moll seemingly warrants apparatuses of inspection and examination to verify genital morphology and function. Another occurs as Moll's supposed transgender capacity commutes the encoding of gender from a matter of sartorial expression and toward a matter of sartorial "couchings" and occlusions. In other words, only some forms of sartoriality in the play are thought to express gender while other forms are understood to occlude it. There are, for instance, any number of characters who might be said to pass "through the play in doublet and breeches." To name a few: Sebastian, Goshawk, Greenwit, Jack Dapper, Sir Alexander Wengrave, Sir Davy Dapper, Sir Adam Appleton, Sir Guy Fitzallard, Lord Noland, Sir Beauteous Ganymede, Sir Thomas Long, Hippocrates Gallipot, Openwork, Tiltyard, Neatfoot, Gull, Ralph Trapdoor, Tearcat, Curtalax, and Hanger. There is no reason to believe such characters are, by default, cisgender men except that the play has too "well couched" them to "mark" their bodies as given over to such examination.

One character who is not so "well couched" to "mark" as a eunuch is the gallant Laxton, whose euonym, like that of Moll Cutpurse, identifies him for what he is or is perceived to be: a eunuch, or one who lacks stones. While we can read this identification of Laxton as a eunuch as a transmisogynistic attack on his manhood, many characters in the play treat it as quite literal. When Laxton first appears in the play, Sir Alexander Wengrave tells his servant, "Furnish Master Laxton with what he wants—a stone—a stool, I would say, a stool," and when Laxton insists that he would "rather stand," Sir Alexander translates Laxton's response into a sublimated desire for potency: "I know you had, good Master Laxton. So, so—" (1.1.55–58). Sir Alexander here invites speculation upon the tenderness of the wound of castration and to the discomfort Laxton might have in sitting. Laxton's notoriety for his sexual promiscuity would supplement his notoriety as a eunuch whose eunuchry is both the cause and effect of his sexual desires.[105]

If *Twelfth Night* requires a "hermeneutics of cispicion" to reconstitute its citations of the eunuch, *The Roaring Girl* more forthrightly resists such a reading strategy because it more thoroughly mobilizes the differential relations between bachelor, husband, and eunuch with which this chapter opened. The play dramatizes the desire to see, know, and possess figures coded as eunuchs across two marriage plots, both of which involve such figures, as Varnado has demonstrated, as instrumental facilitators. In one, Moll helps Sebastian secure Mary Fitzallard as wife. Sebastian's plot involves deploying transphobia: his desire for Moll is to appear so anathema and frightening to his father Sir Alexander that his father will embrace Mary Fitzallard as a suitable partner. In another, Laxton courts Prudence Gallipot, who, eventually, rejects him to affirm her marriage to Gallipot, her husband. In each plot, the figure of the eunuch functions as a kind of "narrative prosthesis," what David T. Mitchell and Sharon L. Snyder define as the "perpetual discursive dependency upon disability, [which] lends a distinctive idiosyncrasy to any character that differentiates the character from the anonymous background of the 'norm.'"[106] As we have seen in early modern marital tracts, patriarchal marriage could be conceived as disabling the eunuch through constructing procreative sexuality as marriage's enabling condition. In *The Roaring Girl*, each plot thus utilizes the figure of the eunuch not only to police the boundaries of marriage but also to affirm marriage as a relation between cisgender men and women that is also a relation in danger of encroachment by a eunuch who conceals who they are.

In dramatizing its marriage plots, the play is not subtle about its objects of desire, fascination, and disgust, about whom it believes should marry or remain single. Sebastian's plot only works if those around him believe someone characterized as a eunuch threatens patriarchal marriage. Sebastian forthrightly explains his plans to Mary at the beginning of the play:

> Though wildly in a labyrinth I go,
> My end is to meet thee: with a side wind
> Must I now sail, else I no haven can find,
> But both must sink forever. There's a wench
> Called Moll, Mad Moll, or Merry Moll, a creature
> So strange in quality, a whole city takes
> Note of her name and person.—All that affection
> I owe to thee, on her, in counterfeit passion,
> I spend to mad my father; he believes
> I dote upon this roaring girl, and grieves
> As it becomes a father for a son
> That could be so bewitched; yet I'll go on
> This crooked way, sigh still for her, feign dreams
> In which I'll talk only of her: these streams
> Shall, I hope, force my father to consent
> That here I anchor, rather than to rent
> Upon a rock so dangerous. (1.1.98–111)

Imagining his device as a maritime adventure, and playing the chaser, Sebastian positions himself as a kind of world traveler who courts the eunuch off England's shores only to abandon that "side wind" to return home. The conceit casts Moll across a range of gender, species, and mineral matter: Moll becomes "a wench," "a creature," a "her," "this roaring girl," and "a rock so dangerous." By courting one whose person troubles a range of classificatory systems, Sebastian means to resolve, or rather short-circuit, his father's concerns over differences in social rank by proliferating matters of difference elsewhere. Rather than mock his father for what will "mad" him, Sebastian only affirms him, acknowledging that what "grieves" (or will) Sir Alexander "becomes a father for a son." In Sebastian's eyes, Moll can be operationalized to divert attention away from Mary and himself, so that their marriage might achieve a patriarch's blessing.

At this point in the play, Sebastian's plan, while it involves Moll, is not yet known by Moll. It is only after Sebastian begins his "counterfeit passion" for Moll, when Moll proclaims so cogently a desire to live a single life, that Sebastian seeks to inform Moll of his designs. He soliloquizes:

This mad girl I'll acquaint with my intent,
Get her assistance, make my fortunes known:
'Twixt lovers' hearts she's a fit instrument,
And has the art to help them to their own.
By her advice, for in the craft she's wise,
My love and I may meet, spite of all spies. (2.2.196–201)

That Sebastian understands Moll as "a fit instrument" literalizes the structural relations this chapter has been tracing between eunuch, bachelor, and husband on the one hand, and between the single life and the married life on the other. Sebastian understands that Moll can function like a eunuch, and thus operate as a necessary tool for securing his marriage with Mary. In that role, Moll helps him realize the necessary classifications of sex central to such a marriage, which, given its legal power and technological function to govern bodies, requires "all spies." Sebastian seeks to redirect those spying eyes of the patriarchal social order to Moll's body and away from Mary's social status.

Sebastian's conception of Moll as "a fit instrument" also literalizes the ideological operations that compound upon the figure of the eunuch even as such conception draws its energy from contemporaneous associations of eunuchry: it imagines Moll as a Byzantine eunuch protecting the marriage bed as well as the eunuch as a sexual body, akin to a "Eunucke dildo," one that brings pleasure but not procreation "twixt lovers' hearts" "and has the art to help them to their own" orgasms.[107] It is this latter meaning of "instrument" that has intratextual resonance in *The Roaring Girl*. The only other time the word "instrument" appears in the play, it functions as a pun on phallic genitalia. When Moll plays the viol later in the play, both Sebastian and Moll make a pun on "instrument" to emphasize its genital meanings in a manner that redoubles the latent viol/vial phallic pun:

*Moll.* . . . Well, since you'll needs put us together, sir, I'll play my part as well as I can: it shall ne'er be said I came into a gentleman's chamber and let his instrument hang by the walls!

*Sebastian.* Why well said, Moll, i'faith; it had been a shame for that gentleman then, that would have let it hang still, and ne'er offered thee it.

*Moll.* There it should have been still then for Moll, for though the world judge impudently of me, I ne'er came into that chamber yet where I took down the instrument myself.

*Sebastian.* Pish, let 'em prate abroad! Thou'rt here where thou art known and loved; there be a thousand close dames that will call the viol an unmannerly instrument for a woman, and therefore talk broadly of thee, when you shall have them sit wider to a worse quality. (4.1.84–98)

Through its series of puns, the scene negotiates the instrumentality of genitalia and reduction of manhood to matters of genital function. Bodies play their parts by having the requisite parts to play. But the "part" Moll willingly plays "as well as [they] can" here is a plural one. Much like the epistle to the reader and the prologue to the play, the scene invites its audiences to speculate upon and fetishize Moll as sexual subject and object, as someone who will not let a gentleman's instrument hang. That pun on the hanging instrument inaugurates a concern over arousal and potency; Sebastian acknowledges the shame of the possibility that such an instrument might "hang still," that it might remain a thing perpetually inert. As Moll plays the viol, Sebastian continues to complicate its meanings as a sexual object, recognizing that it might be an "unmannerly instrument for a woman," which is to say it violates norms of propriety because it is a substitute for the "real deal." The "unmannerly instrument" of the viol is too analogous and homophonically proximate to an unmanly vial, or dildo, a phallus without the potency of testicles. And yet, insofar as the viol is Moll's instrument upon which they play their song, the scene presents an inversion of the synecdochic relation between genital part and gendered whole. The part Moll plays here depends upon what they play: the viol may be taken up as a sign of Moll's gender, but it is not determinative of that gender. In taking up the viol, Moll not only plays the part of a man but also the man's part. Problematically, as Moll does so, they also sing misogynistic songs of spendthrift and adulterous wives. Moll's dreams are patriarchal dreams, denouncing women as gossips, liars, and hypocrites.

In this scene, Moll is dressed in masculine attire playing a viol, and so the scene can reinforce the ways in which the social presentations of gender intimate the inscription of gendered meanings upon the body. The body is read through a series of metonymic, substitutionary relations—from attire, to viol, to genitals. That Moll plays the viol suggests that Moll also does not "have" a vial in the first place, that it must be supplemented through forms of prosthesis, which Will Fisher has shown were central to gendered embodiment in the early modern period.[108] However, this scene also complicates the transparency of the social presentation of gender through such prosthesis. This scene has at first three, and then, with the entrance of Sir Alexander, four people dressed as men. The play means for the audience to understand Moll and Mary as disguised as men while Sebastian and Sir Alexander are not to be so perceived. One obvious marker of gender difference here is naming; that cannot be denied. But I also want to suggest how the relations of the single life and the married life open up and foreclose notions of gendered embodiment and presentation here. Moll facilitates the relationship between Mary and Sebastian; she is an instrument of that relation, one who is external to it but also necessary for its realization. While Moll remains constitutively single, Mary, who is also single but labors to be married, is presented as disguised in a page's clothes supplied by Moll. At this moment, Mary's disguise as a page works to reinforce the play's iteration that Moll's clothing might also operate in similar terms: they, too, might disguise a particular kind of body rather than clothe that body. Taken together, the sartorially of Mary and Moll can be read, especially by the audiences in the scene, to hold an ironic relation to the gendered properties of the body. What might appear to queer or transgress patriarchal gender norms ultimately becomes conducive to them. When Sebastian kisses Mary, who is dressed as a page, Moll observes, "How strange this shows, one man to kiss another," and Sebastian responds, "I'd kiss such men to choose, Moll; / Methinks a woman's lip tastes well in a doublet" (4.1.45–47). Sebastian, in fact, revises Moll's reading of gender here. Where Moll reads two men kissing, Sebastian insists he kisses a "woman's lip." But even here a metonymic relation holds: the labial part of "a woman's lip" is and is not a genital sign. As Sebastian and Mary kiss, the problem of marrying across status lines—the original problem of the marriage plot—disappears from view as Moll surfaces the homoerotic connection, which Sebastian then reorients into a heteroerotic one that will anticipate his eventual marriage.

Throughout most of *The Roaring Girl*, Moll services the patriarchal marriage of Sebastian and Mary, playing, as it were, a good eunuch. The other eunuch in the play, Laxton, performs the opposite function, attempting to destabilize the patriarchal marriage of the Gallipots. Because Laxton seeks to disrupt a patriarchal marriage, his associations with eunuchry become realized in ways that Moll's own characterization as a eunuch never do. Like Lenton's bachelor, Laxton hopes to sow "his seed in other mens gardens" only to be "made an Eunuch, and consequently been hated by the softer Sex for ever after."[109] While originally open to Laxton's advances, Prudence Gallipot will disable him, calling Laxton "another lame gelding" (4.2.47), and will also come to tell him, "I think thy tail's cut" (4.2.102). Laxton is further humiliated by Moll in a duel, where Moll wounds him and he "yield[s] both purse and body" (3.1.121), an abdication that suggests castration and servitude. Where Moll's association with eunuchry suggests plurality, possibility, and sartoriality, Laxton's association with eunuchry intensifies his castration, humiliation, and fundamental disability. As in *Twelfth Night*, then, we have two eunuchs who, positioned against each other, reinforce patriarchal marriage through their veneration or humiliation. Moll's transgender capacities—however they may be realized— exist because they circulate outside a marriage relation that Moll ultimately protects and defends whereas Laxton's capacities become increasingly circumscribed to the evidence of his castration, which could prevent him from marrying should he want to.

At the end of the play, Moll personally rejects marriage but ultimately abets the patriarchal marital order by pretending to be the kind of eunuch that Laxton tries to be. Where earlier in the play Sir Alexander rejected Mary Fitzallard on grounds of social rank and economic status, he now recoils not at social difference but gender differences. Moll makes this clear when, against Sir Alexander's horror at seeing his son with Moll, Moll states, "Methinks you should be proud of such a daughter— / as good a man as your son" (5.2.152)! The gulling of Sir Alexander here effects his embrace of Mary Fitzallard, whom he praises as "a fair fruitful bride" once she revealed as the true wife of Sebastian (l.204). The play is not subtle in this reorientation of whose body invites speculation: Sir Alexander is thankful that Sebastian is marrying a procreative woman and not Moll, who Sir Alexander conceives as existing outside the category of woman, one who, like a eunuch, only ever approximates the patriarchal categories of a sexed body.

And yet, even as Moll facilitates a patriarchal marriage, in their final embrace of the single life, they gesture toward a future of more radical possibility. The end of the play looks, with Moll, beyond its marriage plot for a kind of abolition of marriage itself. In the final moments of the play, Moll insists again upon the single life, rejecting marriage until "doomsday" (l.225). For Moll, marriage become a viable option only when the social order exists as it otherwise never will:

When you shall hear
Gallants void from sergeants' fear,
Honesty and truth unslandered
Woman manned but never pandered
Cheaters booted but not coached,
Vessels older ere they're broached. (ll.217–22)

Moll will marry, in other words, when marriage does not perpetuate patriarchal systems invested in a carceral state and the sexual exploitation of women and children, when women might be manned, or anyone, for that matter, may have the embodiments they desire. Moll will never marry until marriage does not exist as such. In this respect, Moll looks toward a vision of gender abolition most recently theorized by Marquis Bey. Drawing on the work of Hortense Spillers, Kai M. Green, and Treva Ellison, Bey advocates for "a fugitive *un / gendering*" of "traniflesh." As Bey goes on to explain: "Because gender via hegemonic logics is predicated on being visible to the mind, being material, being biological, being an immutable substance, traniflesh, in getting outside of those walled enclosures that ultimately signify fallacies and arbitrariness, becomes un/gendered. It is not gendered, nor strictly speaking ungendered . . . Un/gendering's fleshiness is an overflow that spills over violent categorization and, instead of being generated by whips and frisks, is the unwhippable and unfriskable displacement of normative violence, the levied critique of normativity we hope to move toward as subjective livability."[110] For Moll, the single life is a livable life. It might be a life where Moll's own embodiment is not governed by a patriarchal insistence upon classifying bodies as those belonging to bachelors, husbands, women, or eunuchs, one less subject to the governing technologies of classification, one where bodies are enlivened by their "traniflesh." And Moll is correct. That would be a kind of "doomsday," a more welcome one, where the single life and the married would be merely two of a myriad of ways to forge gender, sexual, racial, economic, and social relations. It would be a world where marriage itself might be unthinkable as such because the terms that make it thinkable, and the types of manhood that organize its epistemologies, would not or could not be the norm. We, like Moll, like Bey, might imagine and labor for such a world.

# Epilogue

## The Renaissance of the Single Life in the Amatonormative Renaissance

The previous chapters have demonstrated (I hope) that attending to the single life can pluralize our understandings of early modern manhood as well as energize our critiques of early modern (and modern) patriarchal ideologies. The single life was never one thing in early modern England, though early modern patriarchal institutions and norms—from companionate marriage to heteroerotic coupling, from livery companies to universities, from patrilineality to entrepreneurality—sought to inscribe it as the fated pasts to its enduring presents. It would just be a matter of time: what were chaste youths but eventual husbands, bachelor journeymen but master householders, gallant sons but ingenious heirs, incel scholars but melancholic geniuses, and unmarried eunuchs but betrothed bachelors? Patriarchy seeks to take what might be and hammer it into what must.

But as I also hope to have shown, not all evasions from or negotiations of patriarchal institutions result in emancipations that might align a particular iteration of gender with the cultural, social, economic, and biopolitical effectuations of power. Incels may not be patriarchs, but they murder women just the same. Unpatriarchal manhoods can reject patriarchal ideals to relocate, realign, and reinscribe modes of masculine privilege to newly violent, predatory, and deadly ends. Such unpatriarchal forms of manhood we face today—circulated and envisioned through social networks, white supremacist online enclaves, and hyper-masculinist fraternal organizations—have their social and cultural histories that, while not firmly nor genealogically tethered to the early modern past, nonetheless resonate with forms of manhood becoming if not popular, then legible in English renaissance literature and culture.

And sometimes there is more than mere resonance. Modern patriarchy often actively seeks to anchor its present power to an early modern past it labors to excavate. Recent legal rulings in the United States, for example, have confirmed how much the modern patriarchal present depends upon linking its own judgments to early modern historical authority. The 2022 *Dobbs v. Jackson Women's Health* decision, which overturned *Roe v. Wade*, cast off jurisprudential precedent by drawing upon seventeenth-century jurists Sir Edward Coke and Sir Matthew Hale.[1] Even as significant a legal victory in marital rights as that of the 2015 *Obergefell v. Hodges* decision drew upon a marital historiography akin to those I covered in the first chapter. Justice Anthony Kennedy's majority opinion begins, "From their beginning to their most recent page, the annals of human history reveal the transcendent importance of marriage," and then asserts, "Its dynamic allows two people to find a life that could not be found alone, for a marriage becomes greater than just two persons."[2] Kennedy is no poet, nor is he paraphrasing Shakespeare exactly, but he could be, for Shakespeare too insists in sonnet eight that those in marital unions "who all in one, one pleasing note do sing: whose speechless song, being many, seeming one" persuade the single to harmonize with history. According to Kennedy, law must keep up with a history that bears witness to the universal, transhistorical power of marriage. In Kennedy's ruling, marriage—whatever it might mean at any given moment in history—is, nonetheless, history's constant.

There are other ways to understand Kennedy's decision, of course. If marriage would not, historically, recognize a monogamous union between a same-gender couple even if it had in the past recognized relations between different gender, polygamous unions, one might, like Kennedy, simply expand marriage's horizons to include those who have petitioned to be included in marriage's historiographical march into modernity. However, one might also otherwise understand marriage as an inadequate institution to serve as the primary metonym for social order or historical progress. A desire to expand its rights-protecting aegis also hardens its function as just that; as Yasmin Nair observes, "it becomes apparent that what appears to be a wish to bestow dignity upon queers is in fact deeply rooted in a fear and loathing of the unmarried and a neoliberal belief that the addition of private rights tied to the state's munificence will end all social problems."[3] One might, like the single Jaques of *As You Like It*, opt out and claim, "To see no pastime, I. What you would have / I'll stay to know at your abandoned cave" (5.4.205–6). There are other ways of knowing and being outside of marriage's promised happy endings.

What do we do with predominance and preeminence of marriage, and in turn, what might thinking about the various, potential meanings of the single life do to denaturalize the institution? The legal rights inscribed into marriage supplement the cultural dominance of what philosopher Elizabeth Brake calls "amatonormativity," the "disproportionate focus on marital and amorous love relationships as special sites of value, and the assumption that romantic love is a universal goal." According to Brake, amatonormativity "consists in the assumption that a central, exclusive, amorous relationship is normal for humans, in that it is a universally shared goal, and that such a relationship is normative, in that it *should* be aimed at in preference to other relationship types."[4] Modern reality television programs, such as ABC's *The Bachelor* and *Bachelorette*, are perhaps the clearest crystallization of American amatonormativity. The amatonormative can also be thought of as having early modern resonances. While queer theorists and feminist scholars alike have observed how Shakespeare's comedies, for instance, revel in homosocial relationships only to reorganize such relations into heteroerotic coupling, we might also conceive of marriage plots as negotiating, and often affirming, modes of early modern amatonormativity. Amatonormativity, in this sense, can be thought of as an effect of genre. Shakespeare's contribution to marital comedy has left an indelible mark.[5]

In attending to the unpatriarchal manhoods of the single life, this book has sought to unthink the norms of early modern patriarchy and its epistemological frames, and in its recentering of the single life, this book has aimed to reconsider what it is possible to know about early modern literature. It has been a partial project; early modern literature has far more ways of imagining the single life than this book has had the time and space to consider. In his desire to hunt with friends, for instance, the chaste youth Adonis resists the desires of the goddess Venus and affirms modes of relationality the dyadic embrace of amatonormativity cannot grant him. Adonis may index an early modern asexual life or he simply might desire something beyond or besides what coupling with Venus might entail. What becomes available to us when we read Shakespeare's erstwhile alloerotic epyllion with an eye on the affordances of the single life?

Reading for the single life is something less than a method, but taking the single life seriously nonetheless can recalibrate what we think and know about early modern gender and social identity. So I'd like to close this book with a reflective envoi that briefly looks again at the bachelor journeymen I focused on in chapter 2 to recenter sexual practices and epistemologies that lurk just outside of patriarchal amatonormativity. To do so, I turn to a play that ostensibly does not have much sex in it at all: Dekker's *The Shoemaker's Holiday* (1599).

A play full of shoemakers shoemaking, *The Shoemaker's Holiday* is also a text where the bawdy language of its bachelor journeymen rejoices in a sexual epistemology not easily recuperated by the marriage plot that would otherwise structure the play. It is a play where the single life facilitates a "sex life," what Joseph Gamble defines as that which "names the quotidian practices through which we build, maintain, and selectively hold open intimate infrastructures."[6] Where the play's marriage plot would insist upon sex as safely ensconced in the marriage relation, the play's single artisans unfix its meanings from that institution, discussing their sex lives in the language of their labor. Sex is not just practiced, or lived, but worked at. Indeed, sex lives as such in the *Shoemaker's Holiday* remain unthinkable apart from acts of labor in the play, where there is often an unbridled joy in the kinesis of bodies. Reimaginings of the meanings of sex emerge in the play at the same time the shop's bachelor journeymen first take the stage. Upon their original appearance, the shoemakers have pressing business. Ralph, a newly married journeyman of Eyre's shop, has been conscripted to fight in France. Appealing to the young aristocrat Rowland Lacy, Eyre seeks Ralph's exemption, but it is Firk, Eyre's "fine firking journeyman," and Jane, Ralph's wife, who make the most direct appeal.[7] They plead:

> *Firk.* Truly, Master Cormorant, you shall do God good service to let Ralph and his wife stay together. She's a young, new-married woman. If you take her husband away from her a night, you undo her; she may beg in the daytime; for he's as good a workman at a prick and an awl as any is in our trade.
>
> *Jane.* O, let him stay, else I shall be undone!
>
> *Firk.* Ay, truly, she shall be laid at one side like a pair of old shoes else, and be occupied for no use. (1.140–48)

Both Firk and Jane make an economic argument. Firk attests that Ralph is a skilled workman—he is handy with the shoemaker's tools of prick and awl—and as such, provides for both himself and Jane. Ralph's going to war strips Jane of a primary source of economic security, such that, Firk suggests, she will become destitute and turn to begging. This narrative of economic destitution, however, is quickly enfolded by the doublespeak of bawdy. Jane "shall be undone" insofar as Ralph cannot "do" her, perhaps leaving her begging for it. Firk's final comparison of Jane to an old shoe likewise suggests that Ralph's deployment will leave her wanting—"occupied" usually, though not always, suggests a man's copulation with a woman.[8] Firk's bawdy likewise suggests Ralph's skill as a laborer signifies his skill as lover: "prick" is arguably not a pun here so much as it clearly denotes, well, Ralph's prick. Smallwood and Wells suggest "awl" is a homonymic pun on "hole," which would suggest Ralph is skilled at vaginal, oral, or anal intercourse (giving or receiving). But "awl" might suggest Ralph is as good with his hands as he is with his prick. Assessing the abilities of Hans (who is really Rowland Lacy) as a shoemaker, Firk queries, "have you all your tools—a good rubbing-pin, a good stopper, a good dresser, your four sorts of awls, and your two balls of wax, your paring-knife, your hand-and thumb-leathers, and good Saint Hugh's bones to smooth up your work?" (4.83–87). Awls were used for poking holes in leather; the citation of the four sizes can correspond to the four fingers of the hand (also of varying sizes and lengths, and as we will see, it is the shoemaker's hands that are continually privileged). Firk's puns suggest that Ralph is adept at not only phallic but also digital penetration of any number of holes.

At first it seems like the play valorizes the patriarchal household. In Eyre's shoemaking shop, the single lives of the artisans provide valuable know-how to the married couples. Married couples learn what a shop of single artisans know. Ralph's skill as a worker crucially depends not only upon his artisanal mastery but also upon his domestic proficiency. Analogized to a shoe—which she will be metonymically aligned with later in the play when Ralph gives her a pair "made up and pinked with letters for [her] name" as a memento (1.241)—Jane emerges as a passive object to be pricked or to "be laid at one side." Any hint of Jane's sexual agency is, like her social and sexual position upon Ralph's leaving, "undone" in inverse proportion to affirmations of Ralph's own artisanal and sexual skill. Yet the plot will come to contravene in this picture of Ralph's virile sexuality and artisanal mastery when he returns from the wars, as Margery observes, "impotent" (whether this is sexual impotence or specifically an injury of Ralph's left leg is never entirely answered) (10.71). Ralph's disability compromises his procreative virility, but it also elevates and prioritizes other sexual practices. If impotent, if classified as a eunuch even, he and Jane will remain childless, but this does not mean Jane will be sexually unsatisfied. When Ralph mourns that Jane will "be poor indeed / Now I want limbs to get whereon to feed," his fellow journeyman Hodge encourages him: "Limbs? Hast thou not hands, man? Thou shalt never see a shoemaker want bread, though he have but three fingers on a hand" (10.87–89). In other words, without a prick, Ralph can still use his skills with an awl. With their range of sexual knowledge, the single men of the shoemaking shop use their shared lexicon of labor to remind the disabled Ralph of his wide-ranging sexual abilities.

203

A play like *The Shoemaker's Holiday*, then, documents how the single life is not so much subordinate to the married one as it is complementary to, and necessary for, an affirmative and affirming social milieu and sexual epistemology. For if the explicit linking of sex acts with labor practices at first lends itself to a rather conservative model of the patriarchal household, the bachelor journeyman's bawdy can, in its allusive opacities, also create a conceptual space where sex acts that subvert patriarchal order abound. Throughout much of the play, Margery, Eyre's wife, is mocked by the bachelor journeymen Firk and Hodge for her social posturing. This is the case when Firk returns from Guildhall with the news that Eyre is "to be sheriff of the City for this famous year now to come and time now being" (10.123–25). Margery gives Firk threepence for this news, but Hodge reprimands, "But, mistress, be ruled by me, and do not speak so pulingly." Building upon Hodge's critique, Firk explains, "'Tis her worship speaks so, and not she," and further requests, "No, faith, mistress, speak me in the old key. 'To it, Firk,' 'There, good Firk,' 'Ply your business, Hodge'—'Hodge,' with a full mouth—'I'll fill your bellies with good cheer till they cry twang' (ll.141–45)." Firk ventriloquizes Margery to distinguish the two kinds of social authority she claims: her old authority as "mistress" of the shop and her new authority as "Mistress Shrieve" (l.130). He aligns the latter with social posturing ("her worship") and the former with authenticity of self ("she"). Firk's elucidation of Margery's double-speak maps onto and structures the articulation of her sexual pleasure. Speaking "in the old key," Margery becomes the journeymen's mistress in both senses of that term. Those phrases meant to cajole the journeymen in their work also voice her orgasmic pleasure in watching them work, or, more explicitly, in telling her journeymen how to fuck her: "To it, Firk, there, good Firk, Ply, your business, Hodge." The explicit references to Margery's pleasurable but ambiguous denotation of the acts being done privilege a kind of surface reading. That is, at their face value, the phrases Firk cites mean what they seem to mean; it is only through the contextualizing corporeal acts—journeymen working, journeymen fucking, Margery eating, Margery receiving pleasure—that the language of labor is transformed into the language of sex, the language of sex into the language of labor. The puns here depend upon Firk miming acts of work or sex acts. Otherwise, as if through a wall—the crucially opaque double-speak of euphemism—we can only hear Margery's pleasures in having sex without knowing or seeing the acts that her voice directs, though she directs them nonetheless.[9]

As the mechanics of labor practice transverse a semantic threshold to signify sexual acts, what kinds of social and sexual subjects are produced, figured forth, or disarticulated, especially as we might understand them outside the grip of patriarchal marriage and manhood? On the one hand, the bawdy of *The Shoemaker's Holiday* positions its bachelor journeymen—and specifically Firk—as subjects who have access to sexual knowledge, who are inside the room as opposed to outside it. Margery, on the contrary, makes similar bawdy jokes but is unaware she does so. When she tells the grieving Ralph that Jane, his wife, "might have opened her case to me or my husband or to any of my men" (10.100–2), she does not seem to intend the pun. Nonetheless, if we hear the pun, we do so because we are invited to speak the language of the play's single men and women. Turning work into bawdy or interpreting work as sex acts, Firk exercises a proficiency of a symbolic domain that Margery does not have, yet she is also invited to participate in a set of relations and sex acts that revel in her pleasure and sexual directives.

One effect of Firk's bawdy, however, is an interpellation of him as a fixed social subject, as one who, unlike so many in the play, does not or cannot aspire to a higher social rank.[10] And yet he is happy to remain single. While the play might otherwise situate Firk as fixed in the social hierarchy, he is anything but static. His is a life of energy and activity, of kinesis. When bawdy puns ally the mechanics of labor practices to sex acts, they tend to privilege activity—the doing of the deed—over any telos framing that activity. Without marriage as a perceived end, the value of both labor and sex find meaning in the acts themselves. In a profound way, the bawdy of the bachelor journeymen in *The Shoemaker's Holiday* removes sex from systems of social meaning, rendering it an act without narrative, a performance outside regimes of patriarchy's procreativity or productive purposes. This paradoxical relationship that the play's bawdy establishes between productive labor and nonprocreative sex acts is nowhere more clearly seen than in the journeymen who "firk" and "yerk." Firk's very name is an index of meanings of artisanal, sexual, and physical activity. The *OED* indicates that as a noun "firk/ferk" can mean "a smart sudden blow or stroke, as with a whip; a flick, slip; a cut or thrust (with a sword)" as well as "a trick, dodge, subterfuge. Also, a freak, prank, caprice" and "a dance."[11] As a verb, "firk/ferk" means, "to bring, carry, conduct; to urge, press hard; to drive, drive away," with adverbs, "to drive, force, or move sharply and suddenly *off, out, up*; to cut *off* (some one's head)" or "to drive or 'ferret' *out* (vermin), to clear *out* (a burrow, etc.; to move about briskly; to dance, jig; to flaunt or frisk about; to be lively, frisky)," as well as "to beat, whip, lash, trounce, drub."[12] Smallwood and Wells translate "yerk" as to "sew (leather)" or "stich."[13] With his journeymen making shoes, Eyre prods them with, "Yerk and seam, yerk and seam" (7.94–95), a phrase that, in addition to signifying the stitching of leather, mimics sonically the repetitive puncturing and pulling of thread. Firk's response is, like so many of his ripostes, bawdy; he tells Eyre, "For yerking and seaming let me alone, an I come to't" (l.96). Aligning the movements of the stitching hand with the pulling and plunging of the masturbating one, Firk asserts his mastery of his craft as a form of sexual autonomy and even privacy. But Firk may be more explicit than most editors give him credit for, as most interpret "seam," when they do not take it as self-evident, to mean "to sew the seam or seams of; to fasten or join on, *together, up* with a seam or seams."[14] This meaning is surely available here, but is it also redundant if "yerk" means to stich. Attention to the material practices of shoemaking suggests another possibility. "Seam" can mean the application of lugubrious oils, a treating of the leather. A contemporary meaning of "seam" was "fat, grease" or "hog's lard," denotations that resonate with the current labor of Firk, who, claiming to be making shoe's for Sybil, is reprimanded by Eyre for busying his "workmanly fingers with the feet of kitchen-stuff and basting ladles" (l.91–92). Eyre's favorite slur for women, and one he applies to Margery as well, is "kitchen-stuff," a material that as, Natasha Korda observes, "was a kind of female currency, collected in the kitchen by women who then sold it to chandlers (who used it to make candles), or to tanners, curriers, and shoemakers, who used it as an inexpensive substitute for high-grade tallow in tanning leather."[15] Firk, then, might also be suggesting that his masturbatory yerking is lubricated by the shop's seam or that seam/semen is the product of vigorous yerking.[16] However, his retort to Eyre also reconstitutes Eyre's misogynistic, classist slur, extracting it from a domestic economy and reconstituting it within an erotic one. "Kitchen-stuff" is, for Firk, not to be denigrated; it is desirable and useful for various kinds of labor.

So it is that for bachelor journeymen, labor is never only work in the play and tools are never just tools, that yerking and firking in the shop is never just about making shoes but making a life outside the norms of patriarchal amatonormativity. It is a consistent pattern in the play that scenes of bachelor journeymen laboring encode tableaux of sex, so much so that it can seem that Dekker only stages journeymen working to make bawdy jokes in a manner that enriches even those married journeymen. Scenes of shoemaking transform into sex scenes and back again. In *The Shoemaker's Holiday*, bachelor journeymen are (forgive me) hard at work.

Consider a final exchange. Hodge, Ralph, and Firk are again in the shop working on shoes, when Hodge (who has now been promoted from foreman to shopkeeper), states, "Tell me sirs, are my cousin Mistress Priscilla's shoes done" (13.20–21)? Hodge's question circumscribes the work the shoemakers perform within the economic relations of the household—shoe as commodity, artisan as producer, and customer as consumer—but just as the economic network of the shop emerges, it is subsumed by Firk's bawdy, which he writes into and over these sets of relations. Firk responds, "Your cousin? No, master, one of your aunts. Hang her; let them alone" (ll.22–23).[17] When Ralph attempts to reinscribe the language of labor back into the network of economic relations, saying "I am in hand with them. She gave charge that none but I should do them for her" (ll.24–25), Firk again returns to sexual puns: "Thou do for her? Then 'twill be a lame doing, and that she loves not. Ralph, thou mightest have sent her to me. In faith, I would have yerked and firked your Priscilla. [*Sings*] Hey down a-down derry.—This gear will not hold" (ll.26–30). While Firk draws upon words associated with labor—yerking and firking—it is unclear what Firk imagines doing with Priscilla. While any number of acts are imaginable, the specific sexual acts Firk has in mind—if indeed he has any in particular in mind—are not identifiable, for even if yerking and firking suggests vaginal sex, they do not, as we have seen, exclusively denote this act. The variety of sex acts cited, made possible, or otherwise imagined here might be added to those sexual and intimates practices—chin chucking, thigh sex, and cunnilingus—that Will Fisher has shown to have their own histories and social contingencies in the early modern period.[18] But here, the materialization of the sex act could be staged through the mechanics of yerking and firking shoes, that is, through the work of producing them, such that, like Jane's shoe, Priscilla's shoes would operate as a metonym for her body. I pause at this scene, however, because of the ways the language among the journeymen modulates between signifying their acts of labor and signifying possible sex acts. This building of ambiguity culminates in Firk's use of the word "gear," which, as Smallwood and Wells note, "could have a range of applications."[19] "This gear" is most likely a stage prop, a tool or piece of shoemaking equipment, but perhaps also Priscilla's shoes themselves. While Ralph's lameness is here transposed upon "this gear," the texture of the joke depends heavily upon how an audience reads the symbolic registers of that object's incapacity, an incapacity that is given new capacities, however, in the bawdy language of the bachelor journeyman Firk.

I realize that, in this final foray of elucidating the possible sex acts of the play's bachelor journeymen, I risk being what Stanley Wells might call a "lewd interpreter."[20] Yet I want to maintain that attending to the single life in early modern literature, and, moreover, thinking through its pluralities and contradictions, can reveal new ways of imagining manhood. In this case, materializing the sex acts of shoemakers and bachelor journeymen in this play gives us points of contact upon which histories of sexuality and theorizations of early modern sex might be constructed, and thus aids us in rethinking what is normative, practiced, habitual, and possible in terms of early modern sexuality outside of patriarchal ideals. The bawdy language of the play's bachelor journeymen might even function as a kind of counterdiscourse to the utopian plot of Eyre's economic rise. Ronda Arab has argued that the play valorizes "the procreative abilities of a commoner," and that it goes further than many contemporary plays in representing sex because it "links lineage production directly to sexual contact with a wife, thus taking its place in the emerging naturalization of heterosexuality."[21] But I think Arab overstates the naturalization of heterosexuality in the play, at least as it aligns with or might be realized through patriarchal marriage. The only procreative persons in the play are not the commoners but the elites. Sir Roger and Sir Hugh are the only patriarchs with children, and only when Simon Eyre supplants Oatley as Lord Mayor and attains an elite position does he imagine himself within a procreative social order; "Mark this old wench, My King," Eyre tells Henry V, "I danced the shaking of the sheets with her six-and-thirty years ago, and yet I hope to get two or three young Lord Mayors ere I die. I am lusty still. Sim Eyre still" (21.29–32). Eyre's euphemism for sex is notable because it repeats Firk's own identification of what Rose and Lacy will do on their wedding night—but it is not one he ever applies to himself or to the other journeymen. Being queried of the whereabouts of Rose and Lacy, Firk explains to Sir Hugh, "Mistress Rose and he [Lacy] are by this time—no, not so, but shortly are to come over one another with 'Can you dance the shaking of the sheets?'" (16.81–83). Both Eyre and Firk temporally circumscribe this sex act to the wedding night, which suggests Eyre has explicitly *not engaged in* procreative sex since his wedding night "six-and-thirty years ago," though now that he has economic security, he hopes to father sons. In other words, when Eyre was a shoemaker, any sex he and Margery had was, whatever it was, not explicitly procreative.

The early modern period certainly reified and institutionalized the notion of companionate marriage as both natural and normal, but its literature, in its various negotiations with patriarchal manhood and representations of the single life, imagined alternative ways of knowing and being. There are, to be sure, numerous ways to resist the damage and violence of both past and present patriarchal norms, but one such way is to analyze closely how the single life of men takes shape within and against those ideals, and, in some cases, fragment them into other possibilities that may yet be ameliorative, valorous, pleasurable, and just. Early modern literature might yet give us some ideas of what unpatriarchal manhood might yet be, what the pluralities of the single life might look like, then and now.

# Notes

INTRODUCTION

1. William Shakespeare, "Sonnet 1," in *Shakespeare's Sonnets*, ed. Stephen Booth (New Haven, CT: Yale University Press, 1977), 1, line 1, hereafter cited parenthetically by sonnet number and line number.

2. Michael Cobb, *Single: Arguments for the Uncoupled* (New York: New York University Press, 2012), 4.

3. Instead of prioritizing the subject's youth, we might also prioritize his complexion (as scholars do for the "dark lady") and refer to him as the fair man or the white man. For the ways Shakespeare's sonnets are suffused with crafting racialized whiteness, see Kim F. Hall, "'These Bastard Signs of Fair': Literary Whiteness in Shakespeare's Sonnets," in *Post-Colonial Shakespeares*, ed. Ania Loomba and Martin Orkin (New York: Routledge, 1998), 65–83, and more recently Imtiaz Habib, "'Two Loves I Have of Comfort and Despair': The Circle of Whiteness in the *Sonnets*," in *White People in Shakespeare: Essays on Race, Culture, and the Elite*, ed. Arthur Little Jr. (New York: Bloomsbury, 2023), 29–44. There is no shortage of criticism on Shakespeare's sonnets, and I will not pretend that I can cover all of it. In his book *Shakespeare and Queer Representation*, Stephen Guy-Bray provides a useful summary, noting, "this early group of sonnets has often been called the reproduction or procreation sonnets, as they are mainly, although not exclusively, exhortations to a young man to marry and have children—with noticeably more emphasis on the having children part than on the marrying part." He's right—the *exhortations* are less about marrying, but the interrogations circulate around or are inaugurated by the citing of marital status. But it should also be said the question of marriage is in these sonnets from the beginning, as Guy-Bray also observes that the word "contracted" in Sonnet 1 implies the young man is married to himself—or to at least parts of himself (his bright eyes, and the eye / I pun already intimates the single life as an insular perversion of a married one). See *Shakespeare and Queer Representation* (New York: Routledge, 2021), 128–30. In his reading of the opening sonnets of the sequence, Garret A. Sullivan argues that they are invested in processes of memory and forgetting, and argues "the procreation sonnets are revealed to be dialogic and agonistic; they record a conflict between the poet and the young man that hinges upon opposing notions of beauty, selfhood, and immortality." I do not disagree with Sullivan, though I would put more emphasis on what he consigns to a footnote,

namely that "it is obviously procreation within marriage that is valorized here, as an illegitimate child would not work to maintain the 'fair house' of the young man's dynastic identity. It is for this reason that these seventeen poems are often referred to as the "marriage sonnets." See "Voicing the Young Man: Memory, Forgetting, and Subjectivity in the Procreation Sonnets," in *The Companion to Shakespeare's Sonnets*, ed. Michael Schoenfeldt (New York: Blackwell, 2007), 333, 342n22. While I have never heard of or seen these sonnets referred to as the "marriage sonnets," that they circulate around a question of marital status is too obvious and so has largely remained uninterrogated or consigned to footnotes.

4. Thomas Cogan, *The Haven of Health* (London, 1584), 248–49.

5. As a demographic matter, E. A. Wrigley and R. S. Schofield note the percentage of never-marrying individuals rises and falls in early modern England, sometimes sharply, but for significant portions of time, the never marrying could be a quarter of the population or more, and they suggest economic reasons: "A rise in the proportion never marrying during the later sixteenth and early seventeenth centuries is not surprising in view of the very steep fall in real wages during the period, though the very high absolute level reached may come as a surprise." See *The Population History of England, 1541–1871: A Reconstruction*. (Cambridge, MA: Harvard University Press, 1981), 263. Because this book is interested in literary representations, the question of proportion of the population that is unmarried at any given point, while interesting, is not central to its arguments.

6. Mario DiGangi, *Sexual Types: Embodiment, Agency, and Dramatic Character from Shakespeare to Shirley* (Philadelphia: University of Pennsylvania Press, 2011), 3, 4.

7. See Ari Friedlander, *Rogue Sexuality in Early Modern English Literature: Desire, Status, Biopolitics* (Oxford: Oxford University Press, 2022), 3, 4.

8. DiGangi, *Sexual Types*, 5.

9. Alexandra Shepard, "From Anxious Patriarchs to Refined Gentlemen? Manhood in Britain, circa 1500–1700," *Journal of British Studies* 44, no. 2 (April 2005): 82.

10. Shepard, "From Anxious Patriarchs," 291.

11. Shepard is somewhat critical of Connell, however. See Alexandra Shepard, *The Meanings of Manhood in Early Modern England* (Oxford: Oxford University Press, 2006), 250.

12. R. W. Connell, *Masculinities*. 2nd ed. (Berkeley: University of California Press, 2005), 76.

13. R. W. Connell and James W. Messerschmidt, "Hegemonic Masculinity: Rethinking the Concept," *Gender & Society* 19, no. 6 (December 2005): 846.

14. Connell, *Masculinities*, 81.

15. See Ben Griffin, "Hegemonic Masculinity as a Historical Problem." *Gender & History*, vol. 30, no. 2 (July 2018): 382.

16. Sir John Davies, *The Complete Poems of Sir John Davies*, edited by Rev.

Alexander B. vol. 2 (London: Chatto & Windus, 1876), 69. The series of poems from which "The Bacheler" comes—"The Twelve Wonders of the World"—was printed on a series of trenchers, complete with illustration. See *The Twelve Wonders of the World*, 1600–1630, set of Roundels, painted and gilded beech, diam 5 7/8in, Victoria and Albert Museum, London. For the circulation of such trenchers in early modern England, see Mary Anne Caton, "'Fables and Fruit Trenchers Teach as Much': English Banqueting Trenchers, c. 1585–1662," *The Magazine Antiques*, 169, no. 6 (2006): 112–19.

17. On the relation between manhood, honor, and women's gossip, see Elizabeth A. Foyster, *Manhood in Early Modern England: Honour, Sex and Marriage* (New York: Longman, 1999), 55–77.

18. See Elizabeth Freeman, *Time Binds: Queer Temporalities, Queer Histories* (Durham, NC: Duke University Press, 2010), 4.

19. Shepard, *Meanings*, 1–19, 75. For manhood and the mean, see Todd W. Reeser, *Moderating Masculinity in Early Modern Culture* (Chapel Hill: University of North Carolina Press, 2006), 11–49, 121–51. See also Joshua Scodel, *Excess and the Mean in Early Modern English Literature* (Princeton: Princeton University Press, 2002).

20. For example, Ilana Krausman Ben-Amos observes, ""Adolescence—the blossoming or lustful age, as it was more frequently referred to—could begin at the age of 9 but also at 14; youth could span the years between 14, or 18, and up to 25, 28, or simply until marriage." See *Adolescence and Youth in Early Modern England* (New Haven, CT: Yale University Press, 1994), 11.

21. The power of this paradigm for women can be seen too in the trope of its negation: "neither maid, nor wife, nor widow," the claim Ester Sowernam makes in *Ester hath hang'd Haman* (1617), her response to Joseph Swetnam's *Araignment of Lewde, idle, froward, and unconstant women* (1615). Amy M. Froide observes that while this trinity of terms—maid, wife, widow—obtained for women in the literature of the period, the term "spinster" gained purchase in the legal and social texts. Unlike "maid, wife, and widow," "spinster" was more capacious, signifying a social identity that included a degree of economic independence and excluded presumptions of virginity and sexual conduct. See Amy M. Froide, *Never Married: Singlewomen in Early Modern England* (Oxford: Oxford University Press, 2005), 160.

22. Joseph Swetnam, *The Araignment of Lewde, Idle, Froward, and vnconstant women: Or the vanitie of them, choose you whether. With a Commendacion of wise, vertuous and honest Women. Pleasant for married men, profitable for young Men, and hurtfull to none* (London, 1615), 36.

23. See Margreta de Grazia, "The Scandal of Shakespeare's Sonnets," *Shakespeare Survey* 46 (1993): 35–49 and Robert Matz's response, "The Scandals of Shakespeare's Sonnets," *ELH* 77, no. 2 (Summer 2010): 477–508, as well as Kim F. Hall, "'These bastard signs of fair,'" 69–74.

24. See Lawrence Stone, *The Family, Sex and Marriage In England 1500–1800*

(New York: Harper and Row, 1977); Lloyd Bonfield, Richard M. Smith, and Keith Wrightson, eds., *The World We Have Gained: Histories of Population and Social Structure* (London: Blackwell, 1986). Notable exceptions to this trend are Judith M. Bennet and Amy Froide, eds., *Singlewomen in the European Past, 1250–1800* (Philadelphia: University of Pennsylvania Press, 1999). There has not yet been a study expressly devoted to single men in early modern England.

    25. See Mark Breitenberg, *Anxious Masculinity in Early Modern England* (Cambridge, UK: Cambridge University Press, 1996). While Breitenberg does not focus on marital status, of the six chapters of his book, at least four address single men or advocates of the single life. Looking at Robert Burton's *Anatomy of Melancholy*, Francis Bacon's "masculine" prose works, Shakespeare's *Love's Labor's Lost*, and, in part, Shakespeare's androgynous young man of the *Sonnets*, Breitenberg nowhere acknowledges the single life venerated or actually lived by many of his subjects, that their anxiousness does not arise out of the defense of a patriarchal ideal, but might in fact arise from not attaining it. The index of his study includes a category for marriage but not the single life. Studies that have largely been devoted to single men tend to overlook the significance of marital status as a category of social difference. In what remains a useful collection of essays, *Masculinity and the Metropolis of Vice, 1550–1650* (New York: Palgrave, 2010), Amanda Bailey, Roze Hentschell and the collection's contributors consider how geography, specifically the divide between urban and rural masculinities, genders men in English Renaissance literature. Very few of the masculinities accounted for in this study are those of married men, and so the single life is a structuring but elided term throughout the collection.

    26. See Bruce Smith, *Shakespeare and Masculinity* (Oxford: Oxford University Press, 2000), 54–60, 71–93, 86. Part of the problem might be one of the Shakespearean texts upon which Smith focuses. He does not touch upon the sonnets and only references *Venus and Adonis* in passing.

    27. Foyster, *Manhood in Early Modern England,* 2.

    28. While not a work of history, Julie Crawford's work often examines the roles and representations of women in relation to, but also in excess of, marital status. See, for one example, *Mediatrix: Women, Politics, and Literary Production in Early Modern England* (Oxford: Oxford University Press, 2014). See also Amy Froide, *Silent Partners: Women as Public Investors during Britain's Financial Revolution, 1690–1750* (Oxford: Oxford University Press, 2016).

    29. Judith Butler, *Undoing Gender* (New York: Routledge, 2004), 104. Ari Friedlander has made a similar argument about the centrality of marriage to understanding early modern rogue sexuality and the rather porous boundaries between the licit and illicit. As he explains, "Marriage is a crucial context for understanding rogue sexuality, because the former was the central institution through which early modern England configured sex and the social order." Friedlander makes this assertion in his argument

about the ways rogue sexuality abets the early modern construction and valorization of companionate marriage and the ways Milton draws upon sixteenth-century ideas about rogue sexuality to develop his ideas about idealized marital unions. See Friedlander, *Rogue Sexuality*, 151.

30. Michel Foucault, *The History of Sexuality: An Introduction, Vol. 1*, trans. Robert Hurley (New York: Vintage, 1990), 37. Judith Butler draws on, and critiques, Foucault across Butler's oeuvre, however.

31. Attending to the ways bodies and spaces organized public display and private feeling, Thomas King, for example, has argued that the early modern period witnesses a move from a "residual pederasty," which marked the pleasures of courtly, public subordination to a sovereign, to an intimate, private mode of heteronormative feeling, encapsulated in the domestic sphere. King is interested in how the patriarchal society of the early modern period facilitated the gendering of men in relation to heterosexual coupling and who (and what kinds of people, behaviors, and alliances) could be understood as queer as it came to be understood "as the lack or failure of private pleasures." According to King, as early modern English patriarchal culture consolidated around a heteronormative ideal associated with the privacies and intimacies of domesticity, articulations of queer life outside this narrow mode of relationality also became legible. King's work is substantive, but he is variously focused on questions of agency and representation and the terms of subjectivity across historical and political shifts. He in particular considers how courtly theatricality supplements later "articulations" of queer men, and how certain forms of acceptable, pleasurable, and useful political relations come to mark queerness as effeminacy and affectation by the eighteenth century. While I resist King's insistence of historical change developing these shifts, his insight about the ways the marriage, domesticity, coupling lend privacy and publicity to certain gender formations and sexualities is insightful and useful. See Thomas A. King, *The Gendering of Men, 1600–1750: The English Phallus*. vol. 1 (Madison: University of Wisconsin Press, 2004), 4–7. See, also, Thomas A. King, *The Gendering of Men, 1600–1750: Queer Articulations*, vol. 2 (Madison: University of Wisconsin Press, 2008).

32. Merry Wiesner-Hanks, "Forum Introduction: Reconsidering Patriarchy in Early Modern Europe and the Middle East," *Gender & History* 30, no. 2 (August 2018): 321. Wiesner-Hanks surveys a range of relevant conferences and articles on histories of gender and sexuality to document the scarcity of the term and its seeming lack of analytic import.

33. Anthony Fletcher, "Men's Dilemma: The Future of Patriarchy in England 1560–1660," *Transactions of the Royal Historical Society* 4 (1994), 61.

34. See Susan D. Amussen, *An Ordered Society: Gender and Class in Early Modern England* (New York: Columbia University Press, 1988).

35. Thomas Cooper, *Thesaura Linguæ Romanæ et Britannicæ* (London, 1584). See also, Debora Shugar, *Habits of Thought in the English Renaissance: Religion, Politics,*

*and the Dominant Culture* (Toronto: University of Toronto Press, 1997), 218–20.

36. Anthony Fletcher, *Gender, Sex, and Subordination in England 1500–1800* (New Haven, CT: Yale University Press, 1995), xv.

37. See Heidi Hartmann, "The Unhappy Marriage of Marxism and Feminism: Towards A More Progressive Union," in *Women and Revolution: A Discussion of the Unhappy Marriage of Marxism and Feminism*, ed. Lydia Sargent (Boston: South End Press, 1981), 14.

38. In her documentation of medieval and renaissance brewsters, Bennet observes how a change to the brewing industry in the late medieval and early modern period did not result in significant political or social gains for the women, who primarily participated and ran that trade. Bennett shows instead that changes in women's lives did not necessitate a change in women's status because of the flexibility patriarchal social order achieves through "its location in multiple sites; its production as an effect of essential social institutions; its flexibility and endurability; and its powerful strategic use of exclusion, segregation, and division." See Judith M. Bennett, *History Matters: Patriarchy and the Challenge of Feminism* (Philadelphia: University of Pennsylvania Press, 2006), 79.

39. The term "incel" is a portmanteau of "involuntary celibate." It identifies someone, usually a man, who believes they deserve sex but are denied it and blame women in particular for refusing them sexual service. Originally coined as "invcel" by a queer Canadian known online as Alana, the term had been co-opted online by a subculture of heterosexual men by the beginning of the 2000s.

40. While Kahn explicitly draws upon psychoanalytic theory—she says early in the book that Shakespeare and Freud "are both psychologists"—she insists in the "Acknowledgments" that Shakespeare "speaks most perceptively to our modern experience. He does so, I think, because he more than any other writer was aware that he lived in a patriarchy—an awareness we are beginning to share when we look at our own world." See Coppélia Kahn, *Man's Estate: Masculine Identity in Shakespeare* (Berkeley: University of California Press, 1981), 1, xi.

41. Janet Adelman, *Suffocating Mothers: Fantasies of Maternal Origin in Shakespeare's Plays, Hamlet to The Tempest* (New York: Routledge, 1991), 11–37.

42. Dympna Callaghan, *Shakespeare Without Women: Representing Gender and Race on the Renaissance Stage* (New York: Routledge, 2000), 9.

43. Amanda Bailey, *Flaunting: Style and the Subversive Male Body in Renaissance England* (Toronto: University of Toronto Press, 2007), 26.

44. Will Fisher, *Materializing Gender in Early Modern English Literature and Culture* (New York: Cambridge University Press, 2006), 87.

45. Jennifer Low, *Manhood and the Duel: Masculinity in Early Modern Drama and Culture* (New York: Palgrave, 2003).

46. See Ronda Arab, *Manly Mechanicals on the Early Modern Stage* (Selinsgrove, PA: Susquehanna University Press, 2011), 15–27.

47. See Simone Chess, *Male-to-Female Crossdressing in Early Modern English Literature* (New York: Routledge, 2016), 42.

48. Abdulhamit Arvas, "Early Modern Eunuchs and the Transing of Gender and Race," *Journal for Early Modern Cultural Studies* 19, no. 4 (Fall 2019): 117. On the figure of the eunuch, and its various representations in renaissance drama, see Gary Taylor, *Castration: An Abbreviated History of Western Manhood* (New York: Routledge, 2000). Karen E Fields and Barbara J. Fields developed the term "racecraft" to explain how racism, as a form of action, comes to construct race materially and epistemologically. See *Racecraft: The Soul of Inequality in American Life* (New York: Verso, 2014).

49. Holly Dugan, "Early Modern Tranimals: 57312*," *Journal for Early Modern Cultural Studies* 19, no. 4 (Fall 2019): 179, 188.

50. Colby Gordon, "A Woman's Prick: Trans Technogenesis in Sonnet 20," in *Shakespeare / Sex: Contemporary Readings in Gender and Sexuality*, ed. by Jennifer Drouin. (London: Bloomsbury, 2020), 268–89.

51. See Catherine Belsey, *Shakespeare and the Loss of Eden: The Construction of Family Values in Early Modern Culture* (New Brunswick, NJ: Rutgers University Press, 1999), 54.

52. See Stephen Guy-Bray, *Homoerotic Space: The Poetics of Loss in Renaissance Literature* (Toronto: University of Toronto Press, 2002).

53. Catherine Bates, *Masculinity, Gender and Identity in the English Renaissance Lyric*. (New York: Cambridge University Press, 2007). Bates has further demonstrated the ways early modern masculinity aligns with failure by attending to the ways the sixteenth-century metaphor of the hunt compromises and confounds patriarchal ideals of power and mastery. See *Masculinity and the Hunt: Wyatt to Spenser* (Oxford: Oxford University Press, 2016); Per Sivefors, *Representing Masculinity in Early Modern English Satire, 1590–1603: "A Kingdom for a Man."* (New York: Routledge, 2020).

54. James M. Bromley, *Intimacy and Sexuality in the Age of Shakespeare* (New York: Cambridge University Press, 2012), 179.

55. See Melissa E. Sanchez, *Erotic Subjects: The Sexuality of Politics in Early Modern English Literature* (Oxford: Oxford University Press, 2011), and, more recently, *Queer Faith: Reading Promiscuity and Race in the Secular Love Traditions* (New York: New York University Press, 2019).

56. Jennifer Panek, *Widows and Suitors in Early Modern English Comedy* (New York: Cambridge University Press, 2004), 81.

57. Christopher Marlow, *Performing Masculinity in English University Drama, 1598–1636* (New York: Routledge, 2016), 3, 6.

58. Kim F. Hall, *Things of Darkness: Economies of Race and Gender in Early Modern England* (Ithaca, NY: Cornell University Press, 1995), 141, 143.

59. Joyce Green MacDonald, *Women and Race in Early Modern Texts* (New York: Cambridge University Press, 2002), 76.

60. See Dennis Austin Britton, *Becoming Christian: Race, Reformation, and Early Modern English Romance*. (New York: Fordham University Press, 2014), 156.

61. Howard P. Chudacoff, *The Age of the Bachelor: Creating an American Subculture* (Princeton: Princeton University Press, 1999), esp. 3–20, 185–216.

62. John Gilbert McCurdy, *Citizen Bachelors: Manhood and the Creation of the United States* (Ithaca, NY: Cornell University Press, 2009), esp. 1–83.

63. Katherine V. Snyder, *Bachelors, Manhood, and the Novel, 1850–1925* (New York: Cambridge University Press, 1999), esp. 1–63. In an irony surely not lost to students of early modern literature and history, Miles Coverdale, the bachelor-narrator of *Blithesdale Romance*, is the namesake of the sixteenth-century Puritan reformer and translator Miles Coverdale, who did in fact marry.

64. See Eve Kosofsky Sedgwick, *Epistemology of the Closet* (Berkeley: University of California Press, 1990), 44–48.

65. *The Batchelars Banquet: Or A Banquet for Batchelars* (London, 1603).

66. Robert Herrick, *Works of Robert Herrick*, vol. 1, ed. Alfred Pollard (London: Lawrence and Bullen, 1891), 14.

67. Turning to etymology and the meanings of "lesbian" in early modern England, for instance, Paula Blank suggest how language provides surprising and rather queer points of contact and depart with the past. See "The Proverbial 'Lesbian': Queering Etymology in Contemporary Critical Practice," *Modern Philology* 109, no. 1 (August 2011): 108–34.

68. Snyder, *Bachelors*, 20; McCurdy, *Citizen Bachelors*, 3.

69. See "bachelor, n." def. 4a. *OED Online* (New York: Oxford University Press, 2015). The citation is from *The Merchant's Tale*. Snyder, *Bachelors*, 20.

70. See "bachelor, n." def. 1a, 2, 3. *OED Online*. (Oxford: Oxford University Press, 2015).

71. McCurdy, *Citizen Bachelors*, 15.

72. Cited in Eric Josef Carlson, *Marriage and the English Reformation* (Oxford: Blackwell, 1994), 114–15.

73. John Florio, *A World of Wordes, Or a Most copious, and exact Dictionarie in Italian and English* (London, 1598), 35.

74. Florio, *A World*, 112, 281, 282.

75. See Didier Lett, *L'enfant de miracles: Enfance et société au moyen âge, XIIe–XIIIe siècle* (Paris, 1997), cited in Ruth Mazzo Karras, *From Boys to Men: Formations of Masculinity in Late Medieval Europe* (Philadelphia: University of Pennsylvania Press, 2003), 15.

76. The one exception I have found is Francis Lenton, *Characterismi: or, Lentons Leisures. Expressed in Essayes and Characters* (London, 1631), G2r-G3r. To be sure, plenty of characters across character books—including the gallant, the young man, or the prodigal, for example—are unthinkable as types outside of a single life. See, for

example, Nicolas Breton, *The Goode and The Badde, or Descriptions of the Worthies and Vnworthies of this Age* (London, 1616), for characterizations of these types.

77. Sir Thomas Overbury, *A Wife now the widow of Sir Thomas Ouerburie Being a most exquisite and singular poeme, of the choyse of a wife. Whereunto are added many witty characters, and conceyted newes; written by himselfe, and other learned gentlemen his friendes* (London, 1614), A4r.

78. Adam Zucker, *The Places of Wit in Early Modern English Comedy* (New York: Cambridge University Press, 2011), 14.

79. Foucault, *The History of Sexuality*, vol. 1, 40.

80. Price, Lawrence. "The Batchelors Feast," (London, 1636). British Library C.20.f.7.12. EBBA 30015, Patricia Fumerton, dir., English Broadside Ballad Archive (website), accessed September 12, 2013. Those range of pleasures need not be procreative or even relational. Valerie Traub cites this poem to different ends. As Traub notes, in one instance, the ballad is to be played to the tune "With a hie dildo, dill." The nonsense of the tune quickly accretes sexual meanings, as both the husband's pleasing of his wife and the bachelor's pleasures are conditioned "with a hie dildo, dill." See *Thinking Sex with the Early Moderns* (Philadelphia: University of Pennsylvania Press, 2016), 216–22.

81. Frances E. Dolan, *Marriage and Violence: The Early Modern Legacy* (Philadelphia: University of Pennsylvania Press, 2008), 4, 2, 3.

82. Dolan, *Marriage and Violence*, 4.

83. Dolan, *Marriage and Violence*, 2.

84. On the influence of humanism on British Protestant ideas of marriage in the sixteenth and seventeenth centuries, see Margo Todd, *Christian Humanism and the Puritan Social Order* (New York: Cambridge University Press, 1987).

85. Throughout *The Rule of Reason*, Wilson returns to questions of marriage—the appropriate age of marriage, the kind of person men and women should marry—to explain logical forms like induction. Explaining the logic of comparison and contrast, and the distinction of things into their particular kinds, Wilson uses the marriage question:

> Nowe ye shall haue a question set forth, and both the partes of a proposition referred to the places of inuention, that thereby ye maie knowe wherein the places do agree, & wherein they do not. For where as the places agree (that is to saie, al thynges are referred to $y^e$ one, that are referred to the other) there the proposition is good, and the latter parte of the proposition, is truly spoken of the first. But where the places do not agree (that is to saie, some thynges are referred to the one worde, that are not referred to the other) ther the thinges themselues can not agree. I will vse this question for an example. whether it be lawfull for a priest to marie a wyfe or no.

See Thomas Wilson, *The Rule of Reason* (London, 1551), fol. 114r. In the first Book of the *Arte of Rhetorique*, Wilson defines rhetoric and the proceeds to explain the kinds of questions orators must answer. Reconstituting Quintillian, he sets out examples of infinite (universal) and definite (particular) topoi. Here he states:

> Every question or demand in things, is of two sorts. Either it is an infinite question and without end or else it is definite and comprehended within some end. Those questions are called infinite which generally are propounded, without the comprehension of time, place, and person, or any such like; that is to say, when no certain thing is named, but only words are generally spoken. As thus, whether it be best to marry or to live single. Which is better, a courtier's life or a scholar's life. Those questions are called definite which set forth a matter with the appointment and naming of place, time, and person. As thus. Whether now it be best here in England for a priest to marry or to live single. Whether it were meet for the king's majesty that now is to marry with a stranger or to marry with one of his own subjects.

See Thomas Wilson, *The Arte of Rhetorique* (London 1553), fol. 1r–1v. I return to Wilson in chapter 1.

86. See Katharina M. Wilson and Elizabeth M. Makowski. *Wykked Wyves and the Woes of Marriage: Misogamous Literature from Juvenal to Chaucer* (Albany: SUNY Press, 1990).

87. See Edmund Tilney, *The Flower of Friendship: A Renaissance Dialogue Contesting Marriage*, ed. Valerie Wayne (Ithaca, NY: Cornell University Press, 1992), 1–93, 13–29 for the misagomous antecedents, 38.

88. Tilney, *Flower of Friendship*, 105.

89. As Wayne observes, Gaulter, whose name refers to Walter Map, stands in for the medieval misogynist and misogamist tradition. Map's work is cited in *The Wife of Bath's Prologue* as one of those texts in Jankyn's books of wicked wives.

90. The setting of the dialogue is the house of Lady Julia, who has a daughter Lady Isabella (a textual analogue for Queen Elizabeth). While it can be presumed Lady Julia is or had been married, her husband is not present. The narrator also notes "many other Ladyes, and their lincked Mates." Tilney, *Flower of Friendship*, 102.

91. Sedgwick, *Epistemology of the Closet*, 1–47, esp. 40.

92. For some of the contours of it, see Jonathan Goldberg and Madhavi Menon, "Queering History," *PMLA* 120, no. 5 (October 2005): 1608–1617 and Carla Freccero, *Queer / Early / Modern* (Durham, NC: Duke University Press, 2006) as well as Valerie Traub's engagement with their arguments in *Thinking Sex*, 57–81.

93. Foucault, *The History of Sexuality*, vol. 1, 40.

94. Foucault, *The History of Sexuality*, vol. 1, 40.

95. For the enduring appeal of Don Juan in Spanish culture, see Sarah Wright, *Tales of Seduction: the figure of Don Juan in Spanish Culture* (London: I. B. Tauris, 2007). Americans cinema saw a straightening out of this character in the 2013 release *Don Jon* (Relativity Media).

96. Traub, *Thinking Sex*, 85.

97. See Jonathan Ned Katz, *The Invention of Heterosexuality* (Chicago: University of Chicago Press, 1995) and Rebecca Ann Bach, *Shakespeare and Renaissance Literature Before Heterosexuality* (New York: Palgrave, 2007).

98. Sedgwick, *Epistemology*, 183.

99. Sedgwick, *Epistemology*, 188.

100. See Sedgwick, *Epistemology*, 182–213.

101. Lee Edelman, *No Future: Queer Theory and the Death Drive* (Durham, NC: Duke University Press, 2004), 1–32, esp. 21.

102. Jonathan Goldberg, *Sodometries: Renaissance Texts, Modern Sexualities* (Stanford, CA: Stanford University Press, 1992), 9–11.

103. Flachmann, Michael, ed. "The First English Epistolary Novel: *The Image of Idleness* (1555). Text, Introduction, and Notes." *Studies in Philology* 87, no. 1 (1990): 1–74.

104. See R. W. Maslen, "*The Image of Idleness* in the Reign of Elizabeth I," *English Language Notes* 41, no. 3 (2004): 11–23.

105. Sedgwick, *Epistemology*, 194. This is not to say that the nineteenth-century novel did not mobilize particular and culturally specific figures of the bachelor, only that the bachelor is not emergent in accordance with the particular uses Sedgwick identifies: the endemic homosexual panic of bourgeois manhood.

106. John Aubrey, *Brief Lives*, ed. Andrew Clark, 2 vols (Oxford: Clarendon, 1898), 1:96.

107. Jeffrey Masten, *Textual Intercourse: Collaboration, Authorship, and Sexualities in Renaissance Drama* (New York: Cambridge University Press, 1997), 61.

108. Phillip Stubbes, *The Anatomie of Abuses* (London: 1583), 144–45.

109. See Alan Bray, *The Friend* (Chicago: University of Chicago Press, 2003), but also see Mario DiGangi's readings of the licit forms of homoeroticism in *Homoerotics of Early Modern Drama* (New York: Cambridge University Press, 1997).

110. Charles Mills Gayley, *Francis Beaumont: Dramatist, A Portrait, with Some Account of His Circle, Elizabethan and Jacobean, and of His Association with John Fletcher* (London: Duckworth & Co., 1914), 95–96.

111. Gayley, *Francis Beaumont*, 96.

112. Masten, *Textual Intercourse*, 62.

113. See Laura Gowing, *Common Bodies: Women, Touch, and Power in Seventeenth-Century England* (New Haven, CT: Yale University Press, 2013).

CHAPTER 1

1. On the normativity of sexuality, see Jacinthe Flore, "Mismeasures of Asexual Desires," in *Asexualities: Feminist and Queer Perspectives*, ed. Karli June Cerankowski and Megan Milks (New York: Routledge, 2014), 17–34.

2. John Donne, "Elegy 8, To His Mistress Going to Bed," *John Donne's Poetry*, edited by Donald R. Dickson (New York: W. W. Norton, 2007), 35.

3. See Gary Taylor, "Some Manuscripts of Shakespeare's Sonnets," *Bulletin of the John Rylands University Library of Manchester* 68 (1985–86): 211–12.

4. This is not to say that the readings that these variants make explicit are not available in the sonnets. Heather Dubrow has argued that when gendered pronouns, or the lack of them, are taken into account, the narrative most scholars see in the sonnets—in which 1–126 are written to the single man and 127–54 are written to the Dark Lady—is far from definitive. See "'Incertainties now Crown Themselves Assur'd': The Politics of Plotting Shakespeare's Sonnets," *Shakespeare Quarterly* 47, no. 3 (October 1996): 291–305.

5. Valerie Traub has productively examined how the category of sodomy displaces women's desires in the sonnets. Reading the sonnets in terms of the legibility of desire, Traub maintains, "these poems confront (1) the desirability and significance of male desire for men; (2) the difficulties posed for male heteroeroticism in a society that systematically undervalues women; and (3) the necessity of insuring that women's desires accord with those of men, thus harnessing women to patriarchal reproduction." See Valerie Traub, "Sex Without Issue: Sodomy, Reproduction, and Signification in Shakespeare's Sonnets," *Shakespeare's Sonnets: Critical Essays*, ed. James Schiffer. (New York: Garland, 1999), 435.

6. Citations from William Shakespeare, "Venus and Adonis," *The Oxford Shakespeare: The Complete Works*, 2nd ed., ed. Stanley Wells and Gary Taylor (Oxford: Clarendon Press, 2005), lines 4, 34, and 36; hereafter cited parenthetically by line number. See Rebecca Yearling, "Homoerotic Desire and Renaissance Lyric Verse," *SEL* 53, no. 1 (Winter 2013): 58.

7. Richard Rambuss, "What It Feels Like For a Boy: Shakespeare's *Venus and Adonis*," in *A Companion to Shakespeare's Works: The Poems, Problem Comedies, Late Plays*, eds. Richard Dutton and Jean Howard, vol. 4 (Oxford: Blackwell, 2003), 244.

8. Madhavi Menon, "Spurning Teleology in Venus and Adonis," *GLQ* 11, no. 4 (2005): 501, 509.

9. Or as Menon asserts, "Neither Venus nor Adonis nor the horses nor the friends have sex in the poem, but everyone desires something." Menon, "Spurning," 510.

10. On compulsory sexuality, see Elizabeth F. Emens, "Compulsory Sexuality," *Stanford Law Review*, 66, no. 2 (February 2014): 303–86; Kristina Gupta, "Compulsory Sexuality: Evaluating an Emerging Concept," *Signs*, 41, no. 1 (Autumn 2015): 131–54. For an asexual, feminist critique of compulsory (hetero)sexuality, see CJ DeLuzio Chasin, "Reconsidering Asexuality and Its Radical Potential," *Feminist Studies*, 39, no. 2 (2013): 405–26. For the erotics of asexuality, see Ela Przybylo, *Asexual Erotics: Intimate Readings of Compulsory Sexuality* (Columbus: Ohio State University Press, 2019).

11. Janet Adelman, *Suffocating Mothers: Fantasies of Maternal Origin in Shakespeare's Plays, "Hamlet" to "The Tempest"* (New York: Routledge, 1992), 78.

12. Kathryn Schwarz, "Chastity, Militant and Married: Cavendish's Romance, Milton's Masque," *PMLA* 118, no. 2 (March 2003): 270.

13. William Shakespeare, *All's Well that Ends Well*, ed. Susan Snyder (Oxford: Clarendon, 1993), act 4, scene 2, line 2. Hereafter cited parenthetically act number, scene number, line number. I have maintained Snyder's choice of names of "Helen" instead of "Helena" and "Paroles" instead of "Parolles."

14. *The booke of the common praier and administration of the Sacraments, and other rites and ceremonies of the Church: after the vse of the Churche of Englande* (London, 1549), sig. Cc1r-Cc1v.

15. In *Intimacy and Sexuality*, James Bromley argues against reading narrative ends as capturing the processes, intimacies, and sets of relations renaissance literature otherwise makes available, observing, "Only when marriage attempts to assert itself over the entire relational field does it elevate longevity as a signifier of pleasure and value and, in turn, advance itself, somewhat fantastically and fictitiously, as the defining long-term relation." Bromley makes this assertion in relation to Marlowe's *Hero and Leander*, which remains narratively open, but he also brings this interpretive strategy to bear on *All's Well*, a play arguably obsessed with a narrative closure coextensive with monogamous marriage. Bromley offers a compelling reading of the play that focuses on Bertram's socialization through his disavowal of the anus. See *Intimacy and Sexuality* (New York: Cambridge University Press, 2012), 30, 49–65.

16. Lee Edelman, *No Future: Queer Theory and the Death Drive* (Durham, NC: Duke University Press, 2004), 3.

17. Edelman, *No Future*, 17.

18. See Theodora A. Jankowski, *Pure Resistance: Queer Virginity in Early Modern English Drama* (Philadelphia: University of Pennsylvania Press, 2000) and Laurie Shannon, *Sovereign Amity: Figures of Friendship in Shakespearean Contexts* (Chicago: University of Chicago Press, 2002), respectively.

19. Benjamin Kahan, *Celibacies: American Modernism and Sexual Life* (Durham, NC: Duke University Press, 2013), 2.

20. Heather Love, *Feeling Backward: Loss and the Politics of Queer History* (Cambridge, MA: Harvard University Press, 2007), 40.

21. Ela Przybylo and Danielle Cooper, "Asexual Resonance: Tracing a Queerly Asexual Archive," *GLQ* 20, no. 3 (June 2014): 304.

22. Patricia Simons, *The Sex of Men in Premodern Europe* (New York: Cambridge University Press, 2011), 2.

23. Simons, *The Sex of Men*, 2.

24. See Gary Taylor, *Castration: An Abbreviated History of Western Manhood* (New York: Routledge, 2000), 94–100.

25. Simons, *The Sex of Men*, 291.

26. Joshua T. Katz, "Testimonia Ritus Italici: Male Genitalia, Solemn Declarations, and a New Latin Sound Law," *Harvard Studies in Classical Philology* 98 (1998): 183–217. See also Simons, *The Sex of Men*, 105–7.

27. Helkiah Crooke, *Mikrokosmographia: A Description of the Body of Man* (London, 1615), 204. At the end of the seventeenth century, this interpretation still had currency. In his anatomical text, Thomas Gibson similarly notes, "The Stones in Latin are called *Testes*, either because they testifie one to be a man, or because amongst the Romans none was admitted to bear witness but he that had them." *The Anatomy of Humane Bodies Epitomized* (London, 1682), 109.

28. Ambroise Paré, *The Workes of that famous Chirugion Ambrose Parey*, trans. Th. Johnson (London, 1634), 120.

29. For impotency and early modern canon law, see B. J. Sokol and Mary Sokol, *Shakespeare, Law, and Marriage* (New York: Cambridge University Press, 2003), 141–42. I discuss in more detail the relationship of testicles and the gendering of men in chapter 5.

30. Jonathan Gil Harris, "All Swell That End Swell: Dropsy, Phantom Pregnancy, and the Sound of Deconception in *All's Well That Ends Well*," *Renaissance Drama* 35 (2006): 170.

31. Caroline Bicks, "Planned Parenthood: Minding the Quick Woman in *All's Well*," *Modern Philology* 103, no. 3 (February 2006): 330–31.

32. Jennifer Evans, "'They Are Called Imperfect Men': Male Infertility and Sexual Health in Early Modern England," *Social History of Medicine* 29, no. 2 (May 2016): 326–30.

33. Harris argues that Paroles is "phantom pregnancy made flesh," and oddly, supports this assertion by quoting this line about bounding balls, which is one of Shakespeare's most bawdy, and to my mind obvious, testicular puns. See Harris, "All Swell," 181–82.

34. George Whetstone, *An Heptameron of Ciuill Discourses* (London, 1582), sig. C2v.

35. Lars Engle, "Shakespearean Normativity in *All's Well That Ends Well*," in *The Shakespearean International Yearbook*, eds. Graham Bradshaw, Tom Bishop, and Mark Turner 4 (Burlington, VT: Ashgate, 2004), 264–78.

36. *The booke of the common praier*, Cc1r-Cc1v.

37. Jankowski, *Pure Resistance*, 96.

38. Jankowski argues that the Protestant preference for the term "chastity" instead of "virginity" enacts a linguistic effacement of the autonomy of virgin women. As the word comes to describe both unmarried virgins and married women in Protestant discourse (Jankowski does not include unmarried men), the discursive shift "works to destroy the autonomy of the virgin within Protestant discourse and to insure that she be

considered, not as a special entity, but as part of a natural female continuum that proceeds inevitably to marriage as the culmination of social and religious existence." See Jankowski, 96–103, qtd. 103. Oddly, Jankowski focuses on Erasmus's "Defense of his Declamation" and not the *Encomium*, which the "Defense" was defending. This oversight leads her to misapply Erasmus's arguments about the single life of a chaste youth to virginal women and to overlook the subject of the chaste single man (whose it at the center of the *Encomium*) in her reading of the marriage debate.

39. Erasmus, Desiderius. *A ryght frutefull Epystle deuysed by the moste excellent clerke Erasmus in laude and prayse of matrymony*, trans Rychard Tauernour (n.p.: 1536), sig. A4r.

40. For the sonnets' relationship to the *Encomium*, see Katharine M. Wilson, *Shakespeare's Sugared Sonnets* (London: Allen and Unwin, 1974), 46–67. Several scholars have pointed out the connection between the sonnets' young man and Bertram. See M. C. Bradbrook, "Virtue is the True Nobility: A Study of the Structure of *All's Well That Ends Well*," *Review of English Studies* 1, no. 4 (October 1950): 290; G. Wilson Knight, *The Sovereign Flower* (London: Metheun, 1958), 95, 109; Roger Warren, "Why Does It End Well? Helena, Bertram, and the Sonnets," *Shakespeare Survey*, ed. Kenneth Muir, 22 (1970): 79–92, esp. 81–84, where Warren likens Helen to *The Sonnet*'s speaker, Bertram to the young man.

41. Erasmus, *A right frutefull Epystle*, A2r.

42. Thomas Becon, trans. "The preface unto the boke," *The golden boke of christen matrimonye* (1542), sig. A3v.

43. Becon, "The preface," sig. A2r-A2v, sig. A4r.

44. Erasmus, *A right frutefull Epystle*, B1v; Francesco Barbaro, *Direction for Love and Marriage. In Two Books* (London, 1677), 3. This phrase appears in numerous early modern discourses on marriage.

45. Erasmus, *A right frutefull Epystle*, B1v.

46. Desiderius Erasmus, "Defense of His Declamation in Praise of Marriage (1519)," trans. David Sider, in *Daughters, Wives, and Widows: Writings by Men About Women and Marriage in England, 1500–1640*, ed. Joan Larsen Klein (Urbana: University of Illinois Press, 1992), 89–96.

47. See Katharina M. Wilson and Elizabeth M. Makowski, *Wykked Wyves and the Woes of Marriage* (Albany: State University of New York Press, 1990), 3.

48. Thomas Wilson, *The Arte of Rhetorique* (London, 1553), sig. A1r. Wilson uses the question of whether or not priests should marry as an example of a proposition in *The Rule of Reason* as well. See *The Rule of Reason* (London, 1552), fol. 114–23.

49. Wilson, *The Arte of Rhetorique*, sig. A1r.

50. Wilson, *The Arte of Rhetorique*, sig. A1v.

51. For this history, see Margo Todd, *Christian Humanism and the Puritan Social Order* (New York: Cambridge University Press, 1987), 98–100, 206–38.

52. Jonathan Dollimore, *Sexual Dissidence: Augustine to Wilde, Freud to Foucault* (Oxford: Clarendon Press, 1991), 116.

53. Lee Edelman, "Ever After: History, Negativity, and the Social," in *After Sex? On Writing Since Queer Theory*, ed. Janet Halley and Andrew Parker (Durham, NC: Duke University Press, 2011), 111.

54. See Valerie Traub, *The Renaissance of Lesbianism in Early Modern England* (New York: Cambridge University Press, 2002), 218, and also 229–325.

55. Jonathan Ned Katz argues that heterosexuality emerges in the nineteenth and twentieth centuries, but he also narrowly casts heterosexuality in relation to its etymology: "The intimidating notion that heterosexuality refers to everything differently sexed and gendered and eroticized is, it turns out, one of the conceptual dodges that keeps heterosexuality from becoming the focus of sustained, critical analysis. You can't analyze everything." But the problem with heteronormativity is its ubiquity; that's what makes heterosexuality dangerously and perniciously normative. See *The Invention of Heterosexuality* (New York: Dutton, 1995), 14. Rebecca Ann Bach likewise claims the renaissance was "before heterosexuality" by insisting the period was organized by a homosocial (rather than heterosexual) order and by defining it through a series of narrow modes of socialization that Sedgwick troubles. It should be noted that homosociality often abets heteroerotic desire and heterosexuality, especially within patriarchal social orders. Bach's study focuses primarily on tragic drama, and does not entirely grapple with how comic drama negotiates homosocial and heteroerotic relations. See Rebecca Ann Bach, *Shakespeare and Renaissance Literature Before Heterosexuality* (New York: Palgrave, 2007).

56. See Eve Kosofky Sedgwick, *Tendencies* (Durham, NC: Duke University Press, 1993), 10

57. See, for instance, James A. Schultz, *Courtly Love, The Love of Courtliness, and the History of Sexuality* (Chicago: University of Chicago Press, 2006). Schultz's book substantively denaturalizes heterosexuality in the medieval period to distinguish it from courtly love, but it does so by narrowly defining heterosexuality as a coherent sexuality in a manner Sedgwick here troubles.

58. Julie Crawford has argued, for instance, "Marriage in the period, and in Shakespeare's comedies, is as much about the suturing and reconfiguring of economies, households, and relationships as it is about a putatively heterosexual and dyadic culmination." See Julie Crawford, "All's Well That Ends Well, Or, Is Marriage Always Already Heterosexual?" in *Shakesqueer: A Queer Companion to the Complete Works of Shakespeare*, ed. Madhavi Menon (Durham, NC: Duke University Press, 2011), 39.

59. In an essay in a blog post for the *Los Angeles Review of Books*, Greta LaFleur traces such congruities between and vacuities of patriarchy and heterosexuality by reading a *Time Magazine* cover image of Chasten and Pete Buttigieg to question the extent to which the homonormativity the image exudes might be something else, something closer to the ethos of heterosexuality, a "heterosexuality without straight people"

that is also, "significantly, a heterosexuality without women." LaFleur then discusses her "effort to register the fact that heterosexuality has become portable." See "Heterosexuality Without Women," *BLARB* (website) May 20, 2019.

60. Erasmus, *A right frutefull Epystle*, D5v-D6r.

61. Knight, *The Sovereign Flower*, 103–12. R. B. Parker expands Knight's observations to argue *All's Well's* ending reveals that both ideals revise each other, resulting in an ending favoring a pragmatic union over an allegorical concept of either. See "War and Sex in 'All's Well That Ends Well,'" *Shakespeare Survey*, ed. Stanley Wells, 37 (1984), 99–114.

62. G. P., "The praise of Chastity," *The Phoenix Nest, 1593* ed. Hyder Edward Rollins (Cambridge, MA: Harvard University Press, 1931), 13, lines 6, 22.

63. Rebecca Ann Bach, "Tennis Balls: 'Henry V' and Testicular Masculinity, or, According to the 'OED,' Shakespeare Doesn't Have Any Balls," *Renaissance Drama*, 30 (1999/2001): 3–23.

64. Susan Snyder, "Naming Names in *All's Well That Ends Well*," *Shakespeare Quarterly* 43 (1992): 273.

65. See William Shakespeare, *All's Well That Ends Well*, ed. G. K. Hunter (London: Metheun, 1959), 10 n. 123–29. Peggy Muñoz Simonds expands upon Hunter's citations, finding further parallels and larger resonances throughout the play. See "Sacred and Sexual Motifs in *All's Well That Ends Well*," *Renaissance Quarterly*, 42 (1989): 33–59. Snyder adds credence to this reading, expanding upon the textual parallels and seeing thematic connections between the Mars/Venus binary operative in both texts. See Snyder, ed. *All's Well That Ends Well*, 6–8.

66. See, for example, Becon, *The golden boke of christen matrimonye*, sig. A2v, which states, "Lette other prayse the kynde of lyfe, wherby mankynd deayeth and in process of tyme shoulde be utterlye destroyed, yet wyll I commende that manner of lyfe, whiche begetteth and bringeth forth to us excelent kinges, noble Princes, Pryncelyke Dukes, puyssaunt Lordes."

67. Erasmus, *A right frutefull Epystle*, A5r.

68. Erasmus, *A right frutefull Epystle*, D8r.

69. Erasmus, *A right frutefull Epystle*, C8r.

70. William Shakespeare, "Venus and Adonis," *The Norton Shakespeare*, third edition, ed. Stephen Greenblatt (New York: W. W. Norton, 2002), 13, line 168.

71. William Shakespeare, *Sonnets*, ed. Stephen Booth (New Haven, CT: Yale University Press, 1977), Sonnet 6, lines 7–10.

72. Paroles's argument echoes the sonnets in many places. For instance, Sonnet 3 figures the young man's chastity as "the tomb / Of his self-love to stop posterity."

73. See Nicolas Ray, "'Twas mine, 'twas Helen's': Rings of desire in *All's Well, That Ends Well*" in *All's Well, That Ends Well: New Critical Essays*, ed. Gary Waller (New York: Routledge, 2007), 188.

74. Will Stockton, *Playing Dirty: Sexuality and Waste in Early Modern Comedy* (Minneapolis: University of Minnesota Press, 2011), 52.

75. Jonathan Goldberg, *Sodometries: Renaissance Texts, Modern Sexualities* (Stanford, CA: Stanford University Press, 1992), 8.

76. Kathryn Schwarz, "'My Intents are Fix'd,': Constant Will in 'All's Well That Ends Well,'" *Shakespeare Quarterly* 58, no. 2 (Summer 2007): 200.

77. Julia Reinhard Lupton, *Thinking with Shakespeare: Essays on Politics and Life* (Chicago: University of Chicago Press, 2011), 112, 113.

78. See Snyder, ed. *All's Well That Ends Well*, 80 n. 34, who suggests that while the play does not specify the location of the fistula, the location of the heart seems likely given the source material and the King's own language.

79. Crooke, *Mikrokosmographia*, 207.

80. Cathy McClive, "Masculinity on Trial: Penises, Hermaphrodites and the Uncertain Male Body in Early Modern France," *History Workshop Journal*, 68, no. 1 (Autumn 2009): 45–68.

81. Jennifer Evans, *Aphrodisiacs, Fertility and Medicine in Early Modern England* (Suffolk, UK: Boydell Press, 2014), 154–55.

82. Kathryn M. Ringrose, *The Perfect Servant: The Social Construction of Gender in Byzantium* (Chicago: University of Chicago Press, 2004), 51.

83. William Gouge. *Of Domesticall Duties: Eight Treatise* (London, 1622), 181–82.

84. Robert Crofts, *The Lover: or Nuptiall Love* (London, 1638), sig. A7r.

85. The verse reads: "For there are some chaste, which were so borne of *their* mothers bellie, and there be some chaste, which be made chaste by men: & there be some chaste, which haue made them selues chaste for the kingdome of heauen. He that is able to receiue *this*, let him receiue it." "The Holy Gospel of Iesus Christ, according to Matthewe," *The Geneva Bible: A Facsimile of the 1560 Edition* (Peabody: Hendrickson, 2007), fol. 11r. The printed marginalia of the passage notes that the editors have translated "gelded" as "chaste."

86. Michel Foucault, *The History of Sexuality: An Introduction, Vol. 1.* trans. Robert Hurley. (New York: Vintage, 1990), 44.

87. David Scott Kastan, "All's Well That Ends Well and the Limits of Comedy," *ELH* 52 (1985): 579; William Shakespeare, *Much Ado About Nothing*, ed. Claire McEachern (London: Arden, 2006), act 2, scene 3, lines, 226–27, 233.

88. Erasmus, *A right frutefull Epystle*, A4r.

89. Erasmus, *A right frutefull Epystle*, C2v-C2r.

90. David McCandless, "Helena's Bed-Trick: Gender and Performance in *All's Well That Ends Well*," *Shakespeare Quarterly* 45, no. 4 (Winter 1994): 449; Adelman, *Suffocating Mothers*, 83.

91. See, for example, Bicks, "Planned Parenthood," 299, n. 2.

92. See Ray, "Twas Mine," 189; Stockton, *Playing Dirty*, 55–56, and Bromley, *Intimacy and Sexuality*, 49–64.

93. On gems as testicular, see Simons, *Sex of Men*, 169–87. In its roundness, Bertram's ring is also likened to the drum of war, which Bertram understands as a sign of martial chastity. Indeed, the loss of Bertram's ring is anticipated by Paroles's loss of the military drum, a clear symbol of his castration. His "drum so lost" (3.6.47), Paroles is proven a counterfeit soldier and later called "a snipped-taffeta fellow" (4.5.1–2).

94. See Patricia Parker, *Shakespeare from the Margins: Language, Culture, Context* (Chicago: University of Chicago Press, 1996), 185–93, esp. 187.

95. See, for instance, Adelman, *Suffocating Mothers*, 82–85.

Chapter 2

1. William Shakespeare, *Much Ado About Nothing*, Ed. Claire McEachern (London: Arden, 2006), act 1, scene 1, line 230. Hereafter cited parenthetically by act, scene, and line number.

2. Philip D. Collington, "A 'Pennyworth' of Marital Advice: Bachelors and Ballad Culture in *Much Ado About Nothing*," in *Shakespeare's Comedies of Love: Essays in Honour of Alexander Leggatt*, ed. Karen Bamford and Ric Knowles (Toronto: University of Toronto Press, 2008), 30.

3. Natascha Würzbach, *The Rise of the English Street Ballad, 1550–1650*, trans. Gayna Walls (New York: Cambridge University Press, 1990), 46.

4. Jeffrey Masten, *Queer Philologies: Sex, Language, and Affect in Shakespeare's Time* (Philadelphia: University of Pennsylvania Press, 2016), 79.

5. Masten, *Queer Philologies*, 79.

6. Derek Attridge, *Peculiar Language: Literature as Difference from the Renaissance to James Joyce* (New York: Routledge, 2004), 107–11, esp. 109.

7. Quoted in Paula Blank, "The Proverbial 'Lesbian': Queering Etymology in Contemporary Critical Practice. *Modern Philology*, 109, no. 1 (August 2011): 114.

8. H. Joachim Neuhaus, "Structural Semantics, Dictionary Definitions, and Lexical Glosses," in *Shakespeare: Text, Language, Criticism: Essays in Honour of Marvin Spevack*, ed. Bernhard Fabian and Kurt Tetzeli von Rosador (Hildesheim: Olms-Weidmann, 1987), 238.

9. Neuhaus, "Structural Semantics," 238.

10. Neuhaus, "Structural Semantics," 242.

11. Neuhaus, "Structural Semantics," 244.

12. Richard Huloet, *Huloets Dictionarie newelye corrected, amended* (London, 1572), C6r.

13. For the metrics of age and marriage as the primary markers of manhood in the early modern period, see Alexandra Shepard, *The Meanings of Manhood in Early Modern England* (New York: Oxford University Press, 2006), 1–19.

14. Randle Cotgrave, "Bachelier," *A Dictionarie of the French and English Tongues* (London, 1612), H3r.

15. John Cowell, *The Interpreter: or Book Containing the Signification of Words* (London, 1607), H1v. All original abbreviations silently expanded. Cowell's definition is not cited in *OED* for the definition of "bachelor." Instead we find Cowell's definition appearing, verbatim, in Thomas Blount's law dictionary, Νομο-λεξιχον (1691), cited by *OED* when it defines a bachelor as "A junior or inferior member, or 'yeoman,' of a trade-guild, or City Company" (def. 2). Cowell's definition later appears adapted in John Wilkes, *Encylopaedia Londinensis; or Universal Dictionary of Arts, Sciences, and Literature*, xxiv vols, London, 1810. Wilkes says the bachelor of the livery companies "are those not yet admitted to the livery. These companies generally consist of a master, two wardens, the livery and the bachelors, who are yet but in expectation of dignity in the company, and have their function only in attendance on the master and wardens. They are also called *yeomen*." Wilkes, vol. 2, 600.

16. Cowell, *The Interpreter*, H1v.

17. Arab not only observes sixteenth-century English theater had its roots in guild productions, but also argues that laborers, in particular journeymen, most likely supplemented their income by acting in troupes. Following the work of David Kathman, among others, Arab further emphasizes that theater owners and actors alike—including Burbage and Henslowe—came from and were members of the London's livery companies. See *Manly Mechanicals on the Early Modern Stage* (Selinsgrove, PA: Susquehanna University Press, 2011), 27–39; David Kathman, "Grocers, Goldsmiths, and Drapers: Freemen and Apprentices in the Elizabethan Theater," *Shakespeare Quarterly* 55, no. 1 (Spring 2004): 1–49. In the course of tracing the apprenticeship of several players, Kathman documents how John Wilson, who probably played Balthasar in *Much Ado*, earned his freedom of the Grocers.

18. Keith Wrightson, "Estates, degrees, and sorts: changing perceptions of Tudor and Stuart England," in *Language, History and Class*, ed. Penelope J. Corfield (Oxford: Basil Blackwell, 1991), 33.

19. George Puttenham, *The Arte of English Poesie* (London, 1589), 168–69.

20. Cited in Eric Josef Carlson, *Marriage and the English Reformation* (Oxford: Blackwell, 1994), 114–15.

21. Thomas Dekker and John Webster, "Westward Ho," in *The Dramatic Works of Thomas Dekker*, ed. Fredson Bowers, vol. 2 (Cambridge University Press, 1955), 318–403. Act 1, scene 1, lines 40–41. Hereafter cited parenthetically. All in-text citations are from this edition.

22. Bachelor's buttons are "various flowers of round or button-like form," *OED*, "bachelor, n." def. C2. Courting, single men commonly wore such flowers as boutonnieres.

23. John Taylor, *An Armado, or Nauye of 103 Ships & Other Vessels* (London, 1627), B5v.

24. Natalie Zemon Davis examines the institutional aspects of youthful festivity as well as the regulatory function it served in early modern France; see "The Reasons of Misrule: Youth Groups and Charivaris in Sixteenth-Century France," *Past & Present* 50, no. 1 (February 1971): 41–75.

25. Writing just on the heels of Davis, and citing her work in the first sentence of his article, Steven R. Smith first asserted that London apprentices were conceived as adolescents in seventeenth-century England; see "The London Apprentices as Seventeenth-Century Adolescents," *Past & Present* 61, no. 1 (November 1973): 149–61. Ilana Krausman Ben-Amos also focuses on apprentices, though her study broaches the question of age and adolescence more broadly; see *Adolescence and Youth in Early Modern England* (New Haven, CT: Yale University Press, 1994), 86–132. Largely overlooking journeymen, Paul Griffiths similarly characterizes apprentices as youths in his study of youth culture and the problems of socialization in early modern England; see *Youth and Authority: Formative Experience in England 1560–1640* (New York: Oxford University Press, 1996), 27–30, 161–213.

26. Davis notes, for instance, that "organizations of unmarried men in peasant communities . . . were called *varlets* and *varlets à marier* or *compagnons* and *compagnons à marier*; and their organizations were known as *bachelleries* . . . ; Kingdoms of Youth; and in wide areas— . . . Abbeys of Youth (Abbayes de la Jeunesse)." Davis, "Reasons," 50.

27. For Davis's work on journeymen, see Natalie Zemon Davis, "A Trade Union in Sixteenth-Century France," *The Economic History Review* 19, no. 1 (April 1966): 48–69. In her history of sixteenth-century French youth groups, Davis notes the printers' journeymen organized as one such youth group. Davis, "Reasons," 59–60.

28. Town records indicate that English journeymen did marry. Alexandra Shepard notes, for example, that Norwich records prohibited the hiring of journeymen because of an already extant population of journeymen, their wives, and children. See *The Meanings of Manhood* (New York: Oxford University Press, 2003), 209. In her study of early modern Italian journeymen, Sandra Cavallo notes the difference between continental and English laws regarding marriage and journeywork. See "Bachelorhood and Masculinity in Renaissance and Early Modern Italy," *European History Quarterly* 38, no. 3 (2008): 382.

29. For a précis of this development, see John Gilbert McCurdy, *Citizen Bachelors: Manhood and the Creation of the United States* (Ithaca, NY: Cornell University Press, 2009), 25–26.

30. R. H. Tawney and Eileen Power, eds., *Tudor Economic Documents: Being Select Documents Illustrating the Economic and Social History of Tudor England* vol. 1 (New York: Longmans, 1951), 339.

31. Tawney and Power, *Tudor Economic Documents*, 339.

32. Sir Thomas Smith, *De Republica Anglorum*, ed. Mary Dewar (London: Cambridge University Press, 1982), 140, 141.

33. Smith, *De Rpublica Anglorum*, 142.

34. Alexandra Shepard points out, "such young men had far less economic agency than married women since they were more restricted by their dependent status from trading in their own names," and cites an account from Wiltshire in 1611 where one "John Pile was presented, 'for that the liveth at libertie and worketh by the daye, being a singell man being out of covenant [service] one yeare and a quarter." See Shepard, *Meanings*, 207.

35. See Urvashi Chakravarty, *Fictions of Consent: Slavery, Servitude, and Free Service in Early Modern England* (Philadelphia: University of Pennsylvania Press, 2022), 14–44.

36. This division was true for the twelve great companies as well as many of the minor companies, but it was not true to all of them. The Stationers' Company is one notable exception. See Sheila Lambert, "Journeymen and Master Printers in the early Seventeenth Century," *Journal of the Printing Historical Society* 21 (1992): 13–27.

37. See Steve Rappaport, *Worlds within Worlds: Structures of Life in Sixteenth-Century London* (New York: Cambridge University Press, 1989), 219. He thus concludes, "For most men, therefore, the yeomanry *was* the company."

38. For the Merchant Taylors, see Matthew Davies and Ann Saunders, *The History of the Merchant Taylors' Company* (Leeds: Maney, 2004), 41–43. Laetitia Lyell indicates that the Mercers termed their yeomanry the bachelors; see *Acts of Court of the Mercers' Company, 1453–1527* (London, 1936), x–xi. For the Clothworkers use of this term, see A. H. Johnson, *The History of The Worshipful Company of the Drapers of London*, vol. 2 (Oxford: Oxford University Press, 1914), 32; Tracey Hill also notes that the yeomanries of the livery companies were called the bachelors; see *Pageantry and Power: A Cultural History of the Early Modern Lord Mayor's Show, 1585–1639* (Manchester, UK: Manchester University Press, 2010), 100n7.

39. Rappaport estimates journeymen composed, on average, about forty percent of a company's membership from the mid-sixteenth century to the early seventeenth (the remaining sixty percent being composed of householders and liverymen). See Rappaport, *Worlds*, 243, Table 7.2. In 1618, for instance, journeymen of the Clothworkers' Company had significant sway of their yeomanry, and their proportion there only continued to grow throughout the seventeenth century. See Thomas Girtin, *The Golden Ram: A Narrative History of the Clothworkers' Company, 1528–1958* (London: Worshipful Company of Clothworkers, 1958), 90–91.

40. Rappaport, *Worlds*, 224, 327; R. A. Leeson, *Travelling Brothers: The Six Centuries' Road from Craft Fellowship to Unionism* (London: Allen & Unwin, 1979), 64–67.

41. Hill, *Pageantry and Power*, 4, 8.

42. Rappaport, *Worlds*, 226.

43. Sir Walter Sherburne Prideaux, *Memorials of the Goldsmiths' Company Being Gleanings From Their Records Between the Years 1335 and 1815*, vol. 1, 1896, vol. 2, 1897 (London: Eyre and Spottiswoode, Her Majesty's Printers), 1: 80.

44. Prideaux, *Memorials of the Goldsmiths' Company Being Gleanings From Their Records Between the Years 1335 and 1815*, vol. 1, 115.

45. Rappaport, *Worlds*, 226.

46. Ian Archer, *The Pursuit of Stability: Social Relations in Elizabethan London* (New York: Cambridge University Press, 1991), 116–17; Johnson, *The History*, 2: 220–21.

47. Lawrence Manley makes this claim in no uncertain terms, concluding the conferment of bachelorhood in the Lord Mayor's show "marked an important distinction between the men of substance who might eventually attain the livery of their companies and the lesser artisans and shopkeepers who never would." See *Literature and Culture in Early Modern London* (New York: Cambridge University Press, 1995). 262–63. Rappaport emphasizes the conditional and temporal parameters of the conferment, stating, "in great companies a separate livery of the yeomanry, called 'the bachelors,' was created for one year when a member of the company was elected mayor of London." Rappaport, *Worlds*, 226. Rappaport's observation amends an early assumption by W. C. Hazlitt. Reading the Haberdashers' records, Hazlitt concludes the bachelors were members of the livery and not the yeomanry. He comes to this conclusion by inference, using the promotion during the Lord Mayor's show as his measure, admitting, "The text does not state so much; but it is inferable that the persons thus selected [bachelors] became permanent members of the Livery." See *The Livery Companies of London: Their Origin, Character, Development, and Social and Political Importance* (New York: Blom, 1892, 1969), 288. Ian Archer revises Hazlitt, Rappaport, and Manley's conclusions regarding the elite nature of the conferment, noting that there were varying degrees of bachelorhood for this procession and its culminating feast at Guildhall. See Archer, *The Pursuit*, 116–17. Though an early account, records of the Mercers' Company from the late fifteenth and early sixteenth century indicate that "lesser artisans" could be impressed as bachelors. In 1491, one Aleyn Payn, who had just finished his apprenticeship but had not yet been sworn of the Company, "by the Supervisours of the bachelers barge was Charged to do apparell hym selfe accordyng as of olde accustumed with other bachelers, also moo for to attend to bryng the Mayre to Westminster the daye of his presentatcion &c." Aleyn was reprimanded for refusing, and his master, Richard Haddon, was forced to pay a fine and to coerce Payn to fall in line.

48. Hill, *Pageantry and Power*, 62–63.

49. Various editors, including Claire McEachern, gloss "fine" as "finis" or "conclusion." See Shakespeare, *Much Ado*, 165n229 (1.1.229). Of course, reading "fine" as "conclusion" does not preclude resonances with the bachelor's role in the livery company ceremonies.

50. "Diary: 1553 (Jul-Dec) and 1562 (Jul-Dec)," in *The Diary of Henry Machyn: Citizen and Merchant-Taylor of Londonm 1550–1563*, ed. J. G. Nichols (London, 1848), 34–50, 287–98. British History Online (website). Bachelors are also mentioned in 1562 (Jan-June) and 1555 (July-Dec) collations.

51. These engravings can be found in Edward Calver, *Passion and Discretion in Youth and Age* (London, 1641).

52. John H Astington, "The Ages of Man and the Lord Mayor's Show," in *Other Voices, Other Views: Expanding the Canon in English Renaissance Studies*, ed. Helen Ostovich, Mary V. Silcox, and Graham Roebuck, 74–90 (Newark: University of Delaware Press, 1999), 81.

53. Chakravarty, *Fictions of Consent*, 19.

54. Henry Benjamin Wheatley, *The Story of London* (London: J. M. Dent, 1904), 321.

55. Wheatley, *The Story*, 321.

56. Mary Bly, "Playing the Tourist in Early Modern London: Selling the Liberties Onstage," *PMLA* 122, no. 1 (January 2007): 61. Bly's subject is the London liberty of Whitefriars; *Memorials of the Goldsmiths' Company Being Gleanings From Their Records Between the Years 1335 and 1815*, vol. 1, 88.

57. Amanda Bailey and Roze Hentschell, eds. "Introduction: Gendered Geographies of Vice," in *Masculinity and the Metropolis of Vice*. Early Modern Cultural Studies (New York: Palgrave Macmillan, 2010), 2. Such locales identified in this volume include alehouses, the universities of Cambridge and Oxford, playhouses, and St. Paul's Cathedral.

58. Prideaux, *Memorials of the Goldsmiths' Company Being Gleanings From Their Records Between the Years 1335 and 1815*, vol. 2, 82, 83.

59. We should be wary of generalizing about similar residences. However, such a residence suggests that journeymen were not merely wandering workers, or that their only places of residence were the master's home or the networks of inns and alehouses that Peter Clark has so usefully documented. See Peter Clark, *The English Alehouse: A Social History 1200–1830* (London: Longman, 1983), 136.

60. Henry Newcome, *The Diary of the Rev. Henry Newcome, from September 30, 1661, to September 29, 1663*, ed. Thomas Heywood, vol. 18 (Manchester, UK: Chetham Society, 1849), 148.

61. Griffiths, *Youth*, 171.

62. Newcome, *The Diary*, 148n1.

63. Raphael Holinshed, et al., *The First and Second Volumes of Chronicles* (London, 1586), 167.

64. Holinshed, et al, *Chronicles*, 167.

65. Holinshed, et al, *Chronicles*, 167.

66. See Mario DiGangi, *Sexual Types: Embodiment, Agency, and Dramatic Character from Shakespeare to Shirley* (Philadelphia: University of Pennsylvania Press, 2011), 31–39.

67. Eve Kosofsky Sedgwick, *Between Men: English Literature and Male Homosocial Desire* (New York: Columbia University Press, 1985), 1.

68. Sedgwick, *Between Men*, 45–46.

69. See Archer, *Pursuit*, 115.

70. See Kathman, "Grocers," 2, 7–12.

71. William Shakespeare, *A Midsummer Night's Dream*, ed. Harold F. Brooks (London: Arden, 2006), act 1, scene 1, line 1; hereafter cited parenthetically.

72. See "house, n." def. 1 and 2, *OED*. In this case, "house" might mean "home," but it could also refer to a rented room, perhaps even in a public house or alehouse.

73. Thomas Dekker, "The Shoemaker's Holiday," in *The Roaring Girl and Other City Comedies*, ed. James Knowles (New York: Oxford University Press, 2001), 1–65, scene 1, line 130. The dramatis personae identifies Ralph as a "journeyman," but early in the play it is suggested this newly married man is about to become a householder "new entered" (1.155). Thus, his conscription to war with France seems especially egregious because, as will be poignantly realized later in the play when Ralph comes home disabled, he quite literally has his legs cut out from under him right when he is about to venture into business on his own.

74. Ronda Arab observes that while Dekker valorizes a corporeal masculinity in his depiction of laborers in *The Shoemaker's Holiday*, the nostalgic, utopian vision of artisanal community the play casts considerably flattens the hierarchical realities of the workshop, where the patriarchal privilege of masters could be (and were) abused, and where journeymen were more likely to be disenfranchised than to attain householder status. See Arab, *Manly Mechancials*, 56–57.

75. Thomas Dekker and Thomas Middleton, "The Honest Whore, Part 1," in *The Dramatic Works of Thomas Dekker*, ed. Fredson Bowers, vol. 2 (Cambridge, UK: Cambridge University Press, 1955), 1–130, act 1, scene 2, line 91. This specific plot to incite Candido to fury encompasses act 4, scene 3.

76. Alexander Niccholes, *A Discourse of Marriage and Wiving* (London, 1615), A3r.

77. See "bachelry," n. *OED. OED* lists only two sources for this use of the word: Percy's *Reliques* (1499), and Niccholes's treatise. The prefatory poem makes the audience of single men explicit, but that audience is also invoked later in the treatise when Niccholes directly quotes from Francis Bacon's (ca. 1587–1657) "Of Marriage and Single Life," in (1612) in his discourse. Niccholes writes, "One saith, wives are yong mens Mistresses, companions for middle age, and old mens Nurses, so that a man may have a quarrell to marry when hee will." *Discourse*, C3r, cf. Francis Bacon, "Of Marriage and Single Life," in *The Essayes or Counsels Civill and Morall*, ed. Michael Kiernan (New York: Oxford University Press, 1985), 24–26. Read in relation to Bacon's essay, Niccholes's titular "Of Marriage and Wiving" appears an attempt to challenge Bacon's argument that the single life should remain a possibility for early modern men.

78. Niccholes, *A Discourse*, A3r.

79. Niccholes, *A Discourse*, A3r.

80. Mark Breitenberg sees early modern patriarchal anxiety and masculinity as

"redundant," and contends that such anxiety was both a "necessary and inevitable" as well as "productive" condition of patriarchy. See *Anxious Masculinity in Early Modern England* (New York: Cambridge University Press, 1996), 2–3.

81. Jennifer Panek, "Community, Credit, and the Prodigal Husband on the Early Modern Stage," *ELH* 80, no. 1 (Spring 2013): 62.

82. Niccholes, *A Discourse*, A3v-A4r.

83. Niccholes's worry over servants and their indiscretion is not novel invention but a generic commonplace in marriage treatises. William Gouge, for example, argues that servants "corrupt their masters children with their filthy and corrupt communication" and "allure them to stage-plaies, to dice-houses, and other like places, which aver the very bane of youth: and draw them to spend in riot such allowance as their parents allow them." See *Of Domesticall Duties* (London, 1622), 631.

84. On how the apprenticeship system made women especially vulnerable to the advances of both masters and servants, see Laura Gowing, *Common Bodies: Women, Touch, and Power in Seventeenth-Century England* (New Haven, CT: Yale University Press, 2003), 59–65. Borachio's imagining of bachelors includes an age-range that would incorporate both apprentices and journeymen. This grouping complements the counternarrative in Niccholes in which apprenticeship trains boys to be bachelors and not husbands, journeymen and not householders. So long as the desire to live a bachelor coincides with a journeyman's actual living as one, these groups might be imagined as a community. An anonymous late seventeenth century pamphlet similarly enjoins apprenticeship and journeymen in its imagining bachelorhood even as it maintains the social distinction between these two groups. *The Maids Complaint against the Bachelors: or an Easter-Offering for Young Men and Apprentices* (London, 1675) makes distinctions between age and rank even as it weds them together under a designation of marital status. This pamphlet garnered an anonymous response, *The Batchellors Answer to the Maids Complaint, or the Young Men's Vindication* (London, 1675). Both were printed by "J. Coniers, at the *Black-Raven* in *Duck-Lane*."

85. The audience for ballads is notoriously elusive. By arguing that certain ballads appealed to specific groups, I do not mean to insist that a ballad was exclusively intended for them. As Tessa Watt has shown, ballads could be found in alehouses as well as noble manors. For Watt's discussion of the wide circulation of ballads, see *Cheap Print and Popular Piety, 1550–1640* (New York: Cambridge University Press, 1991), 1–10.

86. John Selden, *Table-Talk: Being the Discourses of John Selden, Esq.* (London, 1696), 93.

87. Lawrence Price, "The Batchelors Feast," (London, 1636). British Library C.20.f.7.12. EBBA 30015, Patricia Fumerton, dir., English Broadside Ballad Archive (website). Accessed September 12, 2013.

88. Price, "The Batchelors Feast."

89. Merry E. Wiesner, "'Wandervogels' Women: Journeymen's Concepts of Masculinity in Early Modern Germany," *Journal of Social History*, 24, no. 4 (Summer 1991): 776.

90. "The Lamentation of a new married man," (London, ca. 1630). Pepys Library. Pepys Ballads 1.380–81. EBBA 20176, Patricia Fumerton, dir., English Broadside Ballad Archive (website). Accessed September 12, 2013.

91. See "featly, adv. and adj," def. 1a. *OED* Online (Website).

92. Amanda Bailey, *Flaunting: Style and the Subversive Male Body in Renaissance England* (Toronto: University of Toronto Press, 2007), 45.

93. "The Lamentation of a new married man."

94. "The Lamentation of a new married man." Jennifer Panek cites this ballad in *Widows and Suitors in Early Modern English Comedy* (New York: Cambridge University Press, 2007), 49. For Panek, it exemplifies how marriage made a man honest. The ballad's emphasis on credit, however, aligns with her work on prodigal-husband plays, as well.

95. "The Lamenation of a new married man."

96. On how early modern manhood depended on the control of the sexuality of women as well as the power of that sexuality to destabilize manhood, see Elizabeth A. Foyster, *Manhood in Early Modern England: Honour, Sex and Marriage* (London: Longman, 1999), 55.

97. Gail Kern Paster, *The Body Embarrassed: Drama and the Discipline of Shame in Early Modern England* (Ithaca, NY: Cornell University Press, 1993), 37.

98. Heinrich Bullinger, *The golden boke of christen matrimonye*, trans. Theodore Basille (1543), B4v. "Theodore Basille" was a pseudonym used by the Protestant minister Thomas Becon.

99. Becon is not alone in this complaint, nor he is the only conduct writer to address bachelors. For example, see William Whately, *A Care-Cloth: Or a Treatise of the Cumbers and Troubles of Marriage: Intended to Advise Them That May, To shun them; that may not, well and patiently to beare them* (London, 1624). Throughout this text, Whately warns men about the financial responsibilities of marriage, and that they must enter it with great care even as he decries those who abuse their resources in single living.

100. Benedick's complaint about the lack of aged bachelors might also be a moment of characterization that tells us something about Don Pedro's age; just after Benedick utters these words, Don Pedro walks on stage.

101. The translation, in fact, makes substantial changes to the original. As Faith Gildenhuys indicates, the English version expectedly excises Catholic liturgical and hagiographical references, but the text also revises and updates references to fashion, a revision that continued even as the text was reissued. Faith Gildenhuys, ed., *The Bachelor's Banquet* (Ottawa: Dovehouse, 1993), 22.

102. *The Batchelars Banquet: Or A Banquet for Batchelars* (London, 1603).

103. See, for example, Henry Buttes, *Dyets Dry Dinner* (London, 1599), I3v, where "Goate-flesh" is best "for yong and hot stomackes; not old, nor flegmaticke."

104. Jennifer Low suggests Benedick's challenge "reframes masculine values, redefining the role of both the soldier and the knight," and evidences "a reversion to the ideal of Christian faith, a version of chivalry that privileges interiority and the private realm." *Manhood and the Duel: Masculinity in Early Modern Drama and Culture* (New York: Palgrave, 2003), 28.

105. Jean Howard, *Stage and Social Struggle in Early Modern England* (New York: Routledge, 1994), 66.

## CHAPTER 3

1. Sir Francis Bacon, *The Essaies of Sir Francis Bacon Knight, the Kings Solliciters Generall* (London: 1612), 22–23. Cf. Francis Bacon, "Of Marriage and Single Life," *The Essayes or Counsels Civill and Morall*, ed. Michael. Kiernan (Cambridge, MA: Harvard University Press, 1985), 224–25.

2. See Alexandra Shepard, *Meanings of Manhood in Early Modern England* (New York: Oxford University Press, 2003), 70–90.

3. See "economy, n." def. I.1.a, II.8.b, 11. *OED online*, Oxford University Press, 2021.

4. See "entreprenour, n." and "entrepreneur, n." def. 1, *OED* online, Oxford University Press, 2021.

5. William Rowley and Thomas Middleton, "Wit at Severall Weapons," ed. Michael Dobson, *Thomas Middleton: The Collected Works*, ed. Gary Taylor and John Lavagnino (Oxford: Clarendon, 2007), 980–1026, act 1, scene 1, lines 2–4. All subsequent citations refer to this edition and will be cited parenthetically by act, scene, and line number.

6. See Bradley D. Ryner, *Performing Economic Thought: English Drama and Mercantile Writing, 1600–1642* (Edinburgh: Edinburgh University Press, 2014), 1–7, 77–106.

7. As behavioral economics has rethought the premises of neoclassical economics, the figure of the rational market actor has been supplanted, though this figure remains central to many lay capitalist visions of economic action. For a critique of homo economicus, see Richard H. Thaler, "From Homo Economicus to Homo Sapiens," *Journal of Economic Perspectives* 14, no. 1 (February 2000): 133–41. The self-help genre has a proliferation of books on personal "optimization." For another example, see Emma Isaacs, *The New Hustle: Don't Work Harder, Just Work Better* (New York: McGraw-Hill, 2022).

8. Ingram and Keynes, respectively, qtd in Joseph Persky, "Retrospectives: The Ethology of Homo Economicus," *Journal of Economic Perspectives* 9, no. 2 (Spring 1995), 222.

9. For a description of these qualities, as well as analysis of them from several schools of economic thoughts, see Dante A. Urbina and Alberto Ruiz-Villaverde, "A Critical Review of *Homo Economicus* from Five Approaches," *American Journal of Economics and Sociology* 78, no. 1 (January 2019): 65–67.

10. For the history of this migration and the series of James I's proclamations, see F. J. Fisher, *London and the English Economy*, ed. P. J. Corfield and N. B. Harte (London: The Hambledon Press, 1990), 180–83.

11. See G. E. Mingay, *The Gentry: The Rise and Fall of a Ruling Class* (New York: Longman, 1976)

12. Felicity Heal and Clive Holmes, *The Gentry in England and Wales, 1500–1700* (Stanford, CA: Stanford University Press, 1994), 22.

13. Keith Wrightson, *English Society, 1580–1680* (London: Hutchinson, 1982), 27.

14. See, for example, Jean E. Feerick, *Strangers in Blood: Relocating Race in the Renaissance.* Toronto: University of Toronto Press, 2010.

15. See Hall, *Things of Darkness: Economies of Race and Gender* (Ithaca, NY: Cornell University Press, 1995), 124, and its survey of Elizabethan and Jacobean trade, and the inscription of African enslavement on John Hawkins's coat of arms, 16–24.

16. Sir Thomas Smith, *De Republica Anglorum*, ed. Mary Dewar (New York: Cambridge University Press, 1982), 72.

17. See C. G. A. Clay, *Economic Expansion and Social Change: England 1500–1700, vol. 1. People, Land and Towns* (New York: Cambridge University Press, 1984), 151–54.

18. Smith, *De Republica*, 72.

19. See Lawrence Stone, *The Crisis of the Aristocracy, 1558–1641* (Oxford: Clarendon, 1965), 65–97. Emphasizing the implicit connection between wealth and title, Stone terms this Stuart practice "The Inflation of Honors." See also Heal and Holmes, *The Gentry*, 28–29.

20. Ben Jonson, *Every Man Out of His Humour*, ed. Helen Ostovich (Manchester, UK: Manchester University Press, 2001), act 1, scene 2, lines 7–9. In her note to this line, Ostovich quotes Smith, but does not specifically attribute it to him, though she does treat Sogliardo's lines as emblematic of wealth usurping birth as a measure of gentility. For this quote, Ostovich cites G. W. Prothero, ed., *Select Statutes and other Constitutional Documents Illustrative of the Reigns of Elizabeth and James I* (Oxford, 1963), 179.

21. Beginning with Aristotle, labor was understood as anathema to gentility. Henry Peacham summarizes a widely held contemporary belief when he says, "whosoeuer labour for their liuelihood and gaine, haue no share at all in Nobilitie or Gentry." See *The Compleat Gentleman* (London, 1622), 12–13. Patricia Akhimie has theorized that the marking of, and marks upon, the body were crucial to early modern

English racial formations as well, and further notes how hard hands were a recurring trope in racializing discourses. See *Shakespeare and the Cultivation of Difference: Race and Conduct in the Early Modern World* (New York: Routledge, 2018), 117–50.

22. John Selden, *Table-Talk: Being the Discourses of John Selden, Esq; or His Sense of various Matters of Weight and high Consequence; Relating especially to Religion and State* (London, 1696), 64.

23. See Michelle M. Dowd, *The Dynamics of Inheritance on the Shakespearean Stage* (New York: Cambridge University Press, 2015), 31–75.

24. See Heal and Holmes, *The Gentry*, 311–15.

25. For London as center of conspicuous consumption see, F. J. Fisher, "The Development of London as a Centre of Conspicuous Consumption in the Sixteenth and Seventeenth Centuries," *Transactions of the Royal Historical Society* 30 (December 1948): 37–50. For the changing architectural standards of manorial estates, see Nicholas Cooper, "Rank, Manners and Displays: The Gentlemanly House, 1500–1750," *Transactions of the Royal Historical Society* 12 (2002): 291–310.

26. See Ian Warren, "London's Cultural Impact on the English Gentry: The Case of Worcestershire, c. 1580–1680," *Midland History* 33, no. 2 (December 2008): 170–71. Drawing upon work by historians of county community, Warren notes how contemporary anecdotes about the relationship between proximity to London and the length of a family's dynasty have been proven more or less true. With the exception of Kent, the closer lands were to London, the higher their turnover, and so less the guarantee of dynastic succession. Worcestershire, Warren's focus, falls in the middle of the spectrum in terms of turnover, an effect to be expected given its relative distance from London.

27. Humfrey Braham, *The Institution of a gentleman* (London 1555, rep. 1568), A2v-A3r.

28. Braham, *The Institution*, C1r-C4v.

29. Braham, *The Institution*, C1r-C1v.

30. Braham, *The Institution*, C4r.

31. Braham, *The Institution*, C4r-C4v.

32. John Ferne, *The Blazon of Gentrie: Deuivded into two part. The First named The Glorie of Generositie. The Second Lacyes Nobilitie. Comprehending discourses of Armes of Gentry* (London, 1586), A6r.

33. Ferne, *The Blazon*, sig. A2v.

34. Dowd, *The Dynamics of Inheritance*, 31.

35. Ferne, *The Blazon*, B5r.

36. C. G. A. Clay, *Economic Expansion*, 147. See also Heal and Holmes, *The Gentry*, 62.

37. Francis Beaumont and John Fletcher, *Wit Without Money. A Comedie.* London, 1639, B2r. While the title page lists Beaumont as a coauthor, scholars generally attribute Fletcher as the sole author. Cited by signature parenthetically hereafter.

38. While this chapter does not have the space to focus on the implications of Lance's line here, there is a sense in which he acknowledges that his social status and personhood are tied to property interests. Given this alignment, Lance's formulation of "race of Gentry" evinces Cheryl I. Harris's claim that whiteness functions as property in a legal and historical sense, an effect of property interests, including the acquisition of enslaved persons as property. As Harris argues, "the legal legacy of slavery and of the seizure of land from Native American peoples is not merely a regime of property law that is (mis)informed by racist and ethnocentric themes. Rather, the law has established and protected an actual property interest in whiteness itself, which shares the critical characteristics of property and accords with many and varied theoretical descriptions of property." Harris focuses on American law, but that law's antecedents in British and European Enlightenment ideas on personhood and property are evident. Lance's concerns about losing social rank speaks to how intimately early modern ideas of race, lineage, property, and social proximity cathect, each to the other. See "Whiteness as Property." *Harvard Law Review* 106, no. 8 (June 1993), 1724.

39. Jennifer Panek, *Widows and Suitors in Early Modern English Comedy* (New York: Cambridge University Press, 2004), 95.

40. For the ways widows function allegorically as wealth in these kind of marriage plots, see Elizabeth Hanson, "'There's Meat and Money Too': Rich Widows and Allegories of Wealth in Jacobean City Comedy," *ELH* 72, no. 1 (Spring 2005): 209–38.

41. For the intersections between early modern England's patrilineal economy and drama, see Dowd, *The Dynamics of Inheritance*, 31–75 and 209–55.

42. John Dryden, "An Essay of Dramatic Poesy," in *The Major Works*, ed. Keith Walker (New York: Oxford University Press, 1987), 112.

43. Carl Dennis, "Wit and Wisdom in *Much Ado About Nothing*," *SEL, 1500–1900* 13, no. 2 (Spring 1973): 224. The oldest meaning of wit—"the seat of consciousness or thought, the mind"—was current well into the seventeenth century, as was the more specific denotation of "the faculty of thinking and reasoning in general," what we might call rationality. See "wit, n." def. 1, 2a. *OED* online, December 2013, Oxford University Press.

44. William G. Crane, *Wit and Rhetoric in the Renaissance: The Formal Basis of Elizabethan Prose Style* (New York: Columbia University Press, 1937), 9–12.

45. Martin Butler, *Theatre and Crisis, 1632–1640* (New York: Cambridge University Press, 1984), 159. Though Butler notes that the play was probably written by Middleton, Butler cites *Wit at Severall Weapons* as one play in which Fletcher's genteel concerns are displayed, though parodically, by the Clown, Pompey Doodle.

46. Leo Salingar, *Dramatic Form in Shakespeare and the Jacobeans* (New York: Cambridge University Press, 1986), 143, 148. For Salingar, *Every Man in his Humour* exemplifies the sociability of wit.

47. Ari Friedlander, *Rogue Sexuality in Early Modern English Literature: Desire,*

*Status, Biopolitics* (New York: Oxford University Press, 2022), 70. Friedlander argues that Dauphine and Epicene resemble the stock characters of the cross-biting narratives of cony-catching literature. In these narratives, a man and a woman work together to dupe a man of his money. Typically, one of the pair ingratiates him or herself with the mark while the other fleeces the mark in some way.

48. See Adam Zucker, *The Places Of Wit in Early Modern English Comedy* (New York: Cambridge University Press, 2011), 4–8, 54–72.

49. John Stuart Mill, *The Collected Works*, vol. 4, ed. J. M. Robson (Toronto: University of Toronto Press, 1967), 323

50. Mill, *Collected Works*, 325.

51. Mill, *Collected Works*, 326.

52. Mill, *Collected Works*, 330.

53. See Stone, *The Crisis*, 71–77, esp. 77; Mingay, *The Gentry*, 4–5.

54. See Ben Jonson, *Epicene, or the Silent Woman*, ed. Richard Dutton (Manchester, UK: Manchester University Press, 2003), 169n114.

55. Dowd, *The Dynamics of Inheritance*, 239.

56. Zucker, *The Places of Wit*, 4–5.

57. Dryden, "An Essay," 115.

58. As I explore in chapter 5, laws governing early modern marriage hinged upon a man's virility. Dauphine knows what he is doing when he insists Morose confess his impotency.

59. Marjorie Swann, "Refashioning Society in Ben Jonson's Epicoene," *SEL, 1500–1900* 38, no. 2 (Spring 1998): 300.

60. Michael Shapiro, "Audience vs. Dramatists in Jonson's *Epicoene* and Other Plays of the Children's Troupes," *English Literary Renaissance* 3, no. 3 (1973): 401.

61. Ben Jonson, "The Alchemist," *The Complete Plays of Ben Jonson*, ed. G. A. Wilkes, vol. 3 (Oxford: Clarendon, 1982), 223–356, act 3, scene 4, lines 41–42, hereafter cited parenthetically.

62. See Ryner, *Performing*, 77–105.

63. Clay, 152, points out that while such investments in joint stock companies were available, they were also risky. Hence the continual appeal of land as investment. Sir Perfidious also has land, but he his relationship to it is primarily one of investment and not income. He seeks to put money into it and leverage it for further investment; he does not mean to solely live by it.

64. Anupam Basu, "'Like Very Honest and Substantial Citizens': Cony-Catching as Social Performance," *ELR* 44, no. 1 (Winter: 2014): 48.

65. Karen Helfand Bix, "'Masters of Their Occupation': Labor and Fellowship in the Cony-Catching Pamphlets," in *Rogues and Early Modern English Culture*, eds. Craig Dionne and Steve Mentz (Ann Arbor: University of Michigan Press, 2004), 177.

66. Craig Muldrew, *The Economy of Obligation: The Culture of Credit and Social Relations in Early Modern England* (New York: Macmillan, 1998), 98.

## CHAPTER 4

1. Gail Kern Paster, *Humoring the Body: Emotions and the Shakespearean Stage* (Chicago: University of Chicago Press, 2004), 80

2. Henry Peacham, *Minerva Britanna, Or a Garden of Heroical Deuices, furnished, and adorned with Emblemes and Impresas of sundry natures* (London, 1612), 126.

3. See Bridget Gellert Lyons, *Voices of Melancholy: Studies in literary treatments of melancholy in Renaissance England* (New York: Routledge, 1971), 26–44.

4. Kate Manne, *Entitled: How Male Privilege Hurts Women* (New York: Crown, 2021), 4.

5. Manne looks at incels in both of her books. See *Down Girl: The Logic of Misogyny* (New York: Oxford University Press, 2018), and Manne, *Entitled*, 14–32.

6. See Manne, *Entitled*, 15–16.

7. As I detail, Kate Manne has argued that misogyny should be understood less as a feeling of men and instead as a social effect, produced by patriarchy, that women experience. Misogyny, Manne argues, functions to police patriarchal order by targeting women who do not conform, or are perceived as not conforming, to patriarchal ideals of womanhood. See Manne, *Down Girl*, 49–54.

8. I obviously take the term from Raymond Williams, who defines the term thusly: "We are talking about characteristic elements of impulse, restraint, and tone; specifically affective elements of consciousness and relationships: not feeling against thought, but thought as felt and feeling as thought: practical consciousness of a present kind, in a living and interrelating continuity. We are then defining these elements as a 'structure': as a set, with specific internal relations, at once interlocking and in tension." See *Marxism and Literature* (New York: Oxford University Press, 1977), 132.

9. Manne, *Entitled*, 18.

10. The history of melancholy in early modern England, as many scholars have observed, is one of two entangled, contradictory, and competing discourses on atrabilious disease, both of which run through a medicalized and philosophical tradition. One conception arose from a school of Galenic humoralism that diagnosed melancholy as the product of an overabundance of black bile; the other, its genial form, drawn from Theophrastus and Aristotle, and taken up through Ficino and Petrarch, conceived of it as dispositional, a condition of men of genius across art, politics, and philosophy. For the distinction between these two traditions, see Lawrence Babb, *The Elizabethan Malady: A Study of Melancholia in English Literature from 1580 to 1642* (East Lansing: Michigan State College Press, 1951), 66–67, as well as Drew Daniel, *The Melancholy Assemblage: Affect and Epistemology in the English Renaissance.* New York: Fordham University Press, 2013), 17–25. Scholars of early modern melancholy

have done much to reassess the interplay between these two traditions as well as their gendered histories, moving from psychoanalytic analysis to the cultural histories of early modern diagnostic corpus. Two notable studies are Juliana Schiesari, *The Gendering of Melancholia: Feminism, Psychoanalysis, and the Symbolics of Loss in Renaissance Literature* (Ithaca, NY: Cornell University Press, 1992) and Paster, *Humoring*.

11. Sianne Ngai, *Ugly Feelings* (Cambridge, MA: Harvard University Press, 2005), 3. Ngai here quotes Rei Terada, *Feeling in Theory: Emotion after the "Death of the Subject"* (Cambridge, MA: Harvard University Press, 2001), 57. Terada uses this phrase, almost offhand, to describe Paul de Man's analysis of Rousseau's emotion of fear in his *Essay*, especially as it differs from Derrida's analysis of the same emotion.

12. See Manne, *Entitled*, 17.

13. Thomas Cogan, *The Haven of Health: Chiefely gathered for the comfort of Students, and consequently for all those that haue a care of their health, amplified upon fiue words Hippocrates, Epid 6. Labor, Cibus, Potio, Somnus, Venus* (London, 1584), 245.

14. See Bradley J. Irish, *Emotion in the Tudor Court: Literature, History, and Early Modern Feeling* (Chicago: Northwestern University Press, 2018), 7.

15. Talia Lavin, *Culture Warlords: My Journey in the Dark Web of White Supremacy* (New York: Hatchette, 2020), 115.

16. Laura Bates, *Men Who Hate Women, From Incels to Pickup Artists: The Truth about Extreme Misogyny and How It Affects Us All* (Naperville, IL: Sourcebooks, 2020), 6. The trope of the red pill derives from the 1999 film *The Matrix*, by the Wachowski sisters. Incels appropriate it with no sense of irony. In the film, the hero Neo is given the choice to take a red pill, to see the world as it really is, or to take a blue pill, and so remain in the simulacrum of the "matrix."

17. Bates, *Men Who Hate Women*, 17.

18. Lawrence Babb, "Melancholy and the Elizabethan Man of Letters." *Huntington Library Quarterly* 4, no. 3 (April 1941), 254.

19. Suzanne H. Stein, "Hamlet in Melanchthon's Wittenberg," *Notes and Queries* 56, no. 1 (March 2009): 55.

20. William Shakespeare, *Hamlet*, ed. Ann Thompson and Neil Taylor (London: Arden, 2006), act 1, scene 2, line 85. All subsequent citations refer to this edition and will be cited parenthetically by act, scene, and line number.

21. Elizabeth Hanson, "Fellow Students: Hamlet, Horatio, and the Early Modern University," *Shakespeare Quarterly* 62, no. 2 (Summer 2011): 207.

22. Eric De Barros, "*Hamlet* and the Education of the White Self," in *White People in Shakespeare: Essays on Race, Culture and the Elite*, ed. Arthur Little Jr (New York: Bloomsbury, 2021), 167.

23. John Guillory, "The Bachelor State: Philosophy and Sovereignty in Bacon's

*New Atlantis*," in *Politics and the Passions, 1500–1850*, ed. Victoria Kahn, Neil Saccamanto, and Daniela Coli (Princeton: Princeton University Press, 2006), 51.

24. Guillory, "The Bachelor State," 56.

25. See Pierre Haddot, *What Is Ancient Philosophy?* Trans. Michael Chase (Cambridge, MA: Belknap Press of Harvard University Press, 2002), 55–76, esp. 56.

26. As Guillory draws on Nietzsche, he focuses upon *On the Genealogy of Morality*, and specifically the arguments in his third essay, "What do ascetic ideals mean?" Nietzsche is explicit in his repurposing of Diotima's ladder of love metaphor; he prefaces that essay with an epigram from his own *Thus spoke Zarathustra*: "Carefree, mocking, violent—this is how wisdom wants *us*: she is a woman, all she ever loves is a warrior." See Friedrich Nietzsche, *On the Genealogy of Morality*, ed. Keith Ansell Pearson, trans. Carol Diethe (New York: Cambridge University Press, 1984), 72. The Dutch humanist priest Erasmus similarly mobilizes this trope in a letter to the French humanist Guillaume Budé. As Alan Stewart recounts, Erasmus ribs Budé about the responsibilities of his family life, casting his own singleness as a domestic relationship in which Poverty is his wife and Philosophy his mistress. See *Close Readers: Humanism and Sodomy in Early Modern England* (Princeton, Princeton University Press, 1997), xxxix–xl.

27. Mark H. Curtis most notably charts the influx of the nobility into the universities and the various early modern debates about the effects of it. See *Oxford and Cambridge in Transition* (Oxford: Oxford University Press, 1959). But see also Lawrence Stone, "The Educational Revolution in England, 1560–1640," *Past & Present* no. 28, 1964): 41–80; Elizabeth Russell, "The Influx of Commoners into the University of Oxford before 1581: An Optical Illusion?" *English Historical Review* 92, no. 365 (October 1977): 721–45, as well as Rosemary O'Day, "Universities and Professions in the Early Modern Period," in *Beyond the Lecture Hall: Universities and Community Engagement from the Middle Ages to the Present Day*, ed. Peter Cunningham, Susan Oosthuizen, and Richard Taylor (New York: Cambridge University Press, 2009), 79–102.

28. James Bass Mullinger, *The University of Cambridge from the Royal Injunctions of 1535 to the Accession of Charles the First* (Cambridge, UK: Cambridge University Press, 1884; repr. Johnson Reprint Corporation, 1969), 69.

29. William Harrison, *The Description of England*, ed. Georges Edelen (London, 1587. repr. Ithaca, NY: Cornell University Press, 1968), 70–71.

30. Harrison, *The Description*, 71.

31. Victor Morgan and Christopher Brooke, *A History of the University of Cambridge*, vol. 2, 1546–1750 (New York: Cambridge University Press, 2004), 297–98.

32. Morgan and Brooke, *A History*, 78.

33. Morgan and Brooke, *A History*, 150.

34. Henry Buttes, *Dyets Dry Dinner* (London, 1599), A1r-v.

35. See Morgan and Brooke, *A History*, 304.

36. Robert Burton, *The Anatomy of Melancholy*, vol. 1, ed. by Thomas Faulkner, et al. (New York: Oxford University Press, 1981), 790.

37. Erin Spampinato, "How Does the Literary Canon Reinforce the Logic of the Incel?" *The Guardian* (website), June 4, 2018.

38. David Cote, "Review: Robert Icke's Production of 'Hamlet' Misguidedly Embraces the Prince's Incel-Nature," *The Observer* (website), June 30, 2022, access September 2, 2023.

39. See James Poulos, "Alleged Santa Barbara Killer Elliot Rodger and the Twisted Cult of Modern Masculinity," Daily Beast (website), May 26, 2014. Updated July 12, 2017.

40. Harold Bloom, *Shakespeare: The Invention of the Human* (New York: Riverhead, 1999), 109.

41. Margreta de Grazia provides a robust history of Hamlet's supposed modernity, tracing a turn in criticism in the nineteenth century that came to value the play for its titular character divested of his tragic plot. In the twentieth century, the idea of Hamlet's modernity was intensified by the psychoanalytic readings of Freud and Lacan, the deconstructionist readings of Derrida, and the materialism of Eagleton. See *Hamlet without Hamlet* (New York: Cambridge University Press, 2007), 7–22.

42. T. S. Eliot. "Hamlet and His Problems," in *The Sacred Wood: Essays on Poetry and Criticism* (New York: Barnes and Noble, 1953), 99, 100.

43. See Daniel, *The Melancholy Assemblage*, 126–32.

44. Daniel, *The Melancholy Assemblage*, 135.

45. Williams, *Marxism and Literature*, 102.

46. Williams, *Marxism and Literature*, 102.

47. Williams, *Marxism and Literature*, 105–6.

48. Steven Mullaney, "Mourning and Misogyny: Hamlet, The Revenger's Tragedy, and the Final Progress of Elizabeth I, 1600–1607," *Shakespeare Quarterly* 45, no. 2 (Summer 1994): 140.

49. See Mullaney, "Mourning and Misogyny," 150–54.

50. Manne, *Down Girl*, 61. Manne observes that the word "misogyny" originates in the early modern period. In *Swetnam the Woman-Hater Arraigned by Women* (1620), the anonymous response to Joseph Swetnam's *The Arraignment of Lewde, Idle, Froward, and vnconstant women: Or the vanitie of them, choose you whether* (1615), Swetnam is represented as the character "Misogynos." Manne uses excerpts from both as epigraphs to *Down Girl*, and from *The Arraignment*, again, for her final chapter.

51. Daniel provides a compelling gloss of Hamlet's phrase. See Daniel, *The Melancholy Assemblage*, 120–54.

52. Manne, *Down Girl*, 62.

53. See de Grazia, *Hamlet without Hamlet*, 81, 87.

54. See de Grazia, *Hamlet without Hamlet*, 81–128.

55. Hanson, "Hamlet, Horatio, and the Early Modern University," 221.

56. Hanson, "Hamlet, Horatio, and the Early Modern University," 224.

57. Daniel, *The Melancholy Assemblage*, 152.

58. Daniel, *The Melancholy Assemblage*, 154.

59. "Supreme gentleman" is the phrase Rodger used to refer to himself, and which continually circulates in incel discourse. Cited in Manne, *Entitled*, 15.

60. Burton, *The Anatomy of Melancholy*, vol. 1: 391.

61. Elliot Rodger, "My Twisted World: The Story of Elliot Rodger," in School-shooters (website), 20, 1, Langman Psychological Association, LLC, May 31, 2024.

62. Rodger, "My Twisted World, 1.

63. Rodger, "My Twisted World," 88.

64. Stanley E. Fish, *Self-Consuming Artifacts: The Experience of Seventeenth-Century Literature* (Berkeley: University of California Press, 1972), 330, and Daniel, *Melancholy Assemblage*, 156.

65. Mary Ann Lund has argued that Burton's desire to write a curative text for the social good should be taken seriously, if with some qualifications. See *Melancholy, Medicine, and Religion in Early Modern England* (New York: Cambridge University Press, 2010). Adam Kitzes reads the political currents of *The Anatomy*, especially Burton's engagements with utopianism. See *The Politics of Melancholy from Spenser to Milton*. (New York: Routledge, 2006), 123–50.

66. Susan Wells, *Robert Burton's Rhetoric: An Anatomy of Early Modern Knowledge* (Philadelphia: University of Pennsylvania Press, 2019), 9.

67. See Tristan Bridges and C. J. Pascoe, "Hybrid Masculinities: New Directions in the Sociology of Men and Masculinities," *Sociology Compass* 8, no. 3 (March 2014): 246–58.

68. See Alyssa M. Glace, Tessa L. Dover, and Judith G. Zatkin, "Taking the Black Pill: An Empirical Analysis of the 'Incel,'" *Psychology of Men & Masculinities* 22 no. 2 (2021): 291–95.

69. Burton, *The Anatomy of Melancholy*, vol. 1: 3.

70. Burton, *The Anatomy of Melancholy*, vol. 1: 303.

71. Burton, *The Anatomy of Melancholy*, vol. 1: 304.

72. Burton, *The Anatomy of Melancholy*, vol. 1: 304–5.

73. Burton, *The Anatomy of Melancholy*, vol. 1: 305.

74. Rodger, "My Twisted World," 31.

75. Burton, *The Anatomy of Melancholy*, vol. 1: 306–7.

76. Burton, *The Anatomy of Melancholy*, vol. 1: 307.

77. Burton, *The Anatomy of Melancholy*, vol. 1: 311.

78. Burton, *The Anatomy of Melancholy*, vol. 1: 322.

79. Burton, *The Anatomy of Melancholy*, vol. 1: 323.

80. Rodger, "My Twisted World," 105.

81. Burton, *The Anatomy of Melancholy*, vol. 1: 416, 417.

82. Burton, *The Anatomy of Melancholy*, vol. 1: 417.

83. Burton, *The Anatomy of Melancholy*, vol. 1: 417. Reading this passage through psychoanalytic theory, Juliana Schiesari likewise observes that at this moment in *The Anatomy of Melancholy*, where he focuses on single women, "Burton betrays his own fearful identification with them," but concludes, "the potential danger of confronting his own castration is averted, by his ensuing appropriation of/identification with Pallas." See Schiesari, *The Gendering of Melancholia*, 252.

84. Burton, *The Anatomy of Melancholy*, vol. 1: 417.

85. Burton, *The Anatomy of Melancholy*, vol. 1: 417–18.

86. Rodger, "My Twisted World," 135.

87. Burton, *The Anatomy of Melancholy*, vol. 3: 1.

88. Burton, *The Anatomy of Melancholy*, vol. 3: 2, 5.

89. Lund, *Melancholy*, 28.

90. Pierce Alexander Dignam and Deana A. Rohlinger, "Misogynistic Men Online: How the Red Pill Helped Elect Trump." *Signs* 44, no. 3 (Spring 2019): 595. As Dignam and Rohlinger explain, the trope goes so far as to operate as a kind of identity. It came to organize forums (subreddits) on the reddit website, which were integral to right-wing political organization and mobilization in the 2016 election of Donald Trump.

91. Rodger, "My Twisted World," 112.

92. Social scientists have pointed out the degree to which white nationalists recruit by deploying antifeminism and homophobia to "introduce" young men to white supremacy. See, for instance, Sophie Bjork-James, "Racializing Misogyny: Sexuality and Gender in the New Online White Nationalism," *Feminist Anthropology* 1, no. 2 (2020): 176–83. The ADL also issued a report tracing these trends as well. See the Center for Extremism, "When Women are the Enemy: The Intersection of Misogyny and White Supremacy." ADL (website) 2018. The connections between anti-Black racism, white supremacy, and misogyny have long been explored, however, most notably by bell hooks, *Ain't I A Woman: Black Women and Feminism* (Chicago: Pluto Press, 1987).

93. Rodger, "My Twisted World," 84.

94. Burton, *The Anatomy of Melancholy*, vol. 3: 83–84.

95. For the material dimensions of this metaphor, and its implication in the exchange of court jewels as signifiers of a racialized, aristocratic identity, see Kim F. Hall, *Things of Darkness: Economies of Race and Gender in Early Modern England* (Ithaca, NY: Cornell University Press), 211–53, esp. 214–26.

96. Patricia Akhimie, *Shakespeare and the Cultivation of Difference: Race and Conduct in the Early Modern World* (New York: Routledge, 2018), 49.

97. Akhimie, *Shakespeare*, 53.

98. My analysis of this relation between melancholy and misogyny shares something with Mark Breitenberg's reading of *The Anatomy of Melancholy*. Breitenberg similarly attends to the misogyny in the section on love melancholy, but relates it to Galenic humoralism, which traces the etiology of melancholy as a humoral imbalance imposed by women upon men. In Breitenberg's reading, love melancholics experience melancholy as an invasion of the self by a feminine Other, who must be then purged through misogynist fantasies and fixations. See *Anxious Masculinity in Early Modern England* (New York: Cambridge University Press, 2003), 35–68. Unlike Breitenberg, I do not find this experience as representationally anxiety-inducing, though I do find it productive of patriarchal social order. Instead, following Manne, I find misogyny has having less to do with men's feelings than it does with women's experiences of those feelings.

99. Burton, *The Anatomy of Melancholy*, vol. 3: 220.

100. Burton, *The Anatomy of Melancholy*, vol. 3: 221,

101. Burton, *The Anatomy of Melancholy*, 222.

102. Dignam and Rohlinger, "Misogynistic Men Online," 599.

103. Burton, *The Anatomy of Melancholy*, vol. 3: 229.

104. Bates, *Men Who Hate Women*, 1–53.

105. Burton, *The Anatomy of Melancholy*, vol. 3: 229.

106. Burton, *The Anatomy of Melancholy*, vol. 3: 229.

107. See Christopher Tilmouth, "Burton's 'Turning Picture': Argument and Anxiety in "The Anatomy of Melancholy,"" *Review of English Studies*, New Series, 56, no. 226 (2005): 524–49.

108. Burton, *The Anatomy of Melancholy*, vol. 3: 230. Stephanie Shirilian has qualified Burton's misogyny by showing how Burton, in other moments, has no qualms about describing men behaving as badly as women. Given the asymmetries of these descriptions, and the patriarchal norms governing both the production and reception of *The Anatomy of Melancholy*, I find such qualifications unpersuasive. See *Robert Burton and the Transformative Powers of Melancholy* (Burlington, VT: Ashgate, 2015), 163–67.

## CHAPTER 5

1. Francis Lenton, *Characterismi: or Lenton's Leisures*. London, 1636, G2r-G3r. For a similar dynamic between husband, eunuch, bachelor, see the ballad, "THE FANATICKS BARBER. / OR, / A New Cut for NON-CONFORMISTS. / Being a true Relation of the PARSON that was lately Gelt at Chemsford in Essex, / being taken in Bed with another Mans Wife. / Very proper to be sung in all Corporations of this Nation. / All the Town shan't save thee." British Library. Luttrell Ballads, C.20.f.4. (80). EBBA 36464, Patricia Fumerton, dir., English Broadside Ballad Archive (website).

2. See Judith Butler, *Gender Trouble: Feminism and the Subversion of Identity* (New York: Routledge, 1990), 17.

3. Butler, *Gender Trouble*, 7. It goes without saying that Butler's contributions to

the fields of feminism and queer theory are substantial, but one of the features of their writing that remains the most compelling to me are the series of questions they raise, without entirely answering, their seeding of the atmosphere of inquiry.

4. Paisley Currah, *Sex Is As Sex Does: Governing Transgender Identity* (New York: New York University Press, 2022), 39.

5. Currah, *Sex Is As Sex Does*, 80.

6. Freud's own theories of sexual inversion cite the biologist Eugen Steinbech, who was central to early twentieth endocrinology and eugenics. For this history, the influence of Steinbech upon Freud, and the ways figure of the "child" became central to medicalized notions of gender transition and racialization, see Jules Gill-Peterson, *Histories of the Transgender Child* (Minneapolis: University of Minnesota Press, 2018), 35–58, esp. 49–56. For the continuities between Freud's theory and early modern representations of castration, see Gary Taylor, *Castration: An Abbreviated History of Western Manhood* (New York: Routledge, 2000), 15–17, 85–109.

7. This statement, while a crucial point for my argument here, is part of Butler's larger reformulations of performativity. As Butler explains:

> As a result of this reformulation of performativity, (a) gender performativity cannot be theorized apart from the forcible and reiterative practice of regulatory sexual regimes; (b) the account of agency conditioned by those very regimes of discourse/power cannot be conflated with voluntarism or individualism, much less with consumerism, and in no way presupposes a choosing subject; (c) the regime of heterosexuality operates to circumscribe and contour the "materiality" of sex, and that "materiality" is formed and sustained through and as a materialization of regulatory norms that are in part those of heterosexual hegemony; (d) the materialization of norms requires those identificatory processes by which norms are assumed or appropriated, and these identifications precede and enable the formation of a subject, but are not, strictly speaking, performed by a subject; and (e) the limits of constructivism are exposed at those boundaries of bodily life where abjected or delegitimated bodies fail to count as "bodies." If the materiality of sex is demarcated in discourse, then this demarcation will produce a domain of excluded and delegitimated "sex." Hence, it will be as important to think about how and to what end bodies are constructed as is it will be to think about how and to what end bodies are *not* constructed and, further, to ask after how bodies which fail to materialize provide the necessary "outside," if not the necessary support, for the bodies which, in materializing the norm, qualify as bodies that matter.

Of particular significance to my argument are points c through e. Butler's argument pertains to abstract, though nonetheless historical, categories of "heterosexuality" or "the heterosexual matrix." See *Bodies That Matter: On the Discursive Limits of Sex* (New York: Routledge, 1993), 15–16.

8. See Abulhamit Arvas, "Early Modern Eunuchs and the Transing of Gender and Race," *Journal of Early Modern Cultural Studies* 19, no. 4 (Fall 2019): 116–36;

Mathew Kuefler, *The Manly Eunuch: Masculinity, Gender Ambiguity, and Christian Ideology in Late Antiquity* (Chicago: University of Chicago Press, 2001); Kathryn Ringrose, *The Perfect Servant: Eunuchs and the Social Construction of Gender in Byzantium* (Chicago: University of Chicago Press, 2003); Shaun Tougher, ed. *Eunuchs in Antiquity and Beyond* (Swansea: Classical Press of Wales, 2002) and Shaun Tougher, *The Eunuch in Byzantine History and Society* (New York: Routledge, 2008).

9. See Katherine Crawford, *Eunuchs and Castrati: Disability and Normativity in Early Modern Europe* (New York: Routledge, 2019), 4.

10. Crawford, *Eunuchs and Castrati*, 8.

11. Felix Plater, Abdiah Cole, and Nicholas Culpepper, *Platerus Golden Practice of Physick* (London, 1664), 25. The authors make this observation in relation to possible cures for epilepsy.

12. Marquis Bey, *Black Trans Feminism* (Durham, NC: Duke University Press, 2021), 3.

13. Sokol and Sokol, *Shakespeare, Law, and Marriage* (New York: Cambridge University Press, 2006), 142.

14. Edward Behrend-Martínez, "Manhood and the Neutered Body in Early Modern Spain," *Social History* 38, no. 4 (Summer 2005): 1073.

15. Sokol and Sokol, *Shakespeare, Law, and Marriage*, 142.

16. Jennifer Evans, "'They Are Called Imperfect Men': Male Infertility and Sexual Health in Early Modern England," *Social History of Medicine* 29, no. 2 (May 2016): 311–32.

17. William Gouge, *Of Domesticall Duties: Eight Treatise* (London, 1622), 181–82.

18. For the history of marriage as a history of disability, see Crawford, *Eunuchs and Castrati*, 89–99.

19. Gouge, *Of Domesticall Duties*, 182. Gouge in fact redeploys a long theological tradition of seeking to define marriage as a fundamental procreative relation, one that consolidated around a doctrine of *Cum frequenter*, that is, proof of a procreative ejaculate. For this history, which, in the early modern European context, is most fully articulated in Catholic, not Protestant, theological debates about the nature of marriage, see Crawford, *Eunuchs and Castati*, 70–89.

20. See Robert Crofts, *The Lover: or Nuptiall Love* (London, 1638), sig. A7r. Crofts is also citing and repurposing Erasmus's *Encomium Matrimonii* here, which, as I discussed in chapter 1, was continually cited and recited through the sixteenth and seventeenth centuries.

21. See Thomas Gataker, *A Good Wife Gods Gift: And, Wife Indeed. Two Marriage Sermons* (London, 1623), 5.

22. Currah, *Sex Is As Sex Does*, 80.

23. Robert Samber and Charles Ancillon, *Eunuchism Display'd. Describing all the different Sorts of Eunuchs; The Esteem they have met with in World, and how they came to be made so. Wherein principally is examin'd, whether they are capable of Marriage, and if they ought to be suffer'd to enter into that State. The whole confirm'd by the Authority*

*of Civil, Canon, and Common Law, and illustrated with many remarkable Cases by way of Precedent. Also a Comparison between Signior Nicolini and the Three Celebrated EUNUCHS now at Rome, viz. Pasqualini, Pauluccio, and Jeronimo (or Momo): With several observations on Modern Eunuchs. Occasion'd by a young Lady falling in Love with Nicolini, who sung in the Opera at the Hay-Market, and to whom she had like to have been Married* (London, 1718), 2. In summarizing this text, Crawford observes that Ancillon's arguments come to England a year late to make the marital scandal advertised on the title page an exigent one. Crawford also emphasizes the degree to which Ancillon's s text emphasizes that eunuchs should be demonized because of their various forms of dishonesty, of essentially falsifying their manhood. See Crawford, *Eunuchs and Castrati*, 93–94.

24. Samber and Ancillon, *Eunuchism Display'd*, 8.

25. Samber and Ancillon, *Eunuchism Display'd*, 139, emphasis in original.

26. Samber and Ancillon, *Eunuchism Display'd*, 144.

27. Samber and Ancillon, *Eunuchism Display'd*, 146.

28. Reading J. L. Austin's concept of the performative and his example of "marriage with a monkey," Mel Y. Chen observes "the genericity of 'a monkey' implicates that the monkey threatens being genderless: first, in a general sense, a creature without a gender identity somehow threatens the smooth running of heteronormative society which itself relies on a robust organization of its gender systems; second, a creature without a gender identity must also lack a sex, and thus threaten the possibility of bringing an abject, queer sexuality into (the institution of) marriage." See "Animals Without Genitals," in *The Transgender Studies Reader 2*, ed. Susan Stryker and Aren Z. Aizura (New York: Routledge, 2013), 172. Julia Serano examines the tropes of the deceptive and the pathetic transgender subject as well. See "Skirt Chasers: Why the Media Depicts the Trans Revolution in Lipstick and Heels," in *The Transgender Studies Reader 2*, ed. Susan Stryker and Aren Z. Aizura (New York: Routledge, 2013), 226–33.

29. I am loath to cite Janice Raymond, whose transphobia is virulent and sustained and has caused deep and lasting harm. Her arguments, however, can be found in *The Transsexual Empire* (New York: Teachers College Press, 1994), 83–119.

30. Helkiah Crooke, *Mikrokosmographia: A Description of the Body of Man. Together with the Controversies Thereto Belonging* (London, 1615), 274.

31. Crooke, *Mikrokosmographia*, 274.

32. Butler, *Bodies That Matter*, 13.

33. Currah, *Sex Is As Sex Does*, 83.

34. Crooke, *Mikrokosmographia*, 27–28.

35. Crooke, *Mikrokosmographia*, 200.

36. Crooke, *Mikrokosmographia*, 40–41. Crawford, however, misstates Crooke's position, by taking his recapitulation of counterarguments as his assertion. Citing the 1651 edition of *Mikrokosmographia*, Crawford writes, "English royal physician Helkiah Crooke (1576–1648) was having none of it: 'But for the Testicles there is no

necessity of them, for *Eunuchs* live without them." See Crawford, *Eunuchs and Castra-ti*, 23. The text from Crooke reads: "But there want not adversaries who would thrust them [testicles] out of this rank of dignity; although their arguments are very weak. First they say *Galen* in two places defineth a principall part, in the first by *Necessity*, in the second by *communication of a faculty* or *some common matter*. But for the Testicles there is no necessity of them, for *Eunuchs* live without them; neither is there any faculty proceeding, for the animall faculty proceedeth from the brain, the vitall from the heart, the natural (to which the faculty of procreation is referred) issueth from the Liver the chief of all naturall parts. Moreover from the testicles there is no matter communi-cated to the whole body, for they have no spirits proper unto them, no vessels which run through the body by which it may be conveyed; but these are trifles." See Crooke, *Mikrokosmopgrahia* (London, 1651), 180. Crooke in fact lists the assertion about eu-nuchs that Crawford ascribes to him as part of a series of "trifles" that he then proceeds to refute. As I demonstrate, the argument Crawford associates with French physician André du Laurens—that castration changes the body—is also one made by Crooke. In any case, Crawford and I come to similar conclusions about the anatomization of eu-nuchs, which led to their positions tangential to early modern categories of the human animal and gender normativity.

37. Crooke, *Mikrokosmographia*, 41.

38. Crooke, *Mikrokosmographia*, 45.

39. Crooke, *Mikrokosmographia*, 44–45.

40. Crooke, *Mikrokosmographia*, 199.

41. Crooke, *Mikrokosmographia*, 207.

42. Crooke, *Mikrokosmographia*, 242.

43. Chen, "Animals Without Genitals," 173.

44. C. Riley Snorton, *Black on Both Sides: A Racial History of Trans Identity* (Min-neapolis: University of Minnesota Press, 2017), 20.

45. Crooke, *Mikrokosmographia*, 241.

46. Crooke, *Mikrokosmographia*, 241.

47. Pfeffer goes on to assert that Crooke's "exploration of bodily changes and re-categorization occurs divorced from any sense of embodied knowledge or personal choice. Instead, Crooke identifies heat as the main actor that accounts for the legibility of sexual assignment. In this way, bodily materials become the agents of sexual difference rather than the tools deployed in order to manifest their difference." See Jess R. Pfeffer, "Trans Materiality: Crooke's *Mikrokosmographia*, Sexual Dimorphism, and the Embod-iment of Identity," *Journal of Early Modern Cultural Studies* 19, no. 4, (Fall 2019): 228–29. It is true that heat does play a role in Crooke's discussion of sexual assignment, but his understanding of heat is deeply entangled with the gelded body of the eunuch, and it becomes difficult to dematerialize that body. I would suggest Crooke takes pains to insist bodily materials can and should manifest difference.

48. Patricia Simons, *The Sex of Men in Premodern Europe: A Cultural History* (New York: Cambridge University Press, 2011), 142.

49. Crooke, *Mikrokosmographia*, 241.

50. Crooke, *Mikrokosmographia*, 241.

51. Crooke, *Mikrokosmographia*, 243.

52. Crooke, *Mikrokosmographia*, 272.

53. Current rightwing movements explicitly ally natalism and transphobia as each seek to reify an essentialist understanding of gendered embodiment. For the histories and vectors of fascism, transphobia, and pro-life natalism, see Serena Bassi and Greta LaFleur, "Introduction: TERFS, Gender-Critical Movements, and Postfascist Feminisms," *TSQ: Transgender Studies* Quarterly 9, no. 3 (August 2022): 311–33. C. Libby examines the affective circuits that run through TERF rhetoric and Evangelical Christianity as they relate to constructions of ostensibly "dangerous" trans subjects. See "Sympathy, Fear, Hate: Trans-Exclusionary Radical Feminism and Evangelical Christianity," *TSQ: Transgender Studies Quarterly* 9, no. 3, (August 2022): 425–42. The journalist Schuyler Mitchell also documents these alliances as they run through the United States Supreme Court's *Dobbs* decision, which overturned *Roe v. Wade*. See "The Right's Creeping Pro-Natalist Rhetoric on Abortion and Trans Health Care," *The Intercept* (website), May 17, 2022.

54. See Kim F. Hall, *Things of Darkness: Economies of Race and Gender in Early Modern England* (Ithaca, NY: Cornell University Press, 1995), 4–11, 25–61. See also, Abdulhamit Arvas, "Early Modern Eunuchs and the Transing of Gender and Race," *Journal of Early Modern Cultural Studies* 19, no. 4 (Fall 2019): 116–36.

55. Crooke, *Mikrokosmographia*, 242.

56. Thomas Raynold, *The Byrth of Mankynde, otherwyse named the Womans Booke* (London, 1545), fol. 24r-fol. 24v.

57. Julia Serrano, *Whipping Girl: A Transexual Woman on Sexism and the Scapegoating of Femininity* (New York: Seal Press, 2016), 13.

58. Ambroise Paré, *The Workes of that famous Chirugion Ambrose Parey*, translated out of Latine and Compared with the French.Th. Johnson (London, 1634), 120.

59. Nicholas Culpepper, *A Directory for Midwives, or, A Guide For Women* (London, 1651), 13.

60. Thomas Bartholin, *Bartholinus Anatomy; Made from the Precepts of his Father, and From the Observations of all Modern Anatomists, together with his own.* Published by Nich. Culpeper Gent. And Abdiah Cole Doctor of Physick (London, 1668), Book 1, 57.

61. Gayle Salamon, *Assuming a Body: Transgender and Rhetorics of Materiality* (New York: Columbia University Press, 2010), 98.

62. Taylor, *Castration*, 30.

63. Stephen Orgel, *Impersonations: The Performance of Gender in Shakespeare's England* (New York: Cambridge University Press, 1996), 54.

64. Keir Elam, ed. "Introduction." *Twelfth Night, or What You Will* (New York: Bloomsbury, 2013), 75. Elam further examines Viola choosing to disguise herself as a eunuch, which he treats as an enigma that points in two directions: "out to early modern society and back to the dramatic and theatrical past." Elam is primarily interested in renaissance conduct and behavior, and so does not primarily read the figure of the eunuch in relation to early modern marital or anatomical discourses or in relation to the Ottoman and Muslim contexts of other early modern plays that Arvas surveys. See also Keir Elam, "The Fertile Eunuch: *Twelfth Night*, Early Modern Intercourse, and the Fruits of Castration," *Shakespeare Quarterly* 47, no. 1 (Spring 1996): 3.

65. John Astington. "Malvolio and the Eunuchs: Texts and Revels in *Twelfth Night*," *Shakespeare Survey*, ed. Stanley Wells, 46 (1993): 26, 29.

66. William Shakespeare, *Twelfth Night, or What You Will*, ed. Keir Elam, (New York: Bloomsbury, 2013), act 5, scene 1, lines 255–59, hereafter cited parenthetically.

67. See Stephen Greenblatt, *Shakespearean Negotiations: The Circulation of Social Energy in Renaissance England* (Berkeley: University of California Press, 1988), 66–93, and Stephen Orgel, *Impersonations*, 53–58. Reading Sonnet 20, Colby Gordon has shown how all gender in the early modern period is "pricked" out through technogenetic processes. Bachelor, husband, eunuch, woman, wife: all genders are fabricated. See "A Woman's Prick: Trans Technogenesis in Sonnet 20," in *Shakespeare / Sex: Contemporary Readings in Gender and Sexuality*, ed. Jennifer Drouin (New York: Bloomsbury, 2020), 271–89.

68. Thomas Laqueur, *Making Sex: Body and Gender from the Greeks to Freud* (Cambridge, MA: Harvard University Press, 1992), 115.

69. Sawyer Kemp, "'In That Dimension Grossly Clad': Transgender Rhetoric, Representation, and Shakespeare," *Shakespeare Studies* 49 (2019): 121.

70. Kemp, "'In That Dimension,'" 121.

71. See Ezra Horbury, "Transgender Reassessments of the Cross-Dressed Page in Shakespeare, *Philaster*, and *The Honest Man's Fortune*," *Shakespeare Quarterly* 73, no. 1–2 (Summer 2022): 107. Horbury draws upon and revises Jones and Stallybrass's formulation. See Ann Rosalind Jones and Peter Stallybrass, *Renaissance Clothing and the Materials of Memory* (New York: Cambridge University Press, 2000), 208–15.

72. Jo Henderson-Merrygold, "The Present and Future of Trans Hermeneutics. Viewing Sarah Cispiciously: Cisnormalisation, and the Problem of Cisnormativity." *Society of Biblical Literature Annual Meeting*, Denver, November 17–21. 2018. Conference Presentation. Humanities Commons (website).

73. Patricia Parker, "Was Illyria as Mysterious and Foreign as We Think?" in *The Mysterious and the Foreign in Early Modern England*, ed. Helen Ostovich, Mary V. Silcox, and Graham Roebuck (Newark: University of Delaware Press, 2008), 210. See also Constance Relihan, "Erasing the East from *Twelfth Night*," in *Race, Ethnicity, and Power in the Renaissance*, ed. Joyce Green MacDonald (Vancouver: Farleigh Dickinson

University Press, 1997), 80–94 as well as Su Fang Ng, "The Frontiers of *Twelfth Night*," in *Early Modern England and Islamic Worlds*, ed. Bernadette Andrea and Linda McJannet (New York: Palgrave, 2011), 173–96.

74. Parker, "Was Illyria," 212.

75. See Ambereen Dadabhoy, *Shakespeare through Islamic Worlds* (New York: Routledge, 2023), 176–77, 185. I thank Ambereen for sharing page proofs of her book as I finished this chapter.

76. See Arvas, "Early Modern Eunuchs," 125, 128.

77. See Arvas, "Early Modern Eunuchs," 118–25. See also Jane Hathaway, *Beshir Agha: Chief Eunuch of the Ottoman Imperial Harem* (London: Oneworld, 2006).

78. See Dympna Callaghan, *Shakespeare Without Women* (New York: Routledge, 2000), 49–74, esp. 51.

79. Arvas states, "eunuchs primarily functioned on stage as theatrical curiosities (most likely in blackface)," See Arvas, "Early Modern Eunuchs," 127. Surveying a range of texts, from ancient to early modern, Anston Bosman further observes, "wherever we find a eunuch, we nearly always find a black character as well." See "'Best Play with Mardian': Eunuch and Blackamoor as Imperial Culturegram," *Shakespeare Studies*, ed. Susan Zimmerman 34 (2006): 124.

80. Dadabhoy provides a brilliant reading of the bifurcated gendered spaces of Orsino and Olivia's courts as "a distinguishing feature of Islamicate societies." See Dadabhoy, *Islamic Worlds*, 186, but also 198–200.

81. Gataker, *A Good Wife* 5; Paré, *The Workes*, 120.

82. See Arvas, "Early Modern Eunuchs," 119. See also Ringrose, *The Perfect Servant*, 163–83. Ringrose focuses on Byzantine eunuchs, but the Byzantine Empire should not be confused with the Ottoman Empire even as Shakespeare may as he conjures the various cultural geographies of Illyria and even if eunuchs could serve similar functions in respective imperial courts. See Dadabhoy, *Islamic Worlds*, 192–93.

83. Jeffery Masten, "Editing Boys: The Performance of Gender in Print," in *Redefining British Theatre History: from Performance to Print*, ed. Peter Holland and Stephen Orgel (New York: Palgrave, 2006), 114.

84. Masten, "Editing Boys," 116.

85. There are three references to complexion in the play. Two refer to Malvolio's complexion. The other one is Viola referring to Orsino's complexion. Reading *Twelfth Night* in relation to its Ottoman contexts and source texts, Dadabhoy also concludes the play "position[s] [Malvolio] the play's other eunuch." See Dadabhoy, *Islamic Worlds*, 208.

86. William Shakespeare, *The Merchant of Venice*, ed. Barbara Mowat and Paul Werstine (New York: Simon & Schuster, 2009), act 2, scene 1, lines 1–2. Kim F. Hall discusses early modern tropes of sunburn as they organize both gender and racial difference in the period. While Hall notes that the early European theory that Africans had black

skin because of a supposed overexposure to the sun were discredited by later accounts of travel, they also continued to circulate in a variety of literature. As Hall demonstrates, the concern over sunburn became central to early modern English racial discourses, and especially fears of white Europeans somehow becoming "Black.": "The popularity of the idea that sun caused 'black' skin color may have lasted because the very name 'Aethiope' signified burnt or 'torrid' skin, as many travelers intimated, or, more likely, because it provided an oblique way of addressing fears of miscegenation and the absorption of 'white' Europeans by the foreign other" See *Things of Darkness*, 92–197, esp. 95.

87. Patricia Akhimie, *Shakespeare and the Cultivation of Difference: Race and Conduct in the Early Modern World* (New York: Routledge, 2018), 86.

88. Ng, "The Frontiers," 180.

89. Astington, "Malvolio and the Eunuchs," 26.

90. Arvas, "Early Modern Eunuchs," 120.

91. Michel Baudier, *The History of the Serrail, and of the Court of the Grand Seigneur, Emperour of the Turkes*, translated by Edward Grimeston (London, 1635), 132.

92. For the range of early modern citations of Ottoman imperial enslavement of youths and the role of eunuchry in facilitating social status, see Dadabhoy, *Islamic Worlds*, 187–95.

93. Thomas Middleton and Thomas Dekker, *The Roaring Girl*, ed Paul A. Mulholland (Manchester, UK: Manchester University Press, 1999), act 2, scene 2, lines 35–45. All citations are drawn from this volume, cited hereafter parenthetically.

94. See Heather Hirschfeld, "What Do Women Know?: *The Roaring Girl* and the Wisdom of Tiresias," *Renaissance Drama*, 32 (2003): 123–46.

95. See Marjorie Rubright, "Transgender Capacity in Thomas Dekker and Thomas Middleton's *The Roaring Girl* (1611)," *Journal for Early Modern Cultural Studies* 19, no. 4 (Fall 2019): 48.

96. Rubright, "Transgender Capacity," 48.

97. Christine Varnado, *The Shapes of Fancy* (Minneapolis: University of Minnesota Press, 2020), 51, 52.

98. Simone Chess, *Male-to-Female Crossdressing in Early Modern English Literature: Gender, Performance, and Queer Relations* (New York: Routledge, 2016), 16.

99. Middleton and Dekker, *The Roaring Girl*, 71.

100. Christopher Clary, "Moll's Queer Anatomy: *The Roaring Girl* and Queer Generation," in *Staging Shakespeare for Performance: The Bear Stage*, ed. Catherine Loomis and Sid Ray (Vancouver: Farleigh Dickinson University Press, 2016): 93.

101. Varnado, *The Shapes of Fancy*, 76.

102. Middleton and Dekker, *The Roaring Girl*, 68.

103. Middleton and Dekker, *The Roaring Girl*, 68.

104. Middleton and Dekker, *The Roaring Girl*, 69.

105. As Dympna Callaghan notes, "In advanced cases of venereal disease,

castration was often the only remedy. Surgical removal of the penis (as opposed to the testicles) was not an uncommon last recourse." Callaghan, *Shakespeare Without Women*, 54.

106. David T. Mitchell and Sharon L. Snyder, *Narrative Prosthesis: Disability and the Dependencies of Discourse* (Ann Arbor: University of Michigan Press, 2001), 47.

107. See Thomas Nashe, "The Choise of Valentines, or the Merie Ballad of Nash His Dildo," ed. John S. Farmer," 1899. Project Gutenberg (website), February 16, 2006.

108. See Will Fisher, *Materializing Gender in Early Modern England* (New York: Cambridge University Press, 2007), 1–35, 59–82.

109. Lenton, *Characterismi*, G2r-G3r.

110. Bey, *Black Trans Feminism*, 68.

## EPILOGUE

1. *Dobbs v. Jackson Women's Health*, 19–1392 (2022), 17.

2. *Obergefell v. Hodges*, 556 U.S ___ (2015), 3.

3. Yasmin Nair, "Against Equality, Against Marriage: An Introduction," in *Against Equality: Queer Critiques of Gay Marriage*, ed. Ryan Conrad (Lewiston, ME: Against Equality Publishing Collective, 2010), 2.

4. Elizabeth Brake, *Minimizing Marriage: Marriage Morality, and the Law* (New York: Oxford University Press, 2012), 88–89. I'd like to thank Liza Blake for pointing me to Brake's work.

5. Claire Mortimer, *Romantic Comedy* (New York: Routledge, 2010), 1–10.

6. See Joseph Gamble, *Sex Lives: Intimate Infrastructures in Early Modernity* (Philadelphia: University of Pennsylvania Press, 2023), 1.

7. Thomas Dekker, *The Shoemaker's Holiday*, edited by R. L. Smallwood and Stanley Wells (Manchester, UK: Manchester University Press, 1999), scene 1, lines 132–33. All quotations come from this edition, though hereafter they will be cited parenthetically.

8. See Eric Partridge, *Shakespeare's Bawdy: A Literary and Psychological Essay and a Comprehensive Glossary* (London: Routledge, 1955), 160.

9. The euphemisms in this scene typify the slippages of meaning Valerie Traub sees as occurring both within and across time. As Traub puts it: "Synchronically, many words are polysemic: they possess several potential meanings simultaneously." See Valerie Traub, *Thinking Sex with the Early Moderns* (Philadelphia: University of Pennsylvania Press, 2016), 188.

10. He even admits a type of resignation to this fact. When Hodge explains that several alderman are gravely ill, thus paving the way for Eyre's rise, Firk finds this fact inconsequential, asking how this circumstance has any bearing on his own social position.

11. "firk | ferk, n." *OED Online*. December 2015. Oxford University Press.

12. "firk | ferk, v." *OED Online* (website). December 2015. Oxford University Press.

13. Dekker, *The Shoemaker's Holiday*, 122n94, 157n28; The *OED*, citing this passage, but also finding earlier antecedent, defines "yerk/yark": "to draw stitches tight, to twitch, as a shoemaker in sewing . . . also to bind tightly with cords." It can also mean to beat with a whip. See "yerk, yark, v." *OED Online*. December 2015. Oxford University Press.

14. See "seam, v.2." *OED Online*. December 2015. Oxford University Press.

15. Natasha Korda, "'The Sign of the Last': Gender, Material Culture, and Artisanal Nostalgia in *The Shoemaker's Holiday*," *Journal of Medieval and Early Modern Studies* 43, no. 3 (Fall 2013): 586.

16. Firk is not the only one who alludes to masturbation. When Sybil stops by the shop to tell Lacy [as Hans] to meet Rose, Hodge jokes about Sybl taking "heed of pricking" (because she "stand[s] upon needles"). Sybil's responds: "For that, let me alone. I have a trick in my budget." (13.65–67). As far as I read the performance of this moment, Sybil suggests she has a dildo in the bag upon her arm. (Because "budget" could be slang for the vagina, the joke does not just allude to, but also materializes, the sex act.) For early modern lubricants, their history, and their variety of uses, see Gamble, *Sex Lives*, 57–74.

17. The word "aunt" could be slang for "whore." "aunt, n. def. 3." *Oxford English Dictionary*, Oxford University Press, September 2023. The citation provides the example of Dekker and Middleton's *The Honest Whore Part 1* (1604).

18. Fisher has traced the history and practice of early modern sex acts in a series of articles. See "The Erotics of Chin Chucking in Seventeenth-Century England," in *Sex Before Sex: Figuring the Act in Early Modern England*, ed. James Bromley and Will Stockton (Minneapolis: University of Minnesota Press, 2013), 141–69; "'Wantoning with Thighs': The Socialization of Thigh Sex in England, 1590–1730," *Journal of the History of Sexuality* 24 no. 1 (2015): 1–24; "'Stray[ing] lower where the pleasant fountains lie': Cunnilingus in *Venus and Adonis* and in English Culture, c. 1600–1700," in *The Oxford Handbook of Shakespeare and Embodiment: Gender, Sexuality, and Race*, ed. Valerie Traub (New York: Oxford University Press, 2016), 333–46.

19. Dekker, *The Shoemaker's Holiday*, 157n29–30.

20. Stanley Wells, *Looking for Sex in Shakespeare* (New York: Cambridge University Press, 2004), 10–37.

21. Ronda Arab, *Manly Mechanicals on the Early Modern English Stage* (Selinsgrove, PA: Susquehanna University Press, 2011), 55.

# Bibliography

Adelman, Janet. *Suffocating Mothers: Fantasies of Maternal Origin in Shakespeare's Plays, "Hamlet" to "The Tempest"*. New York: Routledge, 1991.

Akhimie, Patricia. *Shakespeare and the Cultivation of Difference: Race and Conduct in the Early Modern World*. New York: Routledge, 2018.

Amussen, Susan D. *An Ordered Society: Gender and Class in Early Modern England*. New York: Columbia University Press, 1988.

Arab, Ronda. *Manly Mechanicals on the Early Modern Stage*. Selinsgrove, PA: Susquehanna University Press, 2011.

Archer, Ian. *The Pursuit of Stability: Social Relations in Elizabethan London*. New York: Cambridge University Press, 1991.

Arvas, Abdulhamit. "Early Modern Eunuchs and the Transing of Gender and Race." *Journal for Early Modern Cultural Studies* 19, no. 4 (Fall 2019): 116–36.

Astington, John H. "The Ages of Man and the Lord Mayor's Show." In *Other Voices, Other Views: Expanding the Canon in English Renaissance Studies*, edited by Helen Ostovich, Mary V. Silcox, and Graham Roebuck, 74–90. Newark: University of Delaware Press, 1999.

———. "Malvolio and the Eunuchs: Texts and Revels in *Twelfth Night*." *Shakespeare Survey* 46, edited by Stanley Wells (1993): 24–34.

Attridge, Derek. *Peculiar Language: Literature as Difference from the Renaissance to James Joyce*. New York: Routledge, 2004.

Aubrey, John. *Brief Lives*. Edited by Andrew Clark. 2 vols. Oxford: Clarendon, 1898.

Babb, Lawrence. *The Elizabethan Malady: A Study of Melancholia in English Literature from 1580 to 1642*. East Lansing: Michigan State College Press, 1951.

———. "Melancholy and the Elizabethan Man of Letters." *Huntington Library Quarterly* 4, no. 3 (April 1941): 247–61.

Bach, Rebecca Ann. *Shakespeare and Renaissance Literature Before Heterosexuality*. New York: Palgrave, 2007.

———. "Tennis Balls: 'Henry V' and Testicular Masculinity, or, According to the 'OED,' Shakespeare Doesn't Have Any Balls." *Renaissance Drama* 30 (1999–2001): 3–23.

*The Bachelor's Banquet*, edited by Faith Gildenhuys. Ottawa: Dovehouse, 1993.

Bacon, Francis. *The Essayes or Counsels Civill and Morall*, edited by Michael Kiernan. New York: Oxford University Press, 1985.

———. *The Essaies of Sir Francis Bacon Knight, the Kings Solliciters Generall*. London: 1612.

Bailey, Amanda. *Flaunting: Style and the Subversive Male Body in Renaissance England.* Toronto: University of Toronto Press, 2007.

———, and Roze Hentschell, eds. *Masculinity and the Metropolis of Vice.* Early Modern Cultural Studies. New York: Palgrave Macmillan, 2010.

Barbaro, Francesco. *Direction for Love and Marriage: In Two Books.* London, 1677.

Bartholin, Thomas. *Bartholinus Anatomy; Made from the Precepts of his Father, and From the Observations of all Modern Anatomists, together with his own.* Published by Nich. Culpeper Gent. and Abdiah Cole Doctor of Physick. London, 1668.

Bassi, Serena and Greta LaFleur. "Introduction: TERFS, Gender-Critical Movements, and Postfascist Feminisms." *TSQ: Transgender Studies Quarterly* 9, no. 3 (August 2022): 311–33.

Basu, Anupam. "'Like Very Honest and Substantial Citizens': Cony-Catching as Social Performance." *ELR* 44, no. 1 (Winter 2014): 36–55.

*The Batchelars Banquet: Or A Banquet for Batchelars.* London, 1603.

Bates, Catherine. *Masculinity and the Hunt: Wyatt to Spenser.* Oxford: Oxford University Press, 2016.

———. *Masculinity, Gender and Identity in the English Renaissance Lyric.* Cambridge, UK: Cambridge University Press, 2007.

Bates, Laura. *Men Who Hate Women, From Incels to Pickup Artists: The Truth about Extreme Misogyny and How It Affects Us All.* Naperville, IL: Sourcebooks, 2020.

Baudier, Michel. *The History of the Serrail, and of the Court of the Grand Seigneur, Emperour of the Turkes.* Translated by Edward Grimeston. London, 1635.

Beaumont, Francis, and John Fletcher. *Wit Without Money: A Comedie.* London, 1639.

Becon, Thomas, trans. *The golden boke of christen matrimonye.* 1542.

Behrend-Martínez, Edward. "Manhood and the Neutered Body in Early Modern Spain." *Social History* 38, no. 4 (Summer 2005): 1073–93.

Belsey, Catherine. *Shakespeare and the Loss of Eden: The Construction of Family Values in Early Modern Culture.* New Brunswick, NJ: Rutgers University Press, 1999.

Ben-Amos, Ilana Krausman. *Adolescence and Youth in Early Modern England.* New Haven, CT: Yale University Press, 1994.

Bennett, Judith M. *History Matters: Patriarchy and the Challenge of Feminism.* Philadelphia: University of Pennsylvania Press, 2006.

Bennet, Judith M., and Amy Froide, eds. *Singlewomen in the European Past, 1250–1800.* Philadelphia: University of Pennsylvania Press, 1999.

Bey, Marquis. *Black Trans Feminism.* Durham, NC: Duke University Press, 2021.

Bicks, Caroline. "Planned Parenthood: Minding the Quick Woman in *All's Well.*" *Modern Philology* 103, no. 3 (February 2006): 299–331.

Bix, Karen Helfand. "'Masters of Their Occupation': Labor and Fellowship in the Cony-Catching Pamphlets." In *Rogues and Early Modern English Culture*, edited by Craig Dionne and Steve Mentz, 171–92. Ann Arbor: University of Michigan Press, 2004.

Bjork-James, Sophie. "Racializing Misogyny: Sexuality and Gender in the New Online White Nationalism." *Feminist Anthropology* 1, no. 2 (2020): 176–83.

Blank, Paula. "The Proverbial 'Lesbian': Queering Etymology in Contemporary Critical Practice." *Modern Philology* 109, no. 1 (August 2011): 108–34.

Bloom, Harold. *Shakespeare: The Invention of the Human.* New York: Riverhead, 1999.

Bly, Mary. "Playing the Tourist in Early Modern London: Selling the Liberties Onstage." *PMLA* 122, no. 1 (January 2007): 61–71.

*The booke of the common praier and administration of the Sacraments, and other rites and ceremonies of the Church: after the vse of the Churche of Englande.* London, 1549.

Bosman, Anston. "'Best Play with Mardian': Eunuch and Blackamoor as Imperial Culturegram." *Shakespeare Studies* 34 (2006): 123–57.

Bradbrook, M. C. "Virtue is the True Nobility: A Study of the Structure of *All's Well That Ends Well.*" *Review of English Studies* 1, no. 4 (October 1950): 289–301.

Braham, Humfrey. *The Institution of a gentleman.* London 1555, rep. 1568.

Brake. Elizabeth. *Minimizing Marriage: Marriage Morality, and the Law.* New York: Oxford University Press, 2012.

Bray, Alan. *The Friend.* Chicago: University of Chicago Press, 2003.

Breitenberg, Mark. *Anxious Masculinity in Early Modern England.* Cambridge, UK: Cambridge University Press, 1996.

Breton, Nicolas. *The Goode and The Badde, or Descriptions of the Worthies and Vnworthies of this Age.* London, 1616.

Bridges, Tristan, and C. J. Pascoe. "Hybrid Masculinities: New Directions in the Sociology of Men and Masculinities." *Sociology Compass* 8, no. 3 (March 2014): 246–58.

Britton, Dennis Austin. *Becoming Christian: Race, Reformation, and Early Modern English Romance.* New York: Fordham University Press, 2014.

Bromley, James M. *Intimacy and Sexuality in the Age of Shakespeare.* New York: Cambridge University Press, 2012.

Bonfield, Lloyd, Richard M. Smith, and Keith Wrightson, eds. *The World We Have Gained: Histories of Population and Social Structure.* London: Blackwell, 1986.

Bullinger, Heinrich. *The golden boke of christen matrimonye.* Translated by Theodore Basille. 1543.

Burton, Robert. *The Anatomy of Melancholy.* Vols. 1–6, edited by Thomas Faulkner, et al. New York: Oxford University Press, 1981–2001.

Butler, Judith. *Bodies That Matter: On the Discursive Limits of Sex.* New York: Routledge, 1993.

———. *Gender Trouble: Feminism and the Subversion of Identity.* New York: Routledge, 1990.

———. *Undoing Gender.* New York: Routledge, 2004.

Butler, Martin. *Theatre and Crisis, 1632–1640.* New York: Cambridge University Press, 1984.

Buttes, Henry. *Dyets Dry Dinner.* London, 1599.

Callaghan, Dympna. *Shakespeare Without Women: Representing Gender and Race on the Renaissance Stage.* New York: Routledge, 2000.

Calver, Edward. *Passion and Discretion in Youth and Age.* London, 1641.

Carlson, Eric Josef. *Marriage and the English Reformation.* Oxford: Blackwell, 1994.

Caton, Mary Anne. "'Fables and Fruit Trenchers Teach as Much': English Banqueting Trenchers, c. 1585–1662." *Magazine Antiques* 169, no. 6 (2006): 112–19.

Cavallo, Sandra. "Bachelorhood and Masculinity in Renaissance and Early Modern Italy." *European History Quarterly* 38, no. 3 (2008): 375–96.

Chakravarty, Urvashi. *Fictions of Consent: Slavery, Servitude, and Free Service in Early Modern England.* Philadelphia: University of Pennsylvania Press, 2022.

Chasin, C. J. DeLuzio. "Reconsidering Asexuality and Its Radical Potential." *Feminist Studies* 39, no. 2 (2013): 405–26.

Chen, Mel Y. "Animals Without Genitals." In *The Transgender Studies Reader 2*, edited by Susan Stryker and Aren Z. Aizura, 168–77. New York: Routledge, 2013.

Chess, Simone. *Male-to-Female Crossdressing in Early Modern English Literature.* New York: Routledge, 2016.

Chudacoff, Howard P. *The Age of the Bachelor: Creating an American Subculture.* Princeton: Princeton University Press, 1999.

Clark, Peter. *The English Alehouse: A Social History 1200–1830.* London: Longman, 1983.

Clary, Christopher. "Moll's Queer Anatomy: *The Roaring Girl* and Queer Generation." In *Staging Shakespeare for Performance: The Bear Stage*, edited by Catherine Loomis and Sid Ray, 91–102. Vancouver: Farleigh Dickinson University Press, 2016.

Clay, C. G. A. *Economic Expansion and Social Change: England 1500–1700, vol. 1. People, Land and Towns.* New York: Cambridge University Press, 1984.

Cobb, Michael. *Single: Arguments for the Uncoupled.* New York: New York University Press, 2012.

Cogan, Thomas. *The Haven of Health.* London, 1584.

Collington, Philip D. "A 'Pennyworth' of Marital Advice: Bachelors and Ballad Culture in *Much Ado About Nothing.*" In *Shakespeare's Comedies of Love: Essays in Honour of Alexander Leggatt*, edited by Karen Bamford and Ric Knowles, 30–54. Toronto: University of Toronto Press, 2008.

Connell, R. W. *Masculinities.* 2nd ed. Berkeley: University of California Press, 2005.

Connell, R. W., and James W. Messerschmidt. "Hegemonic Masculinity: Rethinking the Concept." *Gender & Society* 19, no. 6 (December 2005): 829–59.

Cooper, Nicholas. "Rank, Manners and Displays: The Gentlemanly House, 1500–1750." *Transactions of the Royal Historical Society* 12 (2002): 291–310.

Cooper, Thomas. *Thesaura Linguæ Romanæ et Britannicæ.* London, 1584.

Cote, David. "Review: Robert Icke's Production of 'Hamlet' Misguidedly Embraces the Prince's Incel-Nature." *The Observer* (website), June 30, 2022, accessed September 2, 2023.

Cotgrave, Randle. *A Dictionarie of the French and English Tongues.* London, 1612.

Cowell, John. *The Interpreter: or Book Containing the Signification of Words.* London, 1607.

Crane, William G. *Wit and Rhetoric in the Renaissance: The Formal Basis of Elizabethan Prose Style.* New York: Columbia University Press, 1937.

Crawford, Julie. "All's Well That Ends Well, Or, Is Marriage Always Already Heterosexual?" In *Shakesqueer: A Queer Companion to the Complete Works of Shakespeare*, edited by Madhavi Menon, 39–47. Durham, NC: Duke University Press, 2011.

————. *Mediatrix: Women, Politics, and Literary Production in Early Modern England.* Oxford: Oxford University Press, 2014.

Crawford, Katherine. *Eunuchs and Castrati: Disability and Normativity in Early Modern Europe.* New York: Routledge, 2019.

Crofts, Robert. *The Lover: or Nuptiall Love.* London, 1638.

Crooke, Helkiah. *Mikrokosmographia: A Description of the Body of Man.* London, 1615.

Culpepper, Nicholas. *A Directory for Midwives, or, A Guide For Women.* London, 1651.

Currah, Paisley. *Sex Is As Sex Does: Governing Transgender Identity.* New York: New York University Press, 2022.

Curtis, Mark H. *Oxford and Cambridge in Transition.* Oxford: Oxford University Press, 1959.

Dadabhoy, Ambereen. *Shakespeare Through Islamic Worlds.* New York: Routledge, 2023.

Daniel, Drew. *The Melancholy Assemblage: Affect and Epistemology in the English Renaissance.* New York: Fordham University Press, 2013.

Davies, Sir John. *The Complete Poems of Sir John Davies.* Edited by Rev. Alexander B. Vol. 2. London: Chatto & Windus, 1876.

Davies, Matthew, and Ann Saunders. *The History of the Merchant Taylors' Company.* Leeds: Maney, 2004.

Davis, Natalie Zemon. "A Trade Union in Sixteenth-Century France." *Economic History Review* 19, no. 1 (April 1966): 48–69.

————. "The Reasons of Misrule: Youth Groups and Charivaris in Sixteenth-Century France." *Past & Present* 50, no. 1 (February 1971): 41–75.

De Barros, Eric. "*Hamlet* and the Education of the White Self." In *White People in Shakespeare: Essays on Race, Culture and the Elite*, edited by Arthur Little Jr., 165–76. New York: Bloomsbury, 2021.

de Grazia, Margreta. *Hamlet without Hamlet.* New York: Cambridge University Press, 2007.

————. "The Scandal of Shakespeare's Sonnets." *Shakespeare Survey* 46 (1993): 35–49.

Dekker, Thomas. *The Shoemaker's Holiday*, edited by R. L. Smallwood and Stanley Wells. Manchester, UK: Manchester University Press, 1999.

————. "The Shoemaker's Holiday." In *The Roaring Girl and Other City Comedies*, edited by James Knowles, 1–65. New York: Oxford University Press, 2001.

Dekker, Thomas, and John Webster. "Westward Ho." In *The Dramatic Works of Thomas Dekker*, edited by Fredson Bowers, vol. 2, 318–403. New York: Cambridge University Press, 1955.

Dekker, Thomas, and Thomas Middleton. "The Honest Whore, Part 1." In *The Dramatic Works of Thomas Dekker*, edited by Fredson Bowers, vol. 2, 1–130. Cambridge, UK: Cambridge University Press, 1955.

Dennis, Carl. "Wit and Wisdom in *Much Ado About Nothing.*" *SEL, 1500–1900* 13, no. 2 (Spring 1973): 223–37.

DiGangi, Mario. *Homoerotics of Early Modern Drama.* New York: Cambridge University Press, 1997.

————. *Sexual Types: Embodiment, Agency, and Dramatic Character from Shakespeare to Shirley.* Philadelphia: University of Pennsylvania Press, 2011.

Dignam, Pierce Alexander, and Deana A. Rohlinger. "Misogynistic Men Online: How the Red Pill Helped Elect Trump." *Signs* 44, no. 3 (Spring 2019): 589–612.

Dolan, Frances E. *Marriage and Violence: The Early Modern Legacy*. Philadelphia: University of Pennsylvania Press, 2008.

Dollimore, Jonathan. *Sexual Dissidence: Augustine to Wilde, Freud to Foucault*. Oxford: Clarendon Press, 1991.

Donne, John. *John Donne's Poetry*. Edited by Donald R. Dickson. New York: W. W. Norton, 2007.

Dryden, John. "An Essay of Dramatic Poesy." In *The Major Works*, edited by Keith Walker, 70–129. New York: Oxford University Press, 1987.

Dubrow, Heather. "'Incertainties now Crown Themselves Assur'd': The Politics of Plotting Shakespeare's Sonnets." *Shakespeare Quarterly* 47, no. 3 (October 1996): 291–305.

Dugan, Holly. "Early Modern Tranimals: 57312*." *Journal for Early Modern Cultural Studies* 19, no. 4 (Fall 2019): 178–205.

Edelman, Lee. "Ever After: History, Negativity, and the Social." In *After Sex? On Writing Since Queer Theory*, edited by Janet Halley and Andrew Parker, 110–18. Durham, NC: Duke University Press, 2011.

———. *No Future: Queer Theory and the Death Drive*. Durham, NC: Duke University Press, 2004.

Elam, Keir. "The Fertile Eunuch: *Twelfth Night*, Early Modern Intercourse, and the Fruits of Castration." *Shakespeare Quarterly* 47, no. 1 (Spring 1996): 1–36.

Eliot. T. S. *The Sacred Wood: Essays on Poetry and Criticism*. New York: Barnes and Noble, 1953.

Emens, Elizabeth F. "Compulsory Sexuality." *Stanford Law Review* 66, no. 2 (February 2014): 303–86.

Engle, Lars. "Shakespearean Normativity in *All's Well That Ends Well*." In *The Shakespearean International Yearbook*, edited by Graham Bradshaw, Tom Bishop, and Mark Turner, vol. 4, 264–78. Burlington, VT: Ashgate, 2004.

Erasmus, Desiderius. *A ryght frutefull Epystle deuysed by the moste excellent clerke Erasmus in laude and prayse of matrimony*. Translated by Rychard Tauernour. 1536.

———. "Defense of His Declamation in Praise of Marriage (1519)." Translated by David Sider. In *Daughters, Wives, and Widows: Writings by Men About Women and Marriage in England, 1500–1640*, edited by Joan Larsen Klein, 89–96. Urbana: University of Illinois Press, 1992.

Evans, Jennifer. *Aphrodisiacs, Fertility and Medicine in Early Modern England*. Suffolk, UK: Boydell Press, 2014.

———. "'They Are Called Imperfect Men': Male Infertility and Sexual Health in Early Modern England." *Social History of Medicine* 29, no. 2 (May 2016): 311–32.

"THE FANATICKS BARBER. / OR, / A New Cut for NON-CONFORMISTS. / Being a true Relation of the PARSON that was lately Gelt at Chemsford in Essex, / being taken in Bed with another Mans Wife. / Very proper to be sung in all Corporations of this Nation. / All the Town shan't save thee." British Library. Luttrell

Ballads, C.20.f.4. (80). EBBA 36464, Patricia Fumerton, dir., English Broadside Ballad Archive (website).

Ferne, John. *The Blazon of Gentrie: Deuivded into two part. The First named The Glorie of Generositie. The Second Lacyes Nobilitie. Comprehending discourses of Armes of Gentry.* London, 1586.

Fields, Karen E., and Barbara J. Fields. *Racecraft: The Soul of Inequality in American Life.* New York: Verso, 2014.

Fish, Stanley E. *Self-Consuming Artifacts: The Experience of Seventeenth-Century Literature.* Berkeley: University of California Press, 1972.

Fisher, F. J. "The Development of London as a Centre of Conspicuous Consumption in the Sixteenth and Seventeenth Centuries." *Transactions of the Royal Historical Society* 30 (December 1948): 37–50.

———. *London and the English Economy,* edited by P. J. Corfield and N. B. Harte. London: Hambledon Press, 1990.

Fisher, Will. "The Erotics of Chin Chucking in Seventeenth-Century England." In *Sex Before Sex: Figuring the Act in Early Modern England,* edited by James Bromley and Will Stockton, 141–69. Minneapolis: University of Minnesota Press, 2013.

———. *Materializing Gender in Early Modern English Literature and Culture.* New York: Cambridge University Press, 2006.

———. "'Stray[ing] lower where the pleasant fountains lie': Cunnilingus in *Venus and Adonis* and in English Culture, c. 1600–1700." In *The Oxford Handbook of Shakespeare and Embodiment: Gender, Sexuality, and Race,* ed. Valerie Traub, 333–46. New York: Oxford University Press, 2016.

———. "'Wantoning with Thighs': The Socialization of Thigh Sex in England, 1590–1730." *Journal of the History of Sexuality* 24 no. 1 (January 2015): 1–24.

Flachmann, Michael, ed. "The First English Epistolary Novel: *The Image of Idleness* (1555). Text, Introduction, and Notes." *Studies in Philology* 87, no. 1 (1990): 1–74.

Fletcher, Anthony. *Gender, Sex, and Subordination in England 1500–1800.* New Haven, CT: Yale University Press, 1995.

Flore, Jacinthe. "Mismeasures of Asexual Desires." In *Asexualities: Feminist and Queer Perspectives,* edited by Karli June Cerankowski and Megan Milks, 17–34. New York: Routledge, 2014.

Florio, John. *A World of Wordes, Or a Most copious, and exact Dictionarie in Italian and English.* London, 1598.

———. "Men's Dilemma: The Future of Patriarchy in England 1560–1660." *Transactions of the Royal Historical Society* 4 (1994): 61–81.

Foucault, Michel. *The History of Sexuality: An Introduction,* vol. 1. Translated by Robert Hurley. New York: Vintage, 1990.

Freccero, Carla. *Queer / Early / Modern.* Durham, NC: Duke University Press, 2006.

Freeman, Elizabeth. *Time Binds: Queer Temporalities, Queer Histories.* Durham, NC: Duke University Press, 2010.

Friedlander, Ari. *Rogue Sexuality in Early Modern English Literature: Desire, Status, Biopolitics.* New York: Oxford University Press, 2022.

Froide, Amy M. *Never Married: Singlewomen in Early Modern England.* Oxford: Oxford University Press, 2005.

———. *Silent Partners: Women as Public Investors during Britain's Financial Revolution, 1690–1750.* Oxford: Oxford University Press, 2016.

Foyster, Elizabeth A. *Manhood in Early Modern England: Honour, Sex and Marriage.* New York: Longman, 1999.

Gamble, Joseph. *Sex Lives: Intimate Infrastructures in Early Modernity.* Philadelphia: University of Pennsylvania Press, 2023.

Gataker, Thomas. *A Good Wife Gods Gift: And, Wife Indeed. Two Marriage Sermons.* London, 1623.

Gayley, Charles Mills. *Francis Beaumont: Dramatist, A Portrait, with Some Account of His Circle, Elizabethan and Jacobean, and of His Association with John Fletcher.* London: Duckworth & Co., 1914.

*The Geneva Bible: A Facsimile of the 1560 Edition.* Peabody: Hendrickson, 2007.

Gibson, Thomas. *The Anatomy of Humane Bodies Epitomized.* London, 1682.

Gill-Peterson, Jules. *Histories of the Transgender Child.* Minneapolis: University of Minnesota Press, 2018.

Girtin, Thomas. *The Golden Ram: A Narrative History of the Clothworkers' Company, 1528–1958.* London: Worshipful Company of Clothworkers, 1958.

Glace, Alyssa M., Tessa L. Dover, and Judith G. Zatkin. "Taking the Black Pill: An Empirical Analysis of the 'Incel,'" *Psychology of Men & Masculinities* 22, no. 2 (2021): 288–97.

Goldberg, Jonathan. *Sodometries: Renaissance Texts, Modern Sexualities.* Stanford, CA: Stanford University Press, 1992.

———. and Madhavi Menon. "Queering History." *PMLA* 120, no. 5 (October 2005): 1608–1617.

Gordon, Colby. "A Woman's Prick: Trans Technogenesis in Sonnet 20." In *Shakespeare / Sex: Contemporary Readings in Gender and Sexuality*, edited by Jennifer Drouin, 268–89. New York: Bloomsbury, 2020.

Gouge, William. *Of Domesticall Duties: Eight Treatise.* London, 1622.

Gowing, Laura. *Common Bodies: Women, Touch, and Power in Seventeenth-Century England.* New Haven, CT: Yale University Press, 2013.

G. P. *The Phoenix Nest, 1593*, edited by Hyder Edward Rollins. Cambridge, MA: Harvard University Press, 1931.

Greenblatt, Stephen. *Shakespearean Negotiations: The Circulation of Social Energy in Renaissance England.* Berkeley: University of California Press, 1988.

Griffin, Ben. "Hegemonic Masculinity as a Historical Problem." *Gender & History* 30, no. 2 (July 2018): 377–400.

Griffiths, Paul. *Youth and Authority: Formative Experience in England 1560–1640.* New York: Oxford University Press, 1996.

Guillory, John. "The Bachelor State: Philosophy and Sovereignty in Bacon's *New Atlantis*." In *Politics and the Passions, 1500–1850*, edited by Victoria Kahn, Neil Saccamanto, and Daniela Coli, 49–74. Princeton: Princeton University Press, 2006.

Gupta, Kristina. "Compulsory Sexuality: Evaluating an Emerging Concept." *Signs*, 41, no. 1 (Autumn 2015): 131–54.

Guy-Bray, Stephen. *Homoerotic Space: The Poetics of Loss in Renaissance Literature*. Toronto: University of Toronto Press, 2002.

———. *Shakespeare and Queer Representation*. New York: Routledge, 2021.

Habib, Imtiaz. "'Two loves I have of comfort and despair': The Circle of Whiteness in the *Sonnets*." In *White People in Shakespeare: Essays on Race, Culture, and the Elite*, edited by Arthur Little Jr, 29–44. New York: Bloomsbury, 2023.

Haddot, Pierre. *What Is Ancient Philosophy?* Translated by Michael Chase. Cambridge, MA: Belknap Press of Harvard University Press, 2002.

Hall, Kim F. "'These Bastard Signs of Fair': Literary Whiteness in Shakespeare's Sonnets." In *Post-Colonial Shakespeares*, edited by Ania Loomba and Martin Orkin, 65–83. New York: Routledge, 1998.

———. *Things of Darkness: Economies of Race and Gender in Early Modern England*. Ithaca, NY: Cornell University Press, 1995.

Hanson, Elizabeth. "Fellow Students: Hamlet, Horatio, and the Early Modern University." *Shakespeare Quarterly* 62, no. 2 (Summer 2011): 205–29.

———. "'There's Meat and Money Too': Rich Widows and Allegories of Wealth in Jacobean City Comedy." *ELH* 72, no. 1 (Spring 2005): 209–38.

Harris, Cheryl I. "Whiteness as Property." *Harvard Law Review* 106, no. 8 (June 1993): 1707–91.

Hartmann, Heidi. "The Unhappy Marriage of Marxism and Feminism: Towards A More Progressive Union." In *Women and Revolution: A Discussion of the Unhappy Marriage of Marxism and Feminism*, edited by Lydia Sargent. Boston: South End Press, 1981.

Harris, Jonathan Gil. "All Swell That End Swell: Dropsy, Phantom Pregnancy, and the Sound of Deconception in *All's Well That Ends Well*." *Renaissance Drama* 35 (2006): 169–89.

Harrison, William. *The Description of England*. Edited by Georges Edelen. London, 1587. repr. Ithaca, NY: Cornell University Press, 1968.

Hathaway, Jane. *Beshir Agha: Chief Eunuch of the Ottoman Imperial Harem*. London: Oneworld, 2006.

Hazlitt, W. C. *The Livery Companies of London: Their Origin, Character, Development, and Social and Political Importance*. New York: Blom, 1892, 1969.

Heal, Felicity and Clive Holmes. *The Gentry in England and Wales, 1500–1700*. Stanford, CA: Stanford University Press, 1994.

Henderson-Merrygold, Jo. "The Present and Future of Trans Hermeneutics. Viewing Sarah Cispiciously: Cisnormalisation, and the Problem of Cisnormativity." *Society of Biblical Literature Annual Meeting*, Denver, November 17–21. 2018. Conference Presentation. Humanities Commons (website).

Herrick, Robert. *Works of Robert Herrick*, vol. 1, edited by Alfred Pollard. London: Lawrence and Bullen, 1891.

Hill, Tracey. *Pageantry and Power: A Cultural History of the Early Modern Lord Mayor's Show, 1585–1639*. Manchester, UK: Manchester University Press, 2010.

Hirschfeld, Heather. "What Do Women Know?: *The Roaring Girl* and the Wisdom of Tiresias." *Renaissance Drama* 32 (2003): 123–46.

Holinshed, Raphael, et al. *The First and Second Volumes of Chronicles*. London, 1586.

Horbury, Ezra. "Transgender Reassessments of the Cross-Dressed Page in Shakespeare, *Philaster*, and *The Honest Man's Fortune*." *Shakespeare Quarterly* 73, no. 1–2 (Summer 2022): 100–120.

Howard, Jean. *Stage and Social Struggle in Early Modern England*. New York: Routledge, 1994.

Huloet, Richard. *Huloets Dictionarie newelye corrected, amended*. London, 1572.

Irish, Bradley J. *Emotion in the Tudor Court: Literature, History, and Early Modern Feeling*. Chicago: Northwestern University Press, 2018.

Jankowski, Theodora A. *Pure Resistance: Queer Virginity in Early Modern English Drama*. Philadelphia: University of Pennsylvania Press, 2000.

Johnson, A. H. *The History of The Worshipful Company of the Drapers of London*, vol. 2. Oxford: Oxford University Press, 1914.

Jonson, Ben. *The Complete Plays of Ben Jonson*. Edited by G. A. Wilkes, vol. 3. Oxford: Clarendon, 1982.

———. *Epicene, or the Silent Woman*, edited by Richard Dutton. Manchester, UK: Manchester University Press, 2003.

———. *Every Man Out of His Humour*. Edited by Helen Ostovich. Manchester, UK: Manchester University Press, 2001.

Kahan, Benjamin. *Celibacies: American Modernism and Sexual Life*. Durham, NC: Duke University Press, 2013.

Kahn, Coppélia. *Man's Estate: Masculine Identity in Shakespeare*. Berkeley: University of California Press, 1981.

Karras, Ruth Mazzo. *From Boys to Men: Formations of Masculinity in Late Medieval Europe*. Philadelphia: University of Pennsylvania Press, 2003.

Kastan, David Scott. "All's Well That Ends Well and the Limits of Comedy." *ELH* 52 (1985): 575–89.

Kathman, David. "Grocers, Goldsmiths, and Drapers: Freemen and Apprentices in the Elizabethan Theater." *Shakespeare Quarterly* 55, no. 1 (Spring 2004): 1–49.

Katz, Jonathan Ned. *The Invention of Heterosexuality*. Chicago: University of Chicago Press, 1995.

Katz, Joshua T. "Testimonia Ritus Italici: Male Genitalia, Solemn Declarations, and a New Latin Sound Law." *Harvard Studies in Classical Philology* 98 (1998): 183–217.

Kemp, Sawyer. "'In That Dimension Grossly Clad': Transgender Rhetoric, Representation, and Shakespeare." *Shakespeare Studies* 49 (2019): 120–26.

King, Thomas A. *The Gendering of Men, 1600–1750: The English Phallus*, vol. 1. Madison: University of Wisconsin Press, 2004.

———. *The Gendering of Men, 1600–1750: Queer Articulations*, vol. 2. Madison: University of Wisconsin Press, 2008.

Kitzes, Adam. *The Politics of Melancholy from Spenser to Milton*. New York: Routledge, 2006.

Knight, G. Wilson. *The Sovereign Flower*. London: Metheun, 1958.

Korda, Natasha. "'The Sign of the Last': Gender, Material Culture, and Artisanal Nostalgia in *The Shoemaker's Holiday*." *Journal of Medieval and Early Modern Studies* 43, no. 3 (Fall 2013): 573–97.

Kuefler, Mathew. *The Manly Eunuch: Masculinity, Gender Ambiguity, and Christian Ideology in Late Antiquity.* Chicago: University of Chicago Press, 2001.

LaFleur, Greta. "Heterosexuality Without Women." *BLARB* (website), Los Angeles Review of Books, May 20, 2019.

Lambert, Sheila. "Journeymen and Master Printers in the early Seventeenth Century." *Journal of the Printing Historical Society* 21 (1992): 13–27.

"The Lamentation of a new married man." (London, ca. 1630). Pepys Library. Pepys Ballads 1.380–81. EBBA 20176, Patricia Fumerton, dir., English Broadside Ballad Archive (website).

Laqueur, Thomas. *Making Sex: Body and Gender from the Greeks to Freud.* Cambridge, MA: Harvard University Press, 1992.

Lavin, Talia. *Culture Warlords: My Journey in the Dark Web of White Supremacy.* New York: Hatchette, 2020.

Leeson, R. A. *Travelling Brothers: The Six Centuries' Road from Craft Fellowship to Unionism.* London: Allen & Unwin, 1979.

Lenton, Francis. *Characterismi: or, Lentons Leisures. Expressed in Essayes and Characters.* London, 1636.

Libby, C. "Sympathy, Fear, Hate: Trans-Exclusionary Radical Feminism and Evangelical Christianity." *TSQ: Transgender Studies Quarterly* 9, no. 3 (August 2022): 425–42.

Love, Heather. *Feeling Backward: Loss and the Politics of Queer History.* Cambridge, MA: Harvard University Press, 2007.

Low, Jennifer. *Manhood and the Duel: Masculinity in Early Modern Drama and Culture.* New York: Palgrave, 2003.

Lund, Mary Ann. *Melancholy, Medicine, and Religion in Early Modern England.* New York: Cambridge University Press, 2010.

Lupton, Julia Reinhard. *Thinking with Shakespeare: Essays on Politics and Life.* Chicago: University of Chicago Press, 2011.

Lyell, Laetitia. *Acts of Court of the Mercers' Company, 1453–1527.* London, 1936.

Lyons, Bridget Gellert. *Voices of Melancholy: Studies in Literary Treatments of Melancholy in Renaissance England.* New York: Routledge, 1971.

MacDonald, Joyce Green. *Women and Race in Early Modern Texts.* New York: Cambridge University Press, 2002.

Machyn, Henry. *The Diary of Henry Machyn: Citizen and Merchant-Taylor of Londonm 1550–1563*, edited by J. G. Nichols. London, 1848. British History Online (website).

Manley, Lawrence. *Literature and Culture in Early Modern London.* New York: Cambridge University Press, 1995.

Manne, Kate. *Down Girl: The Logic of Misogyny.* New York: Oxford University Press, 2018.
———. *Entitled: How Male Privilege Hurts Women.* New York: Crown, 2021.

Marlow, Christopher. *Performing Masculinity in English University Drama, 1598–1636.* New York: Routledge, 2016.

Maslen, R. W. "*The Image of Idleness* in the Reign of Elizabeth I." *English Language Notes* 41, no. 3 (2004): 11–23.

Masten, Jeffrey. "Editing Boys: The Performance of Gender in Print." In *Redefining British Theatre History: From Performance to Print*, edited by Peter Holland and Stephen Orgel, 113–34. New York: Palgrave, 2006.

———. *Queer Philologies: Sex, Language, and Affect in Shakespeare's Time*. Philadelphia: University of Pennsylvania Press, 2016.

———. *Textual Intercourse: Collaboration, Authorship, and Sexualities in Renaissance Drama*. New York: Cambridge University Press, 1997.

Matz, Robert. "The Scandals of Shakespeare's Sonnets." *ELH* 77, no. 2 (Summer 2010): 477–508.

McCandless, David. "Helena's Bed-Trick: Gender and Performance in *All's Well That Ends Well*." *Shakespeare Quarterly* 45, no. 4 (Winter 1994): 449–68.

McClive, Cathy. "Masculinity on Trial: Penises, Hermaphrodites and the Uncertain Male Body in Early Modern France." *History Workshop Journal* 68, no. 1 (Autumn 2009): 45–68.

McCurdy, John Gilbert. *Citizen Bachelors: Manhood and the Creation of the United States*. Ithaca, NY: Cornell University Press, 2009.

Menon, Madhavi. "Spurning Teleology in Venus and Adonis." *GLQ* 11, no. 4 (2005): 491–519.

Middleton, Thomas, and Thomas Dekker. *The Roaring Girl*. Edited by Paul A. Mulholland. Manchester, UK: Manchester University Press, 1999.

Middleton, Thomas. *Thomas Middleton: The Collected Works*, edited by Gary Taylor and John Lavagnino. Oxford: Clarendon, 2007.

Mill, John Stuart. *The Collected Works*, vol. 4, edited by J. M. Robson. Toronto: University of Toronto Press, 1967.

Mingay, G. E. *The Gentry: The Rise and Fall of a Ruling Class*. New York: Longman, 1976.

Mitchell, David T., and Sharon L. Snyder. *Narrative Prosthesis: Disability and the Dependencies of Discourse*. Ann Arbor: University of Michigan Press, 2001.

Mitchell, Schuyler. "The Right's Creeping Pro-Natalist Rhetoric on Abortion and Trans Health Care." *The Intercept* (website). May 17, 2022.

Morgan, Victor, and Christopher Brooke. *A History of the University of Cambridge*. vol. 2. 1546–1750. New York: Cambridge University Press, 2004.

Mortimer, Claire. *Romantic Comedy*. New York: Routledge, 2010.

Muldrew, Craig. *The Economy of Obligation: The Culture of Credit and Social Relations in Early Modern England*. New York: Macmillan, 1998.

Mullaney, Steven. "Mourning and Misogyny: Hamlet, The Revenger's Tragedy, and the Final Progress of Elizabeth I, 1600–1607." *Shakespeare Quarterly* 45, no. 2 (Summer 1994): 139–62.

Mullinger, James Bass. *The University of Cambridge from the Royal Injunctions of 1535 to the Accession of Charles the First*. Cambridge, UK: Cambridge University Press, 1884; repr. Johnson Reprint Corporation, 1969.

Nair, Yasmin. "Against Equality, Against Marriage: An Introduction." In *Against Equality: Queer Critiques of Gay Marriage*, edited by Ryan Conrad, 1–10. Lewiston, ME: Against Equality Publishing Collective, 2010.

Nashe, Thomas. "The Choise of Valentines, or the Merie Ballad of Nash His Dildo." Edited by John S. Farmer, 1899. Project Gutenberg (website), February 16, 2006.

Neuhaus, H. Joachim. "Structural Semantics, Dictionary Definitions, and Lexical Glosses." In *Shakespeare: Text, Language, Criticism: Essays in Honour of Marvin Spevack*, edited by Bernhard Fabian and Kurt Tetzeli von Rosador, 235–45. Hildesheim: Olms-Weidmann, 1987.

Newcome, Henry. *The Diary of the Rev. Henry Newcome, from September 30, 1661, to September 29, 1663*, edited by Thomas Heywood, vol. 18. Manchester, UK: Chetham Society, 1849.

Ng, Su Fang. "The Frontiers of *Twelfth Night*." In *Early Modern England and Islamic Worlds*, edited by Bernadette Andrea and Linda McJannet, 173–96. New York: Palgrave, 2011.

Ngai, Sianne. *Ugly Feelings*. Cambridge, MA: Harvard University Press, 2005.

Niccholes, Alexander. *A Discourse of Marriage and Wiving*. London, 1615.

Nietzsche, Friedrich. *On the Genealogy of Morality*. Edited by Keith Ansell Pearson. Translated by Carol Diethe. New York: Cambridge University Press, 1984.

O'Day, Rosemary. "Universities and Professions in the Early Modern Period." In *Beyond the Lecture Hall: Universities and Community Engagement from the Middle Ages to the Present Day*, edited by Peter Cunningham, Susan Oosthuizen, and Richard Taylor, 79–102. New York: Cambridge University Press, 2009.

Orgel, Stephen. *Impersonations: The Performance of Gender in Shakespeare's England*. New York: Cambridge University Press, 1996.

Overbury, Sir Thomas. *A Wife now the widow of Sir Thomas Ouerburie Being a most exquisite and singular poeme, of the choyse of a wife. Whereunto are added many witty characters, and conceyted newes; written by himselfe, and other learned gentlemen his friendes*. London, 1614.

Panek, Jennifer. "Community, Credit, and the Prodigal Husband on the Early Modern Stage." *ELH* 80, no. 1 (Spring 2013): 61–92.

———. *Widows and Suitors in Early Modern English Comedy*. New York: Cambridge University Press, 2004.

Paré, Ambroise. *The Workes of that famous Chirugion Ambrose Parey*. Translated by Th. Johnson. London, 1634.

Parker, Patricia. *Shakespeare from the Margins: Language, Culture, Context*. Chicago: University of Chicago Press, 1996.

———. Patricia Parker, "Was Illyria as Mysterious and Foreign as We Think?" In *The Mysterious and the Foreign in Early Modern England*, edited by Helen Ostovich, Mary V. Silcox, and Graham Roebuck, 209–33. Newark: University of Delaware Press, 2008.

Parker, R. B. "War and Sex in 'All's Well That Ends Well.'" *Shakespeare Survey* 37, edited by Stanley Wells (1984): 99–114.

Partridge, Eric. *Shakespeare's Bawdy: A Literary and Psychological Essay and a Comprehensive Glossary*. London: Routledge, 1955.

Paster, Gail Kern. *The Body Embarrassed: Drama and the Discipline of Shame in Early Modern England*. Ithaca, NY: Cornell University Press, 1993.

———. *Humoring the Body: Emotions and the Shakespearean Stage*. Chicago: University of Chicago Press, 2004.

Peacham, Henry. *The Compleat Gentleman*. London, 1622.

———. *Minerva Britanna, Or a Garden of Heroical Deuices, furnished, and adorned with Emblemes and Impresas of sundry natures*. London, 1612.

Persky, Joseph. "Retrospectives: The Ethology of Homo Economicus." *Journal of Economic Perspectives* 9, no. 2 (Spring 1995): 221–31.

Pfeffer, Jess R. "Trans Materiality: Crooke's *Mikrokosmographia*, Sexual Dimorphism, and the Embodiment of Identity." *Journal of Early Modern Cultural Studies* 19, no. 4 (Fall 2019): 227–41.

Plater, Felix, Abdiah Cole, and Nicholas Culpepper. *Platerus Golden Practice of Physick*. London, 1664.

Poulos, James. "Alleged Santa Barbara Killer Elliot Rodger and the Twisted Cult of Modern Masculinity." Daily Beast (website), May 26, 2014, updated July 12, 2017.

Price, Lawrence. "The Batchelors Feast." London, 1636. British Library C.20.f.7.12. EBBA 30015, Patricia Fumerton, dir., English Broadside Ballad Archive (website), accessed September 12, 2013.

Prideaux, Sir Walter Sherburne. *Memorials of the Goldsmiths' Company Being Gleanings From Their Records Between the Years 1335 and 1815*, 2 vols. London: Eyre and Spottiswoode, Her Majesty's Printers, 1896–97.

Przybylo, Ela. *Asexual Erotics: Intimate Readings of Compulsory Sexuality*. Columbus: Ohio State University Press, 2019.

Przybylo, Ela, and Danielle Cooper. "Asexual Resonance: Tracing a Queerly Asexual Archive." *GLQ* 20, no 3 (June 2014): 297–318.

Puttenham, George. *The Arte of English Poesie*. London, 1589.

Rambuss, Richard. "What It Feels Like for a Boy: Shakespeare's *Venus and Adonis*." In *A Companion to Shakespeare's Works: The Poems, Problem Comedies, Late Plays*, edited by Richard Dutton and Jean Howard, vol. 4, 240–58. Oxford: Blackwell, 2003.

Rappaport, Steve. *Worlds within Worlds: Structures of Life in Sixteenth-Century London*. New York: Cambridge University Press, 1989.

Ray, Nicolas. ""Twas mine, 'twas Helen's': Rings of desire in *All's Well, That Ends Well*." In *All's Well, That Ends Well: New Critical Essays*, edited by Gary Waller, 183–93. New York: Routledge, 2007.

Raynold, Thomas. *The Byrth of Mankynde, otherwyse named the Womans Booke*. London, 1545.

Reeser, Todd W. *Moderating Masculinity in Early Modern Culture*. Chapel Hill: University of North Carolina Press, 2006.

Relihan, Constance. "Erasing the East from *Twelfth Night*." In *Race, Ethnicity, and*

*Power in the Renaissance*, edited by Joyce Green Mac Donald, 80–94. Vancouver: Farleigh Dickinson University Press, 1997.

Ringrose, Kathryn M. *The Perfect Servant: The Social Construction of Gender in Byzantium*. Chicago: University of Chicago Press, 2004.

Rodger, Elliot. "My Twisted World: The Story of Elliot Rodger." In *Schoolshooters.info* (website), Langman Psychological Association, LLC, May 31, 2024.

Rubright, Marjorie. "Transgender Capacity in Thomas Dekker and Thomas Middleton's *The Roaring Girl* (1611)." *Journal for Early Modern Cultural Studies* 19, no. 4 (Fall 2019): 45–74.

Russell, Elizabeth. "The Influx of Commoners into the University of Oxford before 1581: An Optical Illusion?" *English Historical Review* 92, no. 365 (October 1977): 721–45.

Ryner, Bradley D. *Performing Economic Thought: English Drama and Mercantile Writing, 1600–1642*. Edinburgh: Edinburgh University Press, 2014.

Salamon, Gayle. *Assuming a Body: Transgender and Rhetorics of Materiality*. New York: Columbia University Press, 2010.

Salingar, Leo. *Dramatic Form in Shakespeare and the Jacobeans*. New York: Cambridge University Press, 1986.

Samber, Robert. and Charles Ancillon, *Eunuchism Display'd. Describing all the different Sorts of Eunuchs; The Esteem they have met with in World, and how they came to be made so. Wherein principally is examin'd, whether they are capable of Marriage, and if they ought to be suffer'd to enter into that State. The whole confirm'd by the Authority of Civil, Canon, and Common Law, and illustrated with many remarkable Cases by way of Precedent. Also a Comparison between Signior Nicolini and the Three Celebrated EUNUCHS now at Rome, viz. Pasqualini, Pauluccio, and Jeronimo (or Momo): With several observations on Modern Eunuchs. Occasion'd by a young Lady falling in Love with Nicolini, who sung in the Opera at the Hay-Market, and to whom she had like to have been Married.* London, 1718.

Sanchez, Melissa E. *Erotic Subjects: The Sexuality of Politics in Early Modern English Literature*. Oxford: Oxford University Press, 2011.

———. *Queer Faith: Reading Promiscuity and Race in the Secular Love Traditions*. New York: New York University Press, 2019.

Sedgwick, Eve Kosofsky. *Between Men: English Literature and Male Homosocial Desire*. New York: Columbia University Press, 1985.

———. *Epistemology of the Closet*. Berkeley: University of California Press, 1990.

———. *Tendencies*. Durham, NC: Duke University Press, 1993.

Selden, John. *Table-Talk: Being the Discourses of John Selden, Esq; or His Sense of various Matters of Weight and high Consequence; Relating especially to Religion and State.* London, 1696.

Serano, Julia. "Skirt Chasers: Why the Media Depicts the Trans Revolution in Lipstick and Heels." In *The Transgender Studies Reader 2*, edited by Susan Stryker and Aren Z. Aizura, 226–33. New York: Routledge, 2013.

———. *Whipping Girl: A Transexual Woman on Sexism and the Scapegoating of Femininity*. New York: Seal Press, 2016.

Schiesari, Juliana. *The Gendering of Melancholia: Feminism, Psychoanalysis, and the Symbolics of Loss in Renaissance Literature*. Ithaca, NY: Cornell University Press, 1992.

Schultz, James A. *Courtly Love, The Love of Courtliness, and the History of Sexuality*. Chicago: University of Chicago Press, 2006.

Schwarz, Kathryn. "Chastity, Militant and Married: Cavendish's Romance, Milton's Masque." *PMLA* 118, no. 2 (March 2003): 270–85.

———."'My Intents are Fix'd,': Constant Will in 'All's Well That Ends Well.'" *Shakespeare Quarterly* 58, no. 2 (Summer 2007): 200–227.

Scodel, Joshua. *Excess and the Mean in Early Modern English Literature*. Princeton: Princeton University Press, 2002.

Shakespeare, William. *All's Well That Ends Well*, edited by G. K. Hunter. London: Metheun, 1959.

———. *All's Well that Ends Well*. Edited by Susan Snyder. Oxford: Clarendon, 1993.

———. *The Merchant of Venice*. Edited by Barbara Mowat and Paul Werstine. New York: Simon & Schuster, 2009.

———. *A Midsummer Night's Dream*. Edited by Harold F. Brooks. London: Arden, 2006.

———. *Much Ado About Nothing*, edited by Claire McEachern. London: Arden, 2006.

———. *The Norton Shakespeare*, 3rd edition, edited by Stephen Greenblatt. New York: W. W. Norton, 2002.

———. *The Oxford Shakespeare: The Complete Works*, 2nd ed. Edited by Stanley Wells and Gary Taylor. Oxford: Clarendon Press, 2005.

———. *Shakespeare's Sonnets*. Edited by Stephen Booth. New Haven, CT: Yale University Press, 1977.

———. *Twelfth Night, or What You Will*. Edited by Keir Elam. New York: Bloomsbury, 2013.

Shannon, Laurie. *Sovereign Amity: Figures of Friendship in Shakespearean Contexts*. Chicago: University of Chicago Press, 2002.

Shapiro, Michael. "Audience vs. Dramatists in Jonson's *Epicoene* and Other Plays of the Children's Troupes." *English Literary Renaissance* 3, no. 3 (1973): 400–17.

Shepard, Alexandra. "From Anxious Patriarchs to Refined Gentlemen? Manhood in Britain, circa 1500–1700." *Journal of British Studies* 44, no. 2 (April 2005): 281–95.

———. *The Meanings of Manhood in Early Modern England*. Oxford: Oxford University Press, 2006.

Shirilian, Stephanie. *Robert Burton and the Transformative Powers of Melancholy*. Burlington, VT: Ashgate, 2015.

Shugar, Debora. *Habits of Thought in the English Renaissance: Religion, Politics, and the Dominant Culture*. Toronto: University of Toronto Press, 1997.

Simonds, Peggy Muñoz. "Sacred and Sexual Motifs in *All's Well That Ends Well*." *Renaissance Quarterly* 42 (1989): 33–59.

Simons, Patricia. *The Sex of Men in Premodern Europe*. New York: Cambridge University Press, 2011.

Sivefors, Per. *Representing Masculinity in Early Modern English Satire, 1590–1603: "A Kingdom for a Man."* New York: Routledge, 2020.

Smith, Bruce. *Shakespeare and Masculinity.* Oxford: Oxford University Press, 2000.

Smith, Steven R. "The London Apprentices as Seventeenth-Century Adolescents." *Past & Present* 61, no. 1 (November 1973): 149–61.

Smith, Sir Thomas. *De Republica Anglorum.* Edited by Mary Dewar. London: Cambridge University Press, 1982.

Snorton, C. Riley. *Black on Both Sides: A Racial History of Trans Identity.* Minneapolis: University of Minnesota Press, 2017.

Snyder, Katherine V. *Bachelors, Manhood, and the Novel, 1850–1925.* New York: Cambridge University Press, 1999.

Snyder, Susan. "Naming Names in *All's Well That Ends Well.*" *Shakespeare Quarterly* 43 (1992): 265–79.

Sokol, B. J., and Mary Sokol. *Shakespeare, Law, and Marriage.* New York: Cambridge University Press, 2003.

Spampinato, Erin. "How Does the Literary Canon Reinforce the Logic of the Incel?" *Guardian* (website), June 4, 2018.

Stein, Suzanne H. "Hamlet in Melanchthon's Wittenberg." *Notes and Queries* 56, no. 1 (March 2009): 55–57.

Stewart, Alan. *Close Readers: Humanism and Sodomy in Early Modern England.* Princeton: Princeton University Press, 1997.

Stockton, Will. *Playing Dirty: Sexuality and Waste in Early Modern Comedy.* Minneapolis: University of Minnesota Press, 2011.

Stone, Lawrence. *The Crisis of the Aristocracy, 1558–1641.* Oxford: Clarendon, 1965.

———. "The Educational Revolution in England, 1560–1640." *Past & Present* no. 28 (1964): 41–80.

———. *The Family, Sex and Marriage In England 1500–1800.* New York: Harper and Row, 1977.

Stubbes, Phillip. *The Anatomie of Abuses.* London, 1583.

Sullivan, Garret A. "Voicing the Young Man: Memory, Forgetting, and Subjectivity in the Procreation Sonnets." In *The Companion to Shakespeare's Sonnets*, edited by Michael Schoenfeldt, 331–42. New York: Blackwell, 2007.

Swann, Marjorie. "Refashioning Society in Ben Jonson's Epicoene." *SEL, 1500–1900* 38, no. 2 (Spring 1998): 297–315.

Swetnam, Joseph. *The Araignment of Lewde, Idle, Froward, and vnconstant women: Or the vanitie of them, choose you whether. With a Commendacion of wise, vertuous and honest Women. Pleasant for married men, profitable for young Men, and hurtfull to none.* London, 1615.

Tawney, R. H., and Eileen Power, eds. *Tudor Economic Documents: Being Select Documents Illustrating the Economic and Social History of Tudor England*, vol. 1. New York: Longmans, 1951.

Taylor, Gary. *Castration: An Abbreviated History of Western Manhood.* New York: Routledge, 2000.

———. "Some Manuscripts of Shakespeare's Sonnets." *Bulletin of the John Rylands University Library of Manchester* 68 (1985–86): 210–46.

Taylor, John. *An Armado, or Nauye of 103 Ships & Other Vessels.* London, 1627.

Thaler, Richard H. "From Homo Economicus to Homo Sapiens." *Journal of Economic Perspectives* 14, no. 1 (February 2000): 133–41.

Terada, Rei. *Feeling in Theory: Emotion after the "Death of the Subject."* Cambridge, MA: Harvard University Press, 2001.

Tilmouth, Christopher. "Burton's 'Turning Picture': Argument and Anxiety in 'The Anatomy of Melancholy.'" *Review of English Studies.* New Series 56, no. 226 (2005): 524–49.

Tilney, Edmund. *The Flower of Friendship: A Renaissance Dialogue Contesting Marriage,* edited by Valerie Wayne. Ithaca, NY: Cornell University Press, 1992.

Todd, Margo. *Christian Humanism and the Puritan Social Order.* New York: Cambridge University Press, 1987.

Tougher, Shaun, ed. *Eunuchs in Antiquity and Beyond.* Swansea: Classical Press of Wales, 2002.

———. *The Eunuch in Byzantine History and Society.* New York: Routledge, 2008.

Traub, Valerie. *The Renaissance of Lesbianism in Early Modern England.* New York: Cambridge University Press, 2002.

———. "Sex Without Issue: Sodomy, Reproduction, and Signification in Shakespeare's Sonnets." In *Shakespeare's Sonnets: Critical Essays,* edited by James Schiffer, 431–54. New York: Garland, 1999.

———. *Thinking Sex with the Early Moderns.* Philadelphia: University of Pennsylvania Press, 2016.

Urbina, Dante A., and Alberto Ruiz-Villaverde. "A Critical Review of *Homo Economicus* from Five Approaches." *American Journal of Economics and Sociology* 78, no. 1 (January 2019): 63–93.

Varnado, Christine. *The Shapes of Fancy.* Minneapolis: University of Minnesota Press, 2020.

Warren, Ian. "London's Cultural Impact on the English Gentry: The Case of Worcestershire, c. 1580–1680." *Midland History* 33, no. 2 (December 2008): 156–78.

Warren, Roger. "Why Does It End Well? Helena, Bertram, and the Sonnets." *Shakespeare Survey,* edited by Kenneth Muir, vol. 22 (1970): 79–92.

Watt, Tessa. *Cheap Print and Popular Piety, 1550–1640.* New York: Cambridge University Press, 1991.

Wells, Stanley. *Looking for Sex in Shakespeare.* New York: Cambridge University Press, 2004.

Wells, Susan. *Robert Burton's Rhetoric: An Anatomy of Early Modern Knowledge.* Philadelphia: University of Pennsylvania Press, 2019.

Whately, William. *A Care-Cloth: Or a Treatise of the Cumbers and Troubles of Marriage: Intended to Advise Them That May, To shun them; that may not, well and patiently to beare them.* London, 1624.

Wheatley, Henry Benjamin. *The Story of London.* London: J. M. Dent, 1904.

Whetstone, George. *An Heptameron of Ciuill Discourses.* London, 1582.

Wiesner-Hanks, Merry. "Forum Introduction: Reconsidering Patriarchy in Early Modern Europe and the Middle East." *Gender & History* 30, no. 2 (August 2018): 320–30.

———. [Wiesner, Merry E.] "'Wandervogels' Women: Journeymen's Concepts of Masculinity in Early Modern Germany." *Journal of Social History*, 24, no. 4 (Summer 1991): 767–82.

Wilkes, John. *Encylopaedia Londinensis; or Universal Dictionary of Arts, Sciences, and Literature*, vol. 2. London, 1810.

Williams, Raymond. *Marxism and Literature*. New York: Oxford University Press, 1977.

Wilson, Katharina M. and Elizabeth M. Makowski. *Wykked Wyves and the Woes of Marriage: Misogamous Literature from Juvenal to Chaucer*. Albany: SUNY Press, 1990.

Wilson, Katharine M. *Shakespeare's Sugared Sonnets*. London: Allen and Unwin, 1974.

Wilson, Thomas. *The Arte of Rhetorique*. London 1553.

———. *The Rule of Reason*. London, 1551.

Wright, Sarah. *Tales of Seduction: the figure of Don Juan in Spanish Culture*. London: I. B. Tauris, 2007.

Wrightson, Keith. *English Society, 1580–1680*. London: Hutchinson, 1982,

———. "Estates, Degrees, and Sorts: Changing Perceptions of Tudor and Stuart England." In *Language, History and Class*, edited by Penelope J. Corfield, 30–52. Oxford: Basil Blackwell, 1991.

Wrigley, E. A., and R. S. Schofield. *The Population History of England, 1541–1871: A Reconstruction*. Cambridge, MA: Harvard University Press, 1981.

Würzbach, Natascha. *The Rise of the English Street Ballad, 1550–1650*. Translated by Gayna Walls. New York: Cambridge University Press, 1990.

Yearling, Rebecca. "Homoerotic Desire and Renaissance Lyric Verse." *SEL* 53, no. 1 (Winter 2013): 53–71.

Zucker, Adam. *The Places of Wit in Early Modern English Comedy*. New York: Cambridge University Press, 2011.

# Index